A Man for All Oceans

A Man for All Oceans

*Captain Joshua Slocum
and the First Solo Voyage
Around the World*

Stan Grayson

Tilbury House Publishers
with the
New Bedford Whaling Museum

First hardcover edition: June 2017
ISBN 978-0-88448-548-3
eBook ISBN 978-0-88448-550-6

Library of Congress Control Number: 2017934121

10 9 8 7 6 5 4 3 2 1

Book design by Jon Albertson, www.albertson-design.com

Indexed by Jane Crosen

Printed in the USA

Tilbury House Publishers
12 Starr Street
Thomaston, ME 04861
800-582-1899
www.tilburyhouse.com

New Bedford Whaling Museum
18 Johnny Cake Hill
New Bedford, MA 02740
508-997-0046
www.whalingmuseum.org

"The wonder is that a man with such a limited boyhood education and who had been knocking about the sea nearly ever since should be able to turn to authorship and express himself so forcibly and bluntly."

—Clifton Johnson, 1902

"I find likewise that your printer has been so careless as to confound the times, and mistake the dates of my several voyages, and returns; neither assigning the true year, nor the true month, nor the day of the month: and I hear the original manuscript is all destroyed since the publication of my book: neither have I any copy left: however, I have sent you some corrections, which you may insert if ever there should be a second edition: and yet I cannot stand to them; but shall leave that matter to my judicious and candid readers to adjust it as they please."

—Jonathan Swift, "A Letter from Captain Gulliver to His Cousin Sympson," from *Gulliver's Travels*, 1726

"The sea washes off all the woes of men."

—Joshua Slocum, *Voyage of the Liberdade*, 1890

THE NEW BEDFORD WHALING MUSEUM AND TILBURY HOUSE PUBLISHERS GRATEFULLY ACKNOWLEDGE THE FOLLOWING SUPPORTERS OF *A MAN FOR ALL OCEANS*, WHOSE GIFTS HELPED TO UNDERWRITE THE RESEARCH AND WRITING OF THIS BOOK:

BENEFACTOR

NANCY & JOHN W. BRAITMAYER

PATRONS

In memory of E. GRAHAM WARD

GURDON B. & KATHY WATTLES

SUBSCRIBERS

AMY & ANDY BURNES

BESS & JIM HUGHES

CAROLINE & LARRY HUNTINGTON

CHRISTINE W. PARKS

DOLA HAMILTON STEMBERG

SUPPORTERS

ACUSHNET RIVER SAFE BOATING CLUB

NANCY SHANIK & THOMAS P. BARRY

JANE SLOCUM DELAND

THE ENERSEN FOUNDATION

HOWE ALLEN & TIMOTHY EVANS

FAIRHAVEN HISTORICAL SOCIETY -
In memory of HENRY HOTCHKISS

FAIRHAVEN IMPROVEMENT ASSOCIATION

SHELDON FRIEDLAND, ESQ.

VANESSA & JOHN GRALTON

GLORIA & WALTER HEALEY

JULIE & BAYARD HENRY

LUCILE P. & WILLIAM C.S. HICKS

JESSIE W. & LLEWELLYN HOWLAND III

NINA & JAMES "SHAM" HUNT

GAIL ISAKSEN -
In memory of HENRY HOTCHKISS

PATRICIA A. JAYSON

ANN & D. LLOYD MACDONALD

In memory of MARY & EDWIN
McQUILLAN

NORTHEAST MARITIME INSTITUTE
FOUNDATION

EMILY & JOHN C. PINHEIRO

PEGGY REPASS

NORMAN J. SHACHOY

FRIMA G. & DR. GILBERT L. SHAPIRO

SUE & CALVIN SIEGAL

BONNIE & LOUIS SILVERSTEIN

GENEVIEVE & STEVEN SPIEGEL

In memory of KENNETH TAYLOR

BARBARA & DAVID L. THUN

J. WILLIAM WEEKS

Contents

Introduction

ON JUNE 21, 1927, FOUR WEEKS AFTER Charles Lindbergh flew from New York to Paris, successfully completing the first solo nonstop flight across the Atlantic Ocean, the *New York Times* published a reaction to the flight from the National Geographic Society. "Courage, when it goes alone, has ever caught men's imaginations," said the society. The tribute went on to list a handful of men who, like the Lone Eagle, as Lindbergh became known, had accomplished something extraordinary for the first time. On this short list was Captain Joshua Slocum, the first man to sail alone around the world.

When Slocum made his voyage at the tail end of the nineteenth century, the idea that a small boat could voyage the world's oceans was one that few believed possible, and a voyage *alone* around the world was dismissed as a fool's errand. After Joshua Slocum proved such notions false and then wrote about his circumnavigation with great charm and style, he became, for a time, one of the more famous men in America. His experience, his boat, and the simple, self-sufficient way in which he lived have been an inspiration to sailors and non-sailors ever since, and *Sailing Alone Around the World* has never been out of print since its first publication more than a century ago.

Long before he set off in the *Spray*, Joshua Slocum had clawed his way up from a poor young seaman to a master of sailing ships. His chosen way of life was always dangerous, but he took the dangers in stride and seldom remarked upon them. He had needed all his brain power, sinewy toughness, and timely luck to survive and advance. In fact, the challenges Slocum faced as a sailing ship captain were—perhaps with one exception—greater than anything he confronted on the *Spray* voyage. The only thing he feared—in common with most sailors—was sharks. In Cuba, he once witnessed a shark bite a man in half, which increased his dread. Slocum referred to sharks as "monsters," and he killed them when he could.

During his professional sailing career, Joshua Slocum pioneered new business ventures with vision and enormous energy, only to turn his back on his own ideas. When he was 40 years old, his life was knocked permanently off course by the sudden death of Virginia—Ginny—his first wife, his soul-mate, and the immensely talented and adored young mother of his children. Like so many in those days, Slocum turned to spiritualism for comfort, but he never connected with Virginia beyond the grave, and he never overcame his grief. Then, on a very bad day in a beautiful Brazilian bay, he finally lost everything.

Joshua Slocum's life was such a kaleidoscope of adventure in wild, beautiful, and dangerous places that a skilled novelist would be hard-pressed to invent anything even vaguely like it. His story combined aspects of Richard Henry Dana's *Two Years Before the Mast*, Johann David Wyss's *The Swiss Family Robinson*, and Charles Nordhoff and James Norman Hall's *Mutiny on the Bounty*. Yet Slocum himself, by design, remained a mysterious man. When *Forest and Stream* magazine reviewed *Sailing Alone Around the World* in 1900, the writer noted with some disappointment how little "of his own personal part the sailor-author has to say."

But that was how Slocum wanted it. Charming and outwardly welcoming to his admiring public, Joshua Slocum never was an open book. The inner man always remained hidden where Slocum wanted him—in his painful, tumultuous past that none would ever glimpse in its entirety. His personal life was largely unknown even to his children. Reflecting upon his father in 1953, Garfield Slocum, the youngest of four surviving children, wrote, "He was a mystery to me and will be to my dying day."

While holding back so much, Slocum consistently managed his message in expedient ways. There were good reasons why he concocted, rearranged, or even lied about key events in his past, but the result is that a serious biographer must tread carefully in the effort to gain insight into Slocum's motives, feelings, and actions. Complicating the matter is that Slocum was essentially a Victorian, and there were many things that a Victorian simply didn't talk about, including emotions, details of business or personal relationships, and health issues that now seem mundane but were then considered intimate. Creating a responsible, fact-based portrait of a legendary man who's been dead for 108 years is a daunting challenge.

With Slocum, even biographical details that should be easy are difficult. By virtue of his Nova Scotia birthplace, he is claimed by Canadians as one of their own. Yet he took every opportunity to present himself as an American citizen, although, as will be seen, even his U.S. citizenship is shrouded in misdirection. Slocum always boasted about flying the Stars and Stripes on his ships, yet he well knew this claim was not entirely true.

The place names he used so fluently—and he knew the world like the back of his hand—may now mystify readers. Many places well-known to seamen of his time have different names now, or have ceased to exist, or have changed beyond recognition. And some historical allusions that Slocum took for granted would puzzle most readers today.

In the years following Joshua Slocum's disappearance at sea, readers fascinated by his book and seeking to better know the author found few if any places to turn. While Slocum had been alive, many people had visited the *Spray* and shared a moment in time with the skipper. They listened as the old salt spun a yarn or two, cooked up one of his famous chowders on the galley stove, or gladly autographed a copy of his book, pocketing $2.00 for his trouble. But Slocum's visitors knew no more about the captain after they debarked the *Spray* than they had upon going aboard. Not until 1950, some four decades after Slocum's disappearance, was the first book about him published. It created as many problems as it resolved.

In the introduction to his book *Dead Wake*, about the sinking of the passenger liner *Lusitania*, Erik Larson wrote that "one has to be very careful to sift and weigh the things that appear in books already published on the subject. There are falsehoods and false facts, and these, once dropped into the scholarly stream, appear over and over again, with footnotes always leading back to the same culprits."

The first book about Slocum, written by his eldest son Victor, contains such culprits. There is always the risk, when an offspring writes about a famous parent, that the book will be slanted to place its subject in the most favorable light while entirely overlooking less flattering matters or subjects deemed too personal. Nor does a son or daughter necessarily know all the important life facts about his or her parent, famous or otherwise.

The only one of Slocum's four children to follow the sea, Victor called his book *Capt. Joshua Slocum: The Adventures of America's Best Known Sailor*. Published in 1950, just after Victor's death, the book is flawed by factual errors, occasional confusions of chronology, and omissions. Victor was probably repeating what his father had chosen to share with him over the years, but Joshua had slanted some things and left out others. Still, a careful student of Slocum develops a sense for what can probably be trusted in Victor's book and can then be thankful for details that only an eyewitness could relate.

Six years after Victor's book came Walter Magnes Teller's pioneering biography, *The Search for Captain Slocum*. Teller was 46 years old in 1956, when Scribner's published the book. To his self-appointed search for Slocum the man, Teller brought a curious scholar's dogged diligence and a sensitive writer's insights. He wrote letter after letter seeking information and sought out anyone who had met the captain or had known the *Spray*.

After all his research, Teller did what he could to create a coherent portrait of Joshua Slocum. He presented his facts, made insightful comments, and, importantly, avoided passing judgment. He put together all the pieces he could find. He met Slocum's second wife, Hettie, and "held the hand that had held his." But it was a hand that, for good reasons, had never held Slocum's in the way of Joshua's first wife, the love of his life. There remained unanswered questions, unknown details, empty spaces in the Slocum story. Like any professional, Walter Teller had to decide when enough was enough and when it was time to publish.

Even though we once lived concurrently in Princeton, New Jersey, I did not call Walter until after I'd left town in the early 1980s. I certainly had no plans then of writing a book about Joshua Slocum. I felt that Teller's work had been so thorough that little remained to be added to Slocum's story. Still, I had been picking at the corners of the Slocum legend since the mid-1970s and wanted to sound out Teller, whose work I hold in high regard. He was gracious, even encouraging, when I probed about the possibility of there being more to learn. I will always regret not having become better acquainted with Walter Teller, who died in Princeton in 1993.

It was not until thirteen years after his death that I had discovered enough new material to make me think I could add something new to the Slocum story rather than largely rephrasing what already existed. The resulting article—*The Man Behind the Legend: Reflections on Capt. Joshua Slocum and* Spray—was published by *WoodenBoat* magazine in its September/October 2006 issue (Number 192). Reading that decade-old article today, I am relieved that it possesses only a couple of rather minor errors while presenting some insights and a reasonably objective assessment of a complex man whom all sailors, including myself, hold in high regard.

After writing that article, I continued to explore aspects of Slocum's story, aided enormously by the ever-widening reach of the Internet. I sought letters from Slocum and those who knew him; newspaper articles; court records; shipping news columns; birth, death, and marriage certificates; government documents; archival materials; city directories; and nineteenth-century maps and charts. E-mail messaging made it practical to seek answers to questions in Australia, the Philippines, Alaska, Liverpool, Nova Scotia, New Brunswick, San Francisco, Boston, the southeast coast of Massachusetts, and elsewhere.

Bit by bit my research folders grew in number and content. They filled a small carton, then a larger one, then others. Keeping my workspace organized became a challenge. Little pieces of Joshua Slocum's life began surfacing like flotsam from the depths of his long-hidden past. These bits often clarified questions. Just as often, of course, they demanded more digging.

As I worked through Slocum's story, there emerged the small details that create a man. It became evident that although Joshua Slocum presented himself as humble, he was also, with good reason, very proud. Sometimes his need for recognition got the best of him and emerged as vanity. There were times when he simply couldn't resist showing off his sailing prowess.

Once, at Hong Kong, he sailed his 100-foot square-rigged ship right through the close confines of an anchored British fleet, astounding everyone except, perhaps, himself and Virginia. Of course, he knew just the right place and instant to round up and order the anchor let go. He was simply a magnificent seaman and boat handler. His profound navigational abilities meant that he could find his way around the world without a chronometer if need be. There were times when he felt compelled to demonstrate how much smarter he was than everybody else.

Joshua Slocum was a man with a strong sense of right and wrong who would act immediately to defend himself or to vigorously pursue what he believed was rightfully his due. He had a temper that was *almost* always under control. He felt a strong responsibility for his family's welfare, yet ultimately struggled as a provider. He could be kind and generous or combative. Aboard ship, he was a demanding skipper and strict but fair disciplinarian. He admired capable, cultured, educated people—if they were honest and without pretense—as much as he despised the ignorant, the malingerers, and the wicked.

Slocum knew many of the famous people of his time, including an American president. He was a sociable man but entirely independent, and he fumed under any bureaucratic yoke. He cherished solitude, which, he learned, offered no disappointments. He had a wonderfully dry sense of humor that sustained him when nothing else could. He dealt with the roughest forms of humanity yet could be at home in the highest levels of society. He could happily slice and eat a potato with his big jackknife or converse graciously at a meal served on a white tablecloth with heavy silverware and sparkling crystal.

Several times over the years, I corresponded or spoke with Slocum family genealogist Melville Brown, Joshua's first cousin three times removed. Mel's grandmother, Grace Murray Brown, had been a cousin of Joshua and had shared her important memories and insights in letters to Walter Teller. Mel himself spent years gathering Slocum-related documents. To his great credit, Mel Brown always sought to separate facts from all-too-prevalent fictions, from mere "stories" that have served, and continue to serve, as a basis for so much of what has been wrongly presented about Joshua Slocum. Shortly before his passing in 2016, Mel Brown bequeathed his files to me.

"What do you have?" I asked him.

"Everything," he answered.

In truth, it wasn't everything, because it is unlikely there will ever be everything. But it was enough, when added to my own research, to answer some of the many questions readers have asked after first picking up *Sailing Alone Around the World*, entering its briny world, and emerging from the experience with a sense of wonder, appreciation, and a desire to gain more insight about its author.

The world Joshua Slocum knew has long since passed into history. Those who would seek to define or understand him according to today's standards must fail. His time was so different from our own that he might as well have lived on a different planet. I make no judgments in this book, and I have kept speculation to a minimum, always defining it for the fragile thing it is. No longer should the illusions and mistakes of the past regarding Joshua Slocum continue to be propagated. My goal is the historian's goal, the biographer's goal—to tell Slocum's story truthfully based not on dubious memories or sometimes tantalizing hearsay or opinion, but on the historical record.

What a tale it is!

Stan Grayson
Marblehead, Massachusetts
January 2017

Prologue

SHORTLY BEFORE NOON ON APRIL 24, 1895, a former shipmaster named Joshua Slocum took hold of the throat and peak halyards on a boat named the *Spray* and began hoisting the heavy mainsail. It had been three years since Slocum rebuilt the derelict oyster-dredging sloop where she lay in a backyard in the old Poverty Point neighborhood of Fairhaven, Massachusetts. There, close by the Acushnet River, working in the open, Slocum had hefted a well-sharpened adze and begun his labors at the vessel's keel. Steadily, surely, as the weeks and months passed, he worked his way up the hull and, during the process, became a local celebrity. Neighbors, passersby, fellow captains, fishermen, an occasional journalist, and curious children all stopped to witness and sometimes offer questionable advice to the wiry, bald-headed man with chin whiskers who was resurrecting a wreck.

Now, less than three years after Slocum had launched his rebuilt boat, the *Spray* was docked among the wharves and warehouses of East Boston and he again had an audience, this one composed of waterfront onlookers and newspapermen who had come to report on the start of what to most people seemed a foolhardy idea—a singlehanded small-boat voyage around the world. Slocum's second wife, Hettie, was there, too. She had come to wave good-bye, bringing with her two of Slocum's four children—probably 14-year-old Garfield and 20-year-old Jessie—although Slocum never mentioned their presence in his writings about the voyage.

Finally, the *Spray*'s big main with its long, wooden gaff was hoisted fully, the halyards neatly coiled, the jib raised. Casting off, Slocum made his way through the busy harbor. He tacked to windward of a four-masted schooner lying nearby. Then, moving with the sureness of one to whom seafaring is second nature, he eased the main and jib sheets, and the sails filled with the breeze. Steadily—*eagerly*, a sailor might say—the *Spray* gathered speed.

A reporter for what was then known as Boston's *Daily Globe* wrote that Slocum "came flying by the end of the pier with the wind abeam, so that The *Globe*'s snap-shot artist might have a fair chance. 'Click' went the camera. 'Is it alright,' hailed the captain. 'All right,' was sent back, and then, with a wave of his hand in farewell, the captain turned his attention to his boat, and swung her by the south ferry and down the harbor, with everything a rap full, and a white wake trailing out astern."[1]

By the time he passed Deer Island Light and emerged into Massachusetts Bay, Slocum guessed the *Spray* was making a steady 7 knots, fast going for a vessel of her design. Man and boat now headed northeast along Boston's North Shore. Soon enough, the *Spray* was sailing off Revere and the long, pleasant crescent of sand that, a year later, would become the country's first public beach. He passed the bustling city of Lynn with its many tanneries and shoemaking factories, activities that Slocum knew all too well. "Bold Nahant was soon abeam," Slocum would later write, "then Marblehead was put astern."

After a heart-pounding but successful approach through Gloucester's inner harbor, Slocum made ready to dock singlehanded for the first time in such a crowded place and under the critical eyes of old salts on the wharf. Although he made a perfect landing, he admitted in *Sailing Alone* that "[h]ad I uttered a word it surely would have betrayed me, for I was quite nervous and short of breath." He spent the next two weeks taking aboard provisions and supplies.

Slocum departed Gloucester on what he called a mild day. There was a light southwest wind blowing, and it took the *Spray*, tacking her way toward the harbor mouth, until noon before she cleared Eastern Point. Then Slocum turned northeast. He passed the twin lights on Thacher Island off Rockport and on May 8, with his mainsail double-reefed in a rising wind, made Round Pond, Maine. This was to be Slocum's last port in the United States until he completed his voyage.

On May 9, Joshua Slocum departed the Maine coast and sailed east for Brier Island, Nova Scotia, which he called Briar's Island in *Sailing Alone*. He headed for this little island in the Bay of Fundy for deeply personal reasons; he was returning to the place where his life's voyage had begun. He

---

1 This attempt to photograph a moving boat using the dry plate technology of that time did not result in a published photograph. The next day, August 25, 1895, the *Globe*'s story about Slocum, headlined "To Go Round the World," was highlighted by an illustration of the *Spray* rather than a photo. The very same illustration was used three years later when the *Globe* reported on Slocum's return: "Little Vessel Makes Circuit of Globe." (Photos of posed subjects appeared in the *Globe* as of 1901.)

had been born a Bluenose on a Nova Scotia farm and understood that his childhood there, and later at Brier Island, had shaped him into the man he was. There had been times when Joshua Slocum had denied his birthplace, but this was not one of them. "The very stones on Briar's Island," Slocum wrote, "I was glad to see again, and I knew them all."

CHAPTER 1

Nova Scotia

*"It is nothing against the master if the birthplace
mentioned on his certificate be Nova Scotia."*

—Joshua Slocum, *Sailing Alone Around the World*

ALTHOUGH DESCENDED FROM CAPTAIN SIMON SLOCOMBE, who arrived in
Boston from England in 1701 aboard a ship optimistically named *Success,*
Joshua Slocum was born a third-generation Nova Scotian. The simple reason
for this was the American Revolution.

Soon after his arrival in Massachusetts, Simon married Abigail
Wheetly, and the marriage produced two children. After Abigail's death,
Simon married Elizabeth Casheer and fathered eight more children, one of
whom, John Slocomb, was Joshua Slocum's great-grandfather. Born in
Wrentham Township, Massachusetts, in March 1754, John was 21 years old
in April 1775 when the first shots of the Revolutionary War were fired in
Concord. According to a family genealogy published in 1882 by Charles Elihu
Slocum (a Syracuse, New York, physician), John "remained firm in his loyalty
to England and removed to Nova Scotia to avoid being conscripted into the
continental army."

Charles Slocum's information suggests that John left early in the war rather than during the war's-end emigration of 1783, when some 30,000 Loyalists, freed slaves, and others who no longer fit in the fledgling nation left for Canada. John may have departed as early as 1775 for Halifax, where he married Eleanor Sprague in 1778. Various genealogical sources concur that he left Massachusetts aboard his own ship and was known generally as Captain Slocomb.[1] To his descendants, though, he would be remembered as "John the Exile."[2]

As a Loyalist recognized for his service to England, John Slocomb received in 1784 a substantial land grant in Annapolis County's Township of Digby. Included in the grant were "farm lots" and coastal "fish lots." Ultimately, Slocomb settled on 300 acres in Annapolis County's Wilmot Township[3] on North Mountain, the long, volcano-formed basalt ridge that runs northeast from Brier Island all the way to Cape Split. The mountain defines the northern edge of the fertile Annapolis Valley on one side and overlooks the great Bay of Fundy on the other. In a history of Annapolis County published in 1897, Wilmot Township was said to "contain more good land than any other in the county." The Slocomb farm was on Mount Hanley—spelled Mount Handley in those times—facing the bay.

Today the former Slocomb property lies within an area bordered by Mount Hanley Road, Brown Road, and Elliott (Outram) Road. The old farms have largely returned to woodlands, although some cultivation continues. In the nineteenth century, though, this part of North Mountain was a busy agricultural community with its own grist mill. Situated on Mount Hanley Road were a shoe shop, a one-room school, a store, a Baptist church and, close by, a Methodist church. Grace Murray Brown—a lifelong student of the Slocum family and an admiring young cousin of Joshua Slocum, who insisted she call him uncle—recalled that the "Slocombes were prosperous and ran everything on a large scale, not merely farming but raising cattle, horses and sheep for sale and farming enough to support these creatures as well as their family."

As the farm became productive, John Slocomb used his ship, moored below Mount Hanley in Port George, to carry his produce and that of other

---

1 Slocomb was also a captain in the Annapolis Regiment of Militia.

2 The genealogy's entry for John also notes that, having settled in Annapolis County, he would "journey through the county once or twice each year teaching and exhorting the people in the interest of religion. He was one of the pioneer Methodists in the province and became noted as an able expounder of the scriptures."

3 Today the township is known as Mount Hanley Township.

growers to market in Saint John, New Brunswick, and elsewhere. This sea-faring trade was expanded by John's second son, Joshua Upham Slocomb—known as "Captain Joshua U"—Joshua Slocum's paternal grandfather.

According to family lore, Captain Joshua U had a new trading vessel constructed, a powerful but easily managed brig. This two-masted vessel—the mainmast setting a gaff-rigged fore-and-aft sail in addition to its square sails—was big enough to greatly expand the family's trading business, carrying produce to New York and Baltimore and salt cod to Haiti.

Among the ship's crew was Captain Joshua U's eldest son John, Joshua Slocum's father. John Slocomb met Sarah Jane Suthern,[4] who would become Joshua's mother, while the family-owned brig was anchored at Brier Island. This Bay of Fundy island, roughly 5 miles long and 1½ miles wide, is the southwest terminus of Digby Neck and the westernmost land in Nova Scotia, separated from the mainland by St. Mary's Bay.

Sarah Jane's father, also named John, had served as coxswain aboard the HMS *Aeolus*.[5] This 32-gun frigate was part of a squadron that, two weeks after the Battle of Trafalgar in October 1805, captured a surviving remnant of the French-Spanish fleet destroyed by Admiral Nelson. Joshua Slocum wasn't kidding when he wrote in *Sailing Alone*, "On both sides of my family were sailors."

After his shipboard service, John Suthern was stationed in Halifax, Nova Scotia, where he was assigned duties as a "hulkman," repairing damaged ships including those that took part in the War of 1812. On October 12, 1812, he married Sarah McKenzie, and their daughter Sarah Jane Suthern was born in Halifax on June 24, 1814. Four years later, after John's 1818 discharge from the Royal Navy, the Sutherns moved to Brier Island, where, as a navy pensioner, John Suthern was offered employment as keeper of the Brier Island Lighthouse, referred to by islanders as the "Western Light."

Then, as now, the light was an important aid to navigation at the tide-swept, shipwreck-strewn entrance to the Bay of Fundy. The keeper's job was not an easy one. Not only did the Western Light offer the usual discomforts associated with a lighthouse standing exposed to a harsh environment, it

---

4 The family name suffers from spelling anomalies, not unusual in that era. It also appears in various places as "Southern."

5 This information comes from Mike Suthern, great-great-great-grandson of John Suthern. There is no evidence to support Victor Slocum's suggestion that his maternal grandfather had served aboard HMS *Bellerophon*, the 74-gun ship of the line that was launched in 1786, served in Horatio Nelson's fleet at the Battle of Trafalgar in 1805, and carried Napoleon to his final exile at St. Helena in 1815.

was reported as being "vilely constructed and ill-lit." John Suthern would have recognized these deficiencies immediately, but he served as keeper for several decades. Eventually, in 1832, the structure and its beacon were replaced.[1]

As time passed, John Suthern acquired property in Westport, the island's village, and he and his wife became active members of the community. In 1831, John joined the Brier Island Temperance Society, and his wife soon joined as well. The temperance movement, driven largely by religious fervor, was ascendant then. The crusade to reduce or eliminate the daily and often excessive consumption of hard cider, rum, and whisky was so pervasive that there were three temperance societies on little Brier Island, the population of which may have been around 300 people at the time.[2]

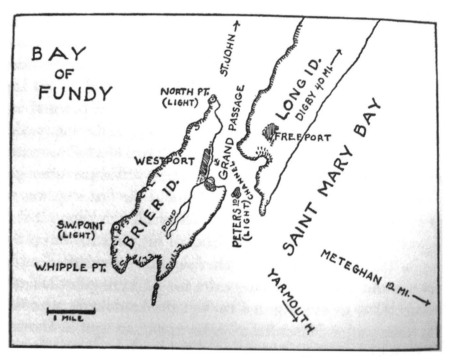

Victor Slocum included this map of Brier Island in his book about his father. Mount Hanley, Joshua Slocum's birthplace, is northeast of Long Island on the Nova Scotia mainland, off the map.

---

1 The new light was a well-made, tapering, wooden octagon painted white with three broad red stripes. It was lost to fire in 1944—a fire possibly set by U-boat saboteurs—and replaced by the current concrete lighthouse. In a nod to John Suthern's long tenure at the light, islanders refer to a distinctive rock formation below the structure as "John's Nose," according to Phil Shea's *Brier Island: Land's End in the Bay of Fundy.*

2 The census of 1838 listed 415 people living on Brier Island. That figure had grown to 678 by 1861, the year Joshua Slocum probably left home.

Historian Dorothy Outhouse noted that "the Temperance Societies in Freeport [on Long Island, facing Westport across the narrow Grand Passage] were very social. They sang temperance songs; members recited temperance related poetry, and those who could play musical instruments and sing solos also did that. There were also temperance societies specifically for children called 'The Band of Hope'. They were run on the same lines as the adult societies but the children had to promise three things: no swearing, drinking or smoking while the adults only had to pledge to no drinking or smoking. My great grandmother grew up in one of the most fervent temperance areas in Nova Scotia. She said one time she was offered a small drink of wine and didn't drink it as she 'had taken the pledge.'"

Not only was temperance an accepted feature of life at the time; so were religious awakenings and revivals. It was at the lighthouse in 1828 that Sarah Jane, at the impressionable age of 14, had "a religious experience" and soon after was baptized at the Brier Island Church.

Sarah Jane Suthern and John Slocomb were married in September 1832, when Sarah was 18 and John 21. According to the Digby County census of 1838, the couple made their home on Brier Island and had two daughters. Although most of the island's men worked as mariners or fishermen, John's profession was given as shoemaker. Grace Murray Brown reported that the raising of cattle at the Mount Hanley farm spawned an ancillary trade. "It was not unusual then for farmers to use the tanned hides of their cattle to make harnesses and boots, and this had become an important sideline on many farms. Boot making was something John Slocomb had learned to do."

This period in Slocomb family life is not reflected in Charles Slocum's genealogy. Dr. Slocum recorded only that the new couple "dwelt near his father's farm in Wilmot [Mount Hanley] for some time." The date of the move from Brier Island to Mount Hanley—some 70 miles northeast along the Bay of Fundy shore—is unknown, but it was likely between 1839 and 1843.

John Slocomb's transition from Brier Island shoemaker to Mount Hanley farmer was a troubled one, and the reason why he attempted the change is unknown. But the move most likely had to do with John's purchase or inheritance of a portion of the family property. In *Sailing Alone Around the World*, Joshua referred just once to the farm, noting that its coming into his father's possession was a "calamity." "[W]hat a load he carried and how he grubbed a living, for us all, out of the old clay farm," Slocum lamented. This woeful remembrance runs contrary to descriptions of the original farm established by John the Exile, but the original grant had been broken up. In today's terms, it had been subdivided.

In his family genealogy, Charles Slocum referred to John Slocomb living "near" rather than "on" the family farm. John the Exile had divided his Mount Hanley property between his middle sons Captain Joshua U and William. Captain Joshua U, in turn, sold pieces to his sons John and Joel. It was Joel, the younger brother and Joshua Slocum's uncle, who settled "on" his father's homestead farm at Mount Hanley. This holding was apparently the more desirable, while John Slocomb's nearby acreage proved a hardscrabble legacy.

At Mount Hanley, on February 20, 1844, the fifth of John and Sarah's eleven children (and the third of the nine who survived childhood) was born. This was a son they named Joshua, presumably for his seafaring grandfather, Captain Joshua U. In *Sailing Alone*, Joshua Slocum does not name his birthplace as Mount Hanley. He wrote, "I was born in a cold spot, on coldest North Mountain," evoking the challenges of simply keeping warm during the winter in what was sometimes referred to as "Nova Scarcity." Slocum aptly described North Mountain as "overlooking the Bay of Fundy on one side and the fertile Annapolis valley on the other."

The Slocum homestead at Mount Hanley as it appeared in September 1947. Ben Aymar Slocum recalled "a blacksmith shop in the yard—plenty of sauerkraut in casks in the shed—hand cut shingles etc." (Photograph by Raymond P. Miller of Swampscott, Massachusetts; courtesy the New Bedford Whaling Museum)

Fifty-five years after his birth, Joshua Slocum wrote in the second paragraph of *Sailing Alone*, "As for myself the wonderful sea charmed me from the first." Charmed by the sea he may have been, but Joshua Slocum spent his first nine years on the farm, learning how to plow a field and shoe a horse well before he learned to box a compass (recite all 32 points of direction on the compass card), splice rope, or tie a seaman's important knots. "Perhaps if Josh had been brought up on the farm, he might never have run away and become the man he did," said Grace Murray Brown.

His father's farm wasn't the only one Joshua worked. In 1902, when Slocum was 58 years old, he granted an interview to the prolific Hadley, Massachusetts, writer and folklorist Clifton Johnson, father of Irving Johnson, the great circumnavigator and sailing author. As is always the case with article writing, Johnson's notes of his Slocum interview were far more extensive than what made it into his final draft, which was published in *Outing* magazine in October 1902 as "Captain Joshua Slocum, the man who sailed alone around the world in a thirty-seven-foot boat." Although Slocum quite purposely left out many details, Johnson's notes reveal much about Slocum's boyhood on Mount Hanley and also about his father.

To Johnson, Slocum described his father as a "jack of all trades." In those times it was common for itinerant cobblers to stop by and make shoes for a family, but John Slocomb, of course, was himself an expert shoemaker. In sugaring season, he tapped the many maple trees on his property, collecting their sap in troughs he made from hollowed-out lengths of locally abundant fir. Then he boiled the sap over an outdoor fire in a big iron kettle to produce maple syrup. Slocum told Johnson that his father was also a capable carpenter and farrier as well as a skilled tanner. Slocum boasted that the "leather [his father] turned out was noted for being a genuine good article."

As was common then, Joshua's time was divided between working to help bring in cash to the family and attending "winter school." Slocum told Johnson that his father read books and owned several, including a large volume on world history that he sometimes loaned to the master of the one-room Mount Hanley school. "J. was only an average scholar," Johnson noted, "but stood well in arithmetic and better still in geog. and on a single occasion he won distinction in spelling."

In 1894, in *Voyage of the Destroyer*, Slocum wrote that, when he was nine, he was "hired out to a local farmer … at three dollars a month." However, he told Johnson that this occurred during summer months starting when he was eight. Throughout his life, the dates Slocum provided interviewers were rather regularly a year or so off, a matter he seemed to deem unimportant. Not all the biographical information he provided was entirely accurate, either.

Johnson wrote that Slocum's memories of being a hired boy included many uncomfortable hours seated on a dried pigskin "aboard an old horse. It was his duty to keep the horse going and he was too small to do this on foot so he rode for many wearisome days on the 'deck' of that old horse 'towing' the harrow up and down the field." The pigskin tended to chafe, and Slocum never forgot how unpleasant he found his fieldwork as a young ploughman.

In what little free time Slocum had, apparently when he was "about eight," he got afloat for the first time in his own craft on a pond adjacent to the local grist mill. This craft was a raft of three spruce logs joined by crossmembers fastened with nails. "Joshua rigged up a mast and sail," Clifton Johnson wrote, "and the rustic vessel carried him many a ... voyage before the breeze; but he always had to pole back." One day, while poling upwind, Joshua lost a knife he had bought at the cost of one day's labor. He marked the spot with his push-pole but never recovered the knife.

THE ONLY REASON Joshua Slocum was not brought up to be a farmer was that his father sold his property to his younger brother Samuel for 175 pounds "lawful money of Nova Scotia" on October 10, 1853. Within a few months after the sale, John moved with Sarah and their children back to Brier Island. This final break from the ancestral land is not elaborated upon in the family history and went largely unremarked in Victor Slocum's book about his father. He wrote only that his grandfather "had exchanged his Wilmot farm for a boot shop in Westport."

The primary reason the Slocombs departed Mount Hanley was said to be Sarah Jane's health. Records in the Westport Baptist Church reveal that "after passing through various afflictions and trials in the loss of children ... the family removed from Hanley Mountain to Westport on Feb. 8th." (The year was presumably 1854.)

According to Grace Murray Brown, her grandmother Naomi—a daughter of Captain Joshua U and wife of John Gates, who owned land adjacent to the Slocomb farm—"went daily to help dear Sarah when she was so frail with babies demanding so much care." She wrote that "John made the break away to Brier Island on account of his wife's dying condition. It was natural for her to want to be with her parents, brother, and sisters." Sarah Jane's frailty appears to have echoed that of her mother. When Sarah

Suthern died at age 77 in 1863, it was said that "for upwards of 20 years her health was very delicate."

Joshua Slocum's only oblique mention of his mother was the sharing of a memory of hearty flapjacks cooked in a big open fireplace. Years later, visitors to the *Spray* would remember Slocum serving them flapjacks that were "as thick as your foot." Grace Murray Brown had "no recollections of Uncle Josh talking of his mother" but believed that Sarah was "very lovely and a gentle soul.... Sarah was ill most of her married life—too many children coming too closely."

The move to Westport took Sarah home to the Suthern family's embrace and assistance. For Joshua, the move was likely exciting. No longer was he looking at the Bay of Fundy from a farm on a mountain. Now he was living right next to it. Slocum attended the school at Westport, but how long he remained in school is uncertain. According to Victor Slocum, when Joshua was 10, "that was the last of [his] schooling." Joshua claimed in his interview with Clifton Johnson that he "went regularly until he was 14," but this was almost certainly nothing more than a false boast.

Slocum's schooling ended when John Slocomb decided it was necessary for his son to work in the boot shop. While today this might appear to have been a selfish act—the sort of cruel fate one encounters in a Dickens novel—it would not have been considered out of the ordinary in a time when it was unusual for boys to continue their schooling past the age of 12. Three or four years of schooling was generally deemed sufficient in mid-nineteenth-century Nova Scotia.

Westport on Brier Island as Joshua Slocum knew it, looking north across Grand Passage toward Long Island. (Courtesy Islands Historical Society)

Joshua certainly learned to read and write in his few winters of school. While his punctuation would always leave something to be desired, his grammar and spelling might compare favorably to those of many high-school graduates today, and his unembellished handwriting was easy to read. Possibly his mother, his older sisters Elizabeth (b. 1837) and Georgiana (b. 1841), or the Suthern family provided some home-schooling. Always remembering his father's books, Slocum later became a voracious reader with an ability to recall and recite long passages of prose and poetry.

The Slocum boot shop was located on the Westport waterfront, where young Josh could no doubt contemplate how close he was to the sea that charmed him, yet how far he was from venturing upon it as a blue-water sailor. His boyhood experience in boats was like that of other youngsters in the area. Although Slocum probably fished from the deck of a Bay of Fundy schooner, much of his experience involved hand-lining from a locally built dory with other boys and with his father, who may well have built a dory himself.

Before the move to Brier Island, according to Victor Slocum, John Slocomb and his neighbors maintained a "fishing station" below Mount Hanley at what is now known as Cottage Cove, where they stored gear and dories. These boats are said to have been about 13 feet long on the bottom and probably about 17 feet long overall, and handling them in the Bay of Fundy's powerful tidal currents, among the world's strongest, would have required skilled seamanship and sturdy men capable of long stints pulling oars set in wooden tholepins.

John Slocomb fit the mold. He was a stout six-footer toughened by a lifetime of manual labor. In 1882, when he visited his son in New York Harbor, they sat in the cabin of the *Northern Light*, the magnificent square-rigged ship of which Joshua was then master and part-owner, and talked about the old days. As Joshua later recalled:

> 'Joshua,' said he, 'do you remember the night in the little boat when we rowed all night on a lee shore and the fishing vessels came into port with close-reefed sails?'
> *Didn't I remember it!*

But if he remembered a hard chance in a dory as something dangerous, exciting, and challenging, Joshua Slocum remembered the boot shop in a less favorable light. His son Victor wrote that the boots were "[s]ewn and pegged together … water-tight and well-nigh indestructible. A fisherman could not get on without them.… He became an expert at pegging boots, a task which he hated. If there were anything he hated worse than pegging boots, it was the sight of the soaking vat."

Grace Murray Brown, however, was skeptical of Victor's remarks on the subject of boots. "I think Victor overdid the harsh father part and the 'song of the boot,'" she wrote author Walter Magnes Teller in October 1953. "Many a boot was made in those days without much ado. If John had not known how to adapt himself to the very different life at Brier Island, I don't know how they could have existed."

Joshua's five-year-younger brother Ornan would, like his father, follow the shoemaker profession for much of his life. Joshua, too, would rely on the trade for a time, although he did so reluctantly and almost never admitted it. He knew his destiny lay elsewhere than in his father's shop. As Victor put it, "[H]e so despised the boot shop [that] he began to whittle ship models and to contemplate voyages."

John Slocomb had no sympathy for his son's fascination with the sea, inbred though it was, nor for the boy's model making or his curiosity about the ships that sailed by Brier Island. John expected Joshua to fulfill what he saw as a son's duty. Family memories of John paint a picture of a strict patriarch and a fundamentalist Baptist deacon—in sharp contrast with the Methodist Slocombs and the family's Quaker forebears, the first of whom, Anthony Slocombe, arrived in Boston in 1630 and, 32 years later, dangerously renounced Puritanism to become a member of the Society of Friends.[1]

But John Slocomb was no outlier given the ironbound role religion then played in people's lives in his part of Nova Scotia. After interviewing Slocum about his boyhood, Clifton Johnson noted that "people were religious and all were constant attendees at church. Some were Baptists and mainly all the rest were Methodists, and at each of their churches it was firmly believed the other flock was going to hell. Joshua went to the Baptist church with its square box frame and high pulpit."

John Slocomb was remembered as a man who viewed the world bleakly and in black-and-white terms, and who, when he preached, warned of the ever-lurking devil. Grace Murray Brown referred to him as a "puritan"

---

1 According to family history, Anthony "did unite with them [the Society of Friends] about the year 1662 and … such union was the cause of his removal to Dartmouth [Massachusetts] and his exclusion from the rights of citizenship." His conversion happened only a year or two after the hanging in Boston of Mary Dyer, a devout Quaker who refused to renounce her faith.

and wrote that he "was a stern type unlike the genial forebears and his own brothers, so his children mentioned."

In May 1899, just over a year after completing his circumnavigation, Slocum wrote a letter to his father's ever genial older brother Joel. In this letter to his uncle, one of the few surviving documents in which Slocum mentioned his father at all, he called his father "a fine man." Referring to John Slocomb's controlling nature and his proselytizing, Slocum wrote: "Indeed my father could raise a breeze—but let that go—I forgave it long ago."[1]

But Slocum also made clear how far he had voyaged from the fire and brimstone his father once preached. He had developed his own un-conventional spirituality born of a respect for the sea and for others. "Old sailors," he wrote his uncle, "may have odd ways of showing their religious feelings but there are no infidels at sea. I myself do not care much for your long-faced tyrannical Christian.... Our religion has improved: The days of Cotton Mather have gone by and we'll burn no more witches. Young people will not listen to bigotry. And there is much of it still.... I never cared much for the devil after I grew up and got away to sea—and he is not the keystone in the arch of our religion today."

One seminal event of 1856 stood forth in sharp relief from the father-son conflict. It was one of those childhood experiences that are never for-gotten, and it was among the few personal stories that the always private Slocum shared not only with his children but with some shipmates. As Victor Slocum recounted the event, 12-year-old Joshua "received a thrashing for being caught down cellar putting the finishing touches on a ship model which had taken many furtive moments to make. It was a fine piece of work and the last ship model he was ever to make. His father burst in upon him in a fury, seized the precious work of art (and hope) and dashed it to the ground, smashing yards and masts and utterly destroying the whole thing."

For John Slocomb, stressed by his wife's failing health, caring for his brood, and establishing himself in Westport, this evidence that his son wasn't walking the prescribed straight and narrow path was intolerable. For Joshua, the confrontation was a clear message that he needed to leave home and make his own way.

It is unlikely that Sarah Jane Slocomb could have done much to mediate

---

1 Joel Slocomb was as different from Joshua's fundamentalist father John as two brothers could be. Grace Murray Brown recalled that "Joel was said to favor the Quaker spirit more. Joel was a genial man who radiated kindliness." Joel served for a time as justice of the peace and was known locally as "Uncle Joel." Although fond of travel, he remained on the family homestead for many years.

the conflict between her husband and her son except to offer Joshua a mother's love, and her efforts must have been spread thin. She gave birth three more times after the move to Westport. A daughter, Henrietta, was born on April 26, 1854. A son, Ingram Bill, was born on November 6, 1856. And on February 5, 1860, Sarah gave birth to another daughter, Ella, her eleventh child. Sarah Jane died eleven days later, at age 46. In the church record, it was recorded that "she fell asleep in Jesus, leaving a husband and nine children to mourn her loss." She was buried at Westport's Hilltop Cemetery.

His wife's death did nothing to soften John Slocomb, only making life's burdens and his gloomy outlook worse. "She died," Grace Murray Brown said, "and, John, out of his element, did not prosper.... He had the motherless chicks to manage and had to hold a tight rein … and John, after her death, had to parcel out the younger children among his sisters. Josh left, a high-spirited lad who believed himself badly used by his father."

THE CIRCUMSTANCES of Slocum's departure from Brier Island are obscured in sparse and conflicting information. He may have first tried to escape the island at age 14 in 1858. Returning from this failed attempt to cook aboard a local schooner, he received another "thrashing." But with the death of his mother in 1860, there was nothing left to hold Joshua Slocum to his father's boot shop or, for that matter, to the deck of a Bay of Fundy fishing schooner.

The neatly kept schooner Freeman Colgate, *seen here at Westport, was typical of the vessels Joshua Slocum sailed on as a boy. (Courtesy Islands Historical Society)*

For Clifton Johnson, Slocum so rearranged the story of his youth that he never even mentioned Brier Island or the boot shop. Instead, he fashioned a narrative that better suited his vision of an appropriate upbringing for a sea captain. "Shortly after he built his raft," Johnson wrote, "he began to go out on the sea fishing for cod and mackerel in a small schooner with a crew made up among the neighbors. He continued at home working as a desultory fisherman and farm laborer until he was seventeen, when he 'slithered' off and started life on his own account." If the age was accurate—a big if—this meant that Slocum left Brier Island in 1861.[1]

Apparently, "slither" was the word Slocum found most apt for describing how he left home, as if he had somehow squeezed himself through the bars of a cage. But having escaped down the bay to Yarmouth, Nova Scotia, Slocum wound up working, of all places, in a tannery, where he found himself surrounded once again by the penetrating odor of the vats in which hides were soaked as part of the tanning process. Slocum told Johnson that he began haunting the docks after work and at night.

"He was soon ready to depart the tannery," Johnson noted, "but his employer treated him with great kindness and he was only a little size codfish at the time anyway so he stayed on for six months. Then he went down to a shoe shop in Massachusetts and worked for a winter." These notes by Clifton Johnson are the most important clues regarding Slocum's actions and whereabouts in the period leading up to his first sea voyage.

It is certain that Joshua Slocum was in Yarmouth by 1862. Toward the end of 1862, he made two documented trips from Yarmouth to Boston aboard the 105-ton schooner *Monitor*. The first was in October, and he arrived in Boston a second time on November 1. The entry records indicate that Slocum then claimed Yarmouth as his home, giving his nationality as Canadian. Both documents state correctly that he was born in Nova Scotia, but on one, for some reason, Slocum stated that his birthplace was Yarmouth rather than Mount Hanley. He would make a far more dramatic claim regarding his birthplace in the not-too-distant future.

Slocum's age as given on the entry documents at Boston was correctly stated as 18. The profession given was not seaman or fisherman but mechanic,

---

1 In *Sailing Alone Around the World*, Slocum wrote that, at the time he returned to Brier Island in 1895, he'd not seen the boot shop for 35 years. That would put the year he left Westport as 1860, the year of his mother's death. However, he also wrote that he "had spent eight years of my life as a lad [there]. Because the family appears to have moved to Brier Island in 1854, and because Slocum was so often a year off in dating events, this raises the possibility that Slocum left in 1862.

a term applied to a variety of crafts. Slocum almost certainly chose "mechanic" as having a more satisfying ring than "shoemaker," yet it is also true that shoemakers in Massachusetts had organized themselves in 1859 as the "Mechanics Association."

The most likely reason for Slocum's 1862 entry to the United States is that he had found work as a shoemaker in Natick, Massachusetts. A once-quiet agricultural community west of Boston, Natick had become an important shoe manufacturing center and, together with Lynn, the birthplace of the famous Massachusetts shoemakers' strike that began on George Washington's birthday in 1860 and spread to twenty-five New England towns. Some 20,000 shoe workers walked off their jobs, and Abraham Lincoln, then campaigning for president, publicly supported their right to do so. Men had been earning $3 for a week of 16-hour days in 1857, women only $1. The strike collapsed in April, but not before employers made concessions in pay and union recognition.

How long Slocum remained on the job is unknown, but it was likely in the early spring of 1863 that he returned to Canada. Within a year or so, Natick would play an important and quite unexpected role in Slocum's life and eventually in the lives of some of his siblings and children. But when he returned to Canada in 1863, Slocum's goal was to finally cease making shoes, find a ship, and begin a career as a merchant seaman.

When at last he achieved his goal—when Nova Scotia's bold, rocky, forested coast finally disappeared beneath the horizon—Joshua Slocum found himself embarked not only on his first deep-water voyage but, inevitably, on a voyage of self-discovery. He would reflect upon his youth throughout his life, looking at it from all points of his emotional compass. With hindsight and the broader frame of reference conferred by life experience, Slocum reshaped the events and emotions of childhood in ways that finally made sense to him.

But in whatever manner he reframed his boyhood and his upbringing in the threadbare, unforgiving Nova Scotia of his youth, Joshua Slocum was inevitably, to an important degree, a product of his family and the beautiful but harsh land of his birth. Although Slocum would come to deny his birthplace and stress that he was an American, he always remained a Bluenose at his core. For that matter, it is likely that his knowledge of the stories he'd heard about the principled Simon Slocombe and about John the Exile suggested to Joshua Slocum that Bluenoses and Americans shared similar attributes and core values. In the first paragraph of *Sailing Alone*, he wrote,

"I am a citizen of the United States—a naturalized Yankee, if it may be said that Nova Scotians are not Yankees in the truest sense of the word."

Grace Murray Brown did her best to identify what she thought her beloved "cousin-uncle" owed to his native land. "He was," she wrote, "a worthy son of a long line of captains who could, given a jack knife and wood, find his way home from the ends of the earth. Our Quaker Slocums handed down endurance and versatility, sobriety and love of adventure.... A few generations back on the distaff side came the Bassett wit and later the Farnsworth [Captain Joshua U having married Elizabeth Farnsworth] gift of sarcasm. That could be scathing, along with the penetrating eyes which were surely indicative of his uncommon attributes. He was not an ordinary mortal."

CHAPTER 2

The Western Ocean and Beyond

"It was always melancholy putting to sea with half the crew so stupid with liquor as to be almost helpless."

—Joshua Slocum, 1902 interview with Clifton Johnson

JOSHUA SLOCUM COMMENCED HIS SEAFARING CAREER blessed with a desire for learning, a brilliant mind, and a sturdy physique. Victor Slocum wrote that his father in his late teens weighed 180 pounds, "which backed up a will of iron." Slocum's weight, though, was probably overstated by some 30 pounds. His father John was a six-footer who weighed 200 pounds. Joel Slocum, John's brother, was a big man too, said to weigh 225 pounds. Joshua, however, was about 5 feet 9½ inches tall and more wiry than stout, as he would note at times himself.

But he was very strong and blessed with great powers of endurance, and he did indeed possess an indomitable will. He overcame losses and adversities that would have shattered others. Joshua Slocum was the embodiment of those fabled iron men who sailed the wooden ships.

His hands reflected his life story. Grace Murray Brown remembered Slocum as a "man of polished appearance, immaculate in his dress when ashore, but his hands showed that he had used them in manual labor." Victor Slocum remarked on the hardness of his father's hands. His fingers were long and, when balled into a fist, could deliver a blow akin to being struck by a rock. As Joshua himself liked to say, he possessed a "big fist," which he willingly—sometimes, perhaps, too willingly—employed afloat or ashore. If Joshua Slocum had been a boxer, he would have been one who punched above his weight. In an interview with author Walter Teller in the 1950s, Martha's Vineyard fisherman and Slocum friend Ernest J. Dean remembered Slocum's hands, too. He told Teller: "I think every finger and thumb on both hands was knuckle busted, set back or crooked—they looked worse than the fingers of an old-time ball player."

The hardness and hurts of Slocum's hands told of sometimes desperate struggles aloft on a yard or on a deck facing rough men seeking to take his life. But besides his stone-hard fists, it was Slocum's will and powerful mind that made possible his survival and advancement on the often brutal decks and in the rank, smoke-filled forecastles of a sailing vessel in the latter half of the nineteenth century.

IN COMMON WITH other seamen of his epoch—including merchant-mariner-turned-novelist Joseph Conrad—Joshua Slocum often referred to the Atlantic Ocean as the Western Ocean. According to Victor Slocum, his father's first voyage on the Western Ocean took him from Saint John, New Brunswick, to Dublin aboard what Victor called a "deal droger."[1] The preferred spelling is the Dutch-derived "drogher," a term well-known to nineteenth-century sailors for vessels engaged in a specialized cargo trade. In *Voyage of the Liberdade*, Slocum used the word himself in reference to a "cotton droger" he saw in North Carolina. The ship in Richard Henry Dana's *Two Years Before the Mast* was a "hide drogher," a vessel engaged in the Boston–San Francisco leather trade.

A drogher could also be—in a more derogatory sense—a ship that was slow, clumsy, leaky, or all three. Whichever definition of a drogher fit Slocum's first ship—and perhaps it was both—it's clear that he began his

---

1 In *The Century* magazine version of *Sailing Alone Around the World*, Slocum wrote of seeing a "bullock carrier" during his voyage from Gibraltar to Brazil. The magazine's editors footnoted "carrier" and referenced it as a "droger." When the articles were prepared for publication in book form, the vessel appeared as a "bullock-droger."

seafaring career by coming aboard through the hawsehole[2] of a nondescript, unexceptional vessel. "Deal" was a cargo of finished pine or fir planks, the major export from Saint John, the nineteenth century's most important timber-shipping port in Atlantic Canada. Victor Slocum wrote that "for all her disrepute a deal droger could always get a crew" and that Joshua and a friend found a vessel on their own rather than through a shipping office. But persistent research has yet to reveal the drogher's name. Although Slocum would later remark that he preferred to sail on American-flagged vessels, the drogher's registration also remains unknown. But she could well have been registered at Yarmouth, where Slocum would have encountered her while roaming the docks during his months of work there.

Victor wrote that Slocum and his friend were the only sober crewmen aboard the drogher at the start of its voyage. The Brier Island temperance societies must have been effective, because this was Slocum's first encounter with inebriated men. Although he drank wine on occasion, he, like so many in his family, would always refrain from imbibing spirits. Many years after his voyage on the drogher, as he stocked up the *Spray*, Slocum took aboard a bottle of whisky and a bottle of brandy for what he termed "emergencies." But although he experienced several potentially fatal events during his epic voyage, he returned with the whisky and brandy bottles unopened.

As the drogher entered Dublin Bay (surveyed in 1800 by Captain William Bligh of *Bounty* infamy) and passed the red-painted Poolbeg Lighthouse, Joshua Slocum was judged to be the crewman most fit to take the helm. He told Victor that the drogher was clumsy and needed plenty of forethought by the man at the wheel, but Slocum left a straight wake as he followed the pilot's guidance into Dublin Harbour.

Bolstering this account of Joshua Slocum's first deep-sea voyage is later information from Slocum himself. In Clifton Johnson's notes made during his interviews with Slocum in 1902, he wrote that Slocum "made a fishing voyage. Then he shipped to Dublin as an ordinary seaman." Victor didn't give a date for the voyage and, most unfortunately, Johnson didn't think to ask Slocum himself. But spring or summer of 1863 remains the likeliest time.

Victor Slocum's account of what his father did next diverges significantly

---

2 A sailor who began his career not as an officer or apprentice but as a lowest-ranking seaman was said to have gone to sea through the hawsehole, the opening in the bow through which mooring cables pass. Seamen were said to "sail before the mast" and were berthed in the forecastle, while officers occupied the afterdeck and were quartered in aft cabins.

from the limited documented evidence. Victor reported that his father crossed the Irish Sea to Liverpool and spent two weeks there looking for a ship. He wrote that his father avoided berths on the emigrant-carrying vessels, said to have been crewed generally by the lowest sort of sailors and unfortunate landlubbers who fell prey to the crimps, and instead sought a professionally crewed, comparatively good-paying, British-flagged East India merchant vessel bound for China. Victor said the ship his father found was the *Tanjore*, but while there was indeed a British vessel of that name, there is nothing to connect it or its captain to Joshua Slocum. What's more, the ship's British registry would have conflicted with Slocum's stated preference for American-flagged vessels.

There was good reason at the time to prefer American ships. The American merchant marine had enjoyed mostly uninterrupted success since the birth of the nation, and by 1851, American vessels, clipper ships or not, were generally recognized as faster and more cost efficient than their British counterparts. Captain Arthur H. Clark, who rose through the ranks to command sailing ships and steamships and knew the business inside out, spoke plainly in his brilliant book *The Clipper Ship Era: 1843–1869*:

> No sailing ships of other nationalities could compete with them.... [I]n
> the matter of speed, an American merchantman would make five
> voyages while a British ship was making four of equal length; and as to
> freights, the American ships had the splendid rates to San Francisco all
> to themselves, while from China to England the rates of freight were
> quite double in their favor, as compared with British ships.

But even as Joshua Slocum was establishing his career, economic events, government regulations, technology, and the American Civil War would combine to end the primacy of American-flagged sailing vessels. A financial depression in 1857 resulted in steep declines in tonnage. A. B. C. Whipple wrote in *The Challenge*:

> [A] shipowner could scarcely afford the necessary wages and insurance
> to keep a vessel sailing. Then came the Civil War.... Unable to keep
> their vessels in service, Northern and Southern shipowners sold them
> abroad; nearly a third of America's oceangoing merchant marine was
> snapped up at distress prices by foreigners.... By the end of the war,
> what with the sinkings [by Confederate raiders] and the panic selling,

nearly every one of the few remaining American clippers had gone to foreign owners or to the bottom of the sea.

In 1865, British shipping exceeded American tonnage once again.... During the half century to come, while the U.S. population tripled, U.S. shipping would be reduced to a third of its 1860 tonnage.

While Great Britain felt the effects of the 1857 depression and the Civil War, too, the British government took important measures to promote the construction of iron steamships. Large numbers of these vessels—iron-built, screw-propeller ships that were far superior to wooden sidewheelers—would pay off in Britain's emerging dominance of world sea trade. (The opening of the Suez Canal in 1869 put another very large nail in the coffin of any sailing ship designed for the Far East trade, whatever her nationality.)

Meanwhile, the U.S. government took no steps that would enable its merchant marine, sail or steam, to keep pace. Captain Clark believed that the negative effects of the depression, Confederate raiding vessels, and the Civil War itself were far exceeded in their impact on the demise of American sailing commerce by "irrational and unjust laws" that "performed the gigantic task of driving the American flag from the oceans." Writing in 1909, Clark said: "until these laws are repealed, as those of Great Britain were in 1849, we may hope in vain that the ensign of the United States will be restored to its place upon the sea."[1]

At any event, the scant surviving evidence from 1863 to mid-1864 contradicts the notion that Slocum shipped from Liverpool to Asia in a British-flagged ship. In 1902, Slocum told Clifton Johnson that, after disembarking from the drogher in Dublin, he "spent four years in the Atlantic" and that "[h]is experience was not by any means an unhappy one." Among the most important of the surviving documents from Slocum's early career is the registration book in which his Seaman's Protection Certificate was recorded.

The Seaman's Protection Certificate originated in 1796 with the goal of shielding American seamen from impressment by the British. A certificate

---

1 Clark was referring to long-standing navigation laws and protective tariffs that "have long-since outlived the usefulness they may once have possessed, and completely fail to meet the requirements of the changes in ocean navigation that have taken place.... [T]hey prohibit an American citizen from owning a foreign-built merchant ship. Meanwhile the Protective Tariff so increases the cost of labor and materials ... that the American ship-builder cannot produce a steel or iron vessel at anything like the cost that will enable her to compete successfully with a ship of the same class built in a European shipyard.... [T]he Navigation Laws and Protective Tariff are the millstones between which the American ship-owner and ship-builder presently find themselves ground."

provided a physical description of the sailor and attested to his American citizenship. This verification, however, was easily abused, since a sailor merely needed to appear at the customhouse with a notarized affidavit, a witness, and a 25-cent fee. It was this aspect of the certificate—that it might not be legitimate—that British Navy captains sometimes used as an excuse to impress certificate-bearing American sailors during the Napoleonic Wars—and that in turn was one of the factors that led America to declare war on England in 1812.

By Slocum's time, fear of impressment had been replaced by concern for the decline in jobs available to seamen and the poor conditions prevailing aboard many (though not all) ships. In 1817, the U.S. Congress had passed legislation requiring the crews of American-flagged ships to include two-thirds American citizens, but this law was routinely ignored. Captain Arthur Clark wrote that "no American merchant ship of considerable tonnage was ever manned by native-born Americans in the sense that French, British, Dutch, Norwegian, Swedish, Spanish, or Danish ships are manned by men born in the country under whose flag they sail."

On April 29, 1864, Joshua Slocum received Certificate Number 210, registering him in the District of Boston and Charlestown, Massachusetts. He gave his age as 19 years old, though he was in fact 20. Quite possibly he adjusted his age so as not to be subject to conscription under the Civil War–era Draft Act of March 1863, which required the registration of all males between the ages of 20 and 45, including aliens who intended to become citizens. Slocum also adjusted his birthplace. Instead of giving Mount Hanley or Yarmouth, Nova Scotia, as his place of birth, he listed Natick, Massachusetts, the shoemaking center. He must have believed that someone there, whether a relative, ex-employer, or close workmate, would vouch for him if necessary.

Most likely Slocum falsified his birthplace to bypass the admittedly informal process of naturalization and get straight to the desired end: the citizenship document nominally required by American ship owners and captains. In claiming to have been born in the United States, he was gambling that officialdom would not discover a discrepancy with his entry documents of 1862. He must have been correct in this, for the matter apparently never arose.

When writing *Sailing Alone Around the World*, of course, Slocum could no longer hide where he had been born. He would boast in the fourth sentence of having been born in Nova Scotia and becoming a naturalized U.S.

The "Abstract of Seamen Registered in the District of Boston and Charlestown, during the quarter ending 30th June 1864" lists Joshua Slocum with his stated name, age, height, complexion, and place of birth. Slocum gave both his age and place of birth incorrectly. The certificate Slocum received with this registration has not been found.

citizen.[1] Until then, however, he would consistently claim in official documents and in the press to have been born in Massachusetts. To cite but one of many examples, when Slocum arrived in Gibraltar aboard the *Spray* in May 1895, he told the *Gibraltar Chronicle* that he was "a native of the Massachusetts

---

1 Becoming naturalized was a less formal process in Slocum's time than today, and no more demanding than acquiring citizenship by gaining a Seaman's Protection Certificate. The petition for naturalization was made orally in court. The petitioner appeared with witnesses attesting to his or, very occasionally, her qualifications for citizenship. Doubtless, Slocum believed his Seaman's Protection Certificate was sufficient proof of citizenship.

capital," thus adding Boston to Natick and Yarmouth as places where he claimed to have been born.

As Slocum began his sailing career, he also began changing the spelling of his family name. Fluid spellings of surnames were not unusual in the eighteenth and nineteenth centuries, and this was certainly true of the Slocum family. The name had been spelled Slocombe and Slocumb in addition to Slocomb, and Joshua himself used different spellings on different documents. On his first 1862 Boston visit, Joshua spelled his last name Slocumb. On the second, he spelled it Slocomb. In 1864, when applying for his Seaman's Protection Certificate at Boston, Joshua spelled his name Slocum.

It would take time, however, before "Slocum" became the consistent spelling of Joshua's last name. On May 3, 1864, when he signed on as an able-bodied seaman aboard the brig *S. J. Sanderson*,[1] Joshua spelled his last name "Slocomb," like his father. There is nothing to suggest that he had any motive for the different spellings or that anyone ever questioned them.

The *S. J. Sanderson* was registered in Yarmouth, Nova Scotia. At the time Slocum signed on, the vessel was preparing to sail from Boston for Glasgow, where it arrived on June 21, 1864. The evidence suggests that Slocum's next ship was the 174-foot *Agra*[2] (named for a city in India). Built in Medford in 1862 by J. T. Foster & Company for the prosperous Boston trading firm of Thomas B. Wales & Company, the *Agra* was an impressive vessel. On February 3, 1863, the San Francisco *Daily Evening Bulletin* did a feature article about her noting that "she has most of the new patent conveniences for working the ship, such as patent blocks, capstans, windlass, earrings, jackstays, pumps, double-topsail yards, etc." Such innovative equipment would doubtless have fascinated Joshua Slocum, and he would have soaked up all the information he could about the advantages offered.

Subsequent to her maiden voyage to San Francisco, the *Agra* sailed to Liverpool, London, Glasgow, Melbourne, and Rangoon (now Yangon, Myanmar) during the period 1863–65. In the absence of his name on a currently available crew list from that the period, the evidence linking Joshua Slocum to the *Agra* is Slocum's own testimony. Many years later, at the beginning of

---

1 The ship was lost the following year while carrying a load of bricks, iron pipe, and slate from Glasgow to Jacmel, Santo Domingo (in what is now Haiti), when she grounded on Bird Reef near Antigua on the night of August 2, 1865.

2 Like seemingly everything about this period, the *Agra* voyage has the potential for confusion because there were at least two older British-flagged *Agras* in service at the time. The American vessel may also have switched its registry to Britain subsequent to being sold in August 1863, after which a court case ensued.

his circumnavigation on April 16, 1895, Slocum told a reporter for the *Boston Herald* that it was aboard the *Agra* in mid-Atlantic that he lost his grip while aloft on the upper topsail yard.[3] The newspaper story said that a collision with the main yard broke Slocum's fall and saved his life while leaving a gash over his left eye that remained a scar for life. As would be demonstrated time and again, Joshua Slocum, skillful and determined as he was, sailed with an angel perched on his shoulder. He called it, eventually, "Slocum's luck."

Subsequent to the *Agra*, Slocum's next ship was almost certainly the *Tanjore*—not the British-flagged *Tanjore* Victor referred to but an American vessel owned, like the *Agra*, by the Boston merchant house of Thomas B. Wales. The last 1864 entry in the *Tanjore*'s logbook reveals that she had just completed a return voyage to Boston from Calcutta, and in January 1865, "Joshua Slocumb" signed aboard for a voyage to Hong Kong. Slocum's rank was seaman, at a wage of $50 per month. Slocum received an advance on his wages to purchase one pair of "thin pants," one "grey shirt (flannel)," two undershirts, two pairs of "drawers" (underpants), three pounds of tobacco, and postage for a letter.

Why did 21-year-old Joshua Slocum, who never squandered his pay, need to borrow for necessities when he signed on to the *Tanjore*? The most likely answer, based on later sporadic correspondence and interviews, is that he sent all the money he could home to Brier Island. Particularly during his early days as a seaman and later as a captain, Slocum was cash-poor. He was concerned about the well-being of his siblings and did what he could to assist them financially. Eventually, he helped them leave Nova Scotia for the United States.

The *Tanjore* was under the command of Captain James P. Martin, who, Slocum later wrote, was an expert navigator but disdainful of the crew and "talked through his nose." "Captain M," as Slocum referred to him in *Sailing Alone*, was so bound to the chain of command that he couldn't directly give Slocum a letter that was waiting for him when the ship reached Hong Kong. "But do you suppose he could hand a letter to a seaman?" Slocum wrote. "No, indeed: not even to an ordinary seaman. When we got to the ship he gave it to the first mate; the first mate gave it to the second mate, and he laid it, minchingly [in a grudging manner as if wishing not to touch it], on the capstan head where I could get it!"

---

3 The *Herald* article gave the year of this event as 1861. Whether this was a typo or incorrect information given by Slocum can't be determined. The *Agra* was built in 1862.

Things apparently went well enough aboard the *Tanjore* until the ship, having traversed the Indian Ocean, reached Hong Kong. There, Captain Martin ordered the sailors, as Slocum recalled nearly 40 years later, to unload "the ice cargo in the cool of the mornings and evenings and then aloft or, worse still, over the ship's side in the heat of the day, which in Hong Kong in summer … was intensely hot." The result of Captain Martin's orders, according to Slocum, was that several of the crew died. Slocum himself became so debilitated that he had to leave the *Tanjore* and enter a hospital in Hong Kong, where he spent nine days convalescing. The ship's logbook refers to this event as a "desertion," although the word possibly had a somewhat different connotation then.

Decades later, in an 1899 letter to one of his Century Company editors, Slocum expressed his feelings about the calculations behind Captain Martin's brutal orders: "The crime for which the crew was so inhumanely worked was that each had the high wages of our home port, $50 per month, whereas there at Hong Kong, hundreds of sailors on the beach were begging for the chance to work their passage to any country at all." In other words, dead, incapacitated, or deserting crew could be replaced by much cheaper men. No commentary on the matter from Captain Martin has been found.

In this letter to Century Company editor Clarence Buel, written at Cottage City (Oak Bluffs) on Martha's Vineyard on July 23, 1899, Slocum reported that he sued Captain Martin "and recovered three months extra wages."[1] Slocum wrote: "[T]he editor may think that I have been a little severe on Captain M. of the old 'Tanjore' but it is my only revenge for years of broken health brought on by the captain."[2]

As was his wont, Joshua Slocum chose not to explain his health concerns during and subsequent to the *Tanjore* voyage, nor have any relevant documents been located. It seems likely that he was back aboard for the return voyage from Hong Kong to Boston, but he only made it as far as Batavia (which is now Jakarta, Indonesia). There, again seriously ill with what he termed a "fever," Slocum entered another hospital.[3]

---

1 Efforts to find documents related to this matter have gone unrewarded. If the case was heard at the American consulate in Hong Kong, the documents would likely have been among those destroyed during the Japanese occupation of World War II. The *Tanjore*'s log reveals the money was paid at Hong Kong as of September 16, 1865. The log entry noted simply: "Three month extra wages."

2 Martin is known to have been in command of the *Tanjore* from 1863–65. In 1867 he joined the Boston Marine Society—a benevolent organization founded in 1809—and later served as its president, stepping down in 1887.

3 Slocum may well have contracted malaria, then a common malady in Hong Kong. It would not be

Joshua Slocum's survival in what sailors of that time referred to as "the pest hole of the Dutch East Indies" was a near thing. That he did survive was in large part the result of some now unknown happenstance, seemingly another example of "Slocum's luck." In the hospital, according to Victor, his father "found a good friend in Captain Airy of the steamship *Soushay*, who rescued him."

Aboard the *Soushay*, it is unlikely that Slocum's weak condition permitted him to do more than, perhaps, practice navigation. He was restored to somewhat better health as the vessel plowed her way to ports in the Java Sea, the Banda Sea, the Flores Sea, the South China Sea, the Indian Ocean, the Arafura Sea, and the Timor Sea—all the waters around Indonesia, Vietnam, and finally, Cooktown[4] in Far North Queensland, Australia. Before landing in Cooktown, the *Soushay* stopped at Booby Island.[5] In *Sailing Alone*, Slocum recalled of this event that "I was well enough to crawl on deck.... Had I died for it, I would have seen that island. In those days passing ships landed stores in a cave on the island for shipwrecked and distressed wayfarers. Captain Airy of the *Soushay*, a good man, sent a boat to the cave with his contribution to the general store."

According to Victor Slocum, "Captain Airy would have been glad to have [my father] accept a permanent berth but the fever was still in his bones and the islands were no place for him at that time." As for the *Tanjore*, Joshua Slocum neither forgot nor forgave Captain Martin. In *Sailing Alone*, though, Slocum raised the issue of his illness just once and only in connection with his arrival in the *Spray* at Cooktown on May 31, 1897. "Here I was reminded of distressful days gone by. I think it was in 1866[6] that the old steamship *Soushay*, from Batavia for Sydney, put in at Cooktown.... On her sick-list was my fevered self."

Almost three decades after he left the *Soushay*, Slocum remained outspoken regarding the need to improve the working conditions and treatment of merchant seamen. Even as he was witnessing the death and burial of the age of sail, Slocum addressed the matter of crew welfare at a meeting of the

---

until about 1900 that Hong Kong's "tropical fevers" were identified as malaria carried by a species of mosquito.

4 In 1770, Captain James Cook beached HMS *Endeavour* at Cooktown for repairs after it was damaged by contact with a reef.

5 By the time Slocum sailed the *Spray* past Booby Island in June 1897, a lighthouse had been in operation there for seven years, an important aid to navigation at the entrance to the Endeavour Strait.

6 It might in fact have been the latter part of 1865.

Shipping League held in Washington, D.C., in February 1890. The Associated Press reported that "Capt. Slocum said the present was a dark time for American shipping, and complained that the Government of the United States did not secure redress for American seamen ill-treated abroad."

VICTOR SLOCUM CAN'T BE HELD entirely to blame for the inaccuracies in his account of his father's early days as a merchant seaman. The person most responsible is Joshua Slocum himself. Only rarely did he discuss his career, and when he did he would adjust the narrative as he saw fit—seldom, if ever, giving an accurate and complete rendition. He treated his later career in much the same way. In a 1954 letter to Walter Teller, Slocum's second son, Ben Aymar, wrote of his father: "J.S. was very closed mouth regarding his associates and friends. You had to ask the direct questions [regarding] others of whom he knew or thought to know and his children knew very little of his private life."

According to Clifton Johnson's interview, sometime after leaving the *Soushay*, Joshua Slocum "attained the position of 2nd mate on a vessel bound from San Francisco to Liverpool." Johnson gave no date for this voyage, nor did he ask the name of the ship. Assuming Slocum voyaged to San Francisco from Batavia, he might have arrived there in late 1865 or early 1866 and then signed aboard a ship bound for Liverpool.

Victor Slocum said his father's primary source for acquiring the necessary learning for advancement from able seaman to mate and then to master was *The Epitome of Practical Navigation*, written by London-born cartographer and navigator John William Norie (1772–1843), whose portrait hangs in Britain's National Portrait Gallery. Norie's first edition of the *Epitome* was printed in London in 1803. "Navigation," wrote Norie in his introduction, "is that Art which instructs the mariner in what manner to conduct a ship through the wide and trackless ocean, from one part to another, with the greatest safety, and in the shortest time possible."

The title page of Norie's book detailed the many benefits a smart young seaman like Joshua Slocum would gain from absorbing its contents: "All necessary instruction for keeping a Ship's reckoning at sea with the most approved methods of ascertaining the latitude by meridian or single altitudes; and the longitude by chronometers, or lunar observations."

Norie never stopped improving his book, adding or correcting material as necessary in each new edition. A revised version, *The Complete Epitome of Practical Navigation*, was published in 1852, nine years after Norie's death; in all, there were 22 editions of the work. Victor Slocum, who became an expert navigator himself, said his father's first Norie was published in 1860, but he didn't say when Joshua acquired it.

Among the chapters were Practical Geometry, Plane Trigonometry, Description and Use of Hadley's Sextant, On Finding the Longitude by Chronometers, and much more. Despite the complexity of the book's material, Joshua Slocum apparently soaked up everything Norie had to teach, over 50 chapters and more than 350 pages of demanding material. Chapter Forty-Seven would prove to be of special interest to Slocum. Its title was "Logarithms for finding the declinations for reducing the Moon's or right Ascension to any Time under the Meridian of Greenwich."

Having absorbed and regularly practiced what Norie had to teach, Slocum would put the most esoteric details of what he'd learned to use with astonishing results both before and during his solo circumnavigation. His skill in lunar navigation, considered among a navigator's most challenging tasks, developed over his many years at sea. By the time Slocum set out in the *Spray* in 1895, his genius for taking and interpreting lunar sights was a conjurer's trick that allowed him to joke about using a tin clock for a chronometer while concealing the real manner in which he found his way around the watery planet. In the end, though, he so impressed himself with his lunarian skills that he gave way and shared his pride with readers.

In addition to Norie's book, the young Slocum purchased what Victor Slocum called a "pig-yoke," an archaic disparaging term sometimes used by seamen for the Davis quadrant. This instrument—invented by Elizabethan seafarer Captain John Davis in 1594—was an improvement over the ancient backstaff and astrolabe. It was used to measure the altitude of the sun or moon as a means of determining latitude. The quadrant Slocum bought had a frame made of ebony wood with the two arcs—the parts engraved with numbers—made of ivory.

To understand what impact mastering the Davis quadrant—which used the sun's shadow as its operational basis—might have had on Slocum's navigation skills, consider the following rather daunting description of how the instrument was used:

> [T]he navigator would place the shadow vane anticipating the altitude of the sun. Holding the instrument in front of him, with the sun at his back, he holds the instrument so that the shadow cast by the shadow vane falls on the horizon vane at the side of the slit. He then moves the

sight vane so that he observes the horizon in a line from the sight vane through the horizon vane's slit while simultaneously maintaining the position of the shadow. This permits him to measure the angle between the horizon and the sun as the sum of the angle read from the two arcs. Since the shadow's edge represents the limb of the sun, he must correct the value for the semidiameter of the sun.

The manual and mental dexterity needed to master the Davis quadrant must have instilled in Slocum a profound appreciation for the taking of celestial sights. He would have gained an understanding of the mechanics and geometries on which all celestial navigation relies. It was the sort of understanding that, once absorbed, would always be a ready tool in his chest of seamanship skills.

Aboard ship, Joshua Slocum learned how to use his Davis quadrant and refer to *The Epitome's* mathematical tables to determine latitude. Progressing from the quadrant to a ship's sextant would have reinforced his developing navigation acumen while making the sight-taking process easier. Ultimately, Slocum's natural aptitude coupled with his thorough understanding of the essentials of mathematics and sight-taking produced a celestial navigator of rare genius.

Slocum told Victor that he regarded his promotion to second mate as "the most decisive step in his career, [a] graduation from the hardest school on the sea, and recognition of his ability in seamanship and skill in handling men." But he would not have been promoted had he not mastered navigation.

THANKS TO A PANORAMIC view of Liverpool taken in 1860 by pioneering British photographer G. R. Berry, one can get an accurate idea of the sight that greeted Joshua Slocum as he approached one of Britain's greatest ports, a city he would come to know well. He would have seen a "forest of masts" towering above the ships at anchor in the River Mersey and those lying at the docks that stretched 15 miles along the waterfront.

Slightly over 2,200 sailing ships were then registered in Liverpool, together with 223 steamships. In his novel *Redburn*, published in 1849, Herman Melville wrote of Liverpool's docks, "which in depravity are not to be matched by anything this side of the pit that is bottomless." To give seamen some respite from crimps, thieves, prostitutes, and other landside threats, Liverpool opened a six-story sailor's home in 1852. There seamen could stay in tiny 8-foot by 5-foot "cabins." This sanctuary, such as it was, was severely damaged by a fire on April 29, 1860, and then repaired.

While Slocum's movements after arriving in Liverpool are unknown, indications are that he returned to San Francisco, arriving there in late 1866 or early 1867. Then, according to Victor, "my father decided to cast his lot on the Northwest Coast and to make San Francisco his hailing port with the view to obtaining command of a vessel under the American flag.... While ashore in San Francisco he fell in with the energetic, rough-and-ready life which still pervaded his adopted land."

Victor Slocum wrote that his father "met a Mr. Griffin[1] who built gill-net boats for the salmon fishery on the Columbia River.... Josh became interested in the industry, little dreaming how far it was going to take him.... He made a design for one of these boats, which was an improvement on the existing type, and this model was bought on sight by a cannery owner in Astoria who had boats built from it at his own establishment."

Although Victor Slocum gave no description of the existing gillnetters, he did provide details of his father's design. Carvel-planked, double-ended, and 25 feet long with a 6-foot beam, a centerboard, and a draft of 2½ feet, Slocum's gillnetter set a spritsail on a 16-foot mast stepped in the bow. It sounds exactly like the classic craft one now associates with the type. The Columbia River salmon fishery grew rapidly starting in the mid to late 1860s. By 1900, it was estimated that some 2,500 gillnet boats were at work supplying canneries with salmon. Slocum and a partner—possibly John Griffin—went salmon fishing themselves for a time, and then, according to Victor, "turned their attention to sea otter hunting at Gray's Harbor [Washington]."

Slocum soaked up all his experiences, kept a journal of camp life and the characters he met, and took careful note of what Victor Slocum referred to as the "Makah and Vancouver Island tribes, for whose seamanship he had the greatest respect, and whose canoe seamanship made a decided impression on him.... [They] produced craft as suitable to use, graceful and as true to line as the white man with [his] more convenient appliances and efficient tools."

This period of fishing, sea otter hunting, and observing Native American boatbuilding and boat-handling ended when Slocum was given his first job as a ship's captain. The vessel was a 75-foot coasting schooner named *Montana*. Slocum told Clifton Johnson that this occurred when he was 23,

---

1 The "Mr. Griffin" that Victor mentions appears to have been John D. Griffin who, with Patrick Healy, had a boat shop located on Jackson Street and Pacific Avenue in San Francisco.

in 1867. Notwithstanding the general uncertainty regarding the dates of Slocum's post-*Tanjore* voyaging, 1867 seems too early for his first command. The only shipping records found to date list Slocum as master of the *Montana* in 1869. These shipping news entries for Slocum and the *Montana* report that the vessel carried oats, barley, and potatoes between San Francisco and nearby Half Moon Bay.

According to Victor Slocum, his father did well with the *Montana*. "By sharp application and observation, the peculiar knack of taking advantage of all weather conditions close under the land was soon acquired by the Captain, who was always quick at learning a new technique. In two years of this employment he won the confidence of more important ship owners."

Slocum apparently remained in command of the *Montana* until early November 1869. His ambitions, however, ranged much farther than a coasting schooner could take him. As 1869 drew to a close, he signed off the *Montana* to return to the blue-water life he knew he'd been born to live.

CHAPTER 3

San Francisco

"Presently young Slocum left the Atlantic for the Pacific, voyaged to California, tried salmon fishing in Oregon, went to China and Australia ...."

—Clifton Johnson, 1902, notes from his interview with Joshua Slocum

SAN FRANCISCO IN THE 1860S was transforming itself from the chaotic, often lawless days of the 1849 gold rush and the 1859 silver rush into the "Paris of the West."[1] Its population of 83,000 in 1865 would grow to 178,000 five years later. Street railways were built to move about the sprawling city; one of them, the Omnibus Railroad Company, employed 90 men and maintained 190 horses. There was a National Guard unit, a philharmonic society, a book club, and libraries of which the city was particularly proud.

San Francisco's maritime industry was thriving too. There were steam-ship companies, boatbuilders, shipbuilders, shipping and forwarding agents, marine insurance companies, the boiler and steam-engine builder Pacific Iron Works, a rope walk, and a big dry dock at Hunters Point that would

---

1 The gold rush was spawned by the January 1848 discovery of gold at Sutter's Mill on the American River. The silver rush was sparked by the Comstock Lode discovery.

one day become a naval shipyard. Of course, there were also ship chandlers who stocked what was needed to outfit vessels and crews, and there were ship owners who might give a man like Joshua Slocum employment. Nicholas Bichard was one of those ship chandlers and ship owners.

Bichard family lore relates that Nicholas journeyed to California from Guernsey, in England's Channel Islands, as part of the great wave of prospectors hoping to strike it rich in the gold rush of 1849. Whether he had any luck in the gold fields is unknown, but he proved entrepreneurial and by 1856 was involved in the first of what would become several businesses. By the early 1860s, Bichard was importing anchor chain and anchors, the start of his ship chandlery.

In 1865, two years before the United States purchased Alaska from Russia, Nicholas Bichard was supplying Alaska-caught fish to Israel Kaskow, the first settler in Belvedere, then known as Still Island, on the Sausalito side of the bay. Kaskow's former property is now home to the San Francisco Yacht Club, but in the 1850s, Israel was drying fish there. Bichard soon became involved in marine salvage as well, and would eventually break up the side-wheel steamer *China*. He saved part of the vessel's superstructure, which exists today in its restored Victorian splendor as "China Cabin" on Beach Road in Belvedere.

Bichard then expanded his business activities to include a coal yard in San Francisco and two square riggers, the *Washington* and the *Constitution*.[1] In April 1870, he hired 26-year-old Joshua Slocum to take command of the *Constitution*, a 361-ton bark being readied for a voyage to Mexico. A decade after he had "slithered off" from Brier Island to Yarmouth, Slocum was exactly where he'd dreamed of being, in the captain's cabin of an oceangoing sailing ship.

On April 13, the *Constitution* cleared San Francisco for Guaymas, Mexico. The principal port of the state of Sonora, Guaymas is located in the northeast portion of the Sea of Cortez (Gulf of California). After returning to San Francisco, Slocum was given orders for a voyage to Alaska, where Bichard recognized the potential for immense profits from the fisheries. Slocum sailed for Alaska with the *Constitution* in August, returning in October. The *Daily Alta California* shipping news for October 7 reported: "Arrived Bktine Constitution, Slocum, 23 days from Kodiak, fish, salt, etc. to

---

1 Bichard's shipping interests may have been conducted, at least in part, with J. C. Merrill & Company, a San Francisco merchant house involved, among other things, in regular packet service to Honolulu and Oregon.

N. B. [Nicholas Bichard]."

Less than a month later, on November 3, 1870, the *Constitution* departed San Francisco for Sydney, Australia, on a voyage that changed Joshua Slocum's life forever. On January 9, 1871, just over two months after departing San Francisco, the *Constitution* arrived and tied up at Patent Slip Wharf. The ship's 20 steerage-class passengers debarked, and Laidley, Ireland & Company, Nicholas Bichard's agents in Sydney, saw to the off-loading and distribution of the *Constitution*'s cargo. As for the ship's captain, he hastened to meet a young lady.

How Joshua Slocum met Virginia Albertina Walker is another lost detail of Slocum's life. Virginia's father, William Walker, was born March 2, 1822, at Albany, New York,[2] but he was living in New York City when he married Margaret (also spelled Marguriette) Ann Walker on December 8, 1848. So far as is known, the newlyweds were unrelated, but the coincidence of surname meant that Margaret, who was said to be part Leni-Lenape Indian, didn't have to change her maiden name.

William Walker worked as a "weigher of coal" for the City of New York. He also served as a second lieutenant in the 9th Regiment of New York State Artillery and was a member of Manhattan Fire Engine Company Number 8, located on Nassau Street. His interest in firefighting stayed with him all his life. The couple's first child, Virginia, was said to have been born at Staten Island, where Margaret's family may have lived. The date of Virginia's birth is a matter of some puzzlement, no birth record having been found. Joshua Slocum believed that Virginia was born on August 22, 1849. However, the birth certificate of her younger brother George gives Virginia's birth year as 1851, and this is likely to be correct.

Family lore suggests that William Walker took his wife and baby daughter to California in pursuit of gold, but there is no record of this. If Walker did go to California, he must have seen little reason to stay. The news of the discovery of gold near Bathurst, New South Wales, in February 1851 was heard around the world and sparked a great influx of hopeful prospectors from Europe and the United States. During the next ten years, Australia's population doubled.

The Walkers joined the crowds emigrating to Sydney in, it is thought, 1853. Victor Slocum reported cryptically that his maternal grandfather "did

---

2 Benjamin Aymar Slocum wrote Walter Teller that his maternal grandfather had been born in England, but no evidence has yet been found to support this.

Virginia Albertina Walker prior to her marriage to Joshua Slocum on January 31, 1871, in Sydney. (Courtesy Melville C. Brown)

as well as he could have wished" in the gold fields, but that he subsequently opened a stationery store on Pitt Street in Sydney in 1854. In 1863, though, as he had in New York, William Walker took a municipal job, this one with Sydney's survey department. Walker was a genial man, an amateur thespian who could readily quote long passages from *Hamlet*. Just as he had been a volunteer fireman in New York, he became one in Sydney, too, serving as resident manager of Volunteer Fire Company No. 2.[1] The family cockatoo, Virginia told her children, might at any hour call out, "Fire, fire, Walker, fire."

Slocum's introduction to the Walker family may have been facilitated by another of Nicholas Bichard's captains, T. C. Walker, whose time in San Francisco overlapped Slocum's. During a several-month period in 1868, Captain Walker was master of the ship *Cesarewitch*,[2] making regular runs, usually of 14 to 18 days, from San Francisco to Kodiak, Alaska, returning with a cargo of ice. It's possible that Slocum served aboard the vessel. From August through November 1869, Walker commanded Bichard's barkentine *Constitution*, bringing timber from Teekalet and Port Gamble, Oregon, to the voracious building market in San Francisco. Captain Walker might well have been related to Virginia's father and, if so, may have suggested to Slocum that he look up the Walkers in Sydney.

However the couple met, it was, apparently, love at first sight. "She knew," wrote Victor Slocum, "he was just the kind of man she wanted." Photos of Joshua Slocum as a young man, when he still had his hair, reveal a fine-featured face, steady eyes, and the familiar chin whiskers and mustache. He was handsome, and projected the warmth of a man one would want to be friends with. The young man radiated an entirely different aura from the stern-visaged, stiff, worn-looking old salt who stares out at us from later images.

Like so much of Joshua Slocum's life story, details of his wedding, not to mention his bride's age, are absent or conflicting. Biographer Walter Teller found documentation indicating conclusively who performed the marriage and where: "I, James Greenwood, being Minister of the Bathurst St. Baptist Church, Sydney, do hereby Certify, that I have this day at 56 Upper Ford St,

---

1 Virginia's brother George was born at the fire station in 1859, and so was Virginia's sister Jessie Helena, in 1863.

2 The ship, operated by the Russian-American Company—an Alaskan fur-trading venture established in 1799 whose operations evolved to include farming and cattle raising in Northern California—was the subject of a lawsuit in March 1868 relating to its fraudulent sale. The *Cesarewitch* was a fixture of the San Francisco–Kodiak trade for at least several years.

Terraced homes on Sydney's Buckingham Street shortly after construction was completed in 1871. The Walker family lived at #19. (From the Collection of Mitchell Library, State Library of New South Wales; courtesy Melville C. Brown)

Sydney, duly celebrated Marriage between Joshua Slocum Bachelor, Master Mariner of Massachusetts, United States and Virginia Albertina Walker, Spinster of 19 Buckingham Street, Strawberry Hill, Sydney, after Declaration made as by law required. Dated this 31st day of January, 1871.... The Consent of Mr. Wm. Henry Walker, 19 Buckingham Street, Strawberry Hill, Sydney, was given to the Marriage of Virginia Albertina Walker with Joshua Slocum, the said Virginia Albertina Walker being under the age of Twenty-one years."[1]

Victor Slocum suggested that some drama attended the marriage. Despite the existence of the parental approval form, Victor wrote that "Mr. Walker, on getting wind of what was going on, hailed a carriage and dashed up to the altar just in time to be in at the finish. He was greatly chagrined and never quite forgave the couple.... I once heard [my mother] tell some of her women friends that it 'looked just like an elopement.'"

Virginia died when Victor was 13, and his information was based in part on what his Australian uncle, Virginia's younger brother George, thought he remembered about a wedding that had occurred some six decades earlier. Still, the marriage could indeed have appeared to be an elopement. For some reason, the wedding was not reported in the *Sydney Morning*

---

1 This reinforces Virginia's birth year as 1851, not 1849, and that she was 20 at the time of her marriage.

THE Consent of ___ *Mr Wm Henry Walker* ___

19 Buckingham St, Strawberry Hill, Sydney ___

was given to the Marriage of ___ *Virginia Albertina Walker*

with ___ *Joshua Slocum* ___

the said ___ *Virginia Albertina Walker* ___ being under

the age of Twenty-one years.

___ *Jas. Greenwood* ___ Minister or Registrar.

The form signed by Virginia's father, William Henry Walker, consenting to his daughter's marriage to Joshua Slocum. (Courtesy the New Bedford Whaling Museum)

Herald until Saturday, February 11, 1871, eleven days after the ceremony. "On the 31st January by the Rev. James Greenwood, Captain Joshua Slocum, ship *Constitution*, Boston, Mass, U.S. to Virginia Albertina, daughter of William H. Walker, Survey Department."

By the time of this announcement, the *Constitution* had been back at sea for a week. Nine days earlier, on February 2, the *Sydney Morning Herald* reported that the *Constitution* had been cleared to sail to San Francisco. "Passengers—Mrs. Slocum, Mrs. Thompson, Misses Thompson (2)." Thus, a reader who cared about such things would have learned that there was a Mrs. Slocum before learning there had been a marriage.[2]

Only 26 days had elapsed between Joshua Slocum's arrival in Sydney and his marriage with Virginia. If today this seems a dramatically short time in which to make and carry out a momentous life decision, it was not so extraordinary by nineteenth-century standards or among seamen and their sweethearts. Then, as now, ships earned no money when tied up in port.

---

2 Virginia was accompanied on the voyage by her 11-year-old younger brother, who appeared on the ship's passenger list as Master George Walker.

It was almost certainly the scheduled departure date of the *Constitution*—which Slocum would have been responsible for meeting—that occasioned the rush. In fact, he missed the sailing date. On March 13, 1871, the *San Francisco Bulletin* erroneously reported that the *Constitution* had cleared Sydney on January 31, Joshua and Virginia's wedding day.

Despite the seeming hurry, the newlyweds knew what they were doing. Virginia had met the love of her life, the man for whom she believed she had been destined. She soon grew to possess a seemingly intuitive understanding of her husband's needs and moods. "She knew more about father," remembered Benjamin Aymar Slocum, who was born in 1873 and spent his earliest years close by his mother, "than of herself. They were a husband and wife who could communicate across a crowded room with only a glance."

When the *Constitution* put to sea, Virginia embarked not only upon married life but upon a great transpacific voyage. It wasn't long before Slocum began teaching her celestial navigation. Like the wives of several well-known captains, Virginia learned the craft and proved an able back-up. Ginny, as Slocum called her, combined beauty, courage and, soon enough, an appetite for shark hunting instilled by her husband. Ben Aymar, when old enough, was enlisted by his mother to help in the quest for sharks.

"It was my job to get the shark interested in coming close up," he remembered in a 1954 letter to Walter Teller. "I used a tin can with a string on it to attract the shark close under stern." There, Virginia would dispatch the shark with a single shot from Slocum's .32-caliber Smith & Wesson revolver. "How I loved to see her do it—and without any signs on her part showing superior skill."

After a 90-day voyage, the *Constitution*, carrying a mixed cargo of coal and merchandise, arrived back in San Francisco on May 4, 1871. The Slocums' honeymoon voyage had been a success. However, a rather significant cloud now descended upon Joshua. Almost immediately upon his arrival, he found himself the defendant in Case No. 559, the *United States v. Joshua Slocum*. The case would be heard in the U.S. District Court in San Francisco and, essentially, involved a charge of assault by Slocum upon a member of his crew.[1]

Such charges against captains and mates had been common for at least 20 years by this time. Often enough, the cases were bogus, put together by "sea lawyers" who waited in barrooms for incoming ships and found a

---

1 National Archives and Records Administration at San Francisco, Record Group 21, Series: Criminal Case Files, 1851–1917, NAID: 1768480, Box 34.

sailor with a grievance, real or perceived. When skillfully presented to a jury of landsmen unfamiliar with shipboard practices, such cases often resulted in victory for the sailor.

Some cases had real merit, however. Among the most infamous and, perhaps, most deserved of lawsuits was brought in San Francisco in 1851 by crewmembers of the great clipper ship *Challenge*. On her maiden voyage from New York to San Francisco in 1851, at least nine men had died, some from injuries inflicted by first mate James Douglass, whose behavior was reinforced by the ship's master, Robert Waterman. Waterman, highly regarded by his peers, was forced to support his abusive mate against mutineers. Both Waterman and Douglass were fortunate to escape lynching by a San Francisco mob, but the subsequent court cases resulted in no significant penalties.

The crewmember who sued Joshua Slocum, Michael Robinson, claimed to be a master mariner who'd been stranded in Sydney by misfortune. In his testimony, Robinson said that he had tried to find the *Constitution*'s captain so he could sign aboard. Failing to meet Slocum, Robinson stowed away, appearing—in a disheveled condition—only after the *Constitution* had cleared Sydney Heads. Slocum was less than pleased to have such an event occur on his first voyage with his wife.

"He said I was a dirty, piratical-looking fellow," Robinson testified. "He told me to go wash my hands and sign the articles. He told 2nd mate to put me to duty." At some point thereafter, Robinson ran afoul of Slocum in a serious way. It is not entirely clear what happened, but Slocum felt that the man had been aft where he didn't belong—perhaps trying to look into the quarters he and Virginia occupied—rather than in the forecastle. The result was that Slocum attacked Robinson with a club, striking him several times. It was a beating serious enough to render Robinson unfit for duty for two or three weeks.

The case was scheduled to be heard on May 8, 1871, at 11:00 a.m. This was a problem for Slocum because Nicholas Bichard had placed him in command of the *Washington*, and Slocum expected to be on his way to Alaska on May 6. Therefore he hired attorney Milton Andros, whose office was in San Francisco's federal courthouse. In his letter to the court appointing Andros, Slocum wrote:

> *I am now the master of the American vessel Washington ... and I am intending to sail on Saturday the sixth day of May instant. Note I am a poor man having no means of support except my profession as a*

master mariner, that I have a wife and brothers and sisters that are
dependent on me for support, that not to proceed on the voyage
aforesaid will seriously injure me.

On May 9, 1871, San Francisco's *Daily Evening Bulletin* reported, "The case of the *United States v. Joshua Slocum* summary proceeding for beating and wounding one Michael Robinson on board the American ship *Constitution* is on trial." A few days later, it was reported that Slocum had been found guilty.

This was the first known instance of Slocum finding himself a defendant in such a case, but it would not be the last. Sometimes judgments went in his favor. Sometimes they did not. Whatever the outcome, Slocum always believed stoutly that his actions were necessary to maintain or restore order or to protect life and property. Worse was to come.

Nicholas Bichard wasn't put off by the decision against his captain. Aware of Slocum's salmon-fishing and gillnet-boat experience on the Columbia River, Bichard sent Slocum to Alaska to reap the harvest of its largely untapped waters. Bichard's long experience with the abundance of fish and fur in Alaska made him quick to realize the resources that, since Alaska's purchase by the United States in 1867, were now within U.S. territory. No longer would there be a need to dodge Russian patrol vessels that could impound or confiscate American ships and imprison crews. The *Washington* was among the first American ships since the purchase of Alaska to make a voyage to the dangerous, salmon-rich fishing grounds off the Kenai Peninsula.

With Joshua Slocum on this ambitious voyage into challenging, little-charted waters went his bride and, again, Virginia's brother George Washington Walker. Slocum anchored the *Washington* near the mouth of the Kasilof River,[1] where, after making a tight, looping turn, it flows into Cook Inlet. Around the river mouth is a broad estuary of tidal flats and creeks that gives way to wetlands and meadows. On higher ground back from the meadows were woods and plentiful game, including caribou, bears, and moose, although the latter were sometimes mistakenly referred to by newcomers as elk.

It was a landscape well-known to the Denai'ina Athabascan tribe, whose members, according to local historian Shana Loshbaugh, "had numerous small, sometimes seasonal communities along the seacoast and salmon

---

1 On old Russian maps, the river was referred to variously as Kasilov or Kasilova or Kasilovka.

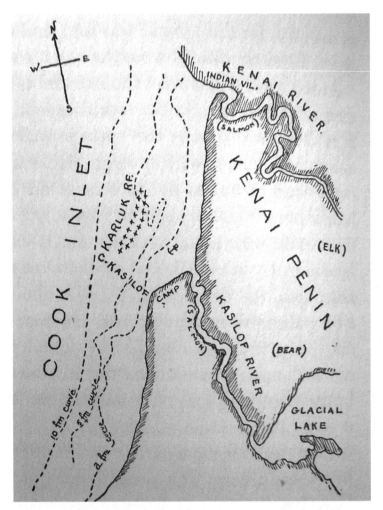

Cook Inlet as described by Joshua Slocum to his son Victor, showing the location of the fishing camp established by the crew of the Washington.

rivers. One village existed just south of the Kasilof River mouth at a place called Humpy Point." Russian settlers had arrived in the area by 1787 and, according to Loshbaugh, were "certainly at Kenai by 1791, where they built a fort that became the seed of a growing community. It was a hub for fur trading, then a Russian Orthodox Church parish seat, and much later a fishing center. In 1871, Kenai would have been inhabited by 'Russianized' natives, mixed-race people, and adventurous new 'Yankees,' all living in clustered cabins with little gardens of cabbages and other hearty vegetables. The U.S. Cavalry had a presence there, dubbed 'Fort Kenay,' but they were so bored they pulled out in 1870 after only 18 months."

Slocum set up a fishing camp on the south side of the river, perhaps at what had been called Humpy Point. His plan was not without risk. Extensive bars of glacial silt make out from the mouth of the Kasilof. Enormous boulders, deposited by glaciers, dot the ground both there and on the shoals at the north and east portions of Cook Inlet. The waters outside the rocky Karluk Reef are swept by 4-knot currents.

Joshua Slocum's safe navigation of a vessel the size of the *Washington* into this area reflected courage and impressive seamanship. Based on what his father told him, Victor Slocum wrote: "To secure sufficient depth of water, the *Washington* had to be anchored about two miles out on an extensive flat which filled the bight between Cape Kasilof and the mouth of the river where the fishing was done.... In this precarious berth the vessel was protected as much as possible from the tidal currents.... [A]lso she derived additional protection from the shelter of Karluk Reef."

Slocum's chosen anchorage was sufficient to protect his ship from the currents outside the reef and from the gale-force winds he knew would buffet them during the stay. The *Washington*'s crew immediately began gillnetting from boats they had built under Slocum's guidance. The whole endeavor was conducted in a wilderness of such beauty that both Joshua and Virginia Slocum remembered it all their lives.

"My mother," wrote Victor Slocum, "never recovered from her admiration and wonder for this Alaskan region. When the weather was clear, across the inlet towered two lofty volcanoes of the Aleutian Range, Mount Redoubt and Mount Iliamna. Beyond the low eastern shores, covered with clumps of timber rose the high Kenai Range, containing large glaciers."

The potential threats weren't all from weather events or bears. Victor Slocum wrote that his mother kept a rifle in her tent for protection against possible intruders from the local community. Once, when her husband approached without hollering a greeting, she prepared to defend herself. Slocum himself had been attacked and mauled by a bear while fishing in British Columbia, according to Victor. At Kenai, Slocum was forced to shoot a huge bear that appeared aggressive and refused to be scared off. The bear's skin eventually wound up as a rug in the home of Slocum's in-laws in Sydney.

But the greatest danger was the weather. An anchor watch remained aboard the *Washington* while the rest of the crew landed impressive numbers of salmon. But neither the shipboard crew nor the *Washington's* anchors proved sufficient to protect the vessel against one of the northwest gales that were not infrequent in the area in early summer. The *Washington*, still riding high in ballast at that early stage of the expedition, dragged both her anchors until she was cast up on the sands.

"I have heard my father say, in speaking of this disaster," Victor Slocum wrote, "that it was reported to him next year that the sand dunes were piled up so high on the seaward side of the vessel that it seemed inconceivable she had ever been afloat." There now commenced an adventure that, while little known at the time—there were no newspapers in the area, and neither Slocum nor Nicholas Bichard had any reason to publicize what happened—became a Slocum family legend. Doubtless no crewmember of the *Washington* ever forgot, either.

News of the event reached San Francisco with the arrival from Kodiak of the schooner *General Harvey*. The loss was briefly reported in a matter-of-fact manner in San Francisco's *The Daily Morning Call* on August 28, 1871, and in the shipping news column of the *Daily Alta California* on August, 27. "June 21 bark *Washington*, Capt. Slocum was wrecked at Pasilo [sic] River, Cooks Inlet." On August 31, the *San Francisco Chronicle* reported: "The bark *Washington*, Captain Slocum, was wrecked on the 21st of last June in Cook's Inlet.... A number of vessels have been wrecked in Cook's Inlet since Alaska came into our possession. It is said that the channels and bars there change every year, so that navigation is very unsafe and dangerous."

But the real story was Slocum's response to the loss of the ship. He kept right on fishing. What Virginia Slocum thought at the time is unknown, but her faith in her husband and her own spirit of adventure would have sustained her. Slocum's plan was to complete the fishing while, at the same time, building another boat using lumber salvaged from the *Washington*. Even as the salmon catch was smoked and prepared for shipment, Slocum set his men to building what Victor described as a 35-foot whaleboat. This boat, with two gillnetters, would be used to get the crew down to Kodiak.

By the time the fishing was complete and the whaleboat had been built, a revenue cutter appeared.[1] "The Captain would accept no other help

---

[1] Established in 1790, the United States Revenue Cutter Service was merged with the United States Lifesaving Service in 1915 to become the Coast Guard. At the time of the *Washington's* loss, the cutter in that part of Alaska was the USRC *Reliance*. Among its duties would have been patrolling to prevent the sale of liquor to the Native American population, which was against federal law.

except to have his wife taken to Kodiak, and in that way she was enabled to make the trip in comfort and safety instead of enduring the hardship of the ship's boats," Victor Slocum wrote. Slocum left behind a skilled wilderness hand named Thompson, known to the crew as "Rocky Mountain Hunter," whose duty it was to protect the valuable salmon until Slocum could return with another vessel.

Once the spring tides had diminished, Slocum and his men pushed off on a voyage of some 200 miles to Kodiak. Their provisions consisted of hardtack and smoked salmon. With the help of fair northerly winds, they made the trip south from Cook Inlet in stages, stopping first in Kachemak Bay, then Cape Elizabeth, then Afognak, and finally Kodiak. There, according to Victor Slocum, a pair of sealing schooners was chartered to go back and fetch Thompson and the salmon catch. Virginia's brother George—a rugged young man who, upon returning to Australia, became a competitive cyclist, swimmer, and rugby player—and the crew returned to San Francisco aboard the familiar *Cesarewitch*, which had come north on another of her ice-harvesting voyages.

The financial result of the *Washington* adventure is unknown. The vessel was lost, and costs were incurred to carry the salmon to San Francisco in other ships. Yet the catch itself was valuable, possibly valuable enough that Bichard still made a profit while also collecting insurance on the *Washington*. Slocum would have gotten back to San Francisco sometime in the autumn of 1871. When he arrived, Bichard put him back aboard the *Constitution* and, on September 2, bought another ship at auction, a schooner named *Page* for which he paid $3,350.

Slocum and Virginia were living aboard the *Constitution* in San Francisco when, in December 1871, they were witness to what the newspaper called a "severe gale." One result was that Slocum became oddly enmeshed in a dispute between two vessels involved in a storm-induced collision. A bark named the *Scotland* that had been anchored off Beale Street dragged her anchor and caused some damage to a British frigate, the *Zealous*. The *Zealous* claimed damages, which were promptly paid.

However, on December 31, 1871, the *Daily Alta California* reported: "It has been demonstrated by Captain Slocum of the bark *Constitution* by actual measurement that the *Zealous* was only 448 yards from the corner of Beale Street Wharf. As the regulations require that she should be 500 yards distant from this point, the money paid in damages will have to be refunded."

Joshua's motive for getting in a small boat and taking the necessary

George Washington Walker, Virginia's athletic younger brother, at the famed Coogee Aquarium and Swimming Baths in Sydney during the early 1890s. (Courtesy Melville C. Brown)

measurements to determine that a British ship was 52 yards closer to the Beale Street dock than port regulations stipulated she should have been was never revealed. But it's a detail that, when put in the context of Slocum's suit against the captain of the *Tanjore* and his readiness to use his "big fist," suggests that he had a very strong sense of right and wrong, even if the matter wasn't really his business. In the case of the *Scotland* and the *Zealous*, Slocum also demonstrated that only *he*—not either captain of the other vessels—had the wit to gather physical evidence. It suggests, too, that there were times when Slocum simply couldn't resist showing off his superior abilities. More dramatic examples would follow.

According to Victor Slocum, his parents were present in San Francisco for the much-anticipated arrival in January of a Japanese delegation to the United States. When the ship carrying the delegation signaled that it would be an hour late, the crowd became restive. Somehow, it fell to Joshua Slocum to provide a bit of entertainment involving a display of marksmanship. It was not unusual for San Franciscans to own a pistol for personal protection, and Slocum carried his .32-caliber Smith & Wesson revolver. This he now used to shoot an unfortunate loon that was feeding near the gathered onlookers. It was something he wouldn't have done in later years, when the only creatures he had no qualms about killing were, as always, sharks.

No records have thus far surfaced regarding the *Constitution's* voyages during 1872, but Victor was born aboard the ship on January 10. Slocum next spent at least two months in command of Bichard's schooner *Page*, taking her on several trips from San Francisco to Alaska and back in February and March 1872. After that, he was back aboard the *Constitution*.

Victor Slocum later learned from his father that the *Constitution* ran for a time as a packet to Honolulu, and on one of these passages, the ship's chronometer broke down. Victor Slocum wrote:

> [T]he mishap made no difference so far as navigation of the vessel was concerned.[1] In fact, upon arriving in San Francisco, it was found that the passage had been unusually short. Mr. Bichard, the owner, who was waiting on the dock, was amazed, and without saying a word about the circumstances of the voyage, turned on his heel, and returned

---

[1] Expertly taken lunar sights supported by mathematical calculations and reference to the appropriate tables could give the best navigators their position without resort to a chronometer. Slocum was already an expert at putting into practice what he had learned in Norie's book on navigation.

with the best chronometer watch, an E. Howard,[2] that money could buy. This he presented to his Captain, both as a mark of appreciation and a guarantee that he would thereafter be protected against accidents by having a second time-piece about.... The chronometer breakdown episode throws a light on the [lunar] navigation of the Spray which has never been very well understood, owing perhaps to the Captain's vagueness on this point.

After his Honolulu runs, Slocum took the *Constitution* on another voyage into the Gulf of California and subsequently to Acapulco. Later in 1872 he made a voyage from Valparaiso, Chile, to Nuku Hiva, the largest of the Marquesas Islands. During a stop for fresh water at Easter Island, Joshua and his wife marveled at the mysterious carved stone images.[3]

ON OCTOBER 20, 1872, a bark named the *B. Aymar* under the command of Captain Elliott arrived in San Francisco and eventually moored at the Mission Street Wharf. There, on November 10, it was reported that the vessel was undergoing a number of repairs that included a new rudderpost. Three days later, when the *B. Aymar* left San Francisco for Burrard Inlet near Victoria, British Columbia, she was under a new master, Joshua Slocum.

No information exists about why Slocum left the *Constitution* and Nicholas Bichard's employment. Possibly there were lingering ill feelings regarding the loss of the *Washington*. As for why Captain Elliott was replaced, the only mention of the *B. Aymar*'s previous voyage noted nothing negative, only that she had experienced "moderate and variable winds all the passage."

As Slocum stood on the afterdeck of the *B. Aymar*, he found himself in command of the first vessel of her size built in Searsport, Maine, at the John Carver yard on the Penobscot River. She was launched in 1840. A grand painting of the bark in the collection of the Penobscot Maritime Museum shows her flying the flag of her owners, Benjamin Aymar & Company, a white field crossed by three rows of red diamonds.

Benjamin Aymar (1791–1876) was among New York's most successful and admired businessmen. *The Old Merchants of New York*, published in 1885, reported that the "house of Benjamin Aymar & Co. did business with all the parts of the world." The family owned at least five ships. Slocum's

---

2 E. Howard & Co. was a Boston maker of fine watches, clocks, and marine timepieces.
3 In 1978, a Christmas Island stamp commemorating Slocum was issued.

Dutch painter Dirk Antoon Teupken's (1801–45) painting of the B. Aymar *shows the newly built ship arriving at the Frisian Island of Texel, Netherlands, in October 1840. Teupken sometimes portrayed his subjects from more than one perspective. Here he depicts the* B. Aymar *sailing to windward as well as off the wind. The house flag of Benjamin Aymar & Company flies at the mizzentop. The name board on the transom reads:* B. Aymar, New York. *Slocum assumed command of the* B. Aymar *in October 1872, exactly 32 years after this painting was made. (Courtesy Penobscot Marine Museum)*

vessel was probably named for Benjamin Aymar's third son, Benjamin, a man who, having no taste for business or shipping, became a farmer.

Initially the *B. Aymar* had carried immigrants from Europe across the Atlantic to New York, but it is thought that the ship began making runs to California during the gold rush and then remained on the West Coast. After signing on as master, Slocum made several runs from San Francisco to Burrard Inlet, which, well before the establishment of the city of Vancouver in 1886, was the port for New Westminster, then the capitol of British Columbia. The area was home to two big sawmills—Moodyville on the inlet's north shore and the Stamp's or Hastings Mill on the south shore—providing lumber for markets along the Pacific Coast and in South America, Australia, Hawaii, China, and England.

It was likely during the early months of 1873 that Slocum received sailing orders to Swatow (now Shantou), a treaty port open for trade with the West in China's Guandong Province. On June 17, 1873, the *B. Aymar*, laden with 8,800 bags of sugar, departed Swatow for the return to San Francisco, which she reached 64 days later. After mooring at Oriental Wharf, Joshua Slocum gave voice to his intense study of the sea in what may have been his first published writing. On August 22, the *Daily Alta California* "Shipping Intelligence" column carried Slocum's account of observations made during his Pacific passage. It was the sort of information only the most serious student of winds and seas would have thought to set down; the sort of vitally useful information that John W. Norie would have applauded; and the sort of information once treasured by astronomer and oceanographer Matthew Fontaine Maury, the U.S. Navy lieutenant who, during an 18-year period before the Civil War, compiled data from ship's logs to produce his remarkable charts tracking the world ocean winds and currents:

> *Per B Aymar—Left Swatow June 17th: experienced strong NE winds in the China Sea; passed through Van Diemen Straits July 3d, with light SW winds, which continued along the coast of Japan: found but little current and sometimes none at all, in the track of the Kurosino [Slocum meant Kuroshio, the north-flowing Japan Current similar to the Gulf Stream] stream; and to venture an humble opinion no one will find the current of much force during those months when the NE trade winds do not blow home; where we found its velocity 28 miles per day in April it was found about 8 in July; from the west of Japan to the meridian of 180, had the wind S and SSE with dense fog; thence to 140 W, light variable winds and calm weather.*

On September 3, 1873, having offloaded her sugar, the *B. Aymar* was chartered by C. L. Taylor & Co., a shipping merchant with offices on California Street in San Francisco, to make a voyage to Melbourne, Australia. Twenty days later, carrying merchandise valued at nearly $43,000 (about $900,000 in today's money), the *B. Aymar* cleared San Francisco. For the first time since her marriage, Virginia was headed back to Australia.

Accompanying Joshua and Virginia, who was again pregnant, was their son Victor, then about 18 months old. In his later book, Victor wrote that the "*Benjamin Aymar* was the first home that I remember." He recalled his parents "promenading the deck in the second dog watch [6:00–8:00

This carte-de-visite image of Virginia was made in the celebrated Sydney studio of Newman Montagu "Monty" Scott (1835–1909), probably during 1874 when the Slocums were in Australia aboard the B. Aymar. Similar in size to a personal calling card, the carte-de-visite— an albumen print on thin paper mounted to a thicker paper card—was popular at the time. Virginia was probably 23 years old when this photo was made. (Courtesy the New Bedford Whaling Museum)

p.m.],” and, later, his father's stories about the very real dangers of pirates and cannibals in the South China Sea and adjacent waters.

The *B. Aymar* arrived in Melbourne on November 27, 1873. There, while Slocum saw to unloading and business matters, it was decided that Virginia and Victor would sail for Sydney. They left Melbourne aboard the *Hero* on December 2, and in Sydney, at her parents’ house, Virginia gave birth to her second son on December 21, 1873. He was named for the ship, Benjamin Aymar Slocum. On the birth certificate, Joshua Slocum's place of birth is listed not as Nova Scotia but, consistent with his Seaman's Protection Certificate, as Massachusetts.[1]

In February 1874, the *B. Aymar* sailed from Newcastle, New South Wales, about 100 miles north of Sydney, for Amoy (now Xiamen), a Chinese treaty port on the country's southeast coast bordering the Taiwan Strait. There, the ship unloaded her cargo and Victor learned to fly kites with Chinese children and was photographed wearing traditional Chinese clothing complete with a tasseled cap. Slocum remained master of the *B. Aymar* well into 1875.

In June 1875, with the ship anchored at Olongapo, Philippines, Virginia gave birth to a daughter named Jessie Helena, in honor of Virginia's sister. But sometime during the latter months of 1875, Benjamin Aymar & Company decided to sell the vessel, and it was purchased by a Shanghai merchant firm. On November 10, the bark was reported to be proceeding to Manila “under charter affected elsewhere,” commanded by a man named Lapham.

The *B. Aymar* was the last ship Slocum didn't own himself or with partners. His departure from her afterdeck marked the start of a new chapter in his life and that of his family. Ashore now in the Philippines, Joshua Slocum would, for a time, exchange the ocean for the jungle and the command of a sailing vessel for the construction of a wooden steamship.

---

1 The birth certificate gave Virginia's age as 23, which would have meant she was born in 1850, not 1849 as has generally been stated. However, as she needed parental permission to marry, the most likely birth year remains 1851.

CHAPTER 4

The Philippine Islands and the Pacific

"Yes sir, we had a stirring voyage and altogether a delightful time on the fishing grounds for every codfish that came in over the rail was a quarter of a dollar clear."

—Joshua Slocum, 1890, on fishing for cod in the Sea of Okhotsk in 1877

ABOUT 60 MILES NORTH AND WEST OF MANILA, at the head of Subic Bay, lies the Philippine city of Olongapo. Although it would be built up by Spain prior to the Spanish-American War and would subsequently become an important U.S. Navy base, Olongapo was a remote jungle town in the 1870s. Crocodiles, boa constrictors, and monkeys crowded the surrounding swamps and jungle, and poisonous centipedes and scorpions lurked underfoot. Neither were the human inhabitants uniformly friendly. Yet it was to

Olongapo, probably during the latter months of 1875, that Joshua Slocum took his wife, infant daughter, and two small boys.

The only source for the Slocums' time at Olongapo is Victor, who would then have been about three years old. He later relied on his father for details of this unusual, uncomfortable, dangerous interlude in Slocum's seafaring career. It was in Manila during or before the sale of the *B. Aymar* that Joshua Slocum met a British businessman named Edward Jackson. Sometime between late 1869 and 1870, Jackson had left London for Manila, where he joined the merchant house of Russell & Sturgis, founded in the 1830s by Bostonian Nathaniel Russell Sturgis (1805–1887).

The trading house was Jackson's day job, but his passion was ship and yacht design. He was especially interested in the speed potential of hulls with comparatively full midship sections that would permit finer lines at the bow and stern. His ideas were considered original enough that he was awarded a patent for "Improvements in the Construction of Ships and Vessels" on November 13, 1872.[1] In a letter published in the May 23, 1873, issue of the British magazine *The Engineer*, Jackson showed the lines for several hulls and, incidentally, cross-sections of several other vessels including the yacht *America*, which he had studied carefully.

The project Jackson and Slocum discussed was the building of a wooden hull for a 150-ton propeller-driven steamship Jackson had designed. Slocum agreed to manage the project at Olongapo, where a shipyard overseen by Chinese shipwrights and employing indigenous Tagalog workers had been operating since the sixteenth century. The yard had a long history of building and repairing big Spanish galleons for voyages from Manila to China for spices and for the rich trade between Manila and Acapulco.

The steamship project would involve labor strife, the planned murder of Slocum's family, an attempt to sabotage the launching of the vessel and, according to Victor, a later attempt on a Manila street to fatally stab Slocum. Typically, Joshua seems to have viewed all these challenges as mere parts of the job, and, as always, he met each one as it came. Virginia, who had been an outdoors sort of girl in Australia, was, if not equally fearless, at least able

---

1 "This Invention relates to a peculiar base for a new form for the hulls of vessels whereby greater safety, handiness, and ease of motion with greater speed in proportion to the power or displacement in vessels of all sizes are obtained." As was the custom then for British inventors overseas, Jackson's patent (#3387) was filed in the name of John Henry Johnson of 47 Lincoln's Inn Fields, County of Middlesex, who was Jackson's agent in the matter. Among other vessels, Jackson is known to have a designed a dredger for the city of Karachi.

to quell her anxieties. She cared for her newborn daughter and the two boys and found ways to cope in an unforgiving environment.

Victor Slocum never forgot his childhood impressions of the night-time jungle noises, insects, and wildlife at Olongapo or his fascination with the framing up of Jackson's hull. But there was trouble from the start. Slocum had paid the corrupt local official in charge at Olongapo to build his family a nipa hut—a raised, thatched dwelling adapted to the tropical environment. Having taken Slocum's money, however, the official found ways to delay construction until Slocum used his big fist and the leather toe of his stout Brier Island boot to get things underway. With the nipa completed, Slocum took the further step of securing it with rattan ropes to stakes driven deep in the ground as a protection against typhoons, an innovation so revolutionary that the local governor came to see it.

Joshua Slocum got along well with the Tagalogs, whom Victor Slocum referred to as "Tagals." The Tagals did much of the grunt work involved in shipbuilding: They felled trees, brought in logs with their water buffalo, and worked as sawyers, laboriously getting out the planks. The Chinese shipwrights were responsible for the fitting together of the components, and it was with them that Slocum's most serious problems developed.

"These particular Chinese," Victor Slocum wrote, "were from the southern coast, and a savage lot. They were under the control of a *patrone* who resented the Jackson contract being given to anyone else, and he planned to either seize or destroy the vessel." Resentment simmered.

Slocum had to make periodic trips back to Manila, and while he was away on one such trip, Virginia and the children were awakened during the night by the shouts of Tagals. Carrying torches and armed with axes, the men formed a protective ring around the Slocum nipa. "The faithful Tagals," Victor explained, "had scented a plot by the Chinese … to murder the family during the Captain's absence."

Meanwhile, work on the vessel continued. One wonders how Joshua Slocum, smart and confident though he was, developed the knowledge to oversee the construction of a ship's hull. He could draw on his small-craft building experience. There had been the gillnetter built to his design on the Columbia River and another gillnetter and a whaleboat on the Kenai peninsula. A key to the project, however, according to Victor, was that both his father and Edward Jackson relied on "Peake's little book on naval architecture." This "little book" was James Peake's *Rudiments of Naval Architecture; an Exposition of the Elementary Principles of the Science, and Their Practical*

Application to Naval Construction; Compiled for the Use of Beginners.

Peake conceived his book to be the first in the English language to cover the subject in a way approachable to those who had not apprenticed in a shipyard nor had any other formal training in vessel design or building. The first edition was published in the 1830s, and the third edition, perhaps the one used by Slocum and Jackson, was released in 1867. Divided into two parts, one on design ("The displacement of a Floating Body considered," etc.) and one on construction ("Description of the several Modes used in Her Majesty's service of uniting the Beams to the Sides of the ship," etc.), the book exhaustively set out the tasks, goals, formulas, and practical considerations of ship design and construction. It speaks to Slocum's genius, and Jackson's, that they could translate Peake's instructions and mathematics into the real thing. For Slocum, the process may have been akin to learning navigation from Norie's book.

Launch day arrived with a plot by the Chinese to sabotage the ship. Although suspicious, Joshua didn't notice that the launch rails had been shifted just enough to stop the hull as it slid down the ways. The plotters' assumption was that big hydraulic jacks would need to be procured from Hong Kong to support the hull and get the ways back into alignment, and they could use the delay to cause further mischief. Instead, the Tagals hitched up enough water buffalo—traditionally used to launch smaller boats—to get the hull afloat undamaged. It was then towed to Manila for installation of the boiler and engine.

The financial details of Joshua Slocum's arrangement with Edward Jackson are largely unknown, and what little is known is confusing. Years later, in a letter, Slocum indicated that severing ties with Benjamin Aymar & Company had left him cash poor. He didn't elaborate, but perhaps the New York merchant house failed to pay him in part or in full for his services. His primary compensation for building the steamship hull was a schooner of Jackson's design, which Jackson handed over after the steamship's successful sea trial.

"I took [the schooner] as a means of retrieving a loss which occurred to me through failure of a heavy House," Slocum wrote, and what a vessel she was! Named *Pato* ("duck" in Spanish), the little schooner—72 feet long on deck with a 15-foot beam and a 9-foot depth of hold—was designed by Edward Jackson along the lines of the American schooner yacht *Sappho*.

Built at the Brooklyn yard of C. & R. Poillon, *Sappho* was a topsail schooner based on the lines of the well-proven *America* launched in 1851.

Designed by William Townsend, the yard's in-house designer, *Sappho* was a big yacht—145½ feet long overall and 274 tons displacement—44 feet longer and 104 tons heavier than the *America*. Two years after her 1867 launching, she was hauled and "hipped," which involved stripping her planking and "padding" her frames. The result was a 14-inch increase in beam, an increase in tonnage to 310, and an 8-foot increase in mast height since the bigger hull could carry more sail.

Under the command of the redoubtable Captain Bob Fish, the *Sappho* made an attention-grabbing transatlantic passage from New York to Queenstown (now Cobh, on the south coast of Ireland) of 12 days, 9 hours, and 36 minutes. Two years later, in 1871, *Sappho*, together with *Columbia*, successfully defended the *America*'s Cup against the British challenger *Livonia*.[1] The widespread publicity garnered by *Sappho* resulted in her design features being published in the day's yachting press. In Manila, Edward Jackson made a close study of the yacht.

Victor Slocum didn't share what changes Jackson made to *Sappho*'s lines to produce the *Pato*. He wrote only that the idea was less to produce a yacht than to be a "commercial experiment," a commercial sailing vessel based on a yacht. But Jackson's re-conception of *Sappho* and the lines he developed based on his own ideas were so impressive that he was awarded a medal at London's 1874 International Exposition.

Although Victor noted that the *Pato* had been "built in the Spanish Philippines by the Chinese," the schooner was not complete when Slocum took possession. "The *Pato* had neither deck nor cabin when I took her," the captain recalled years later. But the hull had been built of teak, ironwood, and mahogany—high-quality species used in the Philippines. Slocum finished her off, adding the deck and accommodations. The only known pictures of the boat, two small profile drawings in Victor's book, show the usual cabinhouse aft. Her rig included a topsail for the mainmast and a staysail that could be set between the top of the foremast and the main topmast. Slocum later called the *Pato* "somewhat oddly rigged."

As was so often the case with Joshua Slocum and bureaucracy, the paperwork for the *Pato* wasn't straightforward. Although the boat was nominally Slocum's property, Edward Jackson, a British citizen, was still listed as her owner when Slocum registered the *Pato* at the British consulate in Manila on February 27, 1877. Thus, the *Pato* could sail under British registry.

---

1 After winning two races, losing one, and being damaged, *Columbia* was replaced by *Sappho*.

Despite his sometime claim that he always sailed under the American flag, neither of Slocum's first transatlantic voyages had been made in American ships. Later, Slocum's experience in the Pacific and the South Seas convinced him that a British-flagged vessel would be treated with more respect than an American flag—a belief that would be disastrously, if erroneously, reinforced in Brazil over a decade later.

A 72-foot schooner was a different sort of craft entirely from the square-rigged sailing ships Slocum had commanded. Her tonnage, by whatever measure one might choose—95 tons by American measurement, 65 tons by English[1]—was a fraction of Slocum's previous vessels. Almost as much yacht as working vessel, the *Pato* was best-suited to fast interisland trade, and Slocum made a few such runs before he was hired to salvage a cargo of tea, camphor, and silks from a British ship that had run onto a reef. This he accomplished just before the vessel slipped off the reef and sank. He was then hired to take a cargo of timber to Hong Kong, and departed Manila on March 3.

With her slick, seaworthy hull, schooner rig and well-cut sails, the *Pato* proved outstanding in windward ability, and dry as well. In rough weather in the Formosa Straits, Slocum's boat much impressed the experienced Chinese junk crews who witnessed her bounding to windward. *Pato* encountered strong northerly gales on the voyage, and by the time she arrived at Hong Kong on March 14, the schooner needed some repairs. It was then that Slocum decided to undertake a cod-fishing expedition north of Japan to Russia's bountiful Sea of Okhotsk (pronounced *oh-kotsk*).

"Hong Kong proved to be a convenient place to fit out," Victor Slocum wrote. "Dories of the Cape Ann model were built by Chinese boat builders, and fishing gear was easily procured. Enough seal poachers, sea otter hunters and other flotsam of the North Pacific were found on the beach to make a fishing crew willing to go on shares. These were of the type that the Captain had come to know on the Northwest Coast and they got on well together."

The *Pato* cleared Hong Kong on April 12, 1877, heading north. Slocum's objective was Petropavlovsk (now Petropavlovsk-Kamchatsky)—the Russian port of entry for the Kamchatka fishing grounds—2,900 miles away. A few days after the *Pato* had entered the Sea of Okhotsk and was steering a northeasterly course past the Kuril Islands toward the Kamchatka Peninsula,

---

1 In one letter, Slocum referred to the *Pato* as a 45-ton vessel, significantly understating her capacity. More information about tonnage can be found in Appendix A.

Victor reported that his mother called him on deck. Virginia was "all aglow with excitement …to see the high, conical peak of Mount Viliushinsky, white and glistening in the morning sunlight, high above the fog drifting upon the sea." Of the ice-capped, volcanic, 7,000-foot-high mountain on the Kamchatka Peninsula, Victor wrote that it was "one of the sights never to be forgotten in one's lifetime."

The richness of the cod fishing wasn't to be forgotten, either. The *Pato's* dories fanned out over the Okhotsk grounds with their trawls and immediately began landing unexpected quantities of fish.[2] As more and more cod were pitched aboard, it became apparent to Slocum that he hadn't brought nearly enough rock salt. Once again, "Slocum's luck" saved the day when he spotted none other than Nicholas Bichard's *Constitution*, just about to head back to San Francisco with her own load of cod. They "were about to shovel overboard enough unused salt to make up the *Pato's* quota," wrote Victor Slocum. "This waste was belayed, and the salt shoveled into the *Pato's* hold."

Two weeks after Slocum's crew started fishing, the *Pato* was loaded with 23,000 pounds of salted cod. Rather than follow the *Constitution* back to San Francisco and accept a sub-premium price from a saturated market, Slocum chose instead to pioneer a new market for Alaskan cod in Portland, Oregon. He stopped first in Victoria, British Columbia, arriving there on September 20, 1877, according to the local newspaper, *The Daily British Colonist*. There Slocum re-registered the *Pato*, though still keeping her under the British flag and Edward Jackson's nominal ownership. After painting his boat's new homeport on the transom—Victoria B.C.— on September 21, Slocum sailed for the Columbia River, where the *Pato* was taken under tow by a sternwheel steamboat, arriving in Portland on or before September 30, 1877.

Victor Slocum recalled an incident sparked by the *Pato's* new homeport. "Some time afterwards, in Oregon, I overhead a couple of bystanders speculating on just what 'B.C.' meant and they seriously concluded that it was 'Before Christ.' … It was not likely that these two had ever heard of British Columbia."

In Portland, Slocum planned to package the codfish himself and market them both on his own and through local merchants. "Genuine Codfish Direct from Okhotsch [sic] Sea" read an ad in the *Morning Oregonian* on

---

2 Victor recalled that the *Pato* carried two stacks of two-man dories lashed to the deck, and one of Victor's profile sketches of the *Pato* shows a nest of four dories. Victor offered no details regarding how many men made up the crew.

October 25, 1877. Recognizing that his catch would be a novelty in Portland compared with the more familiar Atlantic cod, Slocum knew it might take time to sell. What is more, Virginia needed rest. Although Joshua, typically, didn't remark on the event at the time, his wife had given birth to twins during the *Pato's* voyage. In a letter written May 3, 1890, Slocum wrote that "Two of my children were born on this voyage while at Petropolanska [sic]; they were two months old when we arrived at Oregon—4 days old when we began to take in fish."

He neglected to say how soon the twins died after reaching Portland, but it must have been soon after—if not, indeed, while still at sea. Many years later, Ben Aymar Slocum wrote author Walter Magnes Teller that "[t] he ocean is no place to raise a family."

Joshua Slocum thought otherwise, of course. He almost certainly believed that the ocean was not just a good place but the best place to raise a family, and he either gave little thought to the risks Virginia and their babies would face or presumed that the two of them together, both capable people, were, perhaps with some divine intervention, equal to the task. Virginia herself must have been extraordinarily brave and confident. She knew it would be highly unlikely that she would have other women to attend her, let alone a doctor. When she married Joshua Slocum, Virginia signed on for an adventurous, dangerous life that would demand all her strength and courage.

Slocum grounded out the *Pato* beside the Willamette River for some needed repairs, and the family moved ashore in East Portland. At the time, the now-familiar bridges in downtown Portland didn't exist, and the only convenient way to cross the Willamette from East Portland to downtown was by the Stark Street Ferry. Victor remembered the ferry as "a punt which was operated by a winch and chain." Years later, Slocum would recall this ferry in naming a small boat of his own.

Victor wrote that the family lived in rooms in a house owned by Mr. and Mrs. Newhall (or possibly Newell). The *Portland City Directory* for 1878 lists "Slocum J, sea captain" at 55 G Street, between Sixth and Seventh.[1] "The first few months in East Portland were my first and practically my only taste of a regular school," Victor remembered. Most of the early education of the Slocum children was capably done aboard various ships by Virginia.

There was considerable labor involved in preparing the codfish for sale. On November 9, 1877, a weekly named *The New Northwest*, doubtless reflect-

---

1 G Street was renamed S.W. Dewitt Street in 1928.

ing the real or perceived prejudice of the time, reported that "[t]he owner of the schooner *Pato* has employed a number of young girls to do the work in packing fish, and finds them more expert than Chinese, to say nothing of neatness and cleanliness."

In December, *The Oregonian* reported that Slocum had readied the entire cargo. "Samples of these fish have been prepared and left by Captain Slocum at a number of business houses in this city. Those who are experienced in piscatorial matters and have examined the codfish brought on the *Pato* affirm they are in every respect equal, if not superior, to the same species caught on the Atlantic coast." The newspaper reported that, if Slocum's fish met with a good reception, he would return to the fishing grounds for another haul and even contemplate settling down in Portland to "engage permanently in the trade." The paper concluded that "Capt. Slocum's efforts to build up and maintain a most useful industry on this coast should be fostered."

The bulk of the cargo was sold through local merchant Messrs. Allen & Lewis. Slocum said, perhaps with some exaggeration, that he "travelled over the state selling his fish until they were gone, and teaching the people how to cook them. Codfish suddenly became exceedingly popular as a novelty. And were advertised throughout the state."

By late March or early April 1878, the codfish had been sold for what Victor Slocum said was a "handsome profit," but Joshua's suggestion that he might settle in Portland proved to have been either a sales pitch or a passing fancy. It would become evident as time went on that Joshua Slocum had no qualms about thinking out loud to newspaper reporters, well-knowing that some of what he said was really nothing more than speculation.

Now he was after bigger things. He knew that the *Pato*, though a wonderful performer and outstanding sea boat, was not big enough for serious, long-distance commercial trading. Indeed, she was really too small for the sort of voyage just completed, and it was well that she had a skipper of Slocum's abilities to manage her. The schooner was best-suited for inter-island trading, and she was certainly not of sufficient capacity to engage in what Slocum believed would be a highly profitable trade of carrying timber from the Philippines to China, where a new navy of wooden ships was then being built. That was the business in which Slocum was now most interested.

By late March 1878, the Slocums had moved back aboard the *Pato*, Virginia accompanied by a pet canary given to her by her landlady. She named the bird Pete, and the whole family delighted in Pete's cheery voice. Slocum secured a cargo of flour, bread, and oats for Hawaii, where he intended to put the schooner up for sale. Once the *Pato* was loaded at Flanders' Wharf on April 3, he headed down the Columbia to Astoria. There he anchored inside the bar at the river's mouth, waiting for favorable weather to cross the bar, which he accomplished the following day.

The *Weekly Astorian* reported on March 30 that "Capt. Slocum has made many warm friends, who will regret to hear of his departure. He will carry hence the best wishes of this community, and all will unite in the hope that his voyage may prove both pleasant and profitable." The *Pato* reached Honolulu on April 24, 1878, and soon after arrival, Slocum listed the schooner for sale—"with full suit of good sails and new anchor and chain"—with a Honolulu broker. He generated immediate publicity when he agreed to race one of the local vessels, later remembering that the "race at Honolulu in which the *Pato* won was very exciting the whole town turning out to see it."

This ad for Slocum's schooner Pato *appeared in* Honolulu's Pacific Commercial Advertiser *on May 11, 1878. The picture is a generic schooner used in a variety of the paper's ship-related ads.*

While waiting for a buyer, Slocum put his boat back to work. "The schooner built in Manila and lately arrived from Oregon has been put under the Hawaiian flag, and will go on the Kohala route under the command of Capt. Slocumb," reported the *Pacific Commercial Advertiser* on May 4, 1878. These trips from Honolulu to the northwest portion of the big island (Hawaii) and back continued through mid to late June. Then a local planter emerged with an offer for the *Pato*, payment to be made in gold, and Slocum immediately arranged passage for himself and his family to San Francisco, departing on July 1 aboard the German bark *Christine*.

Victor Slocum recalled: "My mother was sitting on the after deck in a wide rattan chair when the bag was tossed into her lap with—'Virginia, there's the schooner.'" The bag held $5,000 in $20 gold pieces.

TIME AND AGAIN throughout his life, Joshua Slocum displayed an interest in and reverence for the old ways. He believed that older was better, and he nurtured this attitude until it became what a critic might call a fetish. He had learned the basics of celestial navigation not with a sextant but with a quadrant invented in Elizabethan times. He'd supervised the construction of a sizable wooden hull using centuries-old methods when iron ships were becoming the rule. Even when it was clear that steam was the future for ocean trade, he stuck with the craft and profession of sail. Years later, when he finally bought his first and only house, he referred to it as among the most "ancient" dwellings on Martha's Vineyard.

In San Francisco, Joshua Slocum discovered for sale a remarkable vessel that also happened to be, he asserted, the oldest American merchant sailing ship afloat.[1] He probably made up his mind in an instant. Soon after he bought the square-rigged *Amethyst*—100 feet long with a beam of 28 feet, depth of hold of 18 feet, and 400 registered tons, according to Victor—Slocum asked Virginia to make a new burgee to fly at the masthead. Over 15 feet long, the pennant was embroidered with white roman numerals—MDCCCXXII—proudly announcing the *Amethyst*'s build year. In the shipping community, the vessel was sometimes called "old 1822." Slocum said the *Amethyst* was known to many as "Old Hickory." Victor wrote that "With the exception of the *Spray* ... this was the most interesting vessel [Joshua] ever had."

That the *Amethyst* was over 50 years old when Slocum bought her underscored what an unusual piece of work she was. It is natural today, and probably even in the nineteenth century when sailing ships were common, to assume that construction details of wooden ships were uniform. But in ships, as in yachts, there were then (and now) builders whose budgets and construction methods produced vessels of exceptional quality, and one of those shipbuilders was Thatcher Magoun. Historian Samuel Eliot Morison referred to Magoun as "second to none among American shipbuilders."

Magoun was born in Pembroke, Massachusetts, on June 17, 1775, the day the British attacked American positions in what became known as the Battle of Bunker Hill. He learned the basics of his trade at the Salem yard of Enos Briggs, whose specialty was large vessels designed for the China trade, a trade route pioneered from Salem. Magoun furthered his education at what would become the Charlestown Navy Yard, where he worked with Joshua Humphrey in lofting the lines for the U.S.S. *Constitution*, "Old Ironsides."

---

1 Slocum may have been unaware that the *Emerald* (1822) was still sailing in 1882. He would also have been unaware of the 93-foot whaling bark *Rousseau*. Built in 1802 for Philadelphia's Stephen Girard, among the country's wealthiest men, the *Rousseau* had been acquired in 1825 by whaling agent George Howland of New Bedford and was still sailing until 1893. "She was the last hulk in New Bedford into the '20s," according to historian Llewellyn Howland III.

"The best thing about the *Amethyst*," Victor Slocum wrote, "was that she was built by Thatcher Magoun....Because of the fact she was the product of that particular builder's yard, her fifty-six years, when my father bought her in San Francisco, did not mean a thing ... [S]he was framed with seasoned live oak, copper fastened, and planked with native white oak.... On going down into the hold you would find shining copper bolt heads in knees, breasthooks, crutches and deadwoods. There are very few remaining examples of this form of construction.... The only one I know of in this country is our frigate *Constitution*."

But Victor Slocum was mistaken in his belief that Magoun had built the *Amethyst*. The best currently available evidence suggests that the *Amethyst* was built in Boston in 1823 by John Robertson. Magoun did launch a ship named for a semiprecious stone in 1822, but this was the 363-ton *Topaz*. Since Victor was specific about the *Amethyst's* construction details, which he saw for himself, it is entirely possible that Robertson (and others), like Magoun, had adopted some of Joshua Humphrey's building methods. Apparently, Lewis & Co. of Boston, the *Amethyst's* first owner, had a budget that permitted live oak components and copper bolt fasteners. Such materials would have contributed to the vessel's long-term integrity given proper maintenance.

Both the *Topaz* and the *Amethyst* sailed at different times for a business entity formed circa 1822 as the Boston and Liverpool Packet Company. Another Medford-built packet, the 366-ton *Sapphire* launched in 1824 by E. and H. Rogers, and the *Emerald*, built at Boston by John Wade circa 1822, also sailed for a time for the packet company. (Because of the vessels' names, the company was sometimes referred to informally as "the jewel line.") Whatever Victor Slocum's confusion was about the *Amethyst*, he likely believed that, with its purchase, his father had united himself to the most fabled ship in the United States, Old Ironsides herself.

To adapt the *Amethyst* to a timber carrier, Slocum arranged to have a loading port constructed in the ship's bow. The ship also needed new decks and new copper sheathing for her bottom. In addition, Slocum ordered a new set of sails for use in heavy weather. Victor recalled that it was standard practice to use the second-best sails in moderate air and the oldest sails if the ship encountered light winds and calms, for the slatting of sails in those conditions was most damaging to sailcloth. While the sails were being built, new running rigging was also assembled.

Since this work would keep the *Amethyst* ashore for some time, Slocum decided to leave Virginia and the children in San Francisco and take the transcontinental railroad (completed nine years before) cross country en route to visit Brier Island. On the train at Altoona, Pennsylvania, he used his big fist to knock out a man who, he felt, was paying unwanted attention to a woman passenger. The railroad provided Slocum with a celebratory meal at a local hotel, and the woman's brother later sent him a note of thanks.

Victor Slocum wrote that this transcontinental rail journey marked the first time his father attempted to write about his travels for a newspaper, the same idea he would try at the outset of his solo circumnavigation. Victor claimed that his father "acted as a correspondent for the *San Francisco Bee*,[1] for he was taking an interest in public affairs and was always writing." Slocum's views on the commercial fishing industry, the treatment of merchant seamen, fair taxation, and other topics would appear from time to time in newspapers wherever he voyaged.

Joshua did not see his father, John, according to Victor, because John had left Brier Island by then and, with his second wife, was living at The Ovens in Lunenburg County.[2] Slocum also visited Boston and his familiar haunt Natick, where some of his siblings had established residence, following in his footsteps. When he departed for his return to California, Slocum took with him his youngest brother, the stalwart, 6-foot, 23-year-old Ingram Bill Slocumb, who had immigrated to the U.S. in 1872, and his youngest sister, 18-year-old Ella, who had gone to Boston as a child in 1871. Both of Slocum's siblings signed aboard the *Amethyst*, Ingram as ship's cook and Ella as a companion to Virginia who would share her work and assist with child care.

The Slocums' stay in San Francisco coincided with the anti-Chinese demagoguery of Denis Kearney. An Irish immigrant, Kearney became a force in the short-lived Workingman's Party and led violent anti-Chinese riots and marches, one of which took him right past the Slocum family's windows at the Clipper Hotel. Victor Slocum wrote, "My father, who had no sympathy for Kearney or his methods, had an over-mature egg ready for him as an expression of his opinion, but my mother dragged father away from the window by the coat tails and told him that if he threw it and hit

---

1 No record of such a paper has been found, and no Slocum byline from this time has been discovered in the *Sacramento Bee*. Slocum told Capt. John Drew that, during his trip east, he went to Washington and was received by President Rutherford B. Hayes, with whom he discussed shipping matters.

2 On January 1, 1863, John Slocomb married Catherine Kreser, the fifth daughter of George Kreser of Lower Granville, Annapolis County, Nova Scotia. (The name was also spelled Kreaser and Creaser.)

Kearney ... the mob would burn down the hotel.... [A]n attack on the Chinese that night was only averted by the appearance of the Militia on the Scene."

One senses from Slocum's letters, in particular, that his thoughts on matters of immigration, race, and religion were not guided by generally accepted prejudices based on ethnicity, skin color, or religious dogma, but instead by whether he believed a person was pulling his weight. Slocum thought everyone deserved a fair shake and even-handed treatment unless and until they proved otherwise.

While he likely developed this attitude on his own, it would have been reinforced by the melting pot that a sailing ship could represent. One need think only of Melville's *Pequot* and its polyglot crew, which included a "heathen" cannibal, a Native American, African Americans, and Caucasians, to get a sense of crew diversity on a nineteenth-century American ship. As for those who didn't measure up to Slocum's expectations—the ignorant, the disorderly, those who were cruel to their horses, oxen, or other beasts—he applied to them a term he'd found in Jonathan Swift's *Gulliver's Travels*. All those sorts of people were "yahoos."

IN THE FINAL DAYS of December 1878, the refurbished *Amethyst* cleared San Francisco for Manila, where Slocum could pursue his plan of freighting timber to China. But he first made a stop in Honolulu, which he reached on January 16, 1879, after an uncomfortable passage thanks to a cumbersome load of what Victor called "rail road iron" (rails for train tracks).[1] Slocum's five paying passengers, planters emigrating to the Hawaiian Islands, were relieved to set foot on terra firma.

At Honolulu, the *Amethyst's* first mate, a competent seaman named Gold from Bath, Maine, signed off to take a skipper's job on a local schooner. Slocum gave Gold a high recommendation, although he had to be sorry to lose a valuable professional mate. In the waning years of commercial sail, men like Gold were becoming fewer and fewer while the number of imposters, incompetents, penniless roughnecks, and criminals grew proportionately. The result, as Joshua Slocum would learn soon enough, could be devastating.

---

[1] Knowing how to properly stow cargoes of different sorts was just one of the challenges that faced a sailing ship master. Victor Slocum wrote that "Railroad iron is considered to be a bad cargo no matter how you take it.... In the effort to stow the cargo in such a way as not to make the vessel too stiff, so much was placed in the 'tween decks that she became crank [displayed a tendency to roll], but not enough to make her unsafe."

This stop in Hawaii was more eventful than Slocum wrote about at the time. Only sporadically, in newspaper articles published in different cities, did Slocum's run-ins with local bureaucrats or individuals or his outspoken beliefs about government emerge. Twenty-four years after this stop in Hawaii, as he was preparing to set off in the *Spray*, he would reveal just how long his memory was regarding real or perceived ill-treatment.

The *Amethyst*'s next stop was Guam, where her fresh water was replenished and a supply of fruits and vegetables was brought aboard. Then Slocum shaped his course for Manila, detouring 200 miles from the shortest route to take advantage of the favorable prevailing winds north of Luzon. On June 3, 1879, the *Amethyst* arrived in Manila, where Slocum arranged a line of credit from the banking house Peele, Hubble and Company.

Several years after the event, in a December 8, 1881 article in the *Boston Journal*, Captain John Drew recalled his astonishment upon seeing the *Amethyst* sail into Manila. Drew's story is among the rare eyewitness accounts of Joshua Slocum and his family aboard one of his ships.

> One day a barque was seen sailing up the bay, a queer old craft for modern sailors to look at, and what was stranger still she flew the American flag. Curiosity was at work at once to find what she could be, for as she glided by there might also be seen a lady's sun-hat and children's curly hair just above the old-fashioned bulwarks. The captain and his barque hailed from San Francisco. He carried his wife and three children. He was a roving genius in every respect.

Although Drew added further confusion regarding when the *Amethyst* had been built—he suggested 1829—he was well aware of her reputation as a speedy vessel and may have known one of her first masters, Captain Jabez Howes. In his article about meeting the *Amethyst* and Slocum at Manila, Drew told a story of Howes making such a fast round trip from Boston to Liverpool that her owner, upon the ship's return (16 days after leaving Liverpool), assumed that Howes had been forced to return to Boston because of trouble. This speedy passage was noted in the *Boston Patriot* newspaper (in May 1829) and elsewhere.

Captain Drew was invited for tea aboard the *Amethyst* and reported that Virginia brought out "her Chinese and Japanese wares. It was as pretty a laid table as I ever saw." Slocum's pride in his wife was unfailing. He told Drew of Virginia having saved first the *Pato* and then the *Amethyst* from certain groundings when anchors failed to hold in sudden storms that arose while Slocum was ashore on business.

From Manila, Slocum sailed south through the Verde Island Passage and into Tayabas Bay. At the time, and into the twentieth century, there stood at the northeast end of the bay a nipa-hut village named Languimanoc.[1] While the village no longer appears on maps, it lay due east of Lucena and close by what is now known as Volcano Island, and it was the home of the merchant from whom Slocum would be purchasing timber.

The logging in the region was similar to that done at Olongapo, with the familiar, narrow-bitted axe and the use of water buffalo to drag felled trees from the forest. Victor Slocum described the process by which logs were floated out to the *Amethyst* and then raised from the water with block and tackle rigged from the jib boom to each end of the log. When level with the loading port, the log was guided into the hold, where it was stowed.

Thus began Joshua Slocum's efforts at the timber trade, a business he would return to again in Brazil, briefly and disastrously, eight years later. The *Amethyst* ranged freely through the waters of Luzon. The labor was as harsh as the environment, and Slocum and his crew had to be careful of enormous boa constrictors—the sight of one of them terrified little Ben Aymar—that might come aboard on a log. There were large centipedes, and Victor received a bite on his bare foot that "swelled up every full moon for several moons."

Virginia, who had given birth to another daughter during the *Amethyst*'s voyage across the Pacific, was unwell when Slocum sailed for Languimanoc. No doubt her pregnancy was one reason why Slocum was eager to bring his sister Ella from Nova Scotia, but nothing suggests that Ella, then 19, had any training or experience as a midwife. On July 17, 1879, Virginia wrote a letter home to her mother describing her health and what had happened at Languimanoc:

> *I have not been able to eat anything till lately. Dear Josh has got me every thing he can think of my hand shakes so now I can hardly write. Dear Mother my Dear little baby died the other day & I expect that is partley the cause, every time her teeth would start to come she would cry all night if I would cut them through the gum would grow together*

---

1 This is the spelling—different from that in Victor's book and in a letter Virginia wrote—that appeared on maps of the time.

again, the night she died she had one convulsion after another I gave
her a hot bath and some medeccine & was quite quiet in fact I thought
she was going to come around when she gave a quiet sigh and was gone.
Dear Josh embalmed her in brandy for we would not leave her in this
horid place she did look so pretty after she died Dearest Mother cannot
write any more"

Slocum continued about his business. The *Amethyst* began making her runs up to Hong Kong—where Virginia bought books to use in teaching the children—and back to Manila. According to Victor, it was during one of these stops at Manila that the son of the Chinese boss at Olongapo spotted Slocum and attempted to stab him. Presumably, Slocum's big fist stopped the assault. Then it was back to Languimanoc for the next load of logs.

Ben Aymar wrote Walter Teller that, on one entry into Hong Kong, Joshua Slocum couldn't resist showing off his ship-handling skills. With Virginia at his side, Slocum, under full sail, threaded the *Amethyst* through a narrow opening between three British warships and a merchant vessel. Ben Aymar recalled:

The admiral of one of Her Majesty's Ships stood at his station looking
for a crash of spars and torn sails. Father just cleared the H.M.S. by
inches—then skillfully cleared the merchant ship by a few inches—
passed on to the vacancy and with 'down helm' swung into the wind
and the 'let go the anchor' order was given. It was then that father
remembered his breach of marine etiquette for he did not salute the
H.M.S. in passing.... Father wrote an apology to the admiral whose
reply read like this—'Any man who can sail a ship under full sail
through a passageway too dangerous to contemplate need not apologize
to the entire British Navy. You are hereby invited to join me aboard the
H.M.S. and the lady who stood beside you on that occasion.'
That may give you a picture of the strength my mother had and of
her judgment valued by Father—one peep from her would have
changed the whole picture.

Not all the voyages were to Hong Kong. September 1880, found the *Amethyst* in Nagasaki, Japan, to take on a load of coal for Vladivostok and Shanghai. In Nagasaki, Slocum engaged in another, though less dramatic, display of his sailing ability. At the time, the U.S.S. *Ticonderoga* and several other vessels were in the harbor, and a race between the sailing tenders of each vessel was arranged. Victor Slocum described the *Amethyst's* launch as a bluff-bowed, square-stern, black-painted, split-lug-rigged, rather battered boat.[1]

He wrote that "the mates turned her bottom up on deck, smoothed her down like glass, and gave her an underwater coating of pot-lead [graphite, the usual treatment then to slicken a bottom]. The split-lug was overhauled and made to set perfectly, and with a racing crew to hold down the weather gunwale, our launch appeared at the line to wait for the gun. There was a smile at first at the rather uncouth appearance of the Yankee competitor, but it wore off soon after the race started. The Yankee just sailed away from the whole of them, as much to the surprise of her own crew as to others."

The *Amethyst* remained a familiar sight in Hong Kong in 1881, but Slocum was looking ahead. He had seen a decline in the demand by the Chinese government for boatbuilding timber. According to Victor, the Chinese had recognized the superiority of the iron warships the Japanese were buying from England, and China now began placing orders for such vessels. Slocum's last voyage as master of the *Amethyst* was to carry gunpowder for the Chinese government to Tainan, the oldest city on Taiwan. Upon his return to Hong Kong, with Virginia again pregnant, Slocum saw what he believed to be a more comfortable and secure future. He acted fast.

---

1 The rig, though perhaps still common at the time, was considered archaic by 1900 and is unfamiliar now. Split-lug referred to a rig with a main and foresail both lashed to the same yard but able to be trimmed separately. It would have provided windward performance similar to a jib-and-mainsail boat. Only one halyard was required—neither sail could be hoisted or lowered without the other—and the yard did not need to be lowered when tacking.

CHAPTER 5

Northern Light

"On a voyage to Java [the Challenge*] smashed into a heavy sea, at 12 knots, that carried away her wheel and the officers' deckhouse, drowning her captain and all of her officers except the third mate, who was crushed by the wreckage but survived."*

—*The Challenge*, A. B. C. Whipple

IN 1877, AT THE URGING OF OUTGOING PRESIDENT ULYSSES S. GRANT, Rutherford B. Hayes appointed John Singleton Mosby as consul to Hong Kong. Mosby, the brilliant and elusive Confederate cavalry commander known as "The Gray Ghost," had so enraged his fellow Virginians by joining the Republican Party and urging postwar reconciliation that his life had been threatened, and in 1878, he left Virginia never to return. In Hong Kong, Mosby began doing his best to root out the rampant corruption he found both in the civil service and among commercial shipping interests, while at the same time overseeing the day-to-day affairs of the consulate.

On March 4, 1881, Mosby was going about his business when Joshua Slocum walked in. Virginia had given birth to a son a day earlier—completing her sixth pregnancy in ten years—and Slocum had come to the consulate to register the newborn as an American citizen. Eight years later, when

Joshua Slocum's voyage in the *Liberdade* became national news, he told reporters, "Little Garfield was born in the port of Hong Kong aboard the *Amethyst*, then the oldest American vessel afloat; he was named by Colonel Mosby, then consul there, as he was registered at the consulate on the day of President Garfield's inauguration." Slocum also told a New York reporter that President Garfield—a Williams College graduate and former congressman and Civil War general—had written his infant son a letter thanking him for the compliment of sharing his name.

While Virginia was recovering from the birth of James Abram Garfield Slocum, Joshua jumped at an opportunity to sell the *Amethyst*. Concerned about the declining timber trade, and perhaps losing interest in other opportunities in Asia, Slocum purchased an ownership share in a much newer and bigger vessel. On June 23, 1881, now 37 years old, he became master and part owner of the 233-foot-long *Northern Light*,[1] which had sailed to Hong Kong from Cardiff, Wales.

In *Sailing Alone*, Slocum wrote: "My best command was that of the magnificent ship *Northern Light*, of which I was part owner. I had a right to be proud of her, for at that time—in the eighties—she was the finest American sailing-vessel afloat."

The *Northern Light* was a ship-rigged moderate clipper, meaning she made some slight compromises in speed to gain carrying capacity. She was not quite as fast as her older namesake, the extreme clipper *Northern Light*, which was built in 1851 by Briggs Brothers in South Boston for the California passenger trade and which, under the command of Captain Freeman Hatch in 1853, sailed from San Francisco to Boston in 76 days 6 hours, the fastest passage ever recorded by a sailing vessel.[2] In 1853, off Cape Horn, the *Northern Light* challenged the extreme clipper *Contest* to a race to Sandy Hook, which she won by three days. Slocum's *Northern Light* was not quite that fast but combined good speed with greater carrying capacity.

---

1 Slocum bought his share in the vessel from her master, Captain John E. Kenney, who returned home in a steamship.

2 In *Ships of the World*, published in 1997, author Lincoln P. Paine referred to the Briggs-built clipper *Northern Light*'s west-to-east passage as "an achievement won by no mortal before or since." Of the voyage's conclusion, Captain Arthur H. Clark wrote in *The Clipper Ship Era*, "Captain Hatch, her commander, was a thorough clipper ship captain, who never allowed his ship to suffer for want of canvas, and on this passage he brought his vessel across Massachusetts Bay before a fresh easterly breeze, carrying her ringtail, studdingsails, and skysails on both sides, alow and aloft, until she was off Boston Light—a superb marine picture and one seldom seen by landsmen even in those days."

DRAWN BY W. TABER.

The Northern Light *bound for Liverpool in 1885 under Joshua Slocum's command, as illustrated by W. Taber in* Sailing Alone Around the World. *Slocum disapproved of this illustration, thinking that it rendered the vessel's sheerline inaccurately and reduced her beauty. He had reason to be proud of this majestic full-rigged ship.*

To reduce crew demand from the ship's full complement of 25 while improving efficiency, the *Northern Light* was equipped with a steam engine in her forward house. The engine could be linked up to handle cargo, pump the bilges, pump water for use against fire, and condense water if necessary. Although Slocum would never seriously consider becoming captain of a steamship, he delighted not only in the labor savings of the *Northern Light*'s steam donkey engine but in the ship's well-equipped workshop fitted with a lathe and all necessary tools. He never lost his flair for mechanics and carpentry.

If the *Amethyst* had linked Slocum to one of the American merchant fleet's oldest ships built by one of Boston's finest builders, his association with the *Northern Light* gave him command of a vessel with many times the *Amethyst*'s carrying capacity. The *Northern Light* had an impressive pedigree, too. Her builder, George Thomas, had established his reputation in Rockland, Maine. There, in 1853, Thomas had launched the clipper ship *Red Jacket*, designed by naval architect Samuel Hartt Pook of Boston. On her first voyage from New York to Liverpool, *Red Jacket*—her figurehead a full-length figure of the Indian chief for whom she was named—averaged 14½

knots, hit 18 knots at times, finished the voyage in 13 days 1 hour, and overtook a steamship that had left two days earlier. Equally impressive performances came soon afterward on runs to Australia for the White Star Line.

After completing the *Red Jacket*, Thomas moved from Rockland to
Quincy Point, Massachusetts, where he established a shipyard on the banks
of the Fore River. It was there that the *Northern Light* was launched in 1871.
The *Northern Light* was originally built for Boston ship owners William F.
Weld & Company, whose vessels, collectively, comprised the Black Horse
fleet and sailed under the house flag, a black flying horse on a red field.

By the time the *Northern Light* was built, the day of what had come to
be called "extreme clippers" like the *Red Jacket* had ended, superseded by
"moderate clippers" with similar or greater cargo capacity for a comparable or
smaller length and the same or fewer crew. The Welds kept the *Northern
Light* for nine years before selling her in 1880 to the shipping house of Benner & Pinckney in New York, where the ship was registered. Subsequently,
Sylvanus Blanchard, affiliated with the First National Bank of Boston,
bought a share of the vessel.

Just as he had handled the documents related to Garfield Slocum's
birth, John Mosby handled the paperwork involving Slocum's purchase of
a minority ownership share in the *Northern Light*. Sometime around May
or June 1881, the *Northern Light* sailed from Hong Kong for Manila, where
she took on a cargo of sugar and hemp for Liverpool. Loading sugar in the
hold and hemp on the upper 'tween deck took a month, as everything had to
be carried 2½ miles by 50-foot dugouts to the *Northern Light's* deep-water
anchorage. Finally, on September 5, Slocum got underway for Java, where he
took aboard fresh vegetables, eggs, and chickens. After rounding the Cape
of Good Hope, the *Northern Light* turned north and, on December 18, 1881,
was reported off St. Helena.[1]

The *Northern Light* entered the Mersey on a fog-shrouded Christmas
Eve, "carrying into Liverpool," according to Victor, "the largest shipment of
sugar to date…. Having discharged our sugar we followed the course of
some it through the great refinery; a transition from the crude and sandy
product of the Philippines to crystal lumps ready to drop into the teacup.
We did the same with the hemp, which we followed to the rope walks and
saw our baled fiber of the abaca plant twisted into stout cordage." The Slocum

---

1 Slocum had previously rounded the Cape of Good Hope—for the first time according to the
best-available evidence—on his voyage aboard the *Tanjore* under Captain Martin's command.

This photo of Joshua Slocum circa 1883, when he was 39, is the only known image that shows him when he still had most of his hair. Close examination of an enlargement reveals a scar or swelling above his left eye, the result of a fall from aloft on the Agra. Slocum rarely posed with his left side to the camera. (Courtesy the New Bedford Whaling Museum)

children received a kind of multifaceted, tactile education well beyond the experience of most youngsters then or now.

A wooden sailing ship demanded constant looking after, and maintenance had to be promptly conducted to keep the vessel shipshape and productive. In Liverpool, the *Northern Light* entered the newly opened Langdon Graving Dock where, once the water was drained, the hull bottom was re-coppered. Victor wrote that there was so much tropical growth on the old copper sheathing that the local newspapers remarked about it. He said that botanically oriented English visitors arrived to take home an example of *Lepas anatifera*—goose barnacles—which can grow to be as much as 31 inches long. Such fouling had significantly slowed the *Northern Light* and accounted for the 160 days required to reach Liverpool.

While the *Northern Light*'s bottom was being renewed, Slocum contracted with a rigger to replace the ship's bowsprit. The rigger failed to show up at the appointed time, however, so Slocum and his first mate oversaw the project themselves. When the rigger finally did arrive to find the job completed, he became argumentative and combative and soon found himself on the wrong end of Slocum's big fist. The rigger brought suit and appeared in court much bandaged, with a nurse and doctor in attendance. After listening to both sides, however, the judge adjourned the case until such time as Slocum might return to Liverpool.

From Liverpool, the *Northern Light* made sail for New York, her homeport. There was still much above-deck maintenance to be done, so Slocum chose a more indirect southerly route across the Atlantic, where he could pick up the easterly trade winds rather than battling the prevailing temperate-zone westerlies. After encountering very rough seas in the Bay of Biscay, the *Northern Light* found the fair-weather trades and Joshua put the crew to work in the easy sailing. By the time the *Northern Light* docked at Pier 17 in New York Harbor to offload her cargo, she looked, according to Victor, like a yacht. "Our masts were scraped down, yards painted, standing rigging all tarred down, deck house and bulwarks painted, and decks holy-stoned."

With unloading complete, the *Northern Light*'s topgallant masts were lowered so she could proceed under the Brooklyn Bridge to her berth at Pier 23. Although work on the bridge had begun in the summer of 1869 and wouldn't be complete until a year after the *Northern Light* was towed beneath it, the Slocums never forgot the experience of passing under the span. Victor remembered: "As we came directly under, a painter, suspended underneath in a bosun's chair, reached down and gave our main truck a dab with his brush when our pilot shouted up to ask him how near we were. It was near enough."

Thoughtful as he was, Joshua Slocum might have observed, to himself at least, that the great bridge, both a literal and metaphoric linking of a great city and great country, was one more impediment to his chosen profession. It was a steel-and-stone monument to the start of a new era and the end of an old one—his. Less than three decades before, in "Crossing Brooklyn Ferry," Walt Whitman had addressed future generations of Americans who, he assumed, would be making the daily commute from Brooklyn to Manhattan aboard the ferry just as he was then: "Just as you stand and lean on the rail, yet hurry with the swift current, I stood yet was hurried, / Just as you look on the numberless masts of ships and the thick-stemm'd pipes of steamboats, I look'd." Twenty-one years later, the bridge was under construction that would one day relegate the daily commute across the East River to a fond memory.

Slocum's insistence that the *Northern Light* be perfect in all respects when she reached New York was an explicit recognition of the pride he took in the ship and himself. Quite possibly, too, Slocum expected the *Northern Light*'s majority shareholders to inspect the vessel in New York, and he wanted to impress them. He had arrived at a pinnacle, and he knew it. He had come aboard through the hawsehole of that clumsy lumber drogher in New Brunswick and advanced to the afterdeck with nothing more than his brains, his fists, and ambition. Now he stood as master of a great sailing ship. At his side was an accomplished and beautiful wife who could dispatch a shark with her revolver in one moment, play a piano recital the next, and then turn to the care and teaching of her four children.

"Every day from 9 to 12," Victor wrote, "school was conducted in a consistent manner. Spelling, reading, and arithmetic, suited to our different ages.... Discipline was maintained by a switch stuck over a picture in the cabin and the culprit had to fetch it himself when it was needed, but that, I must say, was not often.... On the Sabbath we had Sunday School."

With the *Northern Light* secure, Slocum and Virginia, accompanied by a number of other captains and their families, took the Fulton Street Ferry to Brooklyn and boarded an excursion train to Manhattan Beach. The posh resort, then five years old, had been developed by the famously anti-Semitic robber baron and Long Island Railroad mogul Austin Corbin. What Slocum may or may not have known about Corbin wasn't recorded,

This carte-de-visite photo of Virginia may have been taken in New York in 1882 or 1883 after the Slocums arrived aboard the Northern Light. *(Courtesy the New Bedford Whaling Museum)*

but Victor remembered that his father was highly critical of the clam chowder they were served—milk wasn't part of the recipe—and the music played by Patrick Gilmore's famous band. Gilmore, an Irish immigrant composer whose band had enlisted in the 24th Massachusetts Volunteers during the Civil War, was offering up classical music. Joshua Slocum, according to Victor, "was fond of the simple and soulful tunes. But Patsy Gilmore got a hand for all that, for my mother enjoyed him."

The *Northern Light* and her colorful master were a story too good to pass up for James Gordon Bennett Jr.'s *New York Herald*. On June 26, 1882, the paper's "Local Miscellany" column introduced New Yorkers to "a typical American ship, commanded by a typical American sailor who has a typical American wife." Although there was nothing typical about any of them, the article offered useful insights on Slocum, his ship, and his lifestyle. "The tautness, trimness, and cleanliness of this vessel, from keelson to truck and from stem to stern are features not common on merchant ships. The neat canvas cover over the steering-wheel bearing the vessel's name and hailing port, worked with silk, is the handiwork of the captain's wife."

The reporter described what he saw aboard. "Mrs. Slocum sat busily engaged with her little girl at needlework. Her baby boy was fast asleep in his Chinese cradle. An older son was putting his room in order and a second son was sketching. The captain's stateroom is a commodious apartment, furnished with a double berth which one might mistake for a black walnut bedstead; a transom upholstered like a lounge, a library, chairs, carpets, wardrobe and the chronometers. This room is abaft the main cabin which is furnished like a parlor. In this latter apartment are the square piano, center table, sofa, easy chairs and carpets, while on the walls hang several oil paintings."

In passing, the reporter noted the *Northern Light*'s library. In fact, this was something in which Slocum took particular pride. Victor estimated that the library held at least 500 books and wrote that his father's study looked like that of "a literary worker or a college professor." The breadth of Slocum's reading and his love for books rivaled or surpassed many with college degrees. There were presidents of countries and high officials who were ignorant in comparison, and Joshua was quick to recognize the fact. He continued to label such people "yahoos."

Joshua invited his father to visit from Boston, where he had moved, and see the *Northern Light*, meet his family, and witness all that he had achieved. It had been a long time since John Slocomb had destroyed Joshua's ship model, thrashed him, and demanded that he spend his time making boots. In 1899, seven years after the visit, Slocum wrote his uncle Joel: "Father came down to see me in my fine ship, the *Northern Light*. She was as beautiful as her name."

There is nothing to indicate—in what few letters or references exist regarding Slocum and his father—that he resented how his father had treated him or ever held a grudge. Given his own insistence on strict discipline and order, Slocum doubtless believed his father had done what he had to do. One can only assume that, for his part, John Slocomb was proud of his son's achievement and, perhaps, astounded by it.[1]

Slocum's 17-year-old half-sister Emma also came to New York to visit, remaining a guest for seven weeks. In an October 28, 1954 letter to Walter Teller, Emma shared her memories of that visit. "[They] took me sight-seeing to the historical and art museums also bought some nice things for me. I seen nothing but happiness between Josh and Virginia."

THE CONTRAST WAS STARK between the genteel domesticity of the Slocum family's life aft and the rough lifestyle of the sailors in the forecastle. For some 12 years now, Slocum had maintained order and brought ships and crews safely to port in the face of every challenge. He was a strict captain, as he had to be, but he was recognized as a fair man who, when necessary, could apply a common touch to disputes and defuse a threatening situation. He was a product of his own experiences before the mast and as a mate, but, with the exception of the Robinson case in San Francisco, he appears to have run taut ships without serious confrontations.

But part of a master's duty included oversight of the mates, who were responsible for getting the crew to perform promptly and efficiently. The mates faced their own challenges, especially as the pool of professional sailors dwindled. Often enough they resorted to "buckoism," the intimidation or beating of sullen, recalcitrant sailors with fists, a belaying pin, or a club. Between 1890 and 1897, 64 known cases of violence and 14 deaths were caused by attacks of mates on seamen, and those were only the reported instances. Until the passage of the White Act in 1898, there was nothing punishable about such treatment unless it was established that there had been no cause.

Few sailors broke out of the vicious cycle of drunkenness and exploita-

---

1 Having himself immigrated to the United States, John Slocomb died at East Boston on September 9, 1887, and was buried at the Woodlawn Cemetery in Everett, Massachusetts.

tion ashore by the crimps—often owners of boardinghouses or bars—who routinely pocketed the men's hard-earned wages. Few mates found an effective way to deal with the sailors other than with threats and beatings. Victor Slocum, a seaman himself, knew the situation intimately. He wrote: "Both the seamen before the mast, and the mates, were rough. A mate who showed a weak spot was worse than useless both to ship and crew. On American ships at that time, the best mates were graduates of the fo'castle having been selected for posts aft on account of their qualities of leadership, not only as seamen but as superior men mentally and physically."

By the 1880s, there were glimmerings of seamen's unions, but it was not until 1915 that passage of the Seaman's Act granted mariners full legal rights. In August 1882, as Joshua Slocum prepared for a voyage to Yokohama, the reality of the day's labor problems came tumbling right over the *Northern Light*'s newly painted bulwarks. Victor Slocum wrote that the supplied men were typical of crews at the time, neither better nor worse.

The crew's first task was to turn to and assist as the ship was towed to Hunter's Point in Queens, a blighted industrial area described by *Harper's Weekly* as a place "of impure gases and foul and dangerous effluvia of every kind … smearing the banks with vile mud and slime, and pouring the stench of the whole in poisonous vapors over densely populated parts of the city." A Standard Oil refinery was there, and the *Northern Light*'s cargo of case oil—wooden cases containing two 5-gallon cans apiece—was loaded by stevedores. (The ship also carried coal and merchandise.) With loading complete, a pilot came aboard, and the ship was taken in tow through Hell's Gate and Long Island Sound to New London, Connecticut. There, on August 5, Slocum ordered the topsails set, a task accomplished by the few crewmen sober and experienced enough to operate the steam donkey engine and complete the task.

The tug cast off the towing hawser as the *Northern Light* began to get underway. Immediately, there was a problem. Although it hadn't been noticed while the ship was under tow, the rudder would not respond to the wheel. Signals to the fast-disappearing towboat weren't acknowledged, and Slocum found himself in a drifting ship with a forecastle full of men who were mostly still semi-comatose or angry about their situation.

Victor Slocum wrote that the first mate, Morrell Knowles—a stocky 29-year-old from Leaford, Delaware—"turned out to be a 'bucko' of the real down east bull type that 'ate 'em alive.' He entered both fo'-castles and chased all hands, drunk or sober, out on deck." To gain some directional control, jibs and foresail were now set and the yards were trimmed using the donkey engine. Signals made to shore resulted in a pilot coming aboard and the appearance of a tugboat named the *C. P. Raymond*.

Mate Knowles assigned a sailor named Frances Murrin to act as leadsman and take soundings, but Murrin took the opportunity to try vainly to run the *Northern Light* aground. With the ship safely anchored at New London, Murrin led the crew in refusing to furl the sails and then demanding to be put ashore.

"They demanded," Victor Slocum wrote, "to be put ashore in the tug. They were down on the mate for his treatment of them…. Their demand to put ashore having been refused, the crew attempted to rush the quarter deck … armed with handspikes and whatever else they could lay hands on…. The Captain intercepted them down on the main deck, on their own level, with a drawn revolver and a cool, clear-cut order to 'Stop at the peril of life.'" Benjamin Aymar never forgot the sight of his mother backing up his father with a pistol in each hand.

Slocum now made the signal for "mutiny aboard," and the revenue cutter *Grant* responded. Accounts of what happened next vary in detail, but the *Northern Light* was about to become a national news story. The crew was locked up in the forecastle, which in the August heat proved so stifling that they feared suffocation. Murrin managed to squeeze out through a window, open the door to the forecastle, and lead the crew aft. "The mate grabbed hold of me," Murrin said later, "and I immediately drew the knife and plunged it into his stomach. I think I stabbed him three times." Order was restored again by the revenue cutter's men, this time with drawn cutlasses. Knowles was carried off to be attended by a naval surgeon, and Murrin was imprisoned.

A few hours later, Joshua Slocum showed up to discuss the matter with Murrin. The *Bangor* [Maine] *Daily Whig and Courier* was among the papers that carried the story:

> Captain: *What caused you to do it?*
> Murrin: *I have nothing against you but the mate is a brute.*
> Captain: *Did the mate ill-treat you?*
> Murrin: *No but he did others.*
> Captain: *Then why did not they or you come to me with a complaint?*
> Murrin: *I've no fault to find with you Captain.*

> *Captain: If the ship had not met with an accident and proceeded on her voyage and not put in at New London, would there have been any trouble on the ship?"*
> *Murrin: No, I guess not Captain.... There will be no more trouble now that I am off.*

While mate Knowles lay dying, repairs were made to the *Northern Light*. A diver was sent down and discovered the ship's lower rudder pintle—one of the bronze pins that were inserted into hull-mounted gudgeons, or sockets and allowed the rudder to rotate—was broken. With the pintle replaced, a new mate was sent aboard by the *Northern Light*'s primary owner in New York, Benner & Pinckney. "This was Mr. Nubagin," Victor Slocum wrote, "a man of entirely different type than his predecessor and with far greater experience."

Slocum now had what his son called a "man to man" discussion with the crew, and the *Northern Light* got underway again seeking the trade winds that would power her down to the Roaring Forties, where west winds would drive her past the Cape of Good Hope. Yet resentment lingered among some of the crew. Victor Slocum wrote that "[t]here was one faction which had sworn to cut the Captain's throat for taking them to sea; and yet another, of less violent intention, which openly maintained that they had to kill Knowles, saying 'If we hadn't, he'd a killed us.'"

Still, by the time they crossed the equator, morale had improved and the *Northern Light* bowled along her course and, south of the Cape of Good Hope, began "running her easting down" in strong winds. They passed south of Tasmania and east of Australia and then turned north toward the Solomon Islands, which were still regarded then as "cannibal islands." It was there that what Victor Slocum called "the top adventure of the voyage" occurred on December 10, 1882. "[W]e sighted this small speck on the lee bow, bobbing like a nautilus on the great grey-blue ocean.... We backed the main yard and drifting down to within heaving distance, gave them a line and hauled them alongside."

What the *Northern Light* had spotted was a 21-foot ship's boat carrying five Gilbert Islanders, all more dead than alive. They had been adrift for 40 days, and seven of their original number had already died. All were missionaries who had been sailing from their home island of Apamama (now Abemama) to Nonouti, an atoll 70 miles to the south in the Kirabati island nation. On their return trip a storm had blown them well off course.

This photo taken at Yokohama shows the Gilbert Islanders rescued by Joshua Slocum aboard the Northern Light. *To the left of Slocum's head are the words, "From the Tropics to Snow at Japan." Below that are the words "note the gloves" and an arrow pointing to the standing islander. The next inscription notes "Near Naked When Rescued." The seated woman is wearing "mother's [Virginia's] clothes." Standing at the right hand of the seated woman is an islander named Whaggie, and seated next to him is "Father's Prince Albert," who has his hands clenched between his thighs for warmth. The photograph was made at Yokohama. Published in local papers, the photo helped publicize the islanders' plight and generated financial support for their return home. (Courtesy the New Bedford Whaling Museum)*

"The Captain," Victor wrote, "speculated on what his chances would be of being made governor of an island, on personally restoring these subjects … but luck was against the conjecture for we made Apamama on a squally night and a sea infested with coral reefs was no place at that time for a big ship."

Slocum landed the castaways 2,700 sea miles away at Yokohama instead, sharing their story with the local newspapers. He berthed them aboard and began canvassing for funds to get them back home, garnering pledges of $750 in one day while a missionary society raised more. Ultimately, the islanders voyaged to San Francisco, where the Pacific Mail Steamship Company offered to transport them and their boat home to Apamama at no charge. Their roundabout 10,000-mile journey home resembled a modern traveler's flight itinerary, except that it was free.

Having been unloaded, the *Northern Light* made ready to depart Yokohama for Manila, where she would load a cargo of sugar and hemp for New York. Unfortunately, this leg of the journey started much like the initial leg down Long Island Sound. Although Slocum did his best to leave a trouble-making crewmember ashore, the U.S. consul in Yokohama apparently denied the request, offering instead to lock up the man while the ship was in port. The crewman, who Victor Slocum described as a "morose and apparently inoffensive young Russian" named Zelanski, fashioned himself a bowie knife and, further alienated by his time in jail, boasted to other crewmembers that he would use it to stab Slocum in the heart.

When the story made it into a newspaper, Slocum found himself on the defense while stating that the crew as a whole was a credit to any vessel. His only request to the consulate was that Zelanski be unarmed when he was returned to the ship, but instead, the moment the man stepped aboard, he drew his knife and made a dash at Slocum. "Although the Captain did not expect the attack and was unprepared," Victor wrote, "his natural alertness enabled him to guard off and to fell his assailant who, the next moment, was ironed around the maintopmast back stay." The *Northern Light* got underway with Slocum standing atop the wheelhouse, carbine in his hands, overlooking a sullen crew. The mood did not improve until Manila, where Zelanski was put ashore.

In August 1883, with the *Northern Light* loaded once again, Slocum set his course for home, aiming first for Anjer Point (now known more generally as Anyer), an Indonesian port at the eastern end of the Sunda Strait. The strait separating the islands of Java and Sumatra connects the Java Sea with the Indian Ocean, and during the nineteenth century it was a place where passing ships were noted and reported to newspaper shipping news editors around the world.

Familiar though he was with these waters, Slocum had no inkling what lay ahead on this particular journey. Neither did the masters of the American ships *Wm. H. Besse* and *Jonathan Bourne*, who were close behind the *Northern Light*. Beneath them as they sailed, the Earth's mantle was preparing the explosion of Krakatoa. "Slocum's luck" was with him the day he led the way toward Anjer Point with the *Besse* and the *Bourne* in line behind him. Victor Slocum, who was 12, remembered well seeing the square-rigged *Besse*, under full sail, shudder to a dead stop in what should have been deep water.

"She had grounded on a reef which had been cast up by submarine volcanic action in the very spot over which we had passed but a quarter of an hour before. The sea was trembling and in bubbles. A lead that was cast came up from the bottom so hot that it melted out the tallow armor [mud or sand would stick to the tallow and tell a navigator the nature of the bottom].... The *Northern Light* braced her yards and came up into the wind, but as the *Bourne* came up astern of the *Besse* and hove to, to offer assistance, we kept off again for Anjer, which was by this time but a few miles distant."

Slocum stopped at Anjer, where the *Bourne*, appearing later, reported that the *Besse* would be towed to Batavia (Jakarta) for repairs that would take several weeks. Upon sailing from Anjer, the *Northern Light* passed Krakatoa, which Victor Slocum wrote "was in the awful majesty of full eruption.... Here a bright fire burned, throwing up a column of black steam and ashes which reached a culminating altitude of seventeen miles by sextant measurement. The fall of ashes made the sea all about white with pumice stone. For days after passing it was washed upon our deck by the lively sea."

Victor had no idea that the "full eruption" he saw was only a prelude. Krakatoa exploded on August 26, 1883, with a noise said to have been the loudest ever heard on the planet. About two-thirds of Anjer disappeared. Tsunamis followed. Ships were carried a mile into jungles, and an estimated 36,000 people were killed. Ben Aymar Slocum wrote Walter Teller, "Had we been three days later in that region we would have been suffocated by the fumes."

The *Northern Light* sailed into and across the Indian Ocean without incident, but as she approached the Cape of Good Hope she met strong westerly gales and such enormous head seas that Slocum decided to heave to and ride out the blow. Victor reported that they were "doing nicely, when the rudder head twisted off, allowing the ship to fall off into the trough of the sea before a jury gear could be rigged to bring her head back into the wind."

The ship wallowed, and gray seas washed over her, starting a serious leak. The steam engine was started to drive the pumps, which worked reasonably well until the bags of sugar in the hold burst and turned the rising bilge into a thick molasses-like mixture that clogged the pumps. By the time the wind and seas moderated, the *Northern Light*, Slocum's great pride, was listing 30 degrees to port and in danger of capsizing.

Victor wrote: "Then orders were given to break hemp out of the upper 'tweendecks and hoist it over the side to counterbalance the weight taken out of the bottom of the ship. Boats were cleared and provisioned for the next emergency, but a few hours work on the hemp caused the ship to regain her stability, or enough to put her out of danger."

The *Northern Light* limped 20 miles into Port Elizabeth, where the ship's company learned the full extent of what had occurred at Krakatoa. Meanwhile, it took two months to recaulk the topsides and repair leaks at the hood ends of the forward planks, where they fastened to the ship's stem. The foremast was rebuilt, and the hemp standing rigging, stretched beyond repair, was replaced with steel wire, proof that Slocum could keep pace with sailing ship technology when he wished to.[1] The ruined cargo had to be removed, and what could be salvaged was restowed. There were changes in the ship's officers, too. The capable first mate, Mr. Nubagin, had been bedridden throughout the Indian Ocean passage and was replaced by a man referred to by Victor as "Mr. MacLean, an energetic Scotsman.... Being a real sailor he was just the man to finish the rigging."

A new second mate (Victor remembered him as third mate) was signed on as well. This was Henry A. Slater, a British ex-convict who had forged papers to pass himself as a ship's officer in good standing. Slater had met some of the *Northern Light*'s crew ashore and hatched a scheme to lead a mutiny and seize the ship. His first act of insubordination, not long after the *Northern Light* sailed on September 20, caused him to be removed from officer status and sent to the forecastle.

Victor wrote: "The Captain appealed to the reason of the crew and said plainly that he considered the man's act to be one of open mutiny and put it up to them to tell him what to do.... The Captain's cool and judicial manner disarmed the malcontents among the number before him ... for they knew they were dealing with a man who did not know fear. The mutineer was called out of line and placed in irons for the safety of the ship during the rest of the voyage home."

Thus, when the *Northern Light* reached New York in November 1883, she finished the voyage as it had begun, with a man in irons. Slocum obtained an arrest warrant for Slater on November 24, and Slater, in turn, sued

---

1 Introduced on Isambard Kingdom Brunel's *Great Britain*, designed in 1838, wire rope offered benefits over hemp. It was thinner in diameter, thus presenting less surface area to be impacted by wind. It was stronger, size for size, than hemp, and it did not require ongoing "setting up" because of stretching. A ship owner who could save even a dollar per day on a vessel's maintenance and operating expenses would have viewed such cost reduction as important. According to Victor Slocum, the *Northern Light*'s "steel wire standing rigging made her look particularly trim, and it certainly added greatly to her windward qualities, the yards bracing up another point." It was recognized that wire rigging was best suited to iron ships, which could better take the strain that could be imposed. Presumably, those who rigged wooden ships with steel wire knew how to set it up without causing damage. Slocum himself did not remark upon the matter.

Slocum for cruelty. Slater claimed that another officer had lied about his plans to mutiny and that his treatment—which he described as near-starvation rations and filthy living conditions for 53 days—was unjustified. His tale found a sympathetic ear both in the press and in court.

The court found for Slater and ordered Slocum to pay a $500 fine—the equivalent of $12,500 in today's money, an amount that hurt Slocum. Slater entered a civil suit, too, only to drop it. On January 12, 1884, the *Nautical Gazette* reported that Slater had "had enough.... I do not blame Capt. Slocum for the treatment I received.... I never gave my authority to enter a civil suit against Capt. Slocum and I do not wish the suit to proceed. I now see that both Capt. Slocum and myself have been made the dupes of the very men who ought to have protected us, and that the whole affair is made to get money out of Capt. Slocum to be distributed among them."

This bizarre turn of events was made even more so when Slater told the *Gazette's* editor that he "had put Slocum in a bad hole, and was in an equally bad hole himself.... He had signed lots [of] papers, but did not know what they were." The story had legs, as journalists still say. Newspaper accounts about real or alleged maltreatment of seamen could quickly make their way from coast to coast across the country. Now, Slater's accusation that unscrupulous lawyers were behind his civil suit made the news, too.

On January 16, 1884, the *Cleveland Herald* reported that Slater, "late second mate of the ship *Northern Light* who prosecuted Captain Joshua Slocum of that ship for inhuman treatment made affidavit that he had been the tool of designing persons to extort money from Slocum, and that he had not authorized his attorneys to institute a civil suit against the captain."

Although the matter seemed to draw to its inconclusive end in January, Slater would make a negative reappearance over a decade later, during Slocum's circumnavigation. Meanwhile Slocum sold his share of the *Northern Light* in January, and in 1885 the remaining owners sold the vessel to a Norwegian company, who renamed the ship *Mathilda*.

According to Frederick C. Matthews's *American Merchant Ships*, the *Mathilda* sailed in the transatlantic oil and timber trade for 20 years. Upon seeing her sometime after that period, Slocum wrote that the great ship had by then, like so many others, been converted into a coal barge. She was, Slocum wrote, "ignominiously towed by the nose from port to port."

CHAPTER 6

Virginia

"I feel most of the time that Virginia is with me."

—Joshua Slocum, 1885 letter to his mother-in-law

THE EDITOR OF *THE NAUTICAL GAZETTE* at the time of the *Slater v. Slocum* lawsuit was Bradley Sillick Osbon.[1] Born in Westchester, New York, in 1827, Osbon spent his early career at sea and was then a *New York Herald* reporter before becoming "editor and proprietor" of the *Gazette* in 1874. Osbon's seagoing experience coupled with his editorship of what was essentially a specialized trade journal gave him a broad perspective on the maritime industry and many of its foremost people.

The impression Osbon formed of Joshua Slocum hardly fit a captain who could be successfully sued by a convict like Henry Slater or a stowaway like Michael Robinson in San Francisco. The *Gazette* editor knew Slocum to be an "A-1 man, a genuine Yankee captain of high reputation." Slocum's peers regarded him highly, and a *New York Tribune* reporter called him "one of the most popular commanders sailing out of this port, both on account of his general capability and his kindness to his crew."

In 1952, Slocum's cousin Grace Murray Brown wrote author Walter

---

1 B. S. Osbon's career included time in the Union Navy. During a stint as Admiral David Farragut's signal officer, Farragut credited him with saving his life and the ship as well.

Teller, "My father met an old seaman in some Chinese port who had sailed under the captain. He said 'Captain Slocum was considered a hard man but no one ever felt unsafe under his command.'" Slocum himself once told a Boston newspaperman, "The old shipmasters treated their crews like intelligent beings, giving them plenty of leeway, but holding them with a strong hand in an emergency. That's my style."

But the days of the "Cape Horn breed," the "shellbacks," were over. Gone were the men who had doubled the capes and crossed the equator under sail; men who knew all the professional sailorman's skills of splicing, knotting, laying aloft in rough weather, handling miles of running rigging, selecting the necessary line from myriad identical belaying pins, clawing in the canvas in a gale, fitting a topgallant mast or getting it down on deck; men who could "hand, reef, and steer." In fact, they had been gone for some 20 years. Robert Waterman, among the most eminent of the clipper ship masters, had seen it coming well before he was lured from retirement in 1851 by the promise of enormous financial gain to sail the largest American clipper, the *Challenge*, in a race from New York to San Francisco against Josiah Perkins Creesy's *Flying Cloud*.

The *Challenge* required a crew of 60 but had only 56, and Waterman was stunned by the sort of men his first mate had assembled. This is how A. B. C. Whipple described them in *The Challenge*, his tour-de-force book about the race:

> Instead of a dozen 'AB's,' he had three. Out of the entire crew, only six men had ever had a hand on a ship's wheel. Half of the crew had never been to sea. Some of the landlubbers had signed on for a free ride to the gold fields. Others were released jailbirds. Most of them had been delivered, drunk and drugged, by New York crimps. Half a dozen of the crewmen were derelicts from European ports, immigrants unable to understand commands in English.

Waterman promptly made the situation worse by firing the first mate and sending him off the ship with the pilot boat. In a most peculiar stroke of fortune, he was almost immediately approached by another boat carrying the first mate of a just-arrived ship, who was afraid to go ashore because he believed several of the crew planned to murder him for his brutality. Waterman signed him on, setting the stage for a disastrous voyage and a riveting tale.

With the passing of the old breed went much of the former fellowship, variable though it was, that had existed in the ships. On American ships, at least, captains relied increasingly on bucko mates infamous for brutality. To British sailors, the American vessels were known as "blood ships" or "hell ships," yet some sailors counted it a perverse honor, a badge of courage, to have sailed in one and survived with the scars to prove it.

There is nothing to indicate that Slocum ever ran a ship in such fashion. He enforced discipline when necessary but also did his utmost to care for sick crewmembers. Ben Aymar recalled that his father, though not a religious man, tried to give crews time off on Sundays. Events suggest that some of Slocum's mates needed more reining in than they got, but it was a tricky thing to balance command authority with compassion. Much depended on the personalities of mates and crews. A tough but fair mate was as vital as he was rare. A crewman with a grudge who could inspire rebellion in the forecastle was dangerous and not uncommon.

"They were amenable to discipline only in the form of force in heavy and frequent doses," remembered Captain Arthur H. Clark in *The Clipper Ship Era*, "despite the theories of those who have never commanded ships or had experience in handling degenerates at sea.... To talk about the exercise of kindness or moral suasion with such men, would be the limit of foolishness; one might as well propose a kindergarten for baby coyotes or young rattlesnakes."

The typical sailor, it was said, "worked like a horse afloat and spent like an ass ashore." It became more and more clear that things needed to change. Ever so slowly, sailors' grievances led to legal protections. When unions were formed, what might have been termed "mutinies" became "labor stoppages," which is what most of them had probably been anyhow.

Slocum's challenges were no different from those of his peers. To cite but one example, when Slocum proudly assumed command of the *Northern Light* in 1882, a Liverpool judge was considering the case of seven crewmen who had "refused to obey the law of command of the Captain." This forced the British ship to turn back. The seven defendants, who had broken ranks with their fellows, claimed that they had done so because the ship was not ready to sail. In response, the mate took the comparatively mild step of putting them on reduced rations. (Though mild in comparison with a beating, reduced rations could and sometimes did become a near-starvation diet of bread and water.)

Such stories were not rare, and a sailor's brief interludes ashore seemed no better. The waterfront news was full of incidents of drunken men stumbling off docks to drown, of sailors stabbing shipmates to death, of men behaving like "asses" and worse. Infesting the whole business were the crimps, who, after fleecing hapless seamen, returned them to another waiting ship and sometimes made a fortune in the process.

By 1884, captains like Slocum, who had started their careers in the 1860s, were having to battle just to hang on to their profession as demand for sailing masters declined and competition for steamship berths increased. As demand decreased, so did the pay. A decade earlier, in 1874, the *Nautical Gazette* had printed an editorial criticizing the tendency of ship owners to cut the wages of ship masters and mates:

> *It is cruel to ask a first class shipmaster to go to sea, to take charge of a first class vessel and cargo for wages ranging from $75 to $125 per month.... Primage [a bonus paid to the captain based on the profit of the cargo] which once constituted a measure of fair income ... is now almost wholly abolished, except perhaps in Eastern owned ships where masters receive 25 to 30 percent more and 5 percent primage. Some of our best clipper captains receive less than $200 per month.*

Still, Slocum had no plan other than pursuing his career under sail. According to Victor, his father had considered seeking a berth aboard a steamship. "For a time after quitting the deck of the *Northern Light*," wrote Victor Slocum, "the Captain looked to steamboating. But the opportunities offered deck officers were limited." Eventually, Slocum concluded that his best opportunity would be to purchase a smaller sailing vessel than the *Northern Light*, a ship like the *Amethyst*, and resume trading on his own account, just as he had done in the Pacific. While Virginia and the children stayed in Natick with Slocum's émigré sisters Alice and Ella, Slocum went looking for another ship. It didn't take him long to find one.

On February 7, 1884, Baltimore's *The Sun* reported: "The bark *Aquidneck* was purchased by Capt. Joshua Slocum, of New Bedford, Mass, for $2,975.... The *Aquidneck* is 138 feet long, 29 feet beam, and 13 feet depth of hold. She was built in Mystic Bridge, Conn. by Hill & Grinnell, in 1865, under the personal supervision and from designs of Capt. Robt. Chesborough, Sr., her first master. Her record as a clipper has no equal at this port.... Capt. Powell, her last master, covered 366 miles in one day with the *Aquidneck*.... The *Aquidneck* is destined to change her course from the Brasils, in which she has always been engaged to the cold seas of the North Pacific. Her purchaser, Capt. Slocum, intends to use her in cod and other fishing in the latitudes of Alaska."

This report on the sale of the *Aquidneck* reveals much about her new owner. Slocum stuck with his tendency to confuse the matter of where he lived. His marriage announcement had said he was from Massachusetts when he was based in San Francisco. Why, having recently been based in New York and with no shore address, but with siblings and father in Boston, did he choose to say he was from New Bedford, where he never had and never would live? And did he seriously plan to make good on what he had told a Portland, Oregon, newspaper several years earlier and build a fishing business there?

The only answer is that Slocum was and would always be vague and misleading about personal details. His reasons—for he must have had them—may have included false information related to his U.S. naturalization and the inconsistencies he had sometimes given regarding his age. As for the suggestion that he would fish in the North Pacific, it was most likely a straw-man proposal that sounded better than saying he didn't yet have a plan. He would do the same later, when he set off in the *Spray* and again when he was asked to speculate about his plans after completing the voyage.

The $2,975 Slocum paid for the *Aquidneck*—roughly $80,000 in today's money—was a substantial sum at a time when a seaman or a laborer on land might earn $250 per year and a skilled carpenter up to $900. It is unclear how much money he carried away from the *Northern Light* investment and his time as her skipper, or whether he still had any gold pieces left from the *Pato*'s sale. It does not appear that he ever laid by any substantial savings—"money in hand," as it was called then—for future contingencies.

Nor, apparently, did he insure his ships. Although Slocum had brought the *Amethyst* through a typhoon in the Pacific and the *Northern Light* through the near fatal storm off the Cape of Good Hope, he had to have known he was always gambling his skill, his luck, and the lives of his family against elements that had claimed so many others. Whether he simply couldn't afford insurance or was guilty of supreme hubris, the consequences would prove devastating in the end.

The 343-gross-ton *Aquidneck* had been laid up for some time when Slocum purchased her at auction. She had "good bones"—a sharp bow, round stern, and fair underwater lines that made her fast and competitive in the coffee trade from Brazil to Baltimore. Slocum knew she was special as soon as he inspected her. Later he would write that she was "a little bark which of all man's handiwork seemed … the nearest to perfection of beauty, and which in speed, when the wind blew, asked no favors of steamers." But the ship needed work. Slocum had her re-caulked and re-coppered, and her hemp standing rigging was replaced. Apparently he was well-satisfied with the steel wire he'd installed on the *Northern Light*, because he used the wire again on the *Aquidneck*.

When the exterior jobs were done, Slocum had the living area spruced up, moved his books aboard, and sent for Virginia and the children. If he had ever seriously considered the North Pacific cod fishery, he now changed his mind and planned to continue the *Aquidneck's* traditional trading route to Brazil. In the spring of 1884, after some five months in suburban Boston recovering from her *Northern Light* experience, Virginia, with her canary Pete and her children, moved aboard her new home.

The *Aquidneck* was a much smaller ship than the 233-foot *Northern Light*. At 138 feet, she was 38 feet longer than the *Amethyst* but comparable in cargo capacity. The *Aquidneck* had comfortable accommodations. Garfield, who was then only three years old, remembered the ship all his life. He wrote Walter Teller that the "saloon on board the *Aquidneck* was a beautiful room, parquetry floor, doors, paneling, and ceiling painted flat white, open scrollwork over the stateroom doors painted light blue and gold…. Also a square grand piano was bolted to the deck." There were comfortable chairs, a skylight, and a cabinet containing a small but necessary armory of repeating rifles and revolvers. To his already large library, Slocum had added more children's books and toys.

In April 1884 or so, the *Aquidneck* headed into the Atlantic and shaped a southerly course for Recife, the capital of the state of Pernambuco in northeastern Brazil. Sheltered by the reef that gave the city its name, Recife was a pleasant commercial trading center. Victor Slocum later remembered picnics ashore and lessons in natural history from his mother. Virginia also happened to be, along with Ben Aymar, the only family member who knew how to swim. Ben Aymar remembered his mother's great interest was "in collecting sea shells—she and I were constantly exploring places visited by us. The Philippine Islands were a gold mine of shells for her."

With the off-loading of cargo complete, Slocum oversaw preparations for a voyage of some 2,500 miles from Recife to Buenos Aires, Argentina. There he hoped to find a cargo for Sydney so Virginia could again see her family. The ship was well on its way, having passed Rio and reached the

Ben Aymar Slocum considered this photograph of his mother to be the best picture of her. It was taken in Yokohama when Virginia was 31 or 32 years old. (Courtesy the New Bedford Whaling Museum)

latitude of Santa Catarina, Brazil, when Virginia became weak. She put aside the embroidery she was working on and went to bed. The hope was that she would feel better by the time they reached Buenos Aires.

The Río de la Plata (River Plate) was not dredged then as it was in later years, and the *Aquidneck* had to anchor some 12 miles from the Buenos Aires waterfront. On the morning of July 25, Virginia was well enough to begin making butter for the long voyage ahead while Slocum took a local sailboat into the city seeking business. Their agreed signal if Virginia felt the need for her husband's immediate return was the blue-and-white signal flag for the letter "J." In this case, of course, it meant Joshua. At some point that morning, the signal was hoisted to flutter in the wind. In a letter to Walter Teller, Ben Aymar wrote that "Father returned about noon and I was called by father at about 8 p.m. to kneel at her bedside as she breathed her last...." It was the kind of scene encountered in Victorian-era novels.

In Virginia's bible, Slocum made an entry for his wife including her dates of birth and death—the 25th of July, 1884. He wrote: "Thy will be done not ours!" Joshua Slocum was suddenly without his soulmate, the children without their mother. Victor remembered that Virginia's canary Pete did not sing again for a long time.

As adults, long after their mother's death, Virginia's children, probably repeating what their father told them, believed that she had suffered from a weakened heart. Heart disease—sometimes labeled "vascular insufficiency"— was a great killer then. Whether or not it was the proximate cause of Virginia's death, the tension- and danger-filled time aboard the *Northern Light*, with its threatening crew and terrible storm, may have weakened Virginia and worsened an underlying health condition. Jessie, the Slocum daughter who was just nine when her mother died, believed that the "sea was too strenuous for her. Whenever there was trouble with the sailors, it told on her. Her heart was not strong."

Virginia's death at a young age, her strong personality, her talents, her bravery, her unique closeness to her husband and children that came from living aboard ships, resulted in unspeakable grief for those she left behind. They were all lost, and Joshua could only do so much to rescue them. In his book, Victor wrote, "There is no need of my looking at a calendar for the date, which sixty-five years ago was written on my heart, never in this life to be effaced." (The year Victor gave in his book is incorrectly given as 1885, not 1884.)

For Joshua, Virginia's sudden death might well have recalled his mother's passing on Brier Island. Yet Virginia was some 10 years younger than Sarah Jane Slocomb had been. Sarah had struggled with various health issues for years—most probably having to do with her regular pregnancies—but Virginia, to outward appearances at least, had seemed strong enough to handle her stressful, hard lifestyle. Joshua Slocum knew how to rescue a leaking, broken ship, bring her safely to port, and fix her up, but he had no idea how to deal with Virginia's sudden decline and shocking death.

Slocum did what had to be done. He went into Buenos Aires and found a man who, as he would later write in *Sailing Alone*, "sold whisky and coffins." Slocum purchased one of the latter. He made arrangements for his wife to be buried in the English Cemetery and ordered a tall stone monument for Virginia's grave. At the top, in gold leaf, was inscribed "Virginia." Below that, the words carved in stone read:

Wife of Captain Joshua Slocum
Died 25 July 1884
Aged 35 years[1]

The grave itself was prettily adorned with flowers. Slocum hired a photographer to take a picture, which he sent to the Walkers in Sydney together with a letter telling them what had happened. Just 13 years earlier, he had sailed away with the Walkers' eldest daughter. Now he was sending them a picture of Virginia's grave.

No longer in need of a cargo for Sydney, Slocum found a shipment bound north to Maceió, Brazil, a one-time sugar plantation north of Rio and 150 miles south of Recife that had become a fast-growing coastal city. The voyage began badly when Slocum, quite uncharacteristically, ran the *Aquidneck* aground in the Río de la Plata. The ship suffered enough damage that he had to borrow money for her repair. At Maceió, however, things improved. Slocum found a cargo for New York, and then he found cooperative winds. The *Aquidneck* chalked up several impressive 350-mile runs, making port in 19 days.

Whatever the *Aquidneck* earned on the voyage to New York could never compensate for what had been lost. For the rest of Joshua Slocum's life, Virginia's absence would hover over him like a heart-breaking shadow. Death

---

[1] The likely inaccuracy of Virginia's age on her memorial is another of those niggling, conflicting details relating to dates and documents that is common to Joshua Slocum. She was probably 33 years old.

in the nineteenth century was most often an intimate event in the family home. Confronting a deceased loved one in the parlor, the shared bed, the kitchen, a ship's cabin, was a fact of life that forced people to deal with their emotions and their own mortality as best they could. The shock, the grief, the usually little-understood reason for the loss of a loved one led many, millions in fact, to turn to spiritualism as a means of attempting to reconnect

Virginia was buried in the English Cemetery in Buenos Aires, but less than 10 years after her burial, the cemetery was taken by eminent domain to become a public square for the growing city, and the monuments were moved to another location. (Courtesy the New Bedford Whaling Museum)

with the departed. In the aftermath of Virginia's going, Joshua too, in his heartbreak, would seek comfort from a spiritualist.

Just over six months after Virginia's death, on February 10, 1885, Slocum visited old friends in Washington, D.C., and while there wrote an emotional letter to his mother-in-law in Sydney. In letters, at least, he was not a man afraid to bare his feelings to those close to him:

Dear Mother,

While I [am] here with mine and Virginia's old friends my heart goes out again for your poor aching heart. I have just been to the art galleries looking at the picture that our dear one looked at a year ago and talked with friends in the society of this great capitol who loved her dearely but who say we will soon meet her in Heaven.

I feel most of the time that Virginia is with me and helping me and that her noble soul is helping support her dear mother. You were not forgotten by your loving Virginia and I doubt not at all but that she is with you and me more now than before—It has pained me tho to have to give up my beautiful wife when we were getting so many enjoyable friends and getting in comfortable circumstances—I would have had some money in hand by this time if I hadn't got crazy and run my vessel onshore. As it is now I am just swimming out of trouble on borrowed money of course the vessel is mine and I may be lucky enough to earn something with her if I do you shall hear from me dear mother, in the meane time George [Virginia's younger brother] must help you ....

The children are just lovely and healthy. I shall strive to do well by my loved ones children I shall try mother to make her Happy in Heaven she was I know happy with me here—she knew that I loved her dearely, and always loved to be in her company—What a terrible separation this has been to me I send you a photo of o[u]r dear ones grave—the name Virginia is in gold and shall be kept in gold as long as I live.

Good by Dear mother We will write you from Brazil ...

Yours in affliction
/s/ Josh

Basing himself in Baltimore, Slocum now undertook a series of voyages to Recife, Pernambuco, with young Victor aboard while the other children stayed with their aunts in Natick. Of the three boys, Victor was the only one who would follow the sea, a decision he said he never regretted. On the last of three trips to Pernambuco, homeward bound, the *Aquidneck* encountered heavy seas raised by a gale in the Gulf Stream, and the main topmast carried away. As efforts were made to trim the yards and gain some semblance of control, the spar, sails, and yards came crashing down over the leeward rail. The crew got everything aboard and kept going with what sails they could carry as the storm—shifting from southwest to northeast and northwest—continued for what Victor said was 10 days. Finally, they accepted a tow into New York where the *Aquidneck* would remain until the damage was repaired and she was seaworthy again in the spring.

Since Virginia's death, Slocum had kept on sailing, doing the best he could. But he knew—the children knew—that things were never going to be the same as when Virginia had been with them. Everyone was still grappling with the incomprehensible, trying to measure what had been lost. It was a process that, for each of them, would last a lifetime.

Years later, in a letter to Walter Teller, looking back on those terrible days following his mother's death and what her loss meant to his father, Benjamin Aymar wrote: "On many occasions mother had proved herself to be very psychic—and had many times reminded father of failures that need not have occurred had he taken her advice. Father learned to understand her powers of intuition and he relied on it fully until she passed on. His ill fortunes gathered rapidly from the time of her death…. Father's days were done with the passing of mother."

Garfield wrote of his impression, "When she died, father never recovered. He was like a ship with a broken rudder."

Slocum, of course, didn't know how to give up. He continued his life under jury-rig, carrying his grief with him as he began sailing the *Aquidneck* again, making more passages to Pernambuco. But financially he was barely holding his own. His visits with spiritualists didn't help. He could ask himself what Virginia might have thought about a situation, what she might have advised him, but doing so was ultimately an empty exercise. He was on his own now, and only he could fashion a solution that might help remake his shattered life in some unfamiliar but advantageous manner.

CHAPTER 7

Nightmare

*"A man will defend himself and his family to the last,
for life is sweet, after all."*

—Joshua Slocum, *Voyage of the Liberdade*

HAVING LOST VIRGINIA, JOSHUA SLOCUM found himself, like his father 24 years earlier, a widower with children who needed care even as he had to earn money to support them. It was a common nineteenth-century dilemma. Possibly the growing recognition of what his father had confronted contributed to Slocum's eventual forgiveness of John Slocomb's long-ago harshness. Now it was Joshua's turn to seek a solution for loneliness and the care of his motherless children.

By the spring of 1885, the *Aquidneck* was repaired at a Brooklyn shipyard, where a new mainmast was built and installed. Victor returned to the ship with his father while Jessie, Ben Aymar, and Garfield stayed in Natick with Joshua's sisters. The *Aquidneck* resumed her trading voyages to South America. Slocum may have earned enough from these voyages to pay for the *Aquidneck*'s earlier repairs in Brazil while also sending money home to cover his children's expenses.

It was during Slocum's time in New York that he met Adam Willis

Wagnalls. In 1877, Wagnalls had joined his Wittenberg College classmate Isaac Kaufmann Funk's publishing company. Both men were Lutheran ministers, and they specialized in religious works. In 1890, however, the company would be renamed Funk & Wagnalls and expanded to publish its successful newsweekly, *The Literary Digest*, followed by *The Standard Dictionary of the English Language* in 1894. The dictionary became a publishing staple that would be followed in 1912 by a soon-to-be famous encyclopedia, thus completing the transformation of a small, highly focused business endeavor into a lucrative New York–based publishing venture.

How Slocum met Wagnalls and his wife Anna is unknown, although they shared an interest in spiritualism. Slocum's interest had been kindled by Virginia, and after her passing, he turned anywhere he could to seek comfort. While visiting the Wagnalls' home, Joshua met the couple's multitalented daughter Mabel, who was 17 years old and working hard at developing herself as a concert pianist, writer, and artist.

Many years later, in a 1925 biography of her mother, Mabel Wagnalls remembered her first meeting with Joshua Slocum: "I had taken a few [art] lessons in America and an old friend of the family, a sea-captain, happening to see an attempt of mine at portrait painting, begged me paint his dear wife, just deceased. I protested my incompetence, but he was too poor to pay a real artist and my work, he said, would suit him no matter how amateurish. He begged me so piteously, with tears in his eyes, that I was obliged to promise at least to try, and to send the result whatever it would be. So I took his wife's photo with me…. By the most painstaking efforts that picture turned out not as bad as I had feared, and in May it was shipped to my father to give the old captain."

While Mabel was working on Virginia's portrait, the winter of 1886 found Slocum back in Massachusetts. It was probably while visiting his sisters Alice and Henrietta ("Etta") in Natick that Slocum met 24-year-old Henrietta Elliott—Hettie—a first cousin of his.[1] One of seven sisters, Hettie was, like Slocum, a native of Mount Hanley. Following the lead of at least three of her sisters, Hettie had left Nova Scotia in 1884 seeking a better, more prosperous future. She was a pretty girl, soft-spoken, a skilled seamstress who had grown up with a spinning wheel and loom. When Slocum met Hettie, she must have seemed the perfect answer to his needs. Grace Murray Brown believed that Hettie was "no doubt bedazzled by [Slocum's]

---

1 Hettie's mother Ruth was a sister of Slocum's father.

attentions when he was considered successful. I think he must have been an ardent person. Certainly [he] was demonstrative in showing affection."

Hettie's sisters were skeptical of the potential union from the outset, perhaps less because of the 20-year age difference between them—for such a gap was not rare in those times—than because of Joshua's profession. If Hettie were to marry him, he would expect her to sail with him as Virginia had. In a letter to Walter Teller, Grace Murray Brown wrote of Joshua and Virginia that "[t]heirs was the love of a man for a woman." Of Joshua and Hettie, she wrote, "The subsequent alliance was to keep a home for his children and himself…. His love for Hettie was not as vital but he seemed very kind and courtly."

Having no clear idea what she was getting into—and perhaps it wouldn't have mattered—Hettie Elliott married Joshua Slocum in Boston on February 22, 1886. Within a few days of the ceremony, Slocum journeyed to New York with his new bride and Garfield. Ben Aymar did not accompany them, pleading instead to remain with his aunt. "Father wept when I begged to be left ashore," he remembered many years later. Ben Aymar's sister Jessie also stayed behind.

The *Aquidneck* had been loaded with case oil and was ready to sail for Montevideo, Uruguay, from New York. The ship, with Victor as mate—he was "strong as a windlass," according to Slocum—was shorthanded. Because freight rates had dropped from already-low levels, Slocum was sailing with a 10-man crew rather the usual 12. "Our foremast hands, six in number," Slocum would write four years later in his first book, *Voyage of the Liberdade*, "were from as many nations, strangers to me and to each other; but the cook a negro, was a native American—to the manner [sic] born. To have so many Americans in one ship was considered exceptional." (He was referring to himself, Hettie, Victor, Garfield, and the cook.)

Although February 28, 1886 was, according to Slocum, "bitter cold and stormy, boding no good for the coming voyage," he decided to "boldly" sail "somewhat against our better judgment." The consequence of this decision was that Hettie's initiation into a seagoing life involved setting off into a 40-knot gale with only a single foresail set that was, Slocum said, "somewhat larger than a table cloth." Within two days, the gale increased to hurricane strength.

Garfield Slocum, who was only five at the time, never forgot the storm. "A hurricane and very angry sea closed in on the *Aquidneck*. It tried hard to send us to Davy Jones's Locker. Father had to work very hard long hours

Garfield Slocum as a child. (Courtesy Melville C. Brown)

without sleep to keep the ship afloat. Hettie, a sailor and myself were in a provisioned boat on the lee side. The ship had a lot of water in her. I have been told that when the ship rolled onto her starboard side, father went out on her port side and nailed a board onto the breach caused by the huge waves."[1] Slocum himself recalled that "[m]ountains of seas swept over the bark in their mad race, filling her decks full to the top of the bulwarks, and shaking things generally." Spare spars that hadn't been doubly lashed down were swept away. The galley was wrecked, and only the bulwarks saved the galley house, the pots, pans, and the cook from going overboard. Slocum later wrote in his irrepressible, dry wit: "It dampens one's feelings, so to speak. It means cold food for a time to come."[2]

Able to find something positive in the worst circumstances, Slocum called it progress when, as the seas continued to wash aboard the *Aquidneck*, the wind began to lose its force and he could set more sail and drive the ship faster, keeping her ahead of the seas. Ten days after leaving New York, she found the northeast trade winds. Dolphins joined her. Victor said they then "rapidly ran out of the hurricane and into normal weather, where all our troubles were forgotten. That is the way with a sailor; it would never do if he took all the jams to heart that he ever got into." But Victor avoided mentioning what his new stepmother felt about how her honeymoon voyage had begun. Neither did Slocum, who was perhaps speaking only for himself when he wrote, "Our hardships were now all forgotten."

Although Slocum didn't remark on it, the difference between the *Aquidneck's* course to Montevideo and the course prescribed by the *Wind and Current Charts* of Matthew Fontaine Maury, first superintendent of the U.S. Naval Observatory prior to the Civil War, was dramatic. Slocum stuck to the traditional route, giving a wide berth to Cape São Roque—the great eastward bulge of the South American continent in northeastern Brazil—from fear of being blown ashore and wrecked on the cape by the southeasterly

---

1 It is hard to know precisely what Garfield was describing here. Perhaps the ship was rolling scupper to scupper, and Slocum could only work on the port-side bulwarks when the starboard side was inundated.

2 In his book, Victor Slocum remembered this episode differently than his father. He claimed that deck seams improperly caulked with pitch alone instead of the usual stranded oakum opened up, and seawater began flooding the hold. The leaks gained on the pumps until there was six feet of Western Ocean inside the *Aquidneck*, and she began losing her buoyancy. He said that when the leak was discovered at the break of the poop deck (where the poop joined the main deck), it was filled with sail cloth strips and lengths of rope. Slocum makes no mention of this. A caulking job such as Victor describes would be criminal, and one supposes that a man of Slocum's temperament would have sought redress.

trade winds south of the equator. "But Maury found that, contrary to popular belief, a narrow band of favorable westerlies ran right down the [South American] coastline," wrote Chester G. Hearn in his *Tracks in the Sea*, recounting Maury's life and work. "So long as a skipper held his ship close to the hitherto dreaded cape, he would make better time." Maury's chart proved that a sailing ship could drastically reduce the time and distance traveled between the U.S. East Coast and South American ports.

By 1848, following a dramatically successful Baltimore-to-Rio-and-back voyage by a ship named the *W.H.D.C. Wright*, ship owners and captains by the thousands were adopting Maury's charts. The charts, with arrows showing wind directions and ocean currents, represented a vast store of hard-won knowledge that could greatly decrease the time, if not the distance, a sailing ship spent at sea. Yet on this 1886 voyage in the *Aquidneck*, Slocum chose the "old-fashioned way," sailing first across the Atlantic to the Cape Verde Islands and there picking up the southeasterly trades that bore him back across to South America.

Slocum reveled in the experience of sailing from the Cape Verdes to Montevideo. *Voyage of the Liberdade*, published in 1890, reveals his first efforts at expressing his emotions in writing. Regarding this leg of the *Aquidneck's* journey, he wrote: "Most delightful sailing is this large, swinging motion of our bark bounding over the waves, with the gale abaft our beam, driving her forward till she fairly leaps from billow to billow, as if trying to rival her companions, the very flying fish."

Recalling his approach to the Río de la Plata, Joshua Slocum provided ample evidence of a master mariner's "weather eye," the ability to observe cloud formations, gauge their meaning, and take appropriate action. In *Voyage of the Liberdade*, he wrote that the *pampeioros* (winds from the great South American plains, the pampas)

> *give ample warning of their approach: the first being an unsurpassed spell of fine weather, with small, fleecy clouds floating so gently in the sky that one scarcely perceives their movements, yet they do move, like an immense herd of sheep grazing undisturbed on the great azure field. All this we witnessed and took into account. Then gradually and without any apparent cause, the clouds began to huddle together in large groups; a sign had been given which the elements recognized. Next came a flash of fire from behind the accumulating masses, then a distant rumbling noise. It was a note of warning, and one that no vessel*

should let pass unheeded. 'Clew up and furl' was the order. To hand all sail when these fierce visitors are out on a frolic over the seas, and entertain them under bare poles, is the safest plan, indeed the best storm sails are bent; even then it is safest to goosewing¹ the tops'ls before the gale comes on.

Just over two months after departing from New York, the *Aquidneck* sailed into Montevideo on May 5, 1886. There she discharged her cargo into lighters that ferried it to warehouses. With that accomplished, Slocum sailed 800 miles up the South American coast to Antonina, Brazil, to load a cargo of *yerba mate* leaves for Buenos Aires. (The leaves, when ground and mixed with hot water, produce a caffeine-rich tea that is a staple drink in South America.)

"From Buenos Ayres," Slocum wrote in *Voyage of the Liberdade*, "we proceeded up the River Platte, near the confluence of the Parena and Paraguay to salve a cargo of wine from the stranded brig *Neovo San Pascual*, from Marseilles."² He discharged the salvaged wine at the fast-growing Argentine port of Rosario, some 186 miles northwest of Buenos Aires up the Río Paraná. And there, in January, in an example of terrible timing, Slocum loaded a cargo of baled hay bound for Rio de Janeiro.

By the time the *Aquidneck* was ready to sail, a cholera epidemic was sweeping Rosario. One of three such outbreaks in Argentina during the second half of the nineteenth century, it would kill 2.5 percent of Rosario's population. In *Voyage of the Liberdade*, Slocum described how one of Rosario's citizens was affected within 48 hours of the disease striking his family. The man had told him, "I sat at my own hearth with wife and three children by my side. Now I am alone in the world. Even my poor house, such as it was, is pulled down." Among those who died were a captain friend of Slocum's and the friendly river pilot who had guided the *Aquidneck* upriver.

---

1 To reduce a square sail's area by hauling up the leeward corner, leaving only the weather edge of the remaining triangle exposed to the wind.

2 Although Slocum was seldom inaccurate about place names, he must here have been referring to the confluence of the Paraná and Uruguay rivers, forming the Río de la Plata, which broadens into an estuary downstream, with Buenos Aires some 20 miles down on the southwest shore and Montevideo a hundred miles farther away on the northeast shore. A trip up the Paraná to the Paraguay River—hundreds of miles into the current of a broad but winding waterway—would have been unfeasible for a square-rigger. In a January 23, 1889 *New York Times* article about the later loss of the *Aquidneck*, Slocum noted that "I was engaged to transfer a cargo of wine from a wrecked vessel in the Río de la Plata to Rosario." Even getting 150 miles up the Paraná to Rosario to discharge the wine was no mean feat.

It was not then understood that people are infected by eating or drinking food or water carrying cholera bacteria. Slocum knew of microbes thanks to his wide reading, but he shared the widespread impression that impure air could be a transmitter of cholera. He did what he could to disinfect the ship, and his family and crew remained healthy. Ashore, however, panic was the immediate reaction to the outbreak.

The Brazilian consul at Rosario now instructed Slocum to sail not for Rio but instead 62 miles southwest of the city to a quarantine station at Ihla Grande. While Slocum was ashore at noon on sailing day getting the necessary papers for his voyage, his newly signed and paid crew stole one or more of the ship's boats and abandoned the vessel. A new crew had to be rounded up. Then, with a pilot aboard, the *Aquidneck* began her trip downriver.

The next day, as the *Aquidneck* sailed with a fair breeze and current toward the ocean, a dog was spotted in the river, desperately swimming. Slocum rescued the animal, a "fine retriever" he called it, and little Garfield now had a new pet. But the next day, a stray cat that had come aboard killed Virginia's canary Pete. Slocum said they mourned the event "almost as the loss of a child." Then, as the *Aquidneck* approached the Atlantic, the pilot proved incompetent, careless, or both, and ran the ship aground on a dangerous shoal called the Martín García Bar. Slocum was fortunate to save his ship, dumping all his fresh water to lighten the *Aquidneck* and then kedging her off before a *pampeiro* struck

Trouble continued at Ihla Grande. Although a British ship named the *Stadacona* was already anchored there, having discharged its own cargo of hay in December, Slocum's arrival was not welcomed. Upon anchoring at the quarantine station on January 7, 1887, he was confronted by a 250-foot-long Brazilian ironclad named the *Aquidiban* (*Aquidiba* in Portuguese). Launched in 1885 at the Samuda Brothers yard in a part of East London on the Thames known as the Isle of Dogs, this Brazilian vessel was under the command of a self-important admiral and politician named Custódio José de Melo, who refused to let the *Aquidneck* remain. Slocum was faced with the prospect of either dumping his cargo overboard or sailing it all the way back to stricken Rosario.

Receiving no useful directive from the hay's owner, Slocum chose the latter course and departed Ihla Grande on January 8 to once again brave the tricky sandbars and bends of the Río Paraná, finally mooring back in Rosario, where he had started. He later called the whole exercise a "ruinous loss … of time and money." He kept the ship's crew on pay during the *Aquidneck*'s prolonged stay at Rosario until, on a Sunday morning after a night of drinking, they became uncontrollable. Crewmen from other ships helped restore order and the rioters were taken off to jail, but now Slocum had to sign on a new group of men. "Crews were picked up here and there," he wrote, "out of the few brothels that had not been pulled down during the cholera, and out of the street or from the fields.... Mixed among them were many that had been let out of the prisons ... so that the scourge should not be increased by over-crowded jails."

Four of the six men Slocum signed aboard the *Aquidneck* were released murderers, highwaymen, or thieves of a lesser order. The remaining two new crewmen, a Dutchman and a Japanese, were honest enough but soon intimidated by the others. Victor remembered the Rosario crew generally as "a hard looking set.... One of them, a burly scoundrel with an ugly sabre cut across his face, was known as 'Dangerous Jack'; while 'Bloody Tommy' was more of a sneak.... [H]e bragged rather unwisely for himself, while helping to dress some mutton on board, that 'he would just as soon cut a man as a sheep.'" Dangerous Jack had been released from his previous ship after punching her captain in the jaw. Slocum advanced both men part of their wages so they could buy some needed clothing, but they spent the money on alcohol instead.

Not until April 9, 1887, when the cholera epidemic was declared over and quarantine restrictions were lifted, could the *Aquidneck* once again clear Rosario for the quarantine station at Ihla Grande. Once more, Slocum made his way down the Río Paraná to the sea. This time he carried no pilot but kept the crew heaving the sounding lead while he picked his way through the bars and shallows with other vessels following in his wake.

For river sailing like this, Slocum drew on his reading of Mark Twain's *Life on the Mississippi*. The book gave, he wrote later, "no end of information on river currents, wind reefs, sand reefs, alligator water,[1] and all that is useful to know about rivers, so that I was confident of my ability." The *Aquidneck* arrived once more at Ihla Grande on April 29, this time with fog, rain, and wind gusts sweeping down from the island's mountains. The authorities fumigated the ship and kept her there eight days before clearing her and the other ships for Rio.

Even then the ordeal wasn't over. The other vessels waiting for clearance

---

1 In *Life on the Mississippi*, Twain reported that, presumably in the early 1800s, so many alligators might be encountered in shallow water that they had to be dredged by a specially equipped vessel to permit a riverboat's passage.

also carried loads of hay, and Slocum aimed to be first into Rio to gain a price advantage. But because the authorities at Ihla Grande had neglected to telegraph Rio that the ships had been cleared, the fort guarding the harbor entrance fired a warning shot and forced Slocum to anchor in difficult water until the all-clear was received. What's more, he received a fine for having arrived without clearance. At last, on May 11, the *Aquidneck* entered Rio and was unloaded. The log entry read, "The cargo was at last delivered and no one was made ill over it."

By now, Hettie may or may not have been seriously questioning her decision to marry Joshua Slocum. As events would soon demonstrate, however, she possessed a quiet, deep inner strength. And it was well that she did, for what had transpired thus far on her first voyage with her new husband would come to seem insignificant in comparison with what lay ahead.

The Slocums found Rio a pleasant city. Hettie bought herself a new hat whose tall shape, when seen at night, unfortunately reminded Slocum of a haystack. They enjoyed themselves until June 1, when the *Aquidneck*, her hold partly filled with flour, kerosene, wine, rosin, pitch, tar, a stationary steam engine and its boiler, and three pianos, sailed for Paranaguá and Antonina, Brazil. On her long voyage north, *pampeiros* overtook the *Aquidneck*, taking away her topgallant masts and knocking her on her beam ends. Slocum was thankful that the ship remained tight, but some damage was done to the cargo, which was not insured. He wrote that, when delivered, "The pianos were fearfully out of tune—suffering, I should say, from the effects of seasickness."

THE NIGHT OF JULY 23, 1887, found the *Aquidneck* anchored by herself in the harbor at Antonina. Slocum would always remember that night as the time "I was called to defend my life and all that is dear to a man." The worst of the new crew, Dangerous Jack and Bloody Tommy, had both, by then, been insolent and even threatening, and Slocum was aware that they were watching him closely. He had long since learned to control any anxiety he may have felt about potentially dangerous crewmen—he couldn't have functioned otherwise—but he did notice that Bloody Tommy wasn't trying to conceal the wicked-looking knife he was carrying.

Slocum "went to sleep ... as usual ... but my wife, with finer instincts, kept awake." Experienced as he was, it hadn't occurred to Slocum that two of the criminals he had taken on as crew were ringleaders in a plan to murder him and his family and steal whatever money was aboard the *Aquidneck*.

Hettie, by contrast, was too worried to sleep. She was wide awake when she heard footsteps on the poop deck, a part of the ship normally forbidden to crewmen. She also heard the rather noisy release of the falls as a ship's boat was partly lowered, and then more footsteps near the door to the cabin.

Slocum was at first skeptical when Hettie woke him up at 10:30, but when she assured him she hadn't been dreaming, he took a .56-caliber repeating carbine from the gun cupboard. The *Aquidneck's* cabin had two entryways, one forward, the other aft. Hettie warned her husband to use the aft door, for she could hear the mutineers at the forward one.

"I knew," Slocum wrote, "that I had to face a mutiny."

From the darkness came a shout demanding that Slocum come on deck. The men were surprised to hear Slocum respond from aft, ordering them forward and warning them that he was armed. Surprised at this, Dangerous Jack attacked. Hoping that he might be able to club the man rather than shoot him, Slocum struck a blow that he thought hard enough "to fell an ox." Instead, he found himself in the grasp of a very powerful man who used one hand to squeeze his throat and the other to try to force him over the ship's rail.

"I could not speak or even breathe," Slocum wrote in *Voyage of the Liberdade*, "but my carbine spoke for me, and the ruffian fell with the knife in his hand that had been raised against me! Resolution proved more than a match for brute force, for I then knew that not only my own life but the lives of others depended on me at this moment." Slocum now ordered the other men forward. Bloody Tommy's response was to raise his arm and leap at Slocum, who shot him, too, "and there on the deck was ended this misadventure! And like the other he fell on the deck with the deadly knife in his hand." In court testimony, it was revealed that each assailant had armed himself with a kevel, a mooring bitt that could be removed from its mount. Each also had a knife.

With Dangerous Jack wounded and Bloody Tommy[1] dead, the other two criminals now went forward. In the morning, the police came aboard and heard about what Victor later called "a night of horror." Slocum was placed on parole. He wasn't jailed, but couldn't leave Antonina until a trial was held. As the *Aquidneck* was loaded with cargo for Montevideo, it was arranged for a Spanish captain and Brazilian crew to sail the vessel there with

---

1 In court testimony, the men's names were given as James Aikin, who had assaulted his previous ship's captain too, and Thomas Maloney (the deceased), who had been in jail for two years in Rio for robbery and attempted murder.

16-year-old Victor serving as "flag captain," an advisory role representing the ship's ownership.

Slocum piloted the *Aquidneck* out of Antonina harbor, then disembarked to return to town and defend himself in court. Whether he was monitored by Brazilian officers is unknown, but the United States consul general in Rio, when reporting the matter of a U.S. citizen being tried for murder in Brazil, remarked on "the imprisonment of Joshua Slocum, Master of said bark [*Aquidneck*]."

The trial by a jury of twelve was held on August 23 and presided over by Antonina's municipal judge João Passos. One of the defense witnesses, a local merchant, testified that the ship's carpenter had told him that two of the crew planned to murder the captain. Slocum named two of the other crew as conspirators with the men who had attacked him. The jury learned that Maloney had been in stocking feet, a presumed aid to stealthy movement. All the assailants had been fully dressed, while Victor, and possibly Slocum as well, were in their sleeping attire.

Care was taken during the proceeding to ensure that Slocum understood all that had been said and translated. Then the jury rendered its verdict, which was reported by Judge Passos: "[The] captain was … unanimously acquitted, the jury recognizing that he had acted in self-defense. In virtue of this decision he was immediately released." In *Voyage of the Liberdade*, Slocum wrote: "Circumstantial evidence came up in abundance to make the case perfectly clear to authorities. There are few who will care to hear more about a subject so abhorrent to all and I care less to write about it…. The trial being for justice and not money, the case was soon finished."

Leaving Hettie and Garfield in Antonina, Slocum took a steamboat to Montevideo, where he found that the *Aquidneck* had been unloaded and preparations were underway to take on a new cargo. The Brazilian crew was a good one, and, the temporary captain having fulfilled his duty, they would remain with the ship. The *Aquidneck* was in fine shape, too, any remaining damage caused by the pre-mutiny pampeiro having been repaired. Things were finally looking promising, and Slocum could look ahead to some semblance of normal life as a ship owner and captain, plying tricky but familiar routes along a South America coastline he now knew well.

But then a bureaucrat at Montevideo intervened. "What overwhelming troubles may come," Slocum wrote, "of having incompetent officials in places of trust." The port official ruled that a change in master of the *Aquidneck* would be treated as if the ship had been sold. In such an instance, the crew was to be paid off and given further money for steamship passage home. Custom of the sea bound a crew to the ship rather than her master, but Slocum paid the men anyway and left it to them to decide if they wished to re-sign for the coming voyage back to Paranaguá, where most of them lived. With one exception, they did. It was a satisfying outcome for Slocum, who now had a homogenous crew of sober professionals.

But the port official now kept everyone waiting for a day before he gave his final approval, and that needless bureaucratic impediment, Slocum wrote later, "doomed" his crew.

"On sailing day," Slocum wrote in *Voyage*, "every man was at his post and all sang 'Cheerily, ho!' and all were happy save one who complained of chills and a fever, but said that he had been subject to this, and that with a dose of quinine, he would soon be all right again. It appeared a small matter. Two days later though, his chills turned to something I knew less about. The next day three more men came down with rigor in the spine and at the base of the brain." The *Aquidneck*'s fine crew had spent its last, needless night ashore in a house infected with smallpox.

Recognizing the symptoms, Slocum immediately turned back to seek help at Maldonado, a coastal city about 70 miles east of Montevideo, in the approaches to the Río de la Plata, but was turned away. More of the crew became incapacitated. His options dwindling, he rode a fair wind to Isla de Flores, some 35 miles west, where there was a quarantine hospital serving nearby Montevideo, but as the *Aquidneck* approached the rocky island she was overtaken by a fierce gale from the east southeast. With too few men left standing to reduce sail, the *Aquidneck*'s sails were carried away, Slocum said, "like autumn leaves." He steered the ship while Victor and the cook treated themselves and the crew with disinfectant.

In the lee of the island, both the ship's anchors were let go and the *Aquidneck* swung into the wind with all cable and chain veered out to provide the best chance of holding. But it wasn't enough. The gale-force winds increased to hurricane strength, and the anchors dragged. One anchor line broke, then the remaining anchor snagged an underwater cable, which at last held the ship in place. In *Voyage*, Slocum wrote that "[t]wo barks not far from us that night, with pilots on board, were lost trying to come through where the *Aquidneck*, without a pilot and with but three hands on deck to work her, came in…. Then, wet, lame, and weary, we fell down in our drenched clothes, to rest as we might—to sleep or to listen to groans of our dying shipmates."

Joshua Slocum suffered through some bad nights at sea during his lifetime, but he called this one as "the most dismal." The next day, the surviving crewmen were at first refused help at Isla de Flores hospital, but eventually, thanks to an order from a man whom Slocum referred to as "the governor of Montevideo," they were admitted. The ship's cook, who had stood by Slocum through it all, died, and when his wife got the news about her husband, she died too, Slocum said, "of grief." The men who had died aboard had to be buried at sea. Finally the *Aquidneck* was towed to Montevideo, where everything the crewmen had owned was burned, and the entire ship was disinfected with carbolic acid.

The cost to Slocum of this disaster was $1,000, but he wrote in *Voyage* that "[w]hat it cost me in health and mental anxiety cannot be estimated by such value." He said the worst part was having to destroy the presents the crewmen had bought in Montevideo to take home to wives now widowed and children now fatherless. He was thankful only that Hettie and Garfield had remained at Antonina.

ONCE THE *AQUIDNECK* was safely anchored again at Antonina, Slocum sent a letter to the U.S. State Department pleading for help in gaining some sort of recompense from Brazil. He felt that he had been unfairly denied *pratique* (port clearance after completion of quarantine) at Ihla Grande back in April, and that this had led to a serious financial loss. On November 4, 1887, Alvey Augustus Adee, the second assistant secretary of state, sent a letter to the U.S. legation at Rio directing it "to investigate and, if undue discrimination against our vessels appear, to ask an explanation.... Act accordingly but don't give the writer room to suppose that we accept his statements and undertake to press his claim without due substantiation of a sound case."

But even before the State Department replied, Slocum, in desperation, wrote to President Grover Cleveland: "Not having reply to my supplication I know not how else to act so I come, Sir, with my case to the first man in all the land. I have sustained a ruinous loss through no fault of mine which bids to throw me out of my home afloat." Slocum would follow up on his petition in a process that, ultimately, would take several years.

The town of Paranaguá, which had been home to most of the *Aquidneck*'s unfortunate crew, lay 12 miles below Antonina, where the Rio Cachoeira broadens into a complex estuary. Across the river from the town, to its north, the Bay of Paranaguá extended 15 miles north into forested lowlands. The bay was then and remains now an area of spectacular beauty. In Slocum's time, there were virgin timber forests around the bay, with logging activity centered at the little town of Guaraquecaba. The region may have reminded Slocum of his days in the lumber trade in Tayabas Bay on Luzon, not quite a decade earlier.

In *Voyage*, Slocum wrote of this period: "[W]e entered on the next venture, which was to purchase and load a cargo of the famous Brazilian wood." Shortly after Christmas 1887, the *Aquidneck* made sail on what should have been a profitable voyage but turned out instead to be short and disastrous. Slocum summed up what happened in a few sentences:

> The bark was ... proceeding across the bay, where currents and wind caught her foul, near a dangerous sandbar, she misstayed[1] and went on the strand. The anchor was let go to club[2] her. It wouldn't hold in the treacherous sands; so she dragged and stranded on broadside where, open to the sea, a strong swell came in that raked her fore and aft for three days, the waves dashing over her groaning hull til at last her back was broke—and why not add heart as well.... After twenty-five years of good service, the Aquidneck here ended her days.... My best skill and energy could not prevail.

No lives were lost, but Slocum's description of the *Aquidneck*'s end, her "groaning," her broken back, her broken heart, may as well have described the death of a loved one. The uninsured *Aquidneck*[3] was wrecked. It was a stunning loss that at once cost Slocum his home, his life's savings, and, ultimately, his livelihood as a merchant captain. The *Aquidneck* disaster, he would later write, left us "as paupers."

---

1 That is to say, she failed to tack or "come about."

2 According to maritime historian W. H. Bunting, "club hauling" meant dropping an anchor with a warp on it when on a lee shore to cast the vessel on the opposite tack..

3 Slocum was operating his vessel on a very tight budget, if not a shoestring, and insurance would have cost a percentage of the vessel's appraised value and that of her cargo. It is possible that, as the *Aquidneck* sailed under the American flag, insurance costs were even higher than they might have been under other registries. Sailor/author Alan Villiers recalled the challenge of finding affordable insurance circa 1930. In *The Way of a Ship*, he wrote that "[t]he American flag was out of the question on the general score of costs. We flew the Finnish flag." One example Villiers provided for insurance costs for a single round-trip voyage from Britain to Australia was eight percent of the vessel's valuation, which was set by the underwriter at 10,000 pounds. The *Northern Light* had carried insurance, but she was owned and operated by a consortium of which Slocum was a member. As a sole owner, Slocum did without.

CHAPTER 8

Liberdade

"In January 1888 the brig Aquidneck, *Captain Slocum, was wrecked at Paranagua off the coast of Brazil. Having no means to pay his passage and that of his family home, the Captain and his two small boys built a tiny craft ...."*

—Frank Leslie's Illustrated Newspaper, June 1, 1889

TO JOSHUA SLOCUM, IT COULD all have seemed like the collapse of a house built of cards. An ill wind, a missed effort to tack or wear ship, a sandbar in a bad place near the mouth of a beautiful bay, and everything came tumbling down. Five years earlier, with Virginia by his side, he had been interviewed by a newspaperman in New York prior to loading valuable cargo for Japan. Around them in the *Northern Light's* living quarters had been a piano, a fine oriental rug on the floor, a well-stocked library, and little Pete the canary singing happily.

Now Slocum was stranded in Brazil with his 26-year-old cousin-wife Hettie, 16-year-old Victor, and six-year-old Garfield, whose memory of the event would forever be that "father lost all of his money and our beautiful home." Their surroundings were not unlike Olongapo, in the Philippines, where Slocum had built a steamship in the jungle. The heat, humidity, and threat of debilitating fevers were much the same.

But the Brazilians at Paranaguá—where the Slocums found themselves in the aftermath of the *Aquidneck* stranding—were friendlier than the Chinese shipwrights in Subic Bay had been. Victor said that one man, "young and sympathetic," invited the Slocums to stay in his house. Still, the financial loss was devastating, the physical and emotional stresses appalling. It was a terrible time. But it was also the sort of situation that brought out the best in Joshua Slocum and gave him a chance to show what he could do, even if he later took some poetic license in his story about this time.

When he wrote The *Voyage of the Liberdade* in 1890, Slocum framed the basic challenge this way: "The plan, in a word, was this. We could not beg our way, neither would we sit idle among the natives. We found that it would require more courage to remain in the far-off country than to return home in a boat, which we then concluded to build and for that purpose." A few months after the voyage had ended, in April 1889, Slocum told the *Baltimore Sun* he had built the *Liberdade* to avoid going into debt for steamship tickets home, a story he would repeat to other newspapers.

While this may have struck Slocum as a dramatic, perhaps even humorous background to the *Liberdade* tale, he much oversimplified what had really happened. Thus, a substantial and irreconcilable difference exists between Joshua's version of why and where the *Liberdade* was built and that of his son Victor. In *Voyage of the Liberdade*, Slocum wrote merely, "The many hindrances encountered in the building of the boat will not be recounted here." The impression one gets is that the *Liberdade* was built ashore after the wreck of the *Aquidneck* and that it was intended as a vessel in which to sail home.

Victor Slocum wrote a far more detailed account of the *Liberdade's* building, however, and there is no obvious reason to doubt his version. In his account, construction of the *Liberdade* had actually begun aboard the *Aquidneck* prior to the wreck, and the boat's original purpose had nothing to do with a long sea voyage home to save the cost of steamship tickets. Victor wrote that the *Liberdade* was conceived as a tender that would be big enough to use in timber gathering. "The trouble was that the [*Aquidneck's*] longboat was not large enough for comfortable timber cruising. If we were going into the Parangua timber business, the *Aquidneck* must have a regular tender. Its construction was immediately decided upon. The length of the boat was limited to the space between the break of the *Aquidneck's* poop aft, to the after side of the fore-deck house."

Describing the vessel's construction, Victor wrote, "Native sawyers, who whipsawed by hand, were put to ripping forty-foot Spanish cedar logs for boat plank. Ironwood, that would sink, was in similar fashion ripped into thicker plank for the partially flat bottom, for a dory-like hull had been decided upon. Natural crooks of another very hard timber were brought in from the forest by the woodsmen for frames. By that time we had the bottom cleated[1] together, the stem made and erected, and the transom up."

Victor's memory was very specific regarding the planking process. "For this work a plank bench was rigged near the rail on the quarter-deck of the *Aquidneck* and protected from sun and rain by an awning. It took the writer about a month to jack-plane those plank, a task which he remembers very well. The plank were then put on lapstreak, without doubt the strongest way to build a boat."

If Victor's version is accurate, and it is far too detailed to think otherwise, the building of the *Liberdade* began before the *Aquidneck* grounding. But could the *Aquidneck* have continued to serve, after her wreck, as a platform for building a 35-foot boat? The answer, apparently, is "yes." In his book, Victor provided a detailed map showing the locations of various events involving the shipwreck. The place of the grounding was some distance off Mel Island (Ilha do Mel), a large island at the entrance to the Bay of Paranaguá. But the bay is a big body of water, and Ilha do Mel didn't provide enough protection against what Joshua Slocum called "a strong swell ... that raked her fore and aft for three days."

But Slocum did say that his heavily damaged ship "floated off at the end of the storm." Victor wrote that the damaged vessel was moved to an anchorage off the town of Paranaguá,[2] and he pinpointed the spot on his map. Presumably, the ship floated on an even keel, which would have been useful to those building a boat on her deck. Victor wrote that the plan was to finish planking the *Liberdade* aboard the *Aquidneck*, lower the hull over the side, and tow it ashore for completion.

In his book, Victor included the whole story of the *Liberdade* voyage as written by his father, but he excluded the first 8½ chapters of *Voyage of the Liberdade* and instead told about the loss of the *Aquidneck* and the building of the *Liberdade* from his own perspective. Perhaps he resented the fact

---

1 Cleats are the transverse strips to which the bottom planks are screwed in standard wooden dory construction.

2 A colonial settlement established in 1648, Paranaguá was an important port in Slocum's time and remains so today.

that his role in building the *Liberdade* was not more fully recognized in his father's version—Joshua Slocum devoted just two laudatory sentences to Victor's work—and took the opportunity to redress the matter 60 years later. Only after describing the *Liberdade's* construction did Victor write, "From this point on I shall let my father tell his story of the *Voyage of the* Liberdade."

As for the *Aquidneck*, Joshua Slocum said only that "I sold the wreck." Victor wrote that, after being sold, the ship ended "her days as a coffee hulk in Santos [a port city some 200 nautical miles north of Paranaguá] where she finally burned."

JOSHUA SLOCUM HAD GOOD SOURCES to draw on for the *Liberdade's* design and construction. He had always taken an interest in small craft wherever he traveled, including the gillnet boats and Native American canoes he had studied in the Pacific Northwest and the many sampans and junks he had admired in Japan and China. He was familiar with the design and construction of the Grand Banks fishermen's dories he had used as a boy and later commissioned in China for the *Pato*. Regarding the *Liberdade*, he wrote: "Her model I got from my recollections of Cape Ann dories and from a photo of a very elegant Japanese sampan, which I had before me on the spot…. Her rig was the Chinese sampan, which is, I consider, the most convenient boat rig in the whole world."

Slocum neglected to describe his designing of the boat—which he always referred to as a "canoe." Even if the *Liberdade's* overall length was, as Victor said, limited by the length of *Aquidneck's* midship deck, Slocum still had to determine the freeboard, the beam, the rake of the stem and transom, the rudder style, and numerous other details. He may well have used the sampan photo as a basis and sketched what he had in mind. The boat was 35 feet long with a beam of 7½ feet, a depth of hold of 3 feet, and a draft of 2 feet 4 inches. She was flat-bottomed with significant rocker toward the stern (upsweep in the bottom aft when viewed in side profile).

Victor and his father both wrote that timber of various species was used as appropriate. The heavy wood saved from the cargo—which Slocum later referred to as ironwood—was used for the bottom after being fashioned into 1¼-inch × 10-inch planks. (Victor remembered the bottom planks as 1½ inches thick.) Much lighter red cedar was used for side and deck planking. Slocum wrote: "This arrangement of exceedingly heavy wood in the bottom, and light on top, contributed much to the stability of the craft. The ironwood was heavy as stone, while the cedar, being light and elastic,

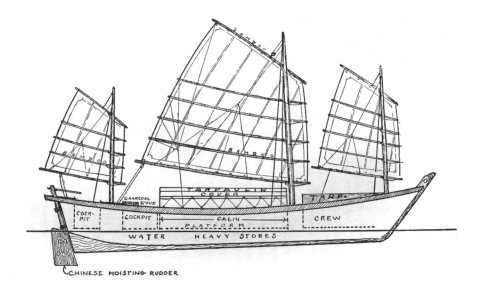

This sail plan and cross section of the Liberdade reflect Victor Slocum's memory of the boat's key features.

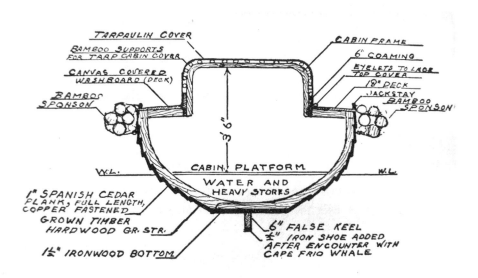

lent buoyancy and suppleness, all we could wish for."

All of the wood that went into the boat—rosewood, mahogany, and bamboo in addition to ironwood and cedar—was durable, rot resistant, and sawn from trees tall enough that full-length planks could be used throughout. Much of the needed metalwork came from the *Aquidneck*, and Joshua Slocum proved ingenious in adapting what he salvaged to new purposes. Some of the copper sheathing plates from the ship's bottom were removed, as were fasteners from the bulwarks and hinges from skylights and doors. Eyebolts, probably used to attach the foot of the ship's gaff-rigged spanker sail,[1] were withdrawn from the wrecked vessel's spanker boom.

Nobody was more aware of the power of the ocean than Joshua Slocum, and he built the *Liberdade* to be both resilient and immensely strong. His life and that of his family depended on this. The planking was fastened to the frames with copper nails, some made from melted-down bottom plates and more bought from Brazilians. Seventy "screw bolts"—more repurposed spanker boom eyebolts—were inserted from inside the hull through the frame and plank and then secured by countersunk nuts. The *Liberdade's* construction would prove itself under severe conditions in the months ahead.

Slocum was a clever and resourceful boatbuilder. According to a cross-section drawing in Victor's book, the *Liberdade* had eight lapstrake planks per side, each precisely fitted against notches in the frames. The side decks were 18 inches wide and covered with canvas that must have come from the *Aquidneck's* sails or spare material. Headroom—from cabin floor to roof—was 4 feet. Berths were located amidships in the cabin, where the motion at sea would be less than if placed forward.

Lashed lengths of bamboo formed sponsons on either side of the hull to add flotation should the boat heel that far. These sponsons appear to have been an invention of Slocum's. Possibly he had come across the idea in his wide reading and study of boats. He wrote that the sponsons made the *Liberdade* "altogether a self-righting [craft] in case of a capsize." Indicating close attention to detail, Slocum calculated that "each joint in the bamboo was an air joint of several pounds buoyant capacity, and we had a thousand joints."

Although the cabin had sturdy sawn hardwood frames and 6-inch-tall wooden coamings where it met the deck, the cabintop was not planked;

---

1 The fore-aft gaff sail of the vessel's aftermost mast.

rather, it was a tightly stretched tarp over light, tough, bamboo stringers running fore and aft. Although similar in theory to a sampan design, the construction was different. Besides being simple and light, the tarp could be rolled up if desired to open the cabin at anchor. Another tarp was rigged over the forepeak area, which Victor labeled the "crew quarters." Hettie, the seamstress, probably sewed the tarps, and she also made the sails on the sewing machine she had brought aboard the *Aquidneck*. "And very good sails they were too," wrote Slocum. Light, tough bamboo was used for the spars.

A profile drawing of the *Liberdade* in Victor's book shows that Slocum copied a Chinese junk rudder, even to the five diamond-shaped holes in the rudder blade that are traditional on junks. Naval architect Cipriano Andrade, an admirer of junks who would one day evaluate the *Spray* for *The Rudder* magazine, said of the junk rudder design in the July 1917 issue of *The Rudder*, "The purpose of these diamond-shaped holes is undoubtedly to let dead water run through to the back of the rudder blade and prevent the accumulation of dead water along the after edge of the rudder." The result was reduced drag and more responsive steering.

A junk's rudder could be hoisted vertically so that the boat could be grounded out, and Slocum included this feature on the *Liberdade* with an ingenious arrangement of semicircular wooden "partners." There was an upper pair and a lower pair of partners, and the members of each pair encircled the rudder shaft but left a wide enough gap for the blade (but not the shaft) to pass through. The rudder could thus be raised vertically when it was in the straight-ahead position.

Slocum built what he called his "microscopic ship" using the toolkit available to him. "To begin with, we had an axe an adz and two saws, one ½ inch auger, one 6-8 and one 3-8 inch auger bit, two large sail needles … a file that we found in an old sail bag washed up on the beach." He had a chalkline but no chalk, so he used finely ground charcoal mixed with water instead. A portion of one of the *Aquidneck*'s smaller jackstays—the iron rod to which square sails were attached—was heated and used to bore holes larger than those that could be made with the available auger bits. A boatbuilder can never have enough clamps, but Slocum had none at all, so he made some from the crooks of guava trees and other trees. River stones were used to keep a sharp edge on the tools.

At least once during the construction process, Slocum fell seriously ill with fever. He had not been altogether well in the months prior to the wreck, writing that he had had to expend "ruinous" amounts on doctor visits.

Slocum called his fever malaria, and he seems to have been susceptible to such maladies since first contracting a fever as a young man in Hong Kong. He was in bed for three days until he began medicating himself with small doses of arsenic from the supply in the ship's medicine chest. "Increasing the doses somewhat, I could feel the beneficial effects hour by hour, and in a few days had recovered from the malady."[1]

The *Liberdade*—"Liberty"—was so named because her launching day was May 13, 1888, when slavery ended in Brazil. An impressive boat, she caught the eye of the local customs officer, who asked Slocum if he would build a new boat for the customhouse or repair the old one, which was in need of a substantial rebuild. It was a tempting offer, but Slocum had to balance the promise of good money against his fear of once again becoming fever ridden.

He was also worried about getting "the passport on which, we thought, depended our sailing." In *Voyage of the Liberdade*, he didn't say why a Brazilian passport would be needed to leave Brazil or why his own papers would not have sufficed. After his return to the United States, however, Slocum told reporters that the "Brazilian port captain announced that he could not grant permission to such a vessel to sail as it had no American registry." Slocum's solution was to procure a local fishing license, with which, he was assured, he could sail anywhere.

To outfit the *Liberdade* for sea, Slocum fashioned an anchor from ironwood, perhaps shaping it after the wooden anchors he'd seen in Asia. Not long before departure, however, he acquired an iron anchor from a local rancher, swapping Hettie's sewing machine for it. Though it must have been a hard trade for Hettie, good ground tackle was critical, and a sewing machine might have seemed a nuisance aboard the *Liberdade*. Ultimately, however, the sewing machine would be much missed.

The *Liberdade*'s three sails, each a different size—the main and foresail had four yards, the mizzen three—could all be instantly reefed by lowering the halyard until the desired yard reached the boom. Its variety of sail combinations and sail areas made Slocum's "canoe" convenient and safe to operate in a wide range of winds.

The boat carried 90 fathoms of anchor cable made locally from vines. The food for the voyage—salt beef, salt cod, salt pork, oranges, bananas,

---

1 Arsenic could be both a "magic bullet" to treat disease and a deadly poison. Beginning in 1786 and continuing for some 150 years, several arsenic-based liquid solutions were used to treat a wide variety of ailments including malaria, arthritis, some cancers, and syphilis.

coconuts, and sugarcane—was stored beneath the floorboards, where it would act as ballast, as were sealed tins of flour, bread, coffee, and tea and 120 gallons of water that could survive a capsize without being spoiled. Fishing nets and hooks were shipped in hopes of augmenting these provisions. Slocum stowed his navigational instruments and charts and his faithful lever-action carbine, a musket, and three cutlasses. A number of books went aboard, including some Shakespeare and Robert Burns. The small library would be augmented during stops along the way, and steamships that the Slocums encountered were generous with magazines.

On June 24, 1888, after shakedown cruises in the bay, Slocum guided the *Liberdade* across the Paranaguá bar and into the South Atlantic. With characteristic insouciance, he sailed right past six ships that had anchored because their skippers felt the seas over the bar were too rough for safe passage. He would show them what *he* could do:

> *The wind from the sou'west at the time was a moderating pampeiro, which brought in a heavy swell from the ocean that broke and thundered on the bar with a deafening roar and grand display of majestic effort. But our little ship bounded through the breakers like a fish—as natural to the elements, and as free!*

Slocum wrote that although the *Liberdade* was stood on her ends in these waves, no sea boarded her. After passing over the bar and squaring away on her course, the boat "flew onward like a bird." By now, Hettie apparently took white-knuckled conditions in stride and stoically hung on. As things settled down, she did most of the cooking on a little charcoal stove in the cockpit just abaft the cabin.

Slocum considered hugging the coast, but it immediately became evident that the seas inshore of what he called "the ten-fathom line" were breaking and dangerous. Farther out, the seas, "though grand, were regular.... In twenty-four hours from the time Parangua Bar was crossed we were up with Santos Heads, a run of 150 miles." Off Santos, however, the *Liberdade* encountered a squall that shredded her sails and forced Slocum into port. There he met an old friend and steamship captain who was departing for Rio the next day, and arranged for Hettie and Garfield to go aboard the *Finance* for this leg of the trip while Slocum and Victor stayed aboard the *Liberdade*, which would be towed the 200 miles to Rio.

Being towed at 12 knots on a 90-fathom-long 1½-inch hawser by a steamship in rough seas was an unpleasant and dangerous proposition. As the seas grew in height and power under gale-force winds, the skipper of the *Finance* began releasing oil to calm the water. Slocum stayed at the helm, gradually assuming the appearance of an oil-soaked bird as he kept his boat on a straight course, for sheering off would have "finished the career of the *Liberdade*.... This canoe ride was thrilling and satisfactory to us all. It proved beyond a doubt that we had in this little craft a most extraordinary sea-boat, for the tow was a thorough test of her seaworthiness."

Garfield and Hettie watched the drama unfold from the steamer. Years later, Garfield remembered in a letter to Walter Teller that they watched "for the *Liberdade* to come up over a huge wave. Father had a lot of nerve, strength and will power. He steered all day and all night. Victor sat in the fore-peak under a tarpaulin, an ax on his lap to cut the hawser in case the *Liberdade* turned over. Father had a lanyard tied to Victor's wrist. Father would pull on it and Victor responded with a pull. Both were wonderful men, plenty of courage and brains and endurance."

In Rio, Slocum learned that his "fishing license could be exchanged for a pass of greater import ... through the office of the Minister of Marine." After encountering the now-familiar bureaucratic delays, he appealed to the American consul for guidance, and eventually, with the help of a Brazilian naval commander, was awarded a *"Passe Especial* [that] had on it a seal as big as a soup plate." Another document with a seal was issued to Slocum by a port official, as was a bill of health. In the spring of 1889, when the *Liberdade* reached New York, Hettie would tell a newspaperman that "Capt. Slocum had obtained a permit to all ports duty-free, from the marine office, and also had been granted permission to sail under the flag of Brazil. They thought it a great honor to allow so small a craft to carry their colors."

Joshua Slocum had learned to speak passable Portuguese and to read it. In *Voyage*, he included a quote from Rio's *Journal Opiz*, for he had taken the opportunity of his stop in the city to tell a major newspaper about the voyage. The paper called Slocum a "cool-headed, audacious American mariner" and described the voyage in dramatic terms. In fact, it *was* dramatic. Small-boat cruising was largely unknown in 1888, and Slocum's long ocean voyage with wife and sons in a self-designed, flat-bottomed 35-footer built under primitive conditions will always remain unique.

Joshua and his family, despite his skills, needed a healthy dose of luck to survive the voyage. Two days out of Rio, a whale that Slocum judged to be 50 or 60 feet long "came up under the canoe, giving us a toss and a great scare." Seven-and-a-half days and 680 miles later, when the *Liberdade* was hauled at Salvador in Brazil's state of Bahia, the keel damage suffered in the whale encounter was obvious. (One of the anchors had been lost, too.) Slocum wrote: "An iron shoe was now added for the benefit of all marine monsters wishing to scratch their backs on our canoe." The boat took on fresh provisions, and Slocum set about "fortifying the canoe against the ravaging worms of the seas we were yet to sail through"—whether with copper sheathing or some other bottom treatment, he did not say.

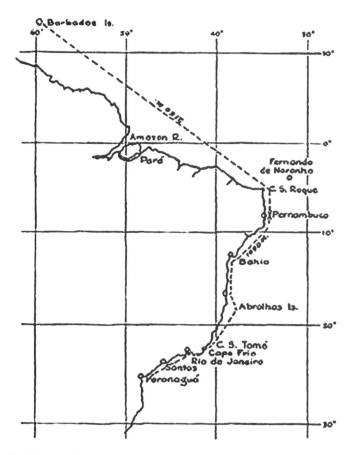

The Liberdade's *voyage from Paranaguá to Barbados as drawn by Victor Slocum. The Slocums made their U.S. landfall at South Carolina, sailed north to overwinter at Washington, D.C., and reached New England the following spring.*

From Bahia (now Salvador), Slocum sailed to Recife, Pernambuco, a pleasant five-day, 390-mile passage in southeast trade winds. The U.S. consulate at Recife took notice of Slocum's voyage and his unresolved claim against Brazil for losses suffered in the *Aquidneck* matter. The consul reported Slocum's situation to the assistant secretary of state in Washington. The voyage's next leg, Pernambuco to Barbados, was 2,150 miles, the longest passage of the trip home. It was also very nearly the last. Between Cape São Roque and the Amazon delta, Slocum made a rare seamanship miscalculation. After encountering heavy seas in a gale from the east southeast, he moved closer inshore in search of calmer seas, and in doing so sailed right over a shoal.

Big, powerful seas broke over the shoal and over the *Liberdade*. Slocum said the waves "bellowed over the shoal! I could smell the slimy bottom of the sea, when they broke! I could taste the salty sand.... This was the greatest danger we had yet encountered. The elasticity of our canoe, not its bulk, saved it from destruction. Her light, springy timbers and buoyant bamboo guards brought her upright again and again through the fierce breakers. We were astonished at the feats of wonder of our brave little craft." Slocum stood to seaward after that and, when the gale subsided, found days of mild trade winds. Their best day's run was 175 nautical miles—an average speed of 7.3 knots, which is more or less top speed for a 35-footer.

Slocum carried more sail than was prudent (at Hettie's urging, he said), and this led to broken main- and foremasts, but they were able to repair both spars and the *Liberdade* carried on, reaching Barbados 19 days after leaving Pernambuco. There Slocum met old friends and decided to remain at the island until hurricane season had passed. The *Liberdade* departed October 7 and, five days and 570 miles later, reached Mayagüez, on the west coast of Puerto Rico. The United States consul there invited the Slocum family to dinner and took them to his father's plantation, where, Hettie said, "we had a charming time."

After a pleasant three days, they departed for the Bahamas by way of Cárdenas, Cuba, navigating with Slocum's customary thoroughness: "Daily observations for determining latitude and longitude were invariably made unless the sun was obscured." Slocum and his son Victor stood alternating six-hour watches throughout the voyage, and either could take a reliable sextant sight while perched atop the cabin. The *Liberdade* averaged an impressive 108 nautical miles per day on the passage.

Their only departure from their passage plan was to skip Nassau, even though Joshua had instructed that his mail be forwarded there. He gave no reason for the change; perhaps he was hoping to avoid a close inspection of their documents. Instead they stopped to replenish their drinking water at tiny, isolated Cay Lobos, a Bahamian island off the Cuban coast. A 148-foot iron lighthouse had been built on the island in 1869, and there were big freshwater storage cisterns there. Slocum sent Victor ashore to fetch water, but the light keeper demanded that "the captain … bring his papers ashore and report."

In *Voyage*, Slocum spent two pages belittling the light keeper. "Thus in a moment was transformed the friend in need to governor of an island." Slocum wrote that his "mate," Victor, normally "attended to the custom reports." It is possible that Victor had documents his father did not, because what Slocum presented was his Brazilian "*Passe Especial*, the one with the big seal on it, written in Portuguese." Apparently it sufficed, and Slocum wasn't required to explain why an American captain was sailing under Brazilian papers on a boat built in Brazil.

Slocum's next landfall was Bimini, but he didn't stop there. He had a fair wind when he entered the Gulf Stream, and with wind and current both favorable, the *Liberdade* covered 220 miles in one day on a course for Cape Romain (which he called Cape Roman), South Carolina. But the fine sailing—Slocum's "canoe" was covering the sea floor at almost 9.2 knots—didn't last. The *Liberdade* struck a derelict floating spar, which "shattered" the keel, then the wind shifted northeast, opposing the Gulf Stream and raising a terrible head sea. Eventually they made landfall south of Cape Romain Light at Bull's Bay, where, rather than battle an adverse tide, they anchored at 8 p.m., 21 days after leaving Mayagüez.

THE HARDSHIPS AND DANGERS faced by Hettie on her honeymoon voyage had apparently suggested to her that she would be happier in the future if her husband turned to farming. Slocum must have agreed to consider the idea, because he said as much in *Voyage*. So he took a special interest in the first people they encountered upon arriving in the United States, farmers working fields along the Santee River.

One in particular, whom Joshua identified as Mr. Anderson, was a Confederate veteran who charmed Slocum with his selflessness and honesty. For his part, Anderson was fascinated by the *Liberdade*. When he learned the reason for the boat's name, he was amazed that Brazil had ended slavery without fighting a civil war. The one-time soldier said to Slocum, "Mister, d'ye know the South were foolish? They had a wah, and they had to free the niggers, too."

But Anderson also shared with Slocum the difficulties he had encountered in starting the farm. The initial idea had been to raise pigs, but the pigs had gotten loose and had to be rounded up by dogs. The pork proved inferior, and the remaining pigs rooted out and ate the farmer's potatoes. Anderson had built a fence to protect his potatoes, which kept out the pigs but not the rats. But Anderson was having better luck with corn.

After listening to a farmer's tale of woe, Slocum wrote that "the resolution which I had made to buy a farm was now shaken and finally dissolved into doubts of the wisdom of such a course." He would have been reminded, too, of his father's failed farming effort at Mount Hanley. It would be another 12 years before Hettie got her wish to live on a farm; it must have seemed like a dream that would never come true.

CHAPTER 9

Fame but Not Fortune

"It was the loss of his Aquidneck *and his subsequent hard luck that made him a writer and he now declares that his troubles were all good fairies in disguise."*

—Clifton Johnson, notes from his 1902 interview of Joshua Slocum

HAVING ARRIVED IN SOUTH CAROLINA near the end of October 1888, Slocum decided to sail on to Washington, D.C., and there spend the winter. The Slocums' first stop after meeting the Anderson family on the shore of the Santee River was Georgetown, South Carolina, where they entered the United States officially. After accepting a tow up the narrow Winyah Bay channel from the passing steamboat *Planter,* they arrived at Georgetown—14 miles above the bay's mouth—late in the afternoon of November 1. There Slocum was told by the quarantine official that the coconuts aboard the *Liberdade* would require the boat to wait until the following day to receive *pratique,* because fruit could not be brought into the state from abroad until after November 1. This bureaucratic idiosyncrasy—all too familiar by now—

irked Slocum, but he mentioned no problem regarding his paperwork.

The unplanned overnight stay at Georgetown meant that Slocum could not accept the *Planter's* offer of a tow back down the bay and through the hazardous entrance shoals into the Atlantic.[1] Having successfully threaded the inlet the following day, the *Liberdade* turned northeast toward the shipwreck-strewn waters off Cape Fear, North Carolina, 70 miles northeast. In favorable weather, the *Liberdade* might have made the passage without incident, but Slocum and his family were not so fortunate. They were overtaken by what Slocum called "gales of considerable violence" at Frying Pan Shoals, which extend from Cape Fear 30 nautical miles into the Atlantic.

To find shelter, Slocum ran into the Cape Fear River—the entrance to which is immediately west of the shoals—and the *Liberdade* waited two weeks at Southport and Wilmington for better weather. Eventually the weather moderated, and the *Liberdade* set off with a cooperative westerly, following a local schooner named the *Packet* whose skipper knew the channel from the Cape Fear River through what was then called Corn Cake Inlet. This put them back in the Atlantic north of Frying Pan Shoals, a significant saving in distance and danger.

The *Liberdade* briefly enjoyed fair sailing as she made her way northward along the Atlantic beach. In *Voyage*, Slocum wrote that the fair breeze lasted for "but a few leagues"—a league being 3 nautical miles—before a northeast gale began building. The seas were dangerous and still building by the time the *Liberdade* was off the entrance bar at New River, and the decision was made to seek refuge from the gale inside. Slocum, irrepressible as always, described their passage over the bar: "[T]he tempest-tossed canoe came sweeping in from sea over the rollers in a delightfully thrilling way. One breaker only coming over us, and even that did no harm more than to give us all the climax soaking of the voyage."

Twenty-one years after the event, Hettie wrote about it in a letter to Mrs. Alfred McNutt, then of Colchester County, Nova Scotia. During their stopover in Barbados, the Slocums had met the McNutts and become friends. Hettie wrote, "We went through drawing 2 feet 4 inches of water where at ordinary time it was a rare thing to have more than twelve inches. We were very glad for we had already had enough of it outside." They anchored in smooth water in the inlet, protected from the roaring seas outside,

---

1 Volume 4 of NOAA's (the National Oceanic and Atmospheric Administration) *Coast Pilot* warns that the shoal-strewn Winyah Bay entrance "is not safe for small craft except in favorable weather. Heavy tide rips prevail … and heavy seas run in moderate weather."

which thundered on the bar. The *Liberdade* remained at anchor nine days.

In 1888, the long, narrow segment of what would eventually become the Intracoastal Waterway[2] connecting New River to Bogue Sound to the northeast was merely a ditch usable only by shoal-draft small craft when the tide served. But after his recent experience in the Atlantic, and perhaps at Hettie's urging, Slocum now planned to somehow get the *Liberdade* through this sheltered inland route. Their course would then take them north through Bogue and Pamlico sounds, thus avoiding the dreaded "outside" passage past Cape Lookout and Cape Hatteras. Slocum wrote that he "set about contrivances to heave the canoe over the shoals" that might be encountered. From a local schooner captain he borrowed a shovel to scoop away mud.

The clouds of the gale proved to have one silver lining. The wind had "so raised the water in the west end of the [Bogue] sound as to fill all the creeks and ditches to overflowing. I hesitated then no longer but headed for the ditch through the marshes on a high tide."

Although the wind out of the west was favorable to the task, any sailor then or now would recognize the challenge of sailing a 35-foot boat, even one of modest draft, through the "ditch." The channel markers that delineate the inland waterway today weren't there to help Slocum. He wrote: "I was getting lost in the maze of sloughs and creeks, which as soon as I entered seemed to lead in every direction but the right one."

Then "Slocum's luck" came to the rescue when they encountered a hunter whose grandfather had dug the ditch and who knew it well. "A bargain was quickly made, and my pilot came aboard.... The entrance to the ditch, then close by, was made with a flowing sheet [the sheets being eased with wind abeam or over the stern quarters], and I soon found that my pilot knew his business. Rush swamps and corn fields we left to port and to starboard." When necessary, Slocum and Victor jumped overboard to push the *Liberdade* over the mud. They spent one night at a fishing camp along the way, where the Slocums listened to stories told by their guide and the fishermen. Slocum said the men all pronounced the *Liberdade*'s voyage from Brazil to be the "greatest thing since the wah."

By now, word of Slocum's 6,000-mile-plus small-boat voyage was getting out. Like a good publicity man, Slocum had done his best to let

---

2 The first edition of what was then called the *Inside Route Pilot* was published by the United States Coast and Geodetic Survey in 1912.

newspapers know of the adventure. Even before leaving Brazil, apparently, he had advised the *New York Herald* of his plans. When the *Liberdade* reached Beaufort, North Carolina, inside Cape Lookout, on November 28, the mayor and townspeople were on the wharf to greet her. On Monday, December 3, Chicago's *Daily Inter Ocean* reported: "Captain Joshua Slocum and family, after a perilous voyage from Brazil ... have touched our coast and are safely sailing northward." It was easy going now.

This image of the Liberdade *was made during the spring of 1889, probably at Washington. Left to right are Joshua, Hettie, Garfield, and Victor. Slocum seems to have adorned the unpainted brown boat with a white stripe that follows the curve of her sheer. A Brazilian flag flies from the mainmast. The* Liberdade's *small, easily reefed junk-style sails made her quickly adaptable to a variety of wind strengths. (Courtesy the New Bedford Whaling Museum)*

As they sailed up the Chesapeake Bay toward the Potomac River, a roasted turkey was the highlight of Christmas dinner. (Presumably the turkey had been cooked ashore, as the *Liberdade's* cookstove was what Hettie called a small iron pot heated by charcoal.) On December 27, 1888, carried along by a southerly breeze, the *Liberdade* arrived at what was then the 6th Street

Wharf in Washington, D.C., and Slocum declared the voyage ended.

The *Milwaukee Daily Journal* carried notice of the *Liberdade's* arrival: "On Thursday, December 27th, there was great excitement when the tiny three-masted vessel *La Liberdad*, anchored at the wharf in Washington." Newspapers in California, Georgia, Missouri, Kansas, North Dakota, Illinois, Idaho, and elsewhere ran stories based on a *New York Herald* cablegram about the *Liberdade*. Captain Joshua Slocum was national news. The voyage was also noted in Nova Scotia, where the *Weekly Monitor* of Bridgetown reported on the *Liberdade* in its May 29, 1889 issue, adding, "Capt. Slocum, as many of our readers know, is a native of Hanley Mountain, this County." Slocum's presence in the capitol caught the attention of famed Civil War photographer Mathew Brady, who made a photographic portrait.

Joshua Slocum sat for this portrait by renowned photographer Mathew Brady when the Liberdade *reached Washington, D.C.*

There is no doubt that Slocum coveted the admiring publicity he generated or that he liked seeing his name in print. He craved recognition of his abilities and felt that he deserved it. Even as a boy he had nurtured vague dreams of glory. In a letter to Clifton Johnson in January 1908, near the end of his life, Slocum wrote, "I often wondered when a boy if I would become famous and see my name on soap advertisements—but this, the real thing is better still."

But publicity did nothing to redress the wrong Slocum felt he had suffered in Brazil. Even before reaching Washington, he had posted another letter in his campaign to recover the financial loss incurred when the *Aquidneck* was turned away from Ihla Grande and forced to return to Rosario because of the cholera outbreak. The British ship ahead of him had been allowed to unload in Rio; why had he been sent away? The correspondence continued in January 1889, by which time Maryland senator Arthur Pue Gorman was involved because the *Aquidneck* had been registered at Baltimore. Slocum proved tireless in his efforts to gain recompense from the Brazilian government, and he would continue the campaign—a weight on his energy and thought—for a long time after leaving Washington.[1]

During the winter of 1888–89, the Slocums stayed in Washington with a friend of Joshua. This may have been Lyman Littlefield, who owned a wharf and storage business in the city. Slocum was popular with his many seagoing colleagues and seemingly had friends everywhere who would speak up for him or help him out in tough times. His presence in Washington gave him the opportunity to attend the American Shipping League meeting of February 6, where he voiced his support for resolutions affirming the need to improve the country's harbors, requesting that U.S. mail be carried only in U.S.-flagged vessels, and seeking additional protections for U.S. seamen abroad.

When spring arrived, Joshua, Hettie, Victor, and Garfield set off again. Upon reaching Baltimore on April 12, 1889, Slocum went to the mayor's office and obtained a permit to display his now famous "canoe" in which, *The Sun* reported, "he made the most marvelous voyage on record." In a January 28 letter to a friend of hers in Nova Scotia, Hettie had written, "The people

---

1 In fact, the British ship *Stadacona* had arrived at Ihla Grande on December 6, 1886, while Slocum had arrived over a month later, on January 7, 1887. In the interim, according to a letter referencing Slocum's case written on September 9, 1890, by Brazil's Minister and Secretary for Foreign Affairs, the Brazilian government had decided "to stop the shipment of all kinds of forage to the ports of Brazil until further orders should be sent."

In Washington, D. C., during the winter of 1889–90, the Slocums sat for a family portrait at the Pennsylvania Avenue studio of J. D. Merritt. Left to right are Victor, Joshua, Hettie, and Garfield. (Courtesy the National Portrait Gallery, Smithsonian Institution.)

in Baltimore are very anxious to see the little craft. We will give them all a chance to see her." Charging admission to see the boat was a way to bring in some cash, an approach Slocum would repeat often with the *Spray.*

Possibly for Hettie's sake, Slocum took the *Liberdade* north "through inland passages,"[2] thus avoiding the unpredictable springtime Atlantic between the Chesapeake Bay and New York Harbor, and the voyage became a pleasure excursion. "Animation of spring clothed the landscape on all sides in its greatest beauty…. And the robin sang even a sweeter trill than ever before heard by the crew, for they listened to it now in the country that they loved."

By the time Slocum reached New York, the *Liberdade* was bigger news than ever. On June 1, 1889, *Frank Leslie's Illustrated Newspaper*, a publication made famous by its wonderful engravings, carried a brief note about the voyage and a rendering of the *Liberdade* at anchor with her sails lowered and neatly contained by lazyjacks. But the most revealing article had appeared earlier when, on May 19, the *New York World* did a feature focusing on Hettie.

The *World* had for years maintained a shipping news office next door

---

2 Slocum was presumably speaking here of a route that followed the Chesapeake and Delaware Canal from the Chesapeake Bay to Delaware Bay, the Delaware River past Philadelphia and Trenton, New Jersey, and the Delaware and Raritan Canal to the Raritan River and thence to New York Harbor.

to the ornate stone Barge Office at the foot of Whitehall Street, near the Battery. The Barge Office was the terminal for the Ellis Island ferry and would serve as an immigration facility in the near future. The *World's* reporter was helped aboard the *Liberdade* by Slocum and found Hettie dressed in "yachting attire" consisting of a dark-blue serge skirt and a blouse trimmed with rows of white braid. She was sitting "in the wee cabin on a plank running the length and raised about three inches from the deck with a blue straw 'sailor hat' in her hand."

The reporter described Hettie as a young and strong woman whose "full brow; bright hazel eyes, a remarkably well-formed 'nez,' [nose] a frank smiling mouth, and a chin expressing both firmness and tenderness, are the features of an oval face which has acquired a rich bronze tint from months of exposure to tropical suns and ocean breezes. Here is the face of a woman who would be capable of the most devoted, intrepid deeds, done in the quietest and most matter-of-fact way, and never voluntarily spoken of afterwards."

The *Herald's* man asked Hettie if she had grown weary and lonely on the voyage. "The loneliness came and went early in the voyage. The weariness grew because it was impossible to get any exercise." Hettie said her most desolate time came after the great send-off the Brazilians had given them at Rio, once the *Liberdade* was well out to sea.

In *Voyage*, Slocum would write: "My wife, brave enough to face the worst storms, as women are sometimes known to do on the sea and on land, enjoyed not only the best of health, but had gained a richer complexion." But good health and a good tan were merely the outward manifestations of the voyage. Had she been asked how she felt, and had she answered frankly, she might well have questioned a number of her husband's decisions. While Slocum had consulted Virginia on a variety of matters and trusted her judgment, there is no indication that he sought out Hettie's input at all. The cumulative effect on Hettie of the dangers and trials she had experienced since her marriage was revealed in her response to the most telling question the reporter asked: "Are you going on another voyage, Mrs. Slocum?"

"Oh, I hope not. I haven't been home in over three years, and this was my wedding journey.... I shall travel by rail. I have had enough sailing to last me for a long time." She meant it, too.

As Slocum made the *Liberdade* ready for the voyage to Massachusetts, Hettie departed with Garfield and took the train to Boston, where she and Garfield moved in with one of her sisters in East Boston and were soon joined by Jessie. It may have been at this time that Hettie took Garfield to

Port George, Nova Scotia, where she left him for a time in her mother's care.

"I attended a school," Garfield remembered, "very cold in the winter—the tide dropped 40 feet. After school I would go down to a beach and work hard gathering scrap iron from old wrecks and take it to a general store where we would turn it in for candy, etc."

Whatever expectations Hettie may have harbored for her life with Joshua Slocum now had to be reassessed in the harsh light of experience. Her relationship with Slocum became by turns difficult and enigmatic. Sometimes their marriage was companionable if not intimate, but at other times it was silent and cool. As time passed, Joshua and Hettie trended into separate lives, cordial in public but often uncommunicative in private. During an era when marriages generally produced a number of children, Hettie never became pregnant.

In an effort to sum up Hettie's relationship with Slocum, Grace Murray Brown wrote Walter Teller, "After the *Aquidneck* wreck, and the voyage home in the *Liberdade*, Hettie found she was not wholly for that life. It was bad all around taking Virginia's place as a wife and trying to do right by the children." As Garfield saw it, his father and stepmother "didn't pull on the same rope." Hettie could hope for nothing approximating a normal life ashore in her own home with Joshua Slocum. In the end, even the manner of his going caused her more trouble.

Eighteen-year-old Victor now left the *Liberdade* to sign aboard the Brazilian Mail Company's steamer *Finance*, the ship that had towed the *Liberdade* in rough weather from Santos to Rio. The *Finance* was conveniently then in New York but headed back south, and so began Victor's seafaring career on a vessel not owned by his father. It would be varied, long, and successful.

IN JUNE 1889, JOSHUA SLOCUM departed New York for New England, alone now aboard the *Liberdade*. After riding the tide through the East River, his first port was New London on Long Island Sound, where, seven years earlier and in a different life, the problems that had plagued Slocum and Virginia aboard the *Northern Light* had begun. He then sailed for New Bedford, where he put the *Liberdade* on display again. Among his visitors was Captain Eben Pierce, a kindly man who would later prove to be a great friend to Joshua Slocum. (Eben spelled his name Peirce, unlike the rest of his family.) Born in Livermore, Maine, Pierce had not only achieved great success as a whaling skipper but had patented a popular and deadly whale "darting gun" before retiring to Fairhaven.

It turned out that Slocum and Pierce had an important "small world" connection. Pierce was the uncle of Captain John Drew, whom Slocum considered a firm friend and role model since their meeting in Manila. Born in Hallowell, Maine, in 1834, Drew had gone to sea at age 15 and become a very successful captain, rounding Cape Horn 14 times and the Cape of Good Hope 40 times during his 45-year career. But it was what Drew did with pen and paper that drew Slocum to him. During the period 1876–89, Drew—under the byline "Kennebecker"—wrote articles about his life at sea for the *Boston Journal*. It was an idea Slocum would try to emulate.

From New Bedford, Slocum sailed to Martha's Vineyard, arriving, as best as islanders could remember later, in "mid-summer." Many years later, on September 23, 1927, Hettie told the *Vineyard Gazette* that she accompanied Slocum on this passage to the island. Neither Hettie nor Slocum remarked on why they went to the Vineyard in the summer of 1889, but they found the island much to their liking. The *Liberdade*, of course, was an exotic interloper among the catboats in the harbor at Oak Bluffs. Nobody who saw her there ever forgot the sight, and the island's observant chronicler, Joseph Chase Allen, recalled the *Liberdade* in a *Vineyard Gazette* article published on June 26, 1959. If accurate, Allen's descriptions indicate that Slocum had made a change to the boat's rig and cabin:

> *Longer than the majority of the catboats, even the largest, she was canoe-shaped, sharp at both ends, with some sheer. The predominating color on and about her was brown, the brown of plug tobacco, or dried autumn leaves.... Her cabin was a hut, of the type seen in pictures of tropical countries, for its rounded 'crowned' top was thatched with some variety of broad leaf, lapping and overlapping to make it weatherproof, although why these leaves did not lift as the wind struck them seemed remarkable.... Her two short masts stood bare, with scarcely a suggestion of rigging, and no sails in sight, either spread or stowed.... Some of the observers probably knew the name of this strange-appearing craft, for it was the Liberdade, Cap'n Joshua Slocum, master, and she had recently come from South America, according to the story.*

Allen didn't see Slocum himself and, in fact, wondered if the boat might have been sold. Nor did he know where the boat went when it departed Martha's Vineyard. That question was answered by Slocum, however, who wrote that he sailed next to Newport, Rhode Island, before heading back to Massachusetts. There, he sailed up the Taunton River to Taunton, the town that his distant ancestor Anthony Slocombe had helped establish in colonial times before being banished to Dartmouth when he joined the Society of Friends. At Taunton the *Liberdade* was hauled out, and the boat and her skipper now "enjoyed the novelty of a 'sail over land.' Then the *Liberdade* moored snug in Boston and her crew spent the winter again among friends." As is so often the case with Slocum, this brief reference in the next-to-last paragraph of *Voyage of the Liberdade* leaves much unsaid.

On November 4, 1889, what was billed, accurately or not, as "the first maritime exhibition ever held in the world" opened in Boston, proclaiming that it was "Open to Exhibits of Everything Connected with Ships and Shipping." The goal was to bring attention to the New England maritime industry and revive the spirit of America's merchant marine, which was mired in the hard times that had overtaken it years earlier. A report published by the exhibition's president, John W. Ryckman, said it would "remain open until January 4, 1890, and it can hardly fail to stimulate an industry in which Americans have always excelled, but which, owing mainly to stupid legislation, has lost its prominence during these later years."

What was described as a "large canal" was built on the ground floor of the exhibition, where canoes and steam or naphtha launches could be tried out. Machinery, windlasses, and buoys were displayed there, and so was the *Liberdade*. The event's report described the *Liberdade* as "that wonderful little craft that Capt. Joshua Slocum and his son built with their own hands, away down on the south-east coast of Brazil, where they were cast away in the ship *Aquidneck* last year. 'My wife made the sails,' said Captain Slocum as he stood in the well of his staunch craft…. We was about three months building of her—me and my son.'"

Joshua Slocum was oppressed by the need to generate income. He viewed the exhibition not only as a venue to bask in his accomplishment but as a place to find a buyer for the *Liberdade*, and he enlisted the aid of exhibition president Ryckman in the effort. On December 16, 1889, Ryckman sent a letter on Slocum's behalf to Professor George Brown Goode, a likeable and highly respected ichthyologist who was then serving as assistant secretary at the National Museum (the Smithsonian), enclosing a photo of the boat, newspaper clippings about the voyage, and even samples of the wood used in the *Liberdade*'s construction. Ryckman wrote:

Capt. Slocum who is poor, is extremely anxious to have her placed permanently in the Smithsonian by purchase. He is willing to sell her cheap and I am positive that it would be one of the most attractive features in the Institution.... Will you kindly advise me at your earliest convenience, if there is not some way by which the Liberdade can be bought by the Institution. It would be a great relief to Capt. Slocum and a great novelty for the Institution.

Slocum, meanwhile, was searching for someone who might fund the purchase and donate the boat to the museum, and he had found a philanthropically minded buyer earlier in December. On December 9 he had written his own letter to the Smithsonian, saying, "The old *Liberdade* was really the gift of Mr. and Mrs. F. [Mr. and Mrs. David W. Fenton of 71 West 12th St., New York City], they having paid me for it more than it cost me, ostensibly for the purpose of putting it where it is. Whether for this or to help me around a corner, more worthy and highly esteemable people it would be impossible to find. I would indeed esteem greatly any acknowledgment you might make to them."

On February 7, 1890, Goode wrote to Slocum, "We shall be glad to accept your proffer of the boat *Liberdade*, and to place it in the Museum building. At present it will be necessary to hang it from the ceiling in the boat hall, but when more space is provided, I have no doubt we shall be able to give it a more prominent position on the floor, with the sails in place. I understood you to say that it could be delivered in Washington, free of cost to us."

The *Liberdade* was given Smithsonian accession number 23,653 and cataloged in the "U.S. National Museum—Division of Mechanical Technology." The cataloging card stated: "Boat Liberdade; Gift from D.W. Fenton who bought it from Capt. Joshua Slocum."

On October 18, 1890, Slocum and the Fentons went to Washington to formally present the *Liberdade* to the Smithsonian. The boat failed to impress at least one curator, Mr. Earle, who called it "merely a curiosity, as it represents no type of naval architecture." This may account for a delay while the museum reconsidered the boat. Ultimately, the cataloging card stated that the accession date was May 13, 1892. Nor would the *Liberdade* enjoy smooth sailing at the U.S. National Museum in the years ahead. A combination of curatorial confusion and Slocum's own inability to manage the situation would seal the fate of "the old *Liberdade*."

CHAPTER 10

East Boston
and Fairhaven

"It was bad all around taking Virginia's place as a wife and trying to do right by the children. Josh had to call on his sisters for help."

—Grace Murray Brown, 1952 letter to Walter Teller

IN *VOYAGE OF THE LIBERDADE*, practicing his usual vagueness, Joshua Slocum wrote that he spent the winter of 1889–90 "among friends." A result has been confusion about whether Slocum and Hettie were living together at a relative's house, separately at the homes of respective relatives, or both. Nor is the confusion lessened by the fact that Hettie's younger sister Odessa—a seamstress who had arrived in Boston in 1879—and Slocum's aunt Naomi Slocombe Gates lived three doors removed from one another, at 61 and 69 Saratoga Street, respectively, in East Boston.[1] Grace Murray Brown wrote to author Walter Teller on October 6, 1952:

---

1 Number 61 Saratoga Street is a two-story, while 69 is a three-story house built after the Civil War by Naomi Gates—daughter of Joshua Upham Slocum (Captain Joshua U) and his wife, Elizabeth Farnsworth—and her husband, John.

After the Liberdade, Hettie and Josh shared a house with her sister Odessa Elliott in East Boston, a few doors from my grandmother's big house and next door to a house my folks had and outgrew.... I [also] remember the family being together at the little house, 61 Saratoga Street. That is the only time we ever saw Victor but Ben, Jessie, and Garfield were around for some time back and forth through the family.

The mansard-roofed triple-decker at 69 Saratoga Street in East Boston—once owned by Slocum's aunt Naomi Gates—as it looked in December 1999. The house at 61 Saratoga was owned by Hettie's sister Odessa. (Photograph by Melville C. Brown)

Jessie herself wrote Teller that "I never heard of Hettie and father being separated except when he went to the West Indies."

Garfield, however, who was nine years old in 1890, remembered spending time in East Boston. He recalled that "Hettie took me to her sister's home in East Boston. I attended a school while I lived there. Hettie, my sister Jessie and myself lived there for awhile, father did not come to that home, don't know where he was. I assume that he was trying to find a job." Ben Aymar remembered of this period that, while he was in Natick with his aunt (Slocum's sister Alice), Jessie and Garfield lived with Hettie. He wrote Walter Teller that, when he visited East Boston, he was "censured to ask no questions, etc."

These living arrangements were less than satisfactory both to Slocum and to Hettie. To Slocum, having to live under someone else's roof was testimony to his failure to provide for his wife and family as expected. Each day he would wonder how a man of his abilities had wound up largely broke and living in someone else's house. He developed bitter feelings toward Hettie's sisters, and those feelings would fester for years. "It irked him," Grace Murray Brown wrote, "not to be as independent as his nature demanded. He was capable of letting his irascible side show up if sufficient provocation was given or even suspected."

For Hettie, who did her best to be a good sport, the situation was an embarrassment that precluded any chance of somehow establishing her own home with her husband. That wouldn't happen for another 13 years. In the meantime, she too nursed resentments, which would build throughout the marriage and sometimes emerge in unpredictable ways.

One thing that Joshua Slocum could do to earn some money, he thought, was to write a book about the *Aquidneck* experience and the long voyage home in the *Liberdade*. Such a book might even further his case against the Brazilian government while appealing to a wide variety of readers. Whether he found paying work during the winter of 1890 is unknown, but he did manage to write *The Voyage of the Liberdade* that winter in East Boston. The hardcover volume was just under 5 inches by 7 inches, bound in green cloth, and printed at Slocum's expense by the Robinson & Stephenson Press in Boston.

Perhaps the first of the few reviews Slocum's book received was published in the Boston *Sunday Globe* of April 27, 1890. It said the book "reads like a romance, but is, nevertheless, the faithful account of the marvelous experiences in the career of that indomitable Yankee tar Capt. Joshua Slocum. How the wonderful little boat, containing the author and his family, made a journey of 7,000 miles in the face of perils calculated to terrify many of the hardiest is told without an attempt at rhetorical garnish, yet with a demeanor that gives it permanent literary value."

A review of more lasting importance appeared on July 5, 1890, in a New York literary magazine, *The Critic: A Weekly Review of Literature and the Arts*. In hindsight, this appears to be one of those remarkably serendipitous events or happy accidents of fate that sets one's course for the future. In Slocum's case, the course would lead, a decade later, to the publication of *Sailing Alone Around the World*.

The *Liberdade* review was written by 32-year-old Joseph Benson Gilder, who, with his sister Jeannette, had founded *The Critic* in 1881. Before embarking on his career as a man of letters, Gilder had spent two years at the U.S. Naval Academy and later worked as a newspaperman, and it was presumably this experience and an ongoing interest in naval matters and the sea, rather than any marketing effort by Slocum, that prompted Gilder to pick up a copy of *Voyage*. "The little book smacks of the sea in more ways than one," Gilder wrote. "It is not only about it but of it…. Ocean breezes shake the leaves of the book as you turn the pages."

The sales prospects for a self-published book written by an amateur without professional editing and distribution were then, as now, unpromising. Slocum's narrative, unpolished but genuine, at least had merit, but how many copies Slocum printed and how long it took to sell them is unknown. One hopes that he printed no more than 500 copies.

The pitfalls of self-publishing are on display in *The Critic's* review. The magazine accompanied each review with information about the publisher and the book's price and availability. In the same issue as the *Voyage* review was a review of *Egyptian Sketches*, by Massachusetts native Jeremiah Lynch, considered a classic in its time. The review was accompanied by price information ($1.75) and the name (Scribner and Welford) and location (New York) of the publisher.

Though Slocum had priced his book at $1, the *Voyage of the Liberdade* review contained no price information, and the publisher information was "Capt. Joshua Slocum, Boston, 69 State St."—a downtown address at the foot of Quincy Market, not far from Faneuil Hall. This homely attribution certainly had the potential to put off interested readers. First they'd have to write to learn the price, and then they'd have to send payment to an unknown individual, not a company. And if anyone did send a payment, it would go to 69 State Street in Boston, where Slocum neither lived nor had relatives. One can only wonder if his aunt Naomi's 69 Saratoga Street, East Boston address was somehow misprinted in *The Critic*, and whether any orders sent to Slocum actually arrived. Having spent money to produce his book without, perhaps, earning an appreciable return, Joshua Slocum was left with little choice but to look for work.

Slocum was no more willing to seek a berth aboard a steamship than he had been six years earlier, after selling his share in the *Northern Light*. He still refused to consider steamships. He told Garfield: "I followed the sea in sailing ships since I was 14 years old," he said. "If I accepted this offer, I would have to get used to steamships and I do not like steamships." He had nothing against steam for others, he said, but steam was not for him. It was a sentiment that would have been familiar to Joseph Conrad, who wrote that steam "lacks the artistic quality of a single-handed struggle with something much greater than yourself."

Some of those who wrote about or remembered Slocum during this period referred to him as being "rudderless." He was without a ship and therefore without the profession in which he took such pride. He was without a job and without a home of his own. Professionally and personally, he was emotionally adrift, too.

Ben Aymar remembered, "During this period, father spent much of his time contacting his former business associates seeking a lead that may lead to something acceptable." But there was nothing acceptable. The end for sailing ships, after long years of decline, had really come years earlier. If today it seems to have been a prolonged, Shakespearean death, it was swift in comparison with the millenia during which men voyaged under sail. "Stretching the period both ways to the utmost," wrote Joseph Conrad, "it [the decline] lasted from 1850 to 1910. Two generations. The winking of an eye. For the pathos of that era lies in the fact that when the sailing ships and the art of sailing them reached their perfection, they were already doomed."

Slocum was simply born too late to reap the rewards that would otherwise have been due to a highly accomplished captain. On March 11, 1853, when Joshua Slocum was nine years old, Donald McKay's *Sovereign of the Seas* accomplished something no sailing ship had ever done before. Slicing her way toward Cape Horn through big seas, en route from San Francisco to New York, the 258-foot clipper, the largest vessel afloat when she was launched in 1852, covered 400 miles in a 24-hour period.[1] When she was wrecked 17 years later in 1869, the day of the clippers had reached its conclusion. That was the same year that Joshua Slocum was enjoying command of his first ship, a schooner, in San Francisco, and also the year in which McKay, who, like Slocum, had been born in Nova Scotia, launched his last clipper ship, *Glory of the Seas*. He had hung on too long.[2]

Joshua Slocum had managed to carve a career as a sailing ship captain

---

1 The exact figure was 411 miles. The ship's speed was calculated to have varied between 16 to as much as 19 or 20 knots.

2 By 1869, in New York City, shipbuilder William H. Webb had long since embraced the future. He had launched his last clipper ship, the *Young America*, in 1853, and within a few years was a leading builder of steamships. Webb built his last square-rigged ship, the *Charles Marshall*, in 1869, and retired in 1872.

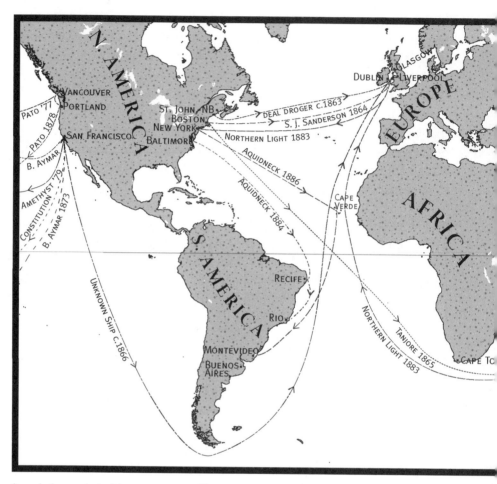

largely because he'd spent most of his time in the Pacific, where a capable man operating his own vessel on low overhead could scrape together a living carrying a variety of cargoes to a variety of ports. But now, in Boston, Slocum's time as a sailing ship captain was irrevocably behind him. At some point during or following the publication of *The Voyage of the Liberdade*, Slocum, according to Ben Aymar, took jobs in local shipyards, a move that would have done little to improve his standing in the eyes of his critical sisters-in-law or even, perhaps, Hettie. She thought she had married a sea captain. Now her husband was walking off down busy Saratoga Street to seek grimy labor.

One day, while working on a vessel, Joshua Slocum was deluged with a mixture of coal and dirt. The once immaculately dressed master of the

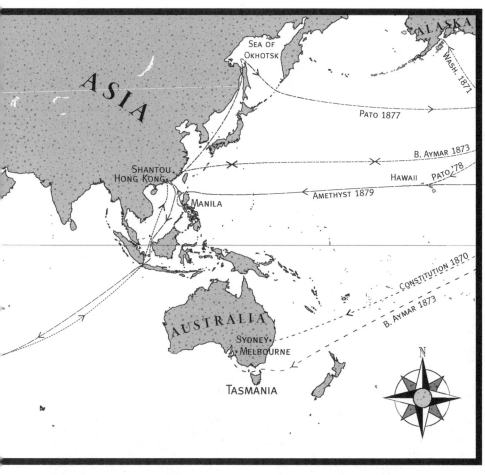

Selected voyages of Joshua Slocum, 1863–1886. Though not a complete record of his voyages as a merchant seaman and captain, the map shows the many ports of call of a sailor who, by 1889, was thoroughly familiar with the world's oceans. The course lines are approximations. The 1866 course line represents the voyage during which Slocum may have received his second-mate papers.

Northern Light had fallen far. Eventually, his wanderings in East Boston brought him to what remained of the shipyard established by Donald McKay. There Slocum worked for a time as a shipwright, but not for long. A newspaperman once asked Slocum about this period and learned why he quit: "They asked me if I belonged to any union. Then they wanted to know what church I was a member of. It cost $50 to get into the union and I hadn't the cash. It didn't seem to suffice that I belonged to God's great church that knew no bounds of creed or sect."

There was more wrong than the nearly nonexistent job market for captains of deep-sea sailing ships or the absence of new orders for such vessels, which had been rendered obsolete by screw-propeller iron steamships. The American economy, while seemingly in an upsurge, was instead teetering on the edge of a terrible collapse that, when it finally came, would be known as the Panic of 1893. A number of complex, interrelated factors, domestic and foreign, led to a run on gold and the failures of 500 banks and thousands of businesses. The question that Joshua Slocum faced upon leaving the East Boston shipyards was simply: What next?

THE OLDEST SECTION of Fairhaven, Massachusetts, dating to colonial times, is Oxford Village, a compact neighborhood on a small point jutting into the Acushnet River above Pope's Island. Construction of the New Bedford–Fairhaven Bridge around 1800 spurred commerce below the bridge, but not at Oxford. While Fairhaven grew, its oldest neighborhood acquired the enduring nickname "Poverty Point."

This image of Fairhaven's Poverty Point was probably made circa 1895. (From the Collection of the Millicent Library)

It was in Oxford Village that retired whaler and inventor Eben Pierce invested in several properties. These included three houses—two of which Pierce built at 31 and 33 Lafayette Street—and an unimproved lot between 23 and 31 Lafayette. The empty lot was bounded on one side by a picket fence (since replaced by a tall hedge) and at its rear by Pilgrim Avenue,[1] which was known as Mara's or Marars Lane at the time. There, sometime around 1885, Pierce hauled ashore an old oyster sloop he'd acquired after it had been abandoned on a beach at Dartmouth. The name in faded white paint on the boat's transom was still readable—*Spray*.

Across Pilgrim Avenue from where the *Spray* was propped up was the shingled house of former shoemaker and Civil War veteran-turned-painter Charles H. Gifford (1839–1902). Inspired by the paintings of Albert Bierstadt, who had lived for a time in New Bedford, Gifford had begun painting Luminist-style landscapes and seascapes. His watercolors and oils found a ready market, and he had earned enough by 1879 to make a painting trip to Ireland, Scotland, and England. Still, he returned to his waterfront house on Poverty Point, where the ever-changing light and river scenes provided endless inspiration.

As time passed, the *Spray* became a fixture of the landscape that Charles Gifford gazed over every day. She was merely the old boat that Eben Pierce had brought home for no reason other than a vague intention to perhaps fix her up someday. For several years she moldered away with little more future ahead of her, apparently, than Poverty Point itself. But then one day, Gifford looked out his window and saw a lean man with chin whiskers walking around the *Spray*.

"COME TO FAIRHAVEN and I'll give you a ship," is how Joshua Slocum immortalized Captain Ebenezer Pierce's offer to make him a gift of the *Spray*. It wouldn't have taken Slocum long to understand that Pierce was offering him not only a boat but a new life. In *Sailing Alone*, Slocum gave the impression that his pivotal meeting with Eben Pierce was a chance encounter in Boston on a "midwinter day of 1892." This version may have pleased Slocum's sense of the serendipitous, and it doubtless simplified the challenge of telling his story, but it was factually incorrect and left much unsaid.

For one thing, even if Slocum had bumped into Eben Pierce by accident

---

1 The street was renamed after the dedication in 1903 of a memorial to John Cook, one of the *Mayflower* pilgrims, who, as Slocum noted in *Sailing Alone*, is buried there. Fairhaven's memorial to Slocum is adjacent to this lot today.

in Boston, as he wrote in *Sailing Alone*, the two men were already acquainted, having met previously aboard the *Liberdade* in New Bedford in mid-August 1890. What's more, as was so often the case, Slocum got the year wrong. It was not 1892. The first clue we have regarding when Slocum left East Boston appeared in the New Bedford *Standard Republican*. The newspaper reported that Slocum was "visiting friends" in the Fairhaven–New Bedford area as of February 19, 1891. This trip to Fairhaven was probably an exploratory visit to see the *Spray*.

What Slocum saw was an old boat propped up beside a yellow shed on Pierce's empty lot, which Slocum called a "pasture." The *Spray* had reportedly already been rebuilt three times. Eben Pierce must have been joking when he said "she wants some work." What she wanted was another total rebuild.

The most useful information about Slocum during this period comes

Poverty Point from the Acushnet River, circa 1895. (From the Collection of the Millicent Library)

from Grace M. Parker, a 22-year-old reporter who interviewed him for an article published in the Boston *Daily Globe* of November 28, 1891, and the New Bedford *Republican Standard* of December 3. By way of background, Parker reported Slocum's friendship with Pierce's nephew, "the marine writer, the late Capt. John Drew,[1] familiar under the name of 'Kennebecker.'"

During his stay with Eben Pierce, Slocum slept, according to a neighbor, in a room over the kitchen. From the house, located at what is now 193 North Main Street, it was only a short walk to the *Spray*, and New Bedford's shipyards were within easy reach across the bridge from Fairhaven. Thus, Slocum could earn money to finance his *Spray* rebuild by taking paying jobs.

Grace Parker reported that Slocum "took up his residence [with Pierce] and went to work in a shipbuilding yard." Though she didn't say when this began, Slocum told her that he moved to Fairhaven after publishing

1 Captain John Drew died December 11, 1890, and was buried in Farmingdale, Maine.

The Voyage of the Liberdade, which was most likely printed as early as April 1891. In *Sailing Alone*, Slocum wrote that he spent 13 months rebuilding the *Spray*, which was launched on June 22, 1892. This supports a start date in May 1891, a time frame that is also supported by pictorial evidence.

Charles Henry Gifford was then 54 years old and certainly had enough life experience to know when an unusual subject presented itself. Joshua Slocum proved willing to sit beside the propped-up *Spray* while Gifford created one of his typically small—9 inches by 13 inches—oil paintings. Gifford never gave the work—now in the collection of the New Bedford Whaling Museum—a title, but if he had titled it, he might simply have called it "Captain Joshua Slocum and the Old Oyster Sloop *Spray*." This painting provides the only available glimpse of what the boat looked like before Slocum set to work on her.

The hull is covered with canvas, which had probably been needed to keep the *Spray* afloat on her five-mile voyage from Dartmouth to haul-out at Poverty Point and had perhaps been left in place for protection from the weather. The son of a ship's carpenter, Gifford knew boats. His painting shows the counter stern seen on Delaware Bay oyster vessels and the straight keel that Slocum would soon modify. In Gifford's painting, Joshua Slocum sits slump-shouldered, a worn man in front of a worn boat in an empty lot covered with grass and wildflowers.

CHAPTER 11

The *Spray*

*"As to her model, in view of what she has done, and of her owner's
liberal praise, it is perhaps best not to discuss it too deeply....
[I]t is that of the ordinary oyster sloop or smack, though with
a fixed keel in place of a centerboard."*

—*Forest and Stream*, August 4, 1900

BECAUSE THERE IS NO RECORD of where, when, or by whom the *Spray* was
built, and because of the manner in which the boat's lines[1] were taken or,
more accurately, not taken post-voyage, a certain mystery will always envelop
what became the most famous of all sailboats. We do know, however, that
the *Spray*—her original and only name—was a centerboard sloop that Eben
Pierce believed had been built around 1817 for oystering in Delaware Bay.[2]

In an appendix to *Sailing Alone Around the World*, Slocum wrote that
"tradition said [the *Spray*] had first served as an oysterman, about a hundred
years ago, on the coast of Delaware. There was no record in the custom

---

1 "Lines" refer to a boat's designed shape as revealed by measurements made at multiple points on her
hull.

2 Naval architect and Smithsonian maritime curator Howard Chapelle's research suggested that boats
like the *Spray* appeared between 1830 and 1840, but Pierce's date can't be discounted.

house of where she was built. She was once owned at Noank, Connecticut, afterward in New Bedford." Since Slocum gave no evidence for his "hundred years ago" remark and generally seemed to think that older was better, it seems safest to stick with Eben Pierce's rough estimate.

Apparently, neither Slocum nor Pierce knew that the boat had spent the years 1871–75 in the waters around Staten Island and New York City, and 1876–78 in Sag Harbor, Long Island. When or how the *Spray* got across Long Island Sound to New England is unknown, but the evidence suggests she arrived there in 1879. Whether or not the boat spent time in Noank, as Slocum suggested, is unknown, nor is there evidence for or against Slocum's assertion to Grace Parker that the *Spray* had been a "caraway [carry-away] boat" used to offload fishing vessels before itself being used for fishing. These statements would have been based on lore passed down to Slocum through Pierce. By 1884, according to Grace Parker's article, the *Spray* had become "disabled and lay for three years on the Dartmouth beach, when she was re-sold to the Fairhaven Captain [Eben Pierce] who kept her uselessly stranded for five years more."

There would have been nothing remarkable about the *Spray* during her working life. She was but one of a great many vessels used in the oyster fishery, which was a big industry on the Delaware Bay during the nineteenth century. "Oysters carpeted the bay," wrote Deborah Cramer in *The Narrow Edge*, her book chronicling the remarkable shorebird, the red knot. "Schooners lined the wharves in Bivalve [New Jersey] at the mouth of the Maurice River. Warehouses, chandleries, and a customs office lined the streets."

By the time Slocum was given the *Spray*, the oyster business employed 4,300 people in New Jersey alone, Americans having developed an enormous appetite for oysters in all their variety. An article in *Marine Fisheries Review* in 1996 reported that by the early 1900s, New Yorkers were consuming "an average of two meals of oysters per person per week." Oyster restaurants were popular, and oysters were prepared in seemingly every way imaginable for breakfast, lunch, and dinner.

Boats used in the fishery ranged from dugout canoes to sharpies, Chesapeake Bay skipjacks, and the centerboard sloops and schooners common to Delaware Bay. Low-sided and broad-beamed with a stout bowsprit, these gaff-riggers were stable boats and good load carriers. They could set several headsails and full or reefed mainsails to haul their dredges under a variety of sail configurations, depending on wind strength. Any fishing boat was often referred to then (and sometimes now) as a "smack," and that is exactly how *Forest and Stream* described the *Spray* in its August 1900 article about Slocum, his just-published book, and his by-then famous boat.

The magazine commented: "In spite of a good amount of deadrise, it is that of the ordinary oyster sloop or small smack.... The bow is of the cod's head type, but the two ends are better balanced in their relative fullness than in many of the old 'cod's head and mackerel tail' sloops." (A so-called cod's head was a bluff, rounded bow that shouldered seas aside rather than slicing through them, while providing more buoyancy and stability forward; a mackerel tail was a tapered underwater shape at the stern that, it was thought, reduced resistance by not dragging the boat's wake along with it—but with a corresponding loss of buoyancy and stability aft.) Then, as now, balance was a key. The *Spray*'s unknown builder was a man who, at least in this instance, produced a hull of great and diverse abilities. Of the stern sections, Slocum observed, "The water leaves her run sharp after bearing her to the last inch, and no suction is formed by undue cutaway."

The *Forest and Stream* article carried no byline, but the insightful commentary was likely the work of indefatigable yachting historian, designer, and small-boat sailor William Piccard Stephens. W. P. Stephens was a regular contributor to the magazine and had the expertise to interpret the *Spray*'s abilities from the lines shown in *Sailing Alone Around the World*. His positive comments were borne out by the *Spray*'s performance. The *Field and Stream* article went on to note, "The overhangs are quite short and the stern is chopped off at the usual smack angle." Slocum appreciated the hull's lack of overhangs, famously warning his readers, "Smooth-water sailors say, 'where is her overhang?' They never crossed the Gulf Stream in a nor'easter, and they do not know what is best in all weathers. For your life, build no fantail overhang on a craft going offshore."

Many years later, in a 1954 letter to Walter Teller, Garfield Slocum recalled that yachtsmen and some fishermen occasionally teased Slocum about the *Spray*'s stern, calling, "'*Spray* ahoy! Did you lose your overhang?' And they would laugh, father would smile. He told me the reason he built the boat without overhang, when mountainous seas struck the stern they would toss the boat ahead without doing any damage."

When Grace Parker interviewed Slocum, he told her that the *Spray* had a reputation as an extraordinary performer. Parker wrote, "The *Spray* was formerly the queen of all speeders in the harbor. It is said that when the

New York yachts[1] were coming into port some years ago and she happened to be returning from a fishing trip, to the infinite disgust of the yachtsmen, at the run [downwind] she passed every flyer in the fleet."

The rebuilding of the *Spray* became a matter of interest to seemingly every boat-oriented man and boy in the New Bedford–Fairhaven area. Henry Howard, superintendent of streets in Fairhaven in 1935, could still remember vividly the day 42 years earlier when he accompanied Joshua Slocum and Eben Pierce to his father's farm just outside town on the New Boston Road. There, Slocum and Pierce selected the "stout oak tree" that would become the *Spray*'s new keel. "Farmer Howard," wrote Slocum of Henry's father, "hauled in this and enough timbers for the frame of the new vessel."

Victor Slocum reported that the *Spray*'s old keel was removed in sections—after sawing through the old floor timbers—without disturbing the stem, sternpost, deadwood, or garboard planks. In this way, Slocum avoided doing anything that might cause the boat to lose the shape formed by the genius of some long-forgotten builder. Slocum told Grace Parker that he saw in the boat "a perfect, but very ancient model." Later, after sailing the *Spray*, he confirmed that first impression, saying, "I was not deceived."

But Slocum's rebuild of the *Spray* did involve a substantial change to the boat's keel. Knowing that he had no need for a centerboard, Slocum did not cut a slot for a board in his new keel.[2] By December 1891, when Parker's article appeared, Slocum had been working for approximately seven months and had made significant progress on the *Spray*. Parker wrote that Slocum "had removed every shred of the old lumber but the frame." Presumably, this meant that Slocum had taken off the old planking and, probably, had already removed the centerboard trunk and replaced the keel. But Slocum must have been joking when he told Parker he would have the *Spray* finished in six weeks. It would take another seven months to complete what was a very big job.

---

1 This is presumably a reference to the New York Yacht Club's annual cruise, a longstanding tradition. The term "speeder" was a colloquialism and need not be taken literally. References to the *Spray*'s performance, including her speed during the circumnavigation, will be found in subsequent chapters and in Appendix B. Suffice it to say here that, in Slocum's expert hands, the boat reeled off performances of which knowledgeable yachtsmen, then or now, would be skeptical.

2 Although the matter cannot be addressed conclusively, it is possible, perhaps likely, that Slocum did reshape the keel. The original keel was probably straight—that is, horizontal. As rebuilt, the *Spray*'s keel was raked, deepest at the very stern. This would have increased the boat's draft and lateral plane, compensating to a degree for the removal of the centerboard. In *Sailing Alone*, Slocum would refer to the aft end of the keel as the *Spray*'s "heel."

Having begun the *Spray* rebuild, Slocum shaped a new three-piece stem from a length of pasture oak so hard that it "afterward split a coral patch in two … and did not receive a blemish." In his book about his father, Victor Slocum went on at some length about pasture oak and its qualities. He lamented that such trees—typically growing alone and unprotected from winds by other trees so their "sinews were hardened by the many gales"—had largely disappeared. "It made a solid keel, stem or sternpost. For steam-bent frames it excelled. A pasture white-oak, steam-bent frame, good and hot, could be tied in a knot. When they became cold, they became hard as a rock. And that was the kind of frame that went into the *Spray*." To heat his steambox, Slocum set up a big cauldron in front of the boat.

Slocum took every opportunity to maximize the strength of his boat. The stem was reinforced, at the suggestion of local whaling captains who came by to critique Slocum's work, with two white oak breasthooks.[3] White oak was also used for the *Spray's* new floors. The boat was planked with 1½-inch Georgia pine planks, an operation that Slocum told his son Victor was "tedious." Right at the turn of the bilge, Slocum used planks that were 3 inches thick, and these beefy strakes must have involved even more tedium—steaming, fitting, and clamping—than the others.

The planking was fastened with copper rivets. Butt blocks—reinforcing wood blocks installed where ends of planks meet—were installed with bolts. Garfield Slocum explained to Walter Teller how his father caulked the *Spray*. "Father filled the seams on top of the cotton wicking (such as the plumbers use) with a mixture of cement and raw linseed oil. It became hard as soon as the salt water contacted the cement."

The deck beams were made of Georgia pine spaced 3 feet apart. To these, the pine deck planks—1½ inches by 3 inches—were fastened with spikes. Fourteen-inch-high white oak stanchions were covered with ⅞-inch white pine planks to form the bulwarks.

Slocum's vision for the *Spray's* cabin arrangement in November 1891 was quite different from the final result. His original intent was to create a boat for taking passengers on what today might be thought of as eco-cruises—one of his several visionary concepts that would be implemented long after his time.

"She will be fitted entirely into a cabin room and can easily accommodate eight or ten people," reported Grace Parker. "These will be chosen from

---

3 The breasthook joins the stem to the topside planking on either side, reinforcing a vessel's bow.

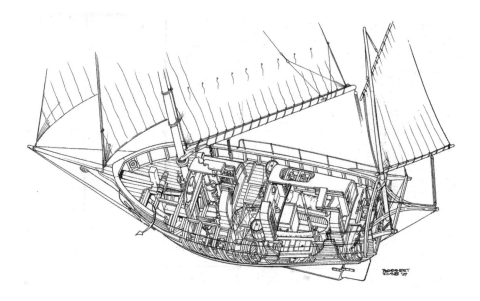

This evocative cutaway illustration of the Spray *shows the boat as imagined by Dutch artist Robbert Das. Slocum's cabin is aft and separated from the forward cabin by the hold that contained water casks and assorted gear. On the bulkhead of Slocum's cabin are shelves for his many books. The rig includes the mizzen sail Slocum installed in the Strait of Magellan.* (*Courtesy Robbert Das*)

among Captain Slocum's friends and will probably be persons who have a genuine love for ocean travel or are scientifically inclined. On her deck will be fitted a large aquarium and a collection of foreign fish, shells and sea vegetation will be made. Because of her diminutive size she can sail almost anywhere, however near the coast, which will be greatly to the advantage of her passengers, for in the clear, smooth waters of the tropics they can see fish or whatever there may be on the sandy bottom they would like to possess."

Sometime during the winter of 1891–92, however, Slocum changed his mind about accommodations. As built, the *Spray* had two deck enclosures, each about 3 feet high. These were the aft cabin—about 10 feet by 12 feet—where Slocum lived, and a forward enclosure that housed the galley and, still farther forward, a pair of berths. Between the two, amidships, was the hold, about 5 feet long fore and aft. In practice, Slocum used the forward berth space primarily to stow sails, anchors (*Spray* carried three, weighing 40, 100, and 180 pounds), and gear. To improve safety given the boat's low bulwarks, Slocum built the *Spray's* distinctive rail. The *Boston Globe* described it as "a stout hard pine rail with stanchions [that] gives a hold for the hands and affords support in a seaway."

The *Spray* was a remarkably shallow 36-foot 9-inch boat, drawing just 4 feet 1 inch. Clearly, Slocum judged the advantages of dispensing with the centerboard and its leak-prone trunk to far outweigh any loss in windward ability. He was, anyhow, an old-school, square-rig sailor more than a fore-and-aft sailor, and he'd spent a career following courses selected to favor a square rigger's best point of sail—off the wind.

The main changes to the hull—and they were as carefully considered as they were crucial—were above the waterline, where Slocum added 12 inches to the freeboard amidships, 18 inches at the bow and 14 inches aft. This raised the boat's sheer and gave her a slab-sided appearance by comparison with the original. The *Spray* was no longer fit for hauling oyster dredges over her higher sides, but she was, in Slocum's opinion, "a better deep-water ship."

The *Spray* was ballasted with cement placed between the frames and held in place with stanchions braced against the deckbeams. Slocum mentions removing three tons of cement when he loaded aboard 30 huge seashells in the Cocos Islands. Having spent his career stowing cargoes for optimal vessel trim, he also considered the weight of the water casks stored in the hold as part of the vessel's ballast.

The *Spray*'s rig was, from first to last, a matter of ongoing development. When Grace Parker interviewed Slocum in 1891, he told her that he was undecided about whether to convert the boat to a schooner or leave her a double-headsail sloop with a long bowsprit and a boom that overhung the transom by at least 4 feet. Despite the penalty of an added mast, gaff, boom, and attendant rigging, a schooner rig would have resulted in a foresail and mainsail that were smaller and easier to manage than the *Spray*'s big main, but he didn't make the change. Instead, the *Spray*'s rig would be refined both during and after the circumnavigation.

Regarding the rig's hardware, Slocum provided few specifics other than to say that "the halyards were rove through ordinary ships' blocks with common patent rollers. Of course the sheets were all belayed aft." Boom and gaff—neither spar having been tapered to reduce weight—were fitted to the mast with jaws, thus eliminating the need for hardware. The mainsail was laced to each spar and was raised on mast hoops.

One must wonder how strenuous it really was, even for the immensely tough and wiry, 146-pound[1] Joshua Slocum, to hoist a gaff-rigged sail that, in its original configuration, must have exceeded 700 square feet. In *Sailing Alone*, Slocum admitted that raising the sail was "no small matter." Garfield Slocum wrote Walter Teller that when he sailed with his father as a boy of 13 in 1894, his father would handle the throat halyard while he, Garfield, took the peak. "It was a job for two people," Garfield wrote. "The mainsail and gaff were heavy. I know it was hard for him to raise it when he was alone." This difficulty would become an important factor, most especially during Slocum's tortuous second passage through the Strait of Magellan.

The *Spray's* robust topping lift—which included a good-sized single block to give Slocum a mechanical advantage—helped him "tame" the boat's big mainsail. Hauling on the topping lift, which ran from the aft end of the boom to the masthead block and then to the deck, took the weight of the

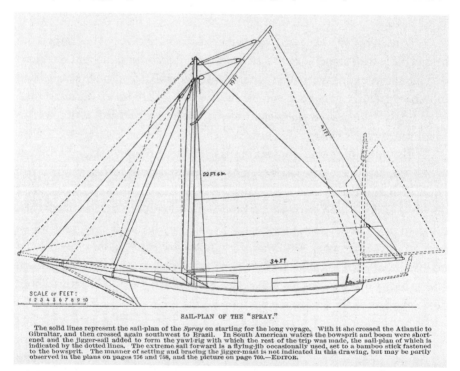

SAIL-PLAN OF THE "SPRAY."

The solid lines represent the sail-plan of the *Spray* on starting for the long voyage. With it she crossed the Atlantic to Gibraltar, and then crossed again southwest to Brazil. In South American waters the bowsprit and boom were shortened and the jigger-sail added to form the yawl-rig with which the rest of the trip was made, the sail-plan of which is indicated by the dotted lines. The extreme sail forward is a flying-jib occasionally used, set to a bamboo stick fastened to the bowsprit. The manner of setting and bracing the jigger-mast is not indicated in this drawing, but may be partly observed in the plans on pages 756 and 758, and the picture on page 760.—EDITOR.

This drawing, originally published in Sailing Alone, *shows the Spray's sail plan as it was upon Slocum's departure (solid lines) and the changes made during the voyage (dotted lines). See Appendix C for more details of rig changes.*

---

1 This is what Slocum told the *Boston Herald* that he weighed at the start of the circumnavigation.

boom when it was time to reef the sail. Working on the *Spray*'s wide and stable deck, Slocum could apparently tuck in a reef in about 10 minutes, which is impressive for one man tying the reef pennants on a sail that would have measured over 30 feet along the boom before being cut down. As a safety measure, he rigged the gaff with a "stout" downhaul that allowed him to add his own muscle to positively dowse the sail, if needed, rather than relying merely on casting off the halyards and allowing gravity to do the job.

An excellent photograph of the *Spray* taken circa 1906 shows the mainsheet rigged through one single and one double block. This arrangement would have given Slocum more mechanical advantage than two single blocks, helping him to trim the sail, but he doubtless would have headed the boat up into the wind as necessary to reduce loads on the main and jib sheets when he needed to adjust them.

Despite her sizable rig, the *Spray* was, according to her skipper, "very easily managed, even in a breeze." Such performance may have been due to what naval architect Cipriano Andrade later called "a theoretically perfect balance," but it also owed something to Slocum's vast experience, sea sense, and innate instincts for what was needed when, and how to do it most efficiently. It would have been an education in seamanship to go sailing with Joshua Slocum, watching his moves while he handled the *Spray* as if she were an extension of his own body.

CHAPTER **12**

"A Pollock in
Each Hand"

*"That the captain is in love with his calling is evident from the
sparkle of the eye when he is talking of the sea."*

—*The Boston Daily Globe*, November 9, 1893

ON JUNE 21, 1892, JOSHUA SLOCUM, presumably with the assistance of Eben
Pierce and friends and a team of horses, dragged the *Spray* in her cradle
across Marars Lane (now Pilgrim Avenue) and launched her into the Acushnet River. There, Slocum wrote in *Sailing Alone*, she "sat on the water like a
swan." The love affair had begun.

Slocum wrote that Pierce accompanied him on the *Spray's* first sea
trial, a sail across Buzzards Bay. A month later, on July 22, the *Spray* served
as the committee boat for the New Bedford Canoe Club's annual regatta.
The race had to be postponed an hour because of high wind and even then
was sailed in what the New Bedford *Evening Standard* called "a gale from the
west." When the festivities concluded that night, "the last group left the scene
of the evening's pleasure and beneath the spangled canopy sailed across the

Acushnet to their homes in the good sloop *Spray*."

Slocum now faced the question of what to do next. As always, there was the need, likely urgent, to earn money. Not only did he have to recoup some of the $553.62[1] he had spent on materials for the *Spray*, he also had to put something aside for Hettie and the children. In *Sailing Alone*, Slocum wrote that he remained in Fairhaven for several months to work on fitting out whaleships, and he spent at least a portion of 1893 fishing in Buzzards Bay. Clifton Johnson's interview notes say that "the first thing he did after the *Spray* was finished was to engage a crew and go on a fishing trip in her. This was a failure. He tried one more time with the same result."

A correspondent for the *Globe* visited Slocum aboard the *Spray* in November 1893 to report on the "unique device invented by Capt. Slocum." The reporter wrote that "Capt. Slocum has been following the fishing business during the past season, and has invented an apparatus for catching mackerel which has not only proved very effective, but shows the inventive genius of the hardy mariner."

The "apparatus" was a 60-foot by 40-foot net, weighted heavily, that Slocum rigged to several points on the *Spray*. Hung vertically over the side with the *Spray* hove to, the net could be gathered up once the mackerel had been attracted to the side of the boat by bait thrown into the water. It is not clear now whether this arrangement might have been worthy of a patent, but the *Globe* reported: "Capt. Slocum says he will not seek to patent his invention, but will be content to give it a name ... [t]he *Spray* spring net, and will claim no royalties for its use."[2]

This article appeared in the *Globe* on November 9 after being published in the *New York Times* on November 6. Slocum told the reporter that he expected "to spend the winter in southern waters his first objective being the West Indies.... He will try for fish of various kinds and may also secure a quantity of shells, sponges and other marine curiosities, which are so abundant in those waters."

But Slocum's idea of spending winters gathering shells—shelling had been a favorite pastime of Virginia—would not be realized until he returned

---

1 This was a substantial sum in 1892. In 1900, the average annual income for all workers was $428. Someone in the building trades might expect to earn about $18 a week, a public school teacher $328 per year. Alas, Slocum didn't provide a breakdown of his expenses for timber, hardware, cordage, mast hoops, and so forth.

2 Slocum would, however, use a spring net to good purpose in the Strait of Magellan, though his quarry then was not fish.

from his circumnavigation. Instead, he decided to forsake the *Spray* and join an odd naval expedition that promised financial rewards almost too good to be true. If this venture worked out, he hoped to earn enough in just three to six months to be set, possibly, for life.

On December 7, 1893, Joshua Slocum accepted command of a 130-foot iron warship, the *Destroyer*, bound for Brazil, where Floriano Peixoto—the second president of the young Brazilian Republic—had been confronted by mutineers in the Brazilian fleet. This revolt, occasioned by the apparently not unjustified claim that Peixoto had seized and remained in power un-constitutionally, was led by two admirals, including Slocum's nemesis in the *Aquidneck* matter, Custódio José de Melo. While government officials were at the opera on the night of September 5, 1893, De Melo seized the naval vessels in Rio's harbor and used the *Aquidaban* to shell the same forts that had prevented Slocum from entering port several years earlier.

President Peixoto appealed for help from the United States, and the U.S. government allowed a mercenary fleet to go to his assistance. Much of the fleet was gathered and paid for by Charles Ranlett Flint, a New York financier who had business interests in Brazil. (Born in Thomaston, Maine, in 1850, Flint would found what became IBM in 1911.) Flint's original plan was to engage a Naval Academy graduate named Guy M. Buck to command the *Destroyer*, with Slocum serving as navigator. When this failed, however, Joshua Slocum accepted the post of "Navigator in Command" of the *De-stroyer*, motivated by money and, perhaps, some vague notion of striking back at De Melo.

On January 28, 1894, the *New York Times* reported that the Brazilian government would pay seamen a $500 bounty and $100 for their service, while officers—depending on their grade—would receive up to $5,000 for their first three months of service and an additional $5,000 for another three months if necessary. Slocum's arrangement was not with Charles Flint but with the Peixoto government, which had contracted to purchase the *Destroyer* and several other vessels, chief among them a hastily converted cargo and passenger hauler that had been built at Newport News, Virginia, in 1893. Originally named *El Cid*, the vessel was renamed the *Nictheroy* (after a town in Brazil) and fitted at New York's Morgan Iron Works with a powerful "dy-namite gun" invented by Polish-American artillery officer Edmund Zalinski.

The *Destroyer* had been designed by iron-clad pioneer John Ericsson, creator of the Union Navy's *Monitor*, and was built at a cost of $50,000 by Ericsson and his partner C. H. Delamater. Launched in 1878, the vessel took its name from its so-called "destroyer system," a bow-mounted "submarine gun" located beneath the waterline. The weapon had proved itself in trials, but the *Destroyer* itself was not designed for an ocean voyage. It was a slender, low-sided harbor-defense vessel with limited coal capacity, and its big stack and slab-sided upper works gave it a top-heavy mien. Slocum's first challenge was to get the *Destroyer* towed from New York to Brazil.

On November 21, 1893, the *New York Times* reported that the *Destroyer* "is in the Erie Basin. She will be towed from this port by some large seagoing tug." A crew of 12 men was recruited. "Better sailors I shall never see," Slocum wrote later. He noted, too, that although it didn't occur to him or his men at the time, his own presence rounded out the ship's company to 13 men. While this was what he called a "fatalistic number"—mariners being notoriously superstitious—he would subsequently, thankfully, adopt it as his *lucky* number.

Air-filled flotation devices known as sponsons were fitted to each side of the *Destroyer* to improve her seaworthiness, and a big oceangoing tug from Boston, the *Santuit*, was engaged as the towboat. Although the *Destroyer* wouldn't be making the trip under its own power—the propeller shaft was disconnected, Slocum noted—a full supply of coal was nevertheless needed to fire the boilers and produce steam for the pumps if needed. A moderate west northwesterly was blowing when the ships set out, but the breeze promptly veered and blew into a storm from the north northeast that raised heavy seas. Soon enough, seams in the *Destroyer*'s topside plating opened up as rivets failed. Water gained on the pumps, and even with the crew bailing by hand to augment the pump discharge, the rising water began extinguishing fires in the boilers.

By this time, Joshua Slocum may well have been telling himself that all his beliefs about steam-powered ships were warranted. "The main hull of the *Destroyer* is already a foot under water, and going down," Slocum would later write about one of the most threatening legs of the journey. That initial battle to stay afloat lasted four days. Even as the *Santuit* resupplied the *Destroyer* with coal, it was discovered that the sponsons, though intended to make the ship safer, were leaky and flooding, and thus making things worse. Slocum later wrote with his characteristic sardonic humor, "He was a clever man who designed those sponsons and saw them constructed in such a manner that both of them didn't fill up together."

Only desperate bailing and pumping by the exhausted crew and the eventual slackening of the storm saved the *Destroyer* from sinking. Victor

The Ericsson harbor defense vessel Destroyer *was towed from New York to Brazil under Slocum's command, nearly sinking in the process. The vessel's "submarine gun" is below the waterline, but one of the torpedoes it could fire is visible on the starboard side. (Courtesy the Library of Congress)*

wrote that when the *Santuit* reached the Caribbean, the decision was taken to steam to leeward of the islands—a longer route—to gain some protection from the Atlantic. It was well they did, for on December 18, the *Destroyer's* best steam pump failed. The *Santuit* then towed the *Destroyer* to Martinique's Fort de Prince, where repairs could be made in dry dock.

When the iron warship was more or less seaworthy again, she was once more put under tow by the *Santuit*, reaching the Brazilian island of Fernando de Noronha on the morning of January 18. From there the strange flotilla proceeded to Pernambuco,[1] arriving on January 20. There the decision was taken to test-fire the *Destroyer's* submarine gun. Not only did the

---

1 Slocum's references to Pernambuco (and Bahia) are now confusing because both are Brazilian states rather than specific cities. Regarding Pernambuco, at least, Slocum was most likely referring to the big port city of Recife. There were times when he did refer to the city by name, but generally he used "Pernambuco."

torpedo fail to launch, but the ship was damaged and again developed a leak when she was put aground so the torpedo could be unloaded. "Though not a severe leak," Slocum wrote, "it was still discouraging."

The *Destroyer* voyage gave Slocum another opportunity to remark upon his lifelong horror of sharks. With the ship still in harbor after being repaired, a crewman identified by Slocum as "Mr. Kuhn," having been advised that no sharks were in the vicinity, decided to go bathing. Slocum warned him to stay aboard: "For the admonition of sailors and sea bathers, generally, I say, put no faith in the yarn about harmless sharks. They are always likely to be about coral reefs and around ships—and they are always *hungry*."

Mr. Kuhn, fortunately, was a strong swimmer and was close enough to the *Destroyer* that he could just clamber aboard before being taken by an 18-foot shark. As the shark made its attack, according to Slocum, it "lashed the sea with his tail like a pleased tiger." This shark was killed by a rifle shot, but three more then appeared to snatch a grease-covered 5-foot-long board and a butter firkin tossed overboard from the galley. "There was no need of further cautioning the crew to keep out of the water.... The monsters, I confess, gave us all a turn," Slocum wrote.

Eventually, on February 13, Slocum and his crew delivered the *Destroyer* at last into Brazilian hands at Bahia (Salvador), but they may as well not have made the voyage at all. President Peixoto refused to pay for the troubled ship and, subsequently, the *Destroyer* was ill-handled and ultimately sunk by an inexperienced crew. By then the Brazilians had already withdrawn Slocum's contract. The "funny war," as it was sometimes called, petered out in March 1894.

On April 16, 1894, the *New York Times* carried an article in which Charles Flint reported the surrender of De Melo, the return of the navy's ships, and President Peixoto's promise of a new election in accordance with the fledgling republic's 1891 constitution. By then, Slocum was well on his way back to New York aboard a Brazilian sailing ship named the *Elma*. He arrived on April 20, apparently with his pockets nearly as empty as when he'd left, to find more bad news awaiting him in East Boston. On December 9, as the *Destroyer* was beginning her dangerous last journey, the Department of State had mailed Slocum its final letter regarding his *Aquidneck* claim against Brazil:

The Brazilian Government denied any liability for damages occasioned by its action, holding that the preservation of the public health was of greater importance than commercial profits.

It is believed that this Government would, in a similar case, adopt the same measures.

This Department therefore, does not feel warranted in taking any further action.

How long Slocum remained in East Boston after his return is unknown, but he had been away from the *Spray* since November and was no doubt anxious to get down to Fairhaven, where his little ship was presumably moored under Eben Pierce's watchful eye. Slocum's reaction to the *Destroyer* episode was to write another book. He began the story with this invocation: "From the quiet cabin of my home on the *Spray,* the reminiscence of a war."

Voyage of the Destroyer seems now to be a curious footnote to Slocum's life and career, a satirical, tongue-in-cheek story that doesn't communicate in a straightforward manner and is marred by jarring digressions. At the time, however, there was public interest in Brazil's strange insurrection, in businessman Flint's involvement, and in the "cardboard squadron" of ships involved. And where there is public interest, there is a possibility of commercial gain.

The book was probably printed and bound by late July. Slocum sent a copy to *Century Magazine* to no avail, but a review in the *Globe* found *Voyage of the Destroyer* amusing—with Slocum's usual dry, sometimes self-deprecating humor—and historically important.

Slocum used made-up names in the book, but that didn't prevent one of the crew from recognizing himself and taking offense. This individual, labeled only as "Sir Charles" in *Voyage of the Destroyer,* was a British soldier-of-fortune named Carlos A. Rivers. Rivers had come off the worse in an altercation with the *Destroyer's* black cook, and Slocum recounted the altercation with relish, milking it for all the entertainment value he could get.

The Boston papers soon carried items noting that Rivers planned to challenge Slocum to a duel. *The Boston Herald* reported that the "lieutenant thirsted for the captain's blood because the latter, in his book … made fun of him." Slocum's response was at once good-humored and serious. "There are my wife's feelings to be thought of. I have always been of the opinion that duelists should consult their wives," he wrote. "It is better that I catch fish than fight him. Just say that I am a man with a big fist."

VOYAGE OF THE DESTROYER

THE DESTROYER AT PERNAMBUCO.
~ FROM ~

NEW YORK TO BRAZIL.

The Voyage of the Destroyer's cover featured a drawing of the vessel with her crew standing atop the superstructure. The ship carried a dory as her tender. (Courtesy the New Bedford Whaling Museum)

After learning Slocum had proposed a bare-knuckled brawl, Rivers, according to the *Herald*, "was never heard from. The captain has given him up for dead." Slocum didn't leave it there, however. He wrote a letter to the *Herald* ridiculing Rivers, and the big fist won by default.

At the end of *Voyage of the Destroyer*, Slocum captured the foolishness, futility, and waste of the cardboard squadron. "[I]t was by the heat of the sun, and by that child of filth, yellow fever, that most lives were lost. In this way, I said, some of the members of our own expedition were taken." The dead included the captain of the *Santuit* and three of the tug's crew, who perished in Brazil in a misbegotten cause.

But mainly, perhaps, the little book says more about Slocum's resilience and optimism than anything else. Among the worst reasons people write and self-publish books is bitterness or a desire for revenge. There is an element of this in *Voyage of the Destroyer*, just as there had been in that part of *Voyage of the Liberdade* relating to the *Aquidneck*'s loss. In both books, however, the lurking strains of righteous anger and bitter self-justification are cloaked in Victorian reticence, good manners, and sardonic humor.

Voyage of the Destroyer is uncomfortable to read, in part because it describes deadly serious events in such a flippant style and in part because one senses how desperate Slocum must have been to undertake such an improbable mercenary endeavor for an improbable employer. Slocum told Victor that 500 copies of the 37-page book were bound. It was a cheaply made book printed on inexpensive paper that became brittle with time.

Slocum biographer Walter Teller could locate only three surviving copies in the 1950s, one of which he himself owned. Another had been presented by Slocum to the Commonwealth State Library in Boston, which still owns it. Slocum also sent a copy to Samuel Pierpont Langley at the Smithsonian, who was said to have given it to the library there, but that copy disappeared. Slocum also gave a copy to the United States Consul in Sydney in 1896. Teller wrote that this copy was "subsequently acquired by the captain's son, Victor, but sometime after the latter's death in 1949, it went to a dealer."

Later, however, a fourth copy surfaced and was purchased by Slocum enthusiast and rare book collector William A. Strauss. "I realized," Strauss wrote, "as soon as he told me that the book was dedicated to the Honorable G. G. Benedict that it did not match with the previously mentioned known three copies.... George Grenville Benedict ... had served as an officer with the 12th Vermont Infantry during the Civil War. Benedict fought at Gettysburg and was a recipient of the Medal of Honor." The inscription to Benedict reveals Joshua Slocum's state of mind when he wrote the book: "The story of the *Destroyer* voyage thrown off hurridly [sic] and when I was not quite over the feeling of outrage."

THE WORDING OF THE FIRST SENTENCE of the introduction to *Voyage of the Destroyer* is worth noting. Slocum didn't write "From the quiet cabin on the *Spray*...." Instead, he wrote "From the quiet cabin of *my home* on the *Spray*...." It was then late April or early May 1894, and Slocum was making it clear that he didn't consider either his sister-in-law's house on Saratoga Street or his aunt's house a few doors away to be his home. He had the *Spray*, and he knew well how to be comfortable in small spaces afloat. He had his own home.

Joshua Slocum's comings and goings between his return from Brazil in April 1894 and his departure on his voyage in April 1895 can't be traced with precision. Reviews of *Voyage of the Destroyer* began appearing in early August, and it may be that Slocum devoted most of June and July to promoting and selling the book. Presumably, it was only after he felt comfortable that the book had been properly launched that Slocum took 13-year-old Garfield with him on a cruise to Maine. Garfield never forgot what he said was the only time his father "complimented me on anything that I did on the *Spray* that I can remember.... Once he said: 'you steer very good.'"

In a letter to Walter Teller written in 1954, Garfield provided one of the few descriptions of Joshua Slocum sailing the *Spray*: "When he was at the helm, he would look aloft at the mainsail peak, he insisted the sail be full of wind, no flutter at the peak, when he told me to steer he would say: 'Keep her full and by.' 'Aye-aye, sir' was my reply. Then he would pace the deck, look at the horizon, look at the sky, at the mainsail peak, then go below to read; he used to read a lot."

This little trip could have ended the *Spray*'s new career almost as soon as it began. Many years after the experience, Garfield remembered what happened while leaving what was probably Pemaquid Beach. Slocum was attempting to make his way past a ledge in light air. It was a situation that any sailor of an engineless boat today would understand and find worrisome.

Garfield wrote, "As the *Spray* almost passed a ledge on the leeward, the powerful undertow lifted her and dropped her on the ledge. The waves tried to finish the *Spray*. Some help came quickly to our aid by land and sea. Father threw a coil of rope to some men on shore. He tied me under my arm pits, held one end of the rope, and told me to jump. The men pulled me to high ground. Other men, in dories, got the *Spray* off, and towed her to a place where father repaired her bottom."

Slocum presumably entered this event in the *Spray's* log but saw no reason to discuss it anywhere else. But he must have recognized the grounding as potentially fatal to have gotten Garfield hauled ashore through the cold Maine water. Perhaps, there was a reasonably heavy swell rolling in that posed a real threat to the boat as well. Slocum owed a lot to those Maine fishermen who, one suspects, took it all as nonchalantly as he did.

Still hoping to generate income from his writing, Slocum took the four-year-old plates for *Voyage of the Liberdade* to Roberts Brothers, the Boston house that had published Louisa May Alcott's *Little Women* in 1868, the American edition of Robert Louis Stevenson's *Treasure Island* in 1884, and *Poems of Emily Dickinson* in 1890. Roberts took on *Liberdade* and printed 1,000 copies of the new edition, which included editorial changes made by Slocum, and illustrations.

According to Walter Teller's research, three differently colored bindings were offered: red, yellow, and blue. In those pre–dust jacket days, the color of a book's binding might sometimes be chosen to coordinate with a room's décor. The price was $1, the equivalent of about $25.95 today. This suggests that book prices have remained largely consistent for well over a century. Slocum received his first copy of the book while aboard the *Spray* at Gloucester, Massachusetts on October 6, 1894. He wrote the publisher to say, "The little book reached me last evening, forwarded from Boston. I think its make-up very neat and modest with altogether a charming appearance."

Slocum's royalty was 10 percent of the book's cover price, which remained an industry standard for another 90 years before being eroded by the deeper discounts commanded from publishers by big wholesalers and big-box retailers.[1] The 10 cents Slocum would have received for each $1 copy sold of *Liberdade* would probably have been a nickel under today's typical royalty schedules.

That said, Roberts Brothers charged Slocum $100 for type changes and for illustrations, thus proving, once again, the daunting reality of those hoping to earn a living wage from writing. That $100 would have been Slocum's entire royalty if the publisher sold all 1,000 copies. However, Slocum asked

---

[1] The largest publishers may still offer a comparable royalty for list-leading authors, but smaller percentages or royalties based on wholesale rather than cover (or list) prices are now the general rule.

The Roberts Brothers edition of Voyage of the Liberdade *with red cloth cover and the illustration stamped in white ink. (Courtesy the New Bedford Whaling Museum)*

to take 500 copies of the press run for himself, gambling that he could sell them and, after covering costs, earn far more than his royalty. Whether he actually took that many copies is unknown.

Details of *Liberdade* sales are sketchy, but some clues about Slocum's involvement survive. On January 9, 1895, after Roberts Brothers supplied Slocum a library of books to take with him on the *Spray*, he wrote a letter thanking company manager Eugene Hardy, who would serve as Slocum's agent and manager during the voyage. He also said, "I will be very glad to take the Liberdades (50) on the terms mentioned."

Ten months later Slocum had apparently sold all 50 copies. He wrote Hardy from Rio de Janeiro reporting he had taken payment for three additional copies and now asked Hardy to send each book to addresses he provided, promising reimbursement later. He was confident he could "sell the balance of the edition by and by on satisfactory terms I think," but there were still copies in inventory when Roberts Brothers was sold to Little, Brown & Company in 1898. Slocum may have eventually purchased these too, for when he displayed the *Spray* at Buffalo's Pan-American Exposition in 1901, he had aboard copies of *Liberdade* for sale at $1 each.

SLOCUM SAILED FROM Gloucester to Boston in October 1894, making one last attempt to generate income from the fishing industry. He told Clifton Johnson that "he bought a load of Pollock at Gloucester, cleaned them himself and sailed with cheerful hope to Boston. He thought he had bought low and planned to sell high. But everything seemed to be against him. He had bought moderately dear and he sold very, very cheap. He sailed all around Boston trying to dispose of his fish…. He walked up to where the *Northern Light* had been built carrying a Pollock by the tail in each hand and took a look at the shipyard. Once he had commanded as fine a ship as ever was launched from the yard—had walked the quarter deck wearing kid gloves and a stovepipe hat—and he thought 'How things have changed.'"

It is not clear when or why Joshua Slocum decided to sail around the world, but Clifton Johnson connected the decision to the failed attempt to earn a profit selling pollock. As always, Slocum cloaked grim times in humor when he spoke with Johnson: "He was discouraged and felt [a need for] a vacation. Why not start off and go around the world in the *Spray*. He was sure he would find it enjoyable. It would be easier than selling fish anyhow. He began to preplan at once and when his plans became known, helpers came forward and he sailed from Boston fairly well equipped except in the matter of money."

Slocum himself at times attributed his voyage to his need to make money. It is entirely possible that Slocum, echoing Captain John Drew, had from the outset hoped to serialize his adventure in a willing newspaper. In its article about Slocum published on April 16, the Boston *Herald* reported: "His voyage is principally for the object of making money by correspondence. He has already closed bargains with the New York *Sun*, Louisville *Courier-Journal* and other newspapers and Roberts Bros., publishers of this city."

Slocum was being less than honest in what he told the paper, however. That January, the *Louisville Courier-Journal*'s managing editor wrote Slocum that "I can not contract with you for the whole of your series of letters.... I shall be glad if consistent with your arrangements to have you submit the letters to us, we to pay for what is used." The New York *Sun* idea didn't work out, and Roberts Brothers was dealing with the *Liberdade* book, not one relating to the voyage.

Slocum's siblings felt that he was making the voyage to escape the past. "They attributed his rather unusual undertaking to an unpleasant experience he had as a sea captain," remembered Herbert L. Coggins, who, as a young-ster, had been a neighbor of the Slocums on Martha's Vineyard. "There had been a mutiny on his ship and he had killed one of the men. Although he was a good mixer, he seemed like an extreme introvert and as I recall either from his conversation or in his book he identified a good deal with Robin-son Crusoe."[1]

With little or no cash to provision and fit out the *Spray*, Slocum be-gan making appeals. He sent an undated letter to Eugene Hardy—possibly between December 1894 and early January 1895—asking for books: "[I] am sure I shall have some time to read and shall require all that I can get in that direction for recreation. Mr. Wagnalls (old acquaintance) of the house of Funk and Wagnalls told me the other day that he would also put me up some. I may be able to pay for all this kindness at some time but not now."

Slocum received a nice selection of books from Hardy by January 9, including Charles Darwin's *The Descent of Man*, Thomas Babington Ma-cauley's *History of England*, Henry Walter Bates's monumental study of South America's rainforests entitled *The Naturalist on the Amazons*, Simon Newcomb's *Popular Astronomy*, poetry books by Alfred Lord Tennyson and Robert Burns, who was a great favorite of Slocum. Slocum's daughter Jessie

---

1 May 4, 1953 letter to Walter Teller.

remembered his other favorite authors including Washington Irving, Mark Twain, Charles Dickens, and Sir Walter Scott.

One of the titles sent by Hardy was newly published by Roberts Brothers, the American edition of *A Strange Career: the life and adventures of James Gladwyn Jebb, by his widow*. Slocum didn't wait until the voyage to read this book, but devoured it immediately. Jebb was a British adventurer whose life played out on a grand scale from India to Mexico and Colorado. Slocum must have identified with Jebb, who, following exhausting efforts to develop silver mines in Colorado, stopped at Boston on his way home to London, where he died at age 50 in 1893.

Jebb's near fatal privations in the Rocky Mountains and the dangers he experienced elsewhere would have fascinated Slocum, who would have noted, too, Jebb's interest in spiritualism and his attendance at séances. Benjamin Aymar said, "Father was converted to spiritual understanding by my mother." The book's conclusion included this passage: "Perhaps from a material point of view, Jack Jebb's life was a failure in that, having set himself to replace the fortune he had lost, he never succeeded in doing so. Still there are failures more noble than success." Slocum wrote Hardy: "Mr. Jebb will be along with me on the voyage."

Adam Wagnalls sent his daughter, Mabel, to deliver his donation of books for the voyage. Mabel well-remembered the troubled captain from their meeting in New York not long after Virginia's death. Now she also presented Slocum with a book she herself had written. *Miserère* would be a source of solace and inspiration to Joshua in the months and years ahead.

A *Boston Herald* article of April 16, 1895, indicated how dire Slocum's financial situation had become. He needed donations not only of books but of foodstuffs and everything else a sailor preparing for a sea voyage required. "Grocers and other tradesmen in Boston have stocked him with supplies."

Among the supplies Slocum took aboard were two barrels of whole-wheat ship's bread or "pilot bread." He told Clifton Johnson that "I put them up in tin cans while they were dry and crisp, and I sealed the cans with solder so the bread was as good three years old as new." Slocum told Johnson that his foodstuffs included coffee, tea, flour, baking soda, salt, pepper, mustard, and curry that he used to season the stews he made. He had butter and condensed milk. He had aboard salt beef and salt pork, ham, and dried codfish. To preserve eggs, Slocum boiled them for a minute to seal the pores of the shells, and found they would "keep for a good many weeks even in a very hot climate."

The *Herald* article also indicates how much Slocum's original voyage plan changed along the way: "He will get more [supplies] in New York. The *Spray* will be towed there by one of L. B. Burnham's tugs, perhaps the *Santuit*, which took the captain to Brazil when the war was on there…. If he can make satisfactory arrangements in New York, Capt. Slocum will cross the Isthmus of Panama; otherwise he will proceed to the Straits of Magellan and then on the south Pacific trade winds through the Indian ocean to the Red sea. Through the Suez Canal and the Mediterranean, he will strike for the Bermudas, then home."

Thinking out loud, as he often did, Slocum shared with the *Herald's* reporter several possible stopping places in the Pacific. He said that he planned to collect "war clubs and other valuable curios." He thought of trying to find the Gilbert Islanders he had rescued 12 years earlier on the *Northern Light*. Still sensitive to the perceived injustice suffered by *Amethyst's* crew in Hawaii 24 years earlier, Slocum told the *Herald* that he might stop in Honolulu, and he referenced the political situation there, the monarchy having been replaced in a coup in 1893.

The new "provisional government" was headed by Sanford Dole who, together with a number of businessmen and sugar planters, had for several years been maneuvering to overthrow the monarchy and replace it with an American-oriented provisional government. A missionary's son born in Hawaii, Sanford Dole had spent one year at Williams College, another in a Boston law office, and eventually received an honorary LLD from Williams in 1897.[1]

Joshua Slocum had had a run-in of some sort with Dole during his time in Hawaii aboard the *Amethyst*. He told the *Herald*: "I know Dole, D---- him, I lost a crew in Honolulu when he was a shyster lawyer there. There are 20,000 Japs there, and I guess if they are stirred up there will be some fun."

In reality, the *Spray's* voyage route would be quite different and its duration far longer than Slocum ever anticipated. And despite his braggadocio, he never went back to Honolulu to "stir things up."

---

1 In November 1897, Sanford Dole's nephew once removed, James Dole (1877–1958), moved to Hawaii. Having completed studies in agriculture at Harvard University's Bussey Institute, Dole founded the Hawaiian Pineapple Company, which later became the Dole Food Company.

CHAPTER **13**

Boston to Gibraltar

"The most picturesque sea voyage of modern times is Captain Joshua Slocum's trip around the world in the Spray.... He went entirely alone, without even a dog or a cat."

—Clifton Johnson, *Good Housekeeping*, February 1903

ON APRIL 22, 1895, A GRAY DAY of showers driven by a brisk easterly wind, Joshua Slocum made his way into Boston where he had business to conduct at the city's impressive Custom House. Built atop 3,100 pilings set into reclaimed land bordering the harbor, the structure resembled a Greek temple. It featured a monumental entrance portico and 36 fluted Doric columns, each one carved from a single piece of granite quarried in Quincy. It was here, 31 years and a lifetime earlier, that Slocum had received his seaman's protection certificate.

Barring deteriorating weather, the captain had determined that he would set sail in the *Spray* on April 24, but before he did, he needed to acquire an important document. The Custom House was home to the Bureau of Navigation, a part of the Department of Commerce and Labor overseeing the district of Boston and Charlestown. The purpose of Slocum's visit was to apply for a yacht license, which would formally recognize the *Spray* as a pleasure boat rather than a commercial vessel. The license specified the yacht's name, her homeport (now Boston rather than Fairhaven), and her calculated tonnage—13.35 gross and 12.70 net tons.[1] Validated at each port Slocum visited, license number 64 would offer proof of the *Spray's* progress around the world. It would also—in theory—exempt the boat from tonnage-based port fees levied on commercial vessels. To Slocum, who was essentially broke when he departed, avoidance of fees was critical.

"He had scarcely ten cents to his name," Clifton Johnson noted regarding Slocum's finances at the time. "He was trusting a good deal to chance, but expected to make something from articles he had arranged to write from time to time for a New York newspaper but this publication went back on its agreement even as he sent in a bill." Slocum certainly couldn't afford the princely sum of $15 to clean and rate his chronometer, but he had other plans in mind for navigation anyway.

Wednesday, April 24, 1895, dawned fair. The barometer was steady at 29.85 inches of mercury, and the temperature was expected to rise into the low 60s. The westerly wind, though, was predicted to be strong, as much as 40 miles per hour in gusts. The *Globe* reporter who covered Slocum's departure called the wind "a fresh westerly breeze."

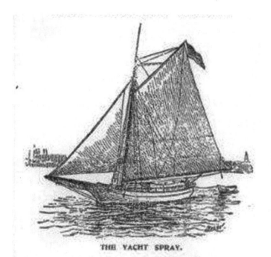

THE YACHT SPRAY.

When the photograph of the Spray *departing East Boston failed to work out, the* Globe *used this engraving. The picture appeared in the newspaper again on August 21, 1895, when the* Spray *reached Gibraltar. By then, however, it was out of date. Slocum had removed the boat's topmast before he departed Yarmouth, Nova Scotia.*

---

1 See Appendix A for remarks on tonnage calculations.

The local newspapers seemed more interested in Slocum's leave-taking and his seemingly outlandish voyage idea than Slocum's attenuated household was. The 1895 *Boston City Directory* listed Slocum as living at 61 Saratoga Street, the home of his sister-in-law Odessa. Hettie was there with 14-year-old Garfield and Jessie, who was 20, but Slocum stayed or visited only as necessary, and none of them considered the house to be a home.

A week before his departure, Slocum was still floating the vague possibility that his wife might accompany him. The *Globe* reported on April 16 that "Capt. Slocum will be alone 'unless,' as he says, 'my wife changes her mind about staying ashore.' This contingency the captain seems to regard as a remote one, however, for he is making all his preparations for a solitary voyage."

Still, on Slocum's sunny, windy departure day, Hettie made her way from her sister's house down East Boston's cobblestone-paved Meridian Street and through Maverick Square to the waterfront. She went not to join her husband but to say good-bye. With her went Garfield and Jessie.

There is no evidence that any of the family considered Slocum to be departing on what could be a historic voyage, nor do surviving letters offer a glimpse into the emotions that Joshua's family may have felt that day. To Hettie, Slocum's departure in the *Spray* was further proof that her husband wasn't ready to settle down and that their lives since the *Aquidneck* disaster had taken sharply divergent courses. From young Garfield and daughter Jessie's points of view, their father was simply heading to sea again and leaving them behind. Years later, in a letter to Walter Teller, Grace Murray Brown wrote, "His children, I have been told, came second to his great love for Virginia." With Virginia gone, nothing would ever compete with the sea for Slocum's full attention. And with the exception of Garfield, the children were young adults.

The *Spray* was tied up at what were then known as the National Docks in East Boston. These docks at the foot of Lewis Street, below busy Maverick Square, were the terminus of the South Ferry that took passengers to downtown Boston. East Boston was bordered entirely by busy wharves, coal yards, warehouses, the shipyards in which Slocum had labored, and ferry landings. The Eastern Railroad Wharf and the Cunard Wharf were adjacent to the National Docks, and the harbor waters were crowded with steamships and with commercial sailing vessels of all descriptions. This chaotic environment invited accidents. Over at Boston's T Wharf, not far from the Custom House, a fishing schooner named the *J. G. Blaine* would collide with the schooner *M. L. Adams* that day, carrying away the *Adams*'s port-side rigging and her foretopmast and damaging the hull. Repair costs were estimated at $500.

Joshua Slocum considered neither crowded Boston Harbor nor a strong wind to be impediments to his departure. High water at Boston came at 10:45 that morning, and he waited until noon, well after the tide had turned, before hoisting the *Spray's* mainsail. "Courage still good?" asked the *Globe* reporter standing on the wharf. "'Just as good as ever', was his hearty reply, as the captain cleared away everything forward and prepared to hoist the jib.... [T]he captain sprang aft to the wheel, trimmed in his jib sheet and was off up the harbor as smoothly as a yacht."

After giving the *Globe's* photographer a chance to capture the *Spray* on film, Slocum left the National Docks behind him. With a fair tide and fair wind, he sailed off down the channel past Bird Island Flats and Governors Island to President Roads and Deer Island at the entrance to Boston Harbor. In *Sailing Alone*, Slocum wrote that as he entered Massachusetts Bay, the wind freshened and the *Spray* was making about 7 knots. He noted drily that, alone as he was, he was already doing better than the skipper and crew of the steamship *Venetian*. He passed the vessel's wreck on a ledge about 3 miles after leaving East Boston. What remained of the *Venetian* and her cargo of 8,000 bags of flour, grain, and canned meats, would be auctioned off in Boston in May.

If Slocum reflected on his youthful days tanning hides and making boots as he sailed past the shoemaking city of Lynn, he kept such thoughts to himself, for that was a part of his life that he kept locked away. Instead, as he sailed along Boston's North Shore, Slocum focused on the beauty of the sea and noted "the sunlight clear and strong." But a west wind on Boston's North Shore is not to be trifled with. The gusts announced themselves, riffling the water and turning it a darker blue. By the time Slocum neared Norman's Woe off Gloucester, scene of the wreck of the *Hesperus* made famous in Longfellow's poem, he had to settle "the throat of the mainsail to ease the sloop's helm, for I could hardly hold her before it with the whole mainsail set. A schooner ahead of me lowered all sail and ran into port under bare poles, the wind being fair.... I saw that some of his sails were gone, and much broken canvas hung in his rigging."

Though this first day of Slocum's great voyage provided boisterous sailing, he arrived safely at Gloucester's picturesque Eastern Point, where the big granite breakwater seen today was under construction. But as he headed toward Ten Pound Island and Gloucester's inner harbor, he admitted to some anxiety. He'd seen a wrecked steamship and a schooner with tattered sails, and if Boston Harbor was crowded with vessels, he knew Gloucester's tight inner harbor would be chockablock with fishing schooners.

In *Sailing Alone*, Slocum admitted that this "was my first experience of coming into port alone, with a craft of any size, and in among shipping.... I hardly know how a calamity was averted, but with my heart in my mouth, almost, I let go the wheel, stepped quickly forward, and downed the jib. The sloop naturally rounded in[to] the wind, and just ranging ahead, laid her cheek against a mooring pile at the windward corner of the wharf, so quietly after all, that she would not have broken an egg."

Safely docked and with his pulse slowed, Slocum could begin thinking about further preparations for the voyage ahead. One item yet to be addressed was his need for a small boat that could be carried aboard the *Spray*. All yachts require a tender suitable for getting from ship to shore, ferrying supplies from the beach, performing maintenance work, or rowing out a kedge anchor should the vessel run aground. What Gloucester offered in abundance, of course, were the famous Cape Ann dories carried aboard fishing schooners. These boats were similar to those Slocum had known as a boy at Mount Hanley and Brier Island, and not unlike the Chinese-built dories he had commissioned for the *Pato* prior to his successful fishing expedition with Virginia in Russian and Alaskan waters.

An 18- or 19-foot dory was far too big and heavy to carry aboard the *Spray*, but Slocum saw potential in what he called a derelict dory that he planned to adapt to his purpose. He cut this dory in half and then fitted a new transom. In *Sailing Alone*, he wrote only that "I made shift to cut a castaway dory in two athwartships, boarding up the ends where it was cut."

That made the job sound easier than it was. The new transom would be far wider than the original, and it needed to make a watertight joint with each of the boat's side and bottom planks. This required careful notching of the transom for each plank and then precisely beveling of the surface where the planks attached so that a flush fit was achieved. At the gunwale, reinforcements, or "knees," were required to join the transom to the topmost hull plank. These knees needed to be fashioned from a hardwood like oak, with the grain running in the appropriate direction.

A Cape Ann or Banks dory is justly renowned for seaworthiness, and its stability increases as it is loaded ever heavier with fish or gear. But Slocum's half-dory could never equal a full-sized version in these attributes and would never be more than a sometimes risky compromise. Still, whatever his

9½-footer lacked in carrying capacity and stability, it could at least be lashed athwartships on the *Spray's* deck. "Manifestly," wrote Slocum in *Sailing Alone*, "there was not room on deck for more than the half of a boat, which, after all, was better than no boat at all, and was large enough for one man." During the voyage, Slocum would acquire a slender South Seas island dugout canoe and, after his return, would replace his half-dory with a shapely, round-bottomed rowing tender.

In Gloucester, as at Boston, Slocum received supplies from well-wishers. He wrote that "many fishing vessels put on board dry cod galore, also a barrel of oil to calm the waves.... They also made the *Spray* a present of a 'fisherman's own' lantern, which I found would throw a light a great distance round.... Then, too, from across the cove came a case of copper paint, a famous antifouling article, which stood me in good stead long after."[1]

Having been given the antifouling paint, Slocum grounded out the *Spray* to coat her bottom, an event that led to what he said was a recurrence of the malaria he had first contracted as a young man in Hong Kong. "So I had to leave there," Slocum wrote Eugene Hardy later, "with the work unfinished, and bide my time."

He departed for Round Pond, Maine, and from there for Brier Island, where his approach proved problematic. As he sailed through the local fishing fleet in the Bay of Fundy, Slocum uncharacteristically asked an anchored fisherman for a compass course to Westport. "The fisherman may have said 'east-south-east,' the course I was steering when I hailed him; but I thought he said 'east-northeast,' and I accordingly changed it to that." They exchanged a few words—the fisherman asking if "I was alone, and if I didn't have 'no dorg nor cat'"—and then Slocum followed his ill-starred compass course into trouble.

In *Sailing Alone*, he wrote that "the *Spray* sailed directly over the southwest ledge [off Brier Island] through the worst tide-race in the Bay of Fundy." The ledge wasn't marked until 1907, when lighted buoy M2 was placed there. In 1895 a chart, compass, local knowledge, and a good idea of one's position were required to navigate the approach to Brier Island. Slocum arrived in Westport on May 13 after what he called "the terrible thrashing I got in the fierce sou'west rip."

Slocum didn't say whether the *Spray* actually struck the ledge, only

---

1 Slocum was referring to the Tarr and Wonson paint manufactory, whose red buildings on Rocky Neck have been a distinctive Gloucester landmark since 1874.

that he "overhauled the *Spray* once more and tried her seams, but found that even the test of the sou-west rip had started [caused a seam or seams to open and leak] nothing." But, in fact, the *Spray* had suffered damage that Slocum chose not to mention in his book. Eight days after the event, on May 21, Slocum wrote to Eugene Hardy at Roberts Brothers, "I am in a grand good place to repair my vessel and do it cheaply. Giving her a great going over!"

In a June 20 letter from Yarmouth, Slocum's next port, he told Hardy that he had "caulked [the *Spray*] all over." Privately he may have been chiding himself for having asked for directions and followed them against his own better judgment. But "Slocum's luck" had seen him through again, and his little ship was still as buoyant as he was and ready for the adventures ahead.

Joshua Slocum never said why he stopped at Yarmouth, but the lay-over did give him a chance to bid a second farewell to Nova Scotia and the town he had considered home during the early 1860s. This visit also offered prospects for wide-ranging publicity, for Yarmouth was the home of Nova Scotia's second-largest fleet of ships and had long since established itself as a commercial and shipbuilding center. The *Halifax Mail Star* published an article about Slocum and his planned voyage on June 24, the reporter noting that Slocum's "little vessel was visited by a large number of our citizens, including many of Capt. Slocum's old shipmates."

In his interview with Clifton Johnson, Slocum said that the "first money he raised on his voyage was at Yarmouth N. S. where a man took a fancy to 3 or 4 books that had been presented the captain by a Boston publisher. With the money he paid for these, the captain bought a barrel of potatoes. Here, too, he made exchange of books for butter with a dairy man." He also wrote Eugene Hardy that "the *Spray* rescued a deacon at Yarmouth … a real live, and good, deep-water baptist deacon! But he was tickled to get on deck & out of the water for all that!"

Slocum included none of this in *Sailing Alone Around the World*, but he did mention that "[a]t Yarmouth, too, I got my famous tin clock, the only timepiece I carried on the whole voyage. The price of it was a dollar and a half, but on account of the face being smashed the merchant let me have it for a dollar." Initially, at least, Slocum avoided mention of using this clock for navigation. Ultimately, though, he couldn't resist making a joke about the clock and navigation that most readers have unfortunately but understandably taken seriously.

The *Spray*'s rig was still on Slocum's mind. The Boston *Daily Globe* article of April 16, 1895, just eight days before the *Spray* began her voyage, reveals that Slocum knew his vessel's rig wasn't optimum for blue-water voyaging. The newspaper reported that the "rig may be changed to something like that of *La Liberdade*, with a battened sail in place of the mainsail and a smaller sail of the same kind on a mizzen mast aft."

Although Slocum continually made changes to the *Spray's* rig, these would never involve a battened mainsail or mizzen. The first change, which came in Yarmouth, was simply to remove the topmast. Slocum lacked a topsail anyhow, and the topmast had only been rigged with flag halyards. Other changes followed over the next several months.

Something else happened in Yarmouth that Slocum didn't write about in *Sailing Alone*. He did mention it more than two months later in a letter to Eugene Hardy, but with such circumspection that Hardy must have been mystified. "A chap in Halifax tried to do me harm," Slocum wrote. "In Yarmouth his representative enjoyed a half hour of the Spray's 'hospitality'—the best she had—And he the next day in Halifax a hundred miles off fired a shot—at my back. A South Sea Islander could not have shown greater treachery."

This "treachery" was, of all things, a newspaper headline. Although the *Mail Star* reporter's story was a straightforward account of Slocum's visit and his plans, the headline—with which the reporter probably had nothing to do—read: "Another Crank at Large." Slocum took offense, and his instinct, as usual, was to respond in writing or with his big fist. "When leaving Yarmouth, therefore," he told Hardy, "I beat a course in for Halifax for, said I, this educated gentleman being such as appears it will be worth my while to enter the port and study the characteristic of the people—one object of the voyage being, as you are aware sir, to gather information."

Doggedly pursuing his South Seas metaphor, Slocum wrote that as he entered Halifax Harbour, he saw "the natives preparing a fire on the beach where I made signs I would land: and not knowing their number or their mode of attack: I hauled off. From that hour until I arrived at Fayal [the island of Faial in the Azores] the *Spray* never ceased going." In other words, Slocum managed to calm himself down regarding the headline that had called him a "crank" and simply sailed away.

In his letter to Hardy, Slocum made it clear that he did not consider Halifax to be "on the hospitable side of the dear old Province." But he made no mention at all of Halifax in *Sailing Alone*, writing only that "I sailed from Yarmouth, and let go my last hold on America." In his log for July 2, 1895, he wrote: "9:30 a.m. sailed from Yarmouth. 4:30 p.m. passed Cape Sable:

distance three cables [3/10ths of a mile] from land. The sloop making eight knots. Fresh breeze N.W."

Joshua Slocum's June 20, 1895, letter to Eugene Hardy made clear that he had yet to really finalize his route around the world. When he announced his initial route in Boston newspapers in mid-April, Slocum said that he planned to sail to Panama and have the *Spray* hauled and taken overland across the isthmus to the Pacific. If that idea proved impractical, he said he would sail down to the Strait of Magellan and reach the Pacific that way. But in his June letter to Hardy, he offered yet more alternatives.

"I think my best way is via the Suez Canal, down the Read [sic] Sea and along the coasts of India in the winter months, calling at Aden and at Ceylon and Singapore taking the S. W. Monsoon next summer up the China Sea. Calling at Hong Kong and other treaty ports in China thence to Japan and on To California. From California I believe I shall cross the Isthmus of Panama. The freight agent of the Panama road wrote me that I could not get over the isthmus we'll see!.... I shall call at Fayal. The Season is just right now to go without the worry from typhoons and monsoons. So I go east instead of west and will roll around the world." Soon enough though, Slocum would change the route of his circumnavigation yet again.

As Slocum headed east on the night of July 5, he watched in some wonder as the fog lifted just long enough for him to see, straight beyond his bowsprit, "the smiling full moon rising out of the sea.... 'Good evening, sir,' I cried; 'I'm glad to see you.' Many a long talk since then I have had with the man in the moon; he had my confidence on the voyage." In the darkness, cold, and fog of the Western Ocean, Slocum was confronting the reality of what lay ahead for him, a lone sailor intent on going around the world.

Always sociable, he now needed tactics to cope with his loneliness. Chatting with the man in the moon was one method. Speaking to an imaginary helmsman as if he were aboard ship at the changing of the watch was another. "Is she on her course?" He gave occasional orders to his son Garfield. He revived what he said was a boyhood practice of singing. He serenaded porpoises, sea turtles, and pelagic birds with chanteys and ditties.

When the fog descended so thick "[o]ne could almost stand on it," the need for increased watchfulness gave Slocum less time to feel lonely. Later, when the wind rose to a gale, he became too busy to be lonely. And as the days at sea turned to weeks and then months, he proved highly adaptable to his new circumstances. He found that he kept himself good company, and his books were constant companions, too. Mr. Pickwick of Dickens, the

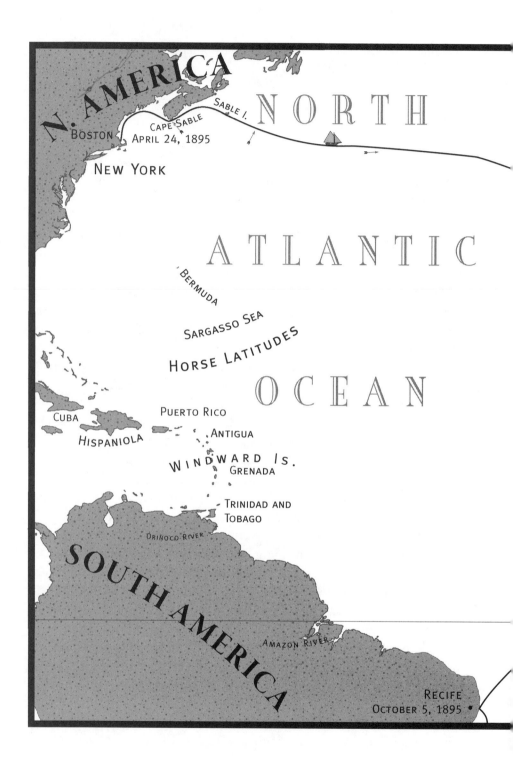

N. AMERICA

NORTH

Sable I.

Cape Sable
Boston   April 24, 1895

New York

ATLANTIC

Bermuda

Sargasso Sea

Horse Latitudes

OCEAN

Cuba

Puerto Rico

Hispaniola   Antigua

Windward Is.
Grenada

Trinidad and
Tobago

Orinoco River

SOUTH AMERICA

Amazon River

Recife
October 5, 1895

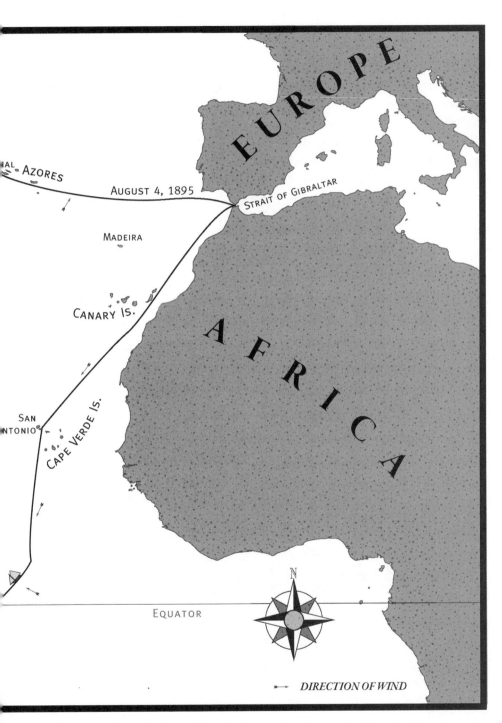

EUROPE

AFRICA

AL. AZORES

AUGUST 4, 1895

STRAIT OF GIBRALTAR

MADEIRA

CANARY IS.

SAN
NTONIO

CAPE VERDE IS.

N

EQUATOR

DIRECTION OF WIND

Slocum's route to Gibraltar and then back across the Atlantic to Recife, capital city of the state of Pernambuco in Brazil.

Yahoos of Lilliput, and many other characters kept him company.

On July 10, Slocum recorded: "eight days at sea, the *Spray* was twelve hundred miles east of Cape Sable." This meant that the *Spray* had been reeling off an impressive 150 miles per day, and Slocum proudly wrote that this performance "for so small a vessel must be considered good sailing." Although such performance could not be maintained throughout the circumnavigation, Slocum's gaff-rigged workboat would log daily runs that would satisfy many present-day cruising sailors equipped with the latest sails and electronic devices. Thanks to her heavy displacement, she did so while offering Slocum a comfortable ride. Once he reached the trade winds and steady sailing, Slocum found the *Spray* to be a dry boat. She took so little spray aboard that he could walk around the deck in slippers.

On the afternoon of July 20, Slocum lowered the *Spray's* anchor at the island of Faial, in the Azores, 18 days after leaving Nova Scotia. Slocum wrote that a young naval officer, resplendently uniformed, had boarded the *Spray* to pilot her into the anchorage in Horta Bay and had managed to foul

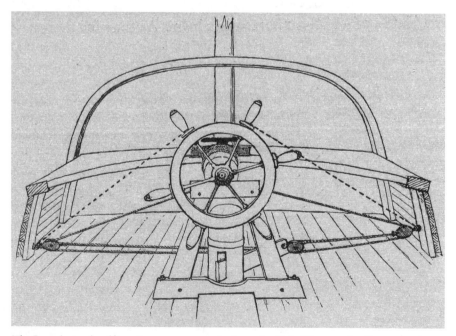

The Spray's simple self-steering arrangement is shown in dashed lines in this illustration from Sailing Alone Around the World. Slocum lashed the wheel on the desired course, and the vessel's exceptional course-keeping ability took care of it from there. The solid lines show the block-and-tackle configuration that transmitted helm changes to the rudder.

several moored vessels and sink a lighter (a small boat for transferring cargo between the shore and anchored vessels) on the way in. The young man then demanded a fee for his services, which Slocum did not pay.

Hoisting a double-reefed mainsail in squally winds on July 24, Slocum departed Horta for Gibraltar, but he didn't get far before an extra-strong gust struck the *Spray* "with such violence that I thought her mast would go." He got the *Spray* pointed into the wind to relieve the pressure on the rig, but not before one of the weather lanyards broke and another stretched so much as to damage the rope fibers within it.[1] Slocum anchored, lowered his mainsail, and had begun making up new lanyards when an oared gig from the custom house appeared, and one of its crew clambered aboard to assist. Always looking on the bright side, Slocum wrote: "[L]et one be without a friend, and see what will happen!"

With his rigging mended, Slocum set sail once more for Gibraltar, the first stop on his planned route through the Mediterranean to the Suez Canal. It was on this passage that, after eating plums and a white cheese given him by the American consul-general at Horta, Slocum was doubled over with cramps. Despite the pain, and rather than heave to, Slocum managed to tie a double reef in the *Spray*'s mainsail, adjust the main and jib sheets to "set her on her course," and finally stumble below into his cabin. In *Sailing Alone*, he famously described the apparition that appeared while he writhed on the cabin floor, incapacitated, as storm-force winds built up. "I saw a tall man at the helm," Slocum wrote. "'Señor,' said he, doffing his cap ...,'I am one of Columbus's crew.... I am the pilot of the *Pinta* come to aid you. Lie quiet, señor captain ... and I will guide your ship tonight.'"

In his delirium, Slocum maintained a conversation with his pilot while heavy seas washed over the *Spray*. Slocum imagined that the breaking seas were boats landing on deck after being thrown off wagons by careless teamsters, and he remembered calling out, "You'll smash your boats, but you can't hurt the *Spray*." Recovering later, he found the *Spray* still obediently sailing the same course she had been on when he had fallen ill. "To my astonishment, I saw now at broad day that the *Spray* was still heading as I had left her.... Columbus himself could not have held her more exactly on her course."[2] The phantom pilot appeared once more as Slocum slept, promising

---

1 In rigs like the *Spray*'s, the shrouds that provided lateral support to the mast were tensioned by means of lanyards rove through holes in wooden deadeyes.

2 Slocum was proud of the *Spray*'s self-steering ability. He wrote: "[N]o man, I think, could stand or sit and steer a vessel around the world." The *Spray*'s hull form, with its wide beam carried well aft

to return later in the voyage. Then he was gone.

Slocum promptly got rid of all the plums aboard, though he made no mention of the cheese. Ben Aymar Slocum later attributed this incident to his father's spiritual side, and perhaps he was right. But it's also true that Columbus's voyages had fired Slocum's imagination when the *Liberdade* was sailing through the Caribbean and Joshua had tried to picture the islands—the New World—as they would have looked to their European discoverer. Columbus had sailed beyond the known world, venturing where the charts of his time said only "There be dragons." For a lonely, feverish, tradition-loving man on a storm-tossed boat in waters familiar to Columbus, what better guide could there be than one of Columbus's captains?

Many years after this event, a cousin of Joshua, the Reverend Joel B. Slocum, mentioned the pilot of the *Pinta* in a talk he gave on loneliness at the Central Baptist Church in Norwich, Connecticut. "To save himself from losing his mind, he invented some little comforting fictions, one of which was that the pilot of the *Pinta*—one of the vessels of Columbus—was at the wheel when he himself could not be." Sometimes, as the voyage progressed, Slocum would pretend that one of his sons was with him.

Slocum anchored at Gibraltar on August 4, 29 days after departing Nova Scotia, and took the opportunity to sell some of the salted pollock left over from his fish-selling failure in Boston. He also wrote the first of his "letters" for the Boston *Globe*, recalling the friendly spirit of the *Pinta*'s pilot. The *Globe* headline reflected the challenge of adapting Slocum's dispatches to the commercial needs of a daily newspaper: "Spook on Spray. Ghost of Columbus' Man Steered the Boat."

Slocum spent three weeks at Gibraltar, where he was feted by the governor, the U.S. consul, and the admiring British naval garrison, which

---

and inherent good balance, was the basis for the boat's course-holding ability. Slocum knew his boat's balance instinctively, but it was eventually verified independently by a naval architect (see Appendix B). Once the sails were trimmed and the rudder angled to hold course, Slocum held the wheel in place with port- and starboard-side lines looped over one of the wheel's spokes. In the steady trade winds Slocum sought for his passages, he could trim the sheets and then leave the wheel untended for days at a time. As for the steering system itself, it was a simple, sturdy wheel-and-drum arrangement relying on a rope secured to blocks mounted at deck level on the bulwarks port and starboard. Victor Slocum emphasized that "[t]he tiller [connected to the rudder head] led aft towards the transom so as to be out of the way." Garfield Slocum offered a rare description of lashing the helm, which he did while sailing with his father from Pemaquid, Maine, to Boston: "I wanted to know whether the *Spray* would hold her course without anyone at the wheel. I saw a black can buoy ahead. I headed the *Spray* for it, lashed the helm and paced the deck. She kept on her course until she came near the buoy, then I removed the ropes from the helm."

The Spray *anchored off Gibraltar as depicted in* Sailing Alone Around the World.

sent down fresh milk daily and fresh vegetables twice weekly. Among the warships in harbor was a 10-month-old 242-foot "torpedo-gunboat" named for the Greek goddess Hebe, "cup-bearer of the gods." Although powered by steam turbines generating 3,500 horsepower, the *Hebe* carried a sailmaker aboard who made a new jib for the *Spray*.

Joshua Slocum was treated as a celebrity by the British Navy personnel at Gibraltar. The admiral in command, Admiral Bruce, had the *Spray* taken in hand and spruced up, and Bruce's wife went aboard for a guided tour. The U.S. consul, Horatio J. Sprague, was another visitor. Slocum couldn't help but think that he might be on to something with his solo voyage.

Slocum used his three weeks at Gibraltar to explore, write more travel letters, and socialize with the British naval officers about a variety of topics including Alfred Thayer Mahan's book *The Influence of Sea Power upon History, 1660–1783*. Published in 1890, the book was already on its way to achieving the enduring impact it would exercise on naval strategy and world power.

But Slocum's new British friends strongly advised him against transiting the Suez Canal and sailing down the Red Sea. Slocum wrote: "By officers of vast experience in navigating these seas, I was influenced to make the change. Long shore pirates on both coasts being numerous, I could not afford to make light of the advice."

Now, Slocum again changed his route. First, he'd had to abandon his initial plan to sail to Panama and have the *Spray* hauled across the isthmus to the Pacific. It was a disappointment that later prompted his enthusiasm for the Panama Canal, though he wouldn't live to see it completed. In Gibraltar, once he gave up on sailing through the Suez Canal and down the Red Sea, he decided to head back across the Atlantic Ocean and sail the *Spray* through the Strait of Magellan to the Pacific. This decision would lead directly to several of the most exciting and life-threatening events of the *Spray* voyage.

CHAPTER 14

Gibraltar to the Río de la Plata

"He crossed the Atlantic and had reached Gibraltar, but hearing there that there were pirates in the Red Sea, he again turned westward, and after a tempestuous passage across the Atlantic, reached Pernambuco, Brazil, on Oct. 5, which was the last heard of him until the news just received [from the Strait of Magellan]."

—New Orleans Daily Picayune, April 12, 1896

ON MONDAY, AUGUST 25, SLOCUM departed Gibraltar at the far end of a Royal Navy tugboat's hawser. The idea was to get the *Spray* well clear of tricky winds that swirl around "the Rock's" 1,400-foot-high mountain and give her a good start toward the Atlantic. There, Slocum planned "to haul offshore well clear of the land, which hereabouts is the home of pirates."

Slocum wrote that his entry into the Atlantic was soon met by a wind that increased to what he called "a furious gale." Worse, he learned that there were, indeed, pirates off Morocco's Atlantic coast. He found himself being chased by a felucca, a speedy, lateen-rigged vessel that quickly began overtaking the *Spray*. Perhaps the best that can be said of Slocum's altering his route to avoid pirates in the Red Sea is that he might find fewer of them along his new route in the wide expanse of the Atlantic.

The wind was simply too strong to continue under full main; even as the pirates gained on him, Slocum was forced to heave to and tie in a reef to reduce sail. Reefing a mainsail the size of the *Spray*'s in a big wind and rough seas would be challenging even in a crewed boat, but Slocum had to do it alone and under intense pressure. The multistep task involved lowering the mainsail partway while supporting the boom with the topping lift, trimming the mainsheet to hold the boom inboard, hauling taut the reefing lines at the sail's tack and clew, and then tying in a dozen or so reefing pendants. Slocum completed the reef in an impressive but exhausting 15 minutes.

Even so, when he finished, the felucca was close enough that he could see the "exhultation on their faces." It was at that moment, Slocum wrote, that a freak wave caused the felucca, which was carrying too much sail, to broach. When the same wave hit the *Spray*, the mainsheet block parted from the boom, which promptly broke near the mast. "How I got the boom in before the sail was torn I hardly know," Slocum wrote. He lowered the main, hoisted the jib, dashed below for his rifle, and returned on deck to find the pirates far behind. They had been dismasted.

Slocum made a temporary but strong repair of the boom as the *Spray* continued offshore under jib and foresail. A flying fish obligingly landed on deck, but Slocum was too tired to even think of dinner. "I do not remember to have been more tired before or since in all my life than I was at the finish of that day," he wrote.

By August 27, all that could be seen of land was two distant mountain peaks, which soon disappeared. The *Spray* sailed on as Slocum congratulated himself. Despite his broken boom and the pirate chase, he thought himself in better condition than Columbus had been when navigating these same waters. Columbus had already been dealing with rumblings of mutiny and a broken rudder, Slocum wrote.

The *Spray* now began her second crossing of the Atlantic toward Recife, the Brazilian port that Slocum knew all too well. He recorded in his log each ship that he met along the way and his disappointment that they seemed in too great a hurry to slow down for a brief gam, or chat. One of these ships came very close to ending the *Spray*'s voyage and, quite likely, Slocum's life.

Slocum was below on an eerily quiet night when he was shocked to hear voices close by. He rushed on deck just in time to see "a white bark under full sail" surge past the *Spray*.

Fear of collision while asleep is among the singlehanded sailor's greatest fears, and it must have come as a shock to Slocum that only his good luck had prevented such an event in the mid-Atlantic. After this narrow escape, he "sat long on the starlit deck that night, thinking of ships, and watching the constellations on their voyage."

Slocum thereafter sharpened his watch, at least during the day. Tough and spry, he climbed the mast on September 14 to have a good look around for approaching ships. He spotted one vessel headed north, well out of signaling distance. Nine days later, the *Spray* was passed by the Boston schooner *Nantasket*, headed for the Río de la Plata. The *Spray*'s antifouling paint must have been working better than the schooner's, for the fish that had been following Slocum now deserted him. "Fishes," he wrote, "will always follow a foul ship."

Forty days after departing Gibraltar, on October 3, Slocum anchored the *Spray* at noon in the harbor at Pernambuco, his first visit since the unfortunate *Destroyer* adventure. In a letter to Eugene Hardy, Slocum wrote that he "lived awful hard coming down." There had been the experience with the pirates and, worse, the near-miss in midocean. "But don't say anything about it," he wrote. As always, Slocum promptly relegated these disturbing events to the past, just more water under the keel.

Slocum was discouraged to learn from Hardy that his travel letters weren't making a big hit in Boston. What was more, Hardy wrote, the *Globe*'s Charles Henry Taylor, Jr., was balking at the price he himself had offered for Slocum's work. Slocum responded that Taylor "agreed on $20 per col for the availables not as a literary production—the high price—but to encourage the enterprise as I understood it and the editor of the *Sunday Sun* said 'all right I'll go you $20.'" Slocum told Hardy he regretted the whole situation and that he had hoped to use some of the money earned "at least to help my little boy." He was probably referring to 14-year-old Garfield, but he would also send money at various times to Victor and, probably, to Hettie for the other children.

In his previous visits to Brazil, Slocum had met a boat enthusiast he named only Dr. Perera. The proprietor of a prominent newspaper in Rio de Janeiro, Perera owned a country estate at Pernambuco and now invited Slocum to visit. Always alert to boats, Slocum wrote that Perera had several

His mustache and chin whiskers bushier than usual, Slocum posed aboard the Spray *after completing what even he admitted was a "rough" passage from Gibraltar to Brazil. The photograph was probably taken in the harbor at Recife, Pernambuco, in October 1895. The boom, which had been unshipped for repair, has yet to be re-installed. The porthole in the* Spray's *cabin was just that—a hole. There was no expensive bronze-rimmed portlight. Instead, the opening could be covered with a tight-fitting wooden plug when necessary to keep out rain or boarding seas. (Courtesy the New Bedford Whaling Museum)*

interesting small craft at his waterfront home, including a Chinese sampan, a Norwegian pram, and a Cape Ann dory. The latter boat, Slocum couldn't help but notice, had once belonged to the *Destroyer*.

If Slocum had not forgotten the *Destroyer* adventure, neither had the Brazilians. The de Melo faction—the rebels he had been hired to defeat—were now in power, and the customs collector at Pernambuco told Slocum he would be charged tonnage fees as if the *Spray* were a commercial vessel rather than a yacht. What Slocum called a "trifling difficulty" in *Sailing Alone* was in fact a tricky, frustrating situation that neither the U.S. consul nor a friendly local businessman found a way to resolve. In the end, an "old merchant friend came to my assistance, advancing the cash direct."

On October 23, having shortened the *Spray's* boom by 4 feet and fitted it with new jaws (semi-circular wooden fittings that hold a boom to its mast), Slocum departed Pernambuco for Rio, arriving there on November 5.

In Rio he met William I. Buchanan, whom President Grover Cleveland had appointed as minister to Argentina in 1894—a meeting both men would have cause to remember.

During this layover, Slocum made his next modification to the *Spray's* rig. In *Sailing Alone*, he wrote that he "had decided to give the *Spray* a yawl rig for the tempestuous waters of Patagonia." Now Slocum installed the distinctive arch that he called a "semi-circular brace to support a jigger [mizzen] mast," but not the mast itself. Slocum didn't explain why he didn't complete the job. It may be that he couldn't scrounge a suitable piece of timber from which to fashion the mast and couldn't afford to buy one. (Captain friends in Rio donated an anchor, anchor cable, and other gear, but not a mast.) The brace transformed the appearance of the *Spray's* stern and became among the boat's most distinctive features.

On November 11, Slocum wrote Eugene Hardy with updates and shared his thoughts about his unhappy experience with the *Boston Globe*. "I hav'nt since the last news from Boston, felt like trying to write for a paper. I thought there was something to young C---- Taylor but I find he is only a rich man's son after all."[1]

Slocum was still cash-poor and was thankful to Hardy for a $20 advance. Sales of the *Liberdade* had also helped. "I will sell the balance of the edition by and by on satisfactory terms I think," he wrote Hardy.

Never one to give up a petition, Slocum now appealed to the "highest lord of the admiralty and ministers, to inquire concerning the matter of wages due me from the beloved *Destroyer*." The predictable response was that he was welcome not to any cash payment but to the ship itself, still lying awash at Bahia (Salvador). Slocum wrote in *Sailing Alone* that "I thanked the kind officer, but declined his offer."

Slocum departed Rio for Montevideo on November 28. It was while recounting this leg of the voyage in *Sailing Alone* that he would deliberately mislead readers about his tin clock. A steamship Slocum encountered "gave the longitude by chronometer as 48° W., 'near as I can make it,'" he wrote. "The *Spray* with her tin clock, had exactly the same reckoning. I was feeling at ease in my primitive method of navigation, but it startled me not a little to find my position by account [by deduced, ded, or "dead" reckoning] verified by the ship's chronometer." Slocum relied throughout the voyage on

---

1 Charles Henry Taylor, Jr., was the son of the *Globe's* famous publisher, Civil War veteran Charles Henry Taylor, and was largely responsible for repositioning the newspaper beginning in 1877.

RECIFE

SOUTH
AMERICA

RIO DE JANEIRO
NOVEMBER 5, 1895

MONTEVIDEO
BUENOS
AIRES   DECEMBER 19, 1895

N

CAPE VIRGINS
FEBRUARY 11, 1896

DIRECTION OF WIND

Slocum's route from Recife to the Strait of Magellan.

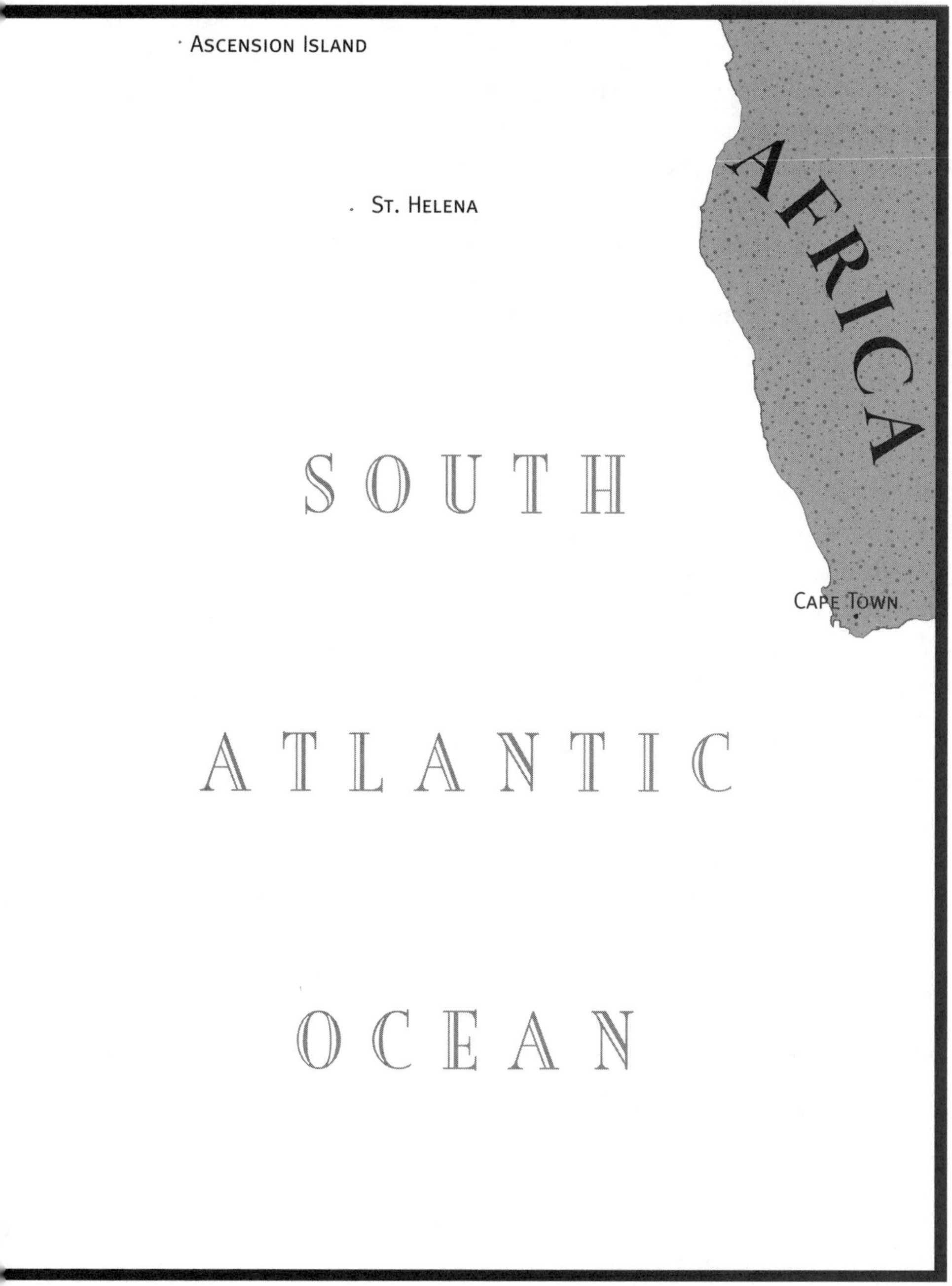

· ASCENSION ISLAND

. ST. HELENA

AFRICA

SOUTH

CAPE TOWN.

ATLANTIC

OCEAN

the patent log towed behind the *Spray*, supplementing it with lunar observations.

Slocum enjoyed fair weather during the first two weeks of this coastwise passage, but on the night of December 11, mistaking vast, moonlit sand dunes for ocean swells, he ran hard aground on a sandbar off the Uruguayan coast. Slocum said the spot was about 7 miles south of the Brazilian border and not far from what he called Fort Teresa. The fort, about 190 miles north of Montevideo, is known to Uruguayans as Fortalesa de Santa Teresa.

Running aground is never pleasant, and Slocum now faced imminent danger as the *Spray* was exposed to ocean swells. He managed to launch his half-dory and row out a kedge anchor, but the *Spray* was already hard aground with the tide falling fast. To prepare for its return, he decided to row out one of his heavier anchors on the end of a 240-foot cable. This ground tackle would provide an unquestionably secure purchase to haul the boat to deeper water when the tide returned.

But carrying this heavy anchor in his tender through the surf was a precarious and exhausting task. The half-dory shipped water, began leaking, and was in danger of sinking by the time he reached the drop point. Slocum lifted the big anchor above his head and tossed it into the sea "just as [the half-dory] was turning over … I suddenly remembered I could not swim." Three times he tried and failed to right his little boat and clamber in without capsizing it again. On his fourth attempt he finally managed it. Now he realized that although the wind was onshore, the current was offshore and he was in a battle for his life.

What saved him, after getting back in the boat and bailing it, was that he'd recovered one of his oars. After attaching another anchor cable to the buoyed end of the first one, he had just enough length to take a single turn around the *Spray*'s windlass. He might have planned it that way, but he well knew "Slocum's luck" had seen him through yet again.

With day breaking, Slocum took shelter from the wind behind a sand dune, where he hoped to get some rest while awaiting the tide's return. This attempt was interrupted by a young man on horseback who discovered the half-dory and was preparing to tow it off the beach when Slocum stood up and greeted him. Thus began the twin challenges of protecting the *Spray* from looters and getting her afloat.

In *Sailing Alone*, Slocum described this fraught affair with his usual humor and lightheartedness. Among those who showed up on the beach from a nearby village was a non-Uruguayan who stole "my revolver and several small articles." Slocum recovered his property, although he did not say whether the big fist was required. As the tide returned, Slocum got the *Spray* afloat with local assistance before a tug sent from Montevideo arrived.

The next day he arrived at Maldonado, the very port from which he'd been turned away eight years before in the smallpox-ridden *Aquidneck*. This time he was welcomed and given fresh eggs, strawberries, milk, and bread by the daughter of the British consul. He gathered fresh mussels and oysters, and thus resupplied, sailed into Montevideo, where he was embarrassed by an enthusiastic welcome of steam whistles and crowds. As ever, people were willing to help, and he was informed by local agents for the Royal Mail Steamship Company that they would see to whatever repairs the *Spray* might require.

The *Spray* was hauled and the extent of her damages assessed. Slocum wrote that the boat's protective keel shoe had been lost to the grounding, and the false keel itself had been damaged, but he did not itemize other damage except to say that some re-caulking was needed. These repairs were expertly seen to, and Slocum's leaky half-dory was repaired, painted green, and restored to better condition than she'd been when Slocum completed her at Gloucester. In *Sailing Alone*, Slocum wrote that "I hardly knew her from a butterfly." Here, too, the *Spray's* forecastle was equipped with "a wonderful makeshift stove ... and in cold, wet days off the coast of Tierra del Fuego, it stood me in good stead."

Across the wide Río de la Plata estuary that divides Uruguay from Argentina is the city of Buenos Aires, which Slocum decided to visit once more after departing Montevideo. With him on this short voyage was an old friend, Captain Howard. Slocum took the opportunity to demonstrate the *Spray's* self-steering ability to this experienced seaman. In *Sailing Alone*, Slocum wrote that Howard "sat near the binnacle and watched the compass while the sloop held her course so steadily that one would have declared that the [compass] card was nailed fast. Not a quarter of a point did she deviate from her course."[1]

---

[1] Slocum gave no indication that he lashed the helm during this demonstration. If he had not, the suggestion is that the *Spray's* balance was so extraordinary that, at least in reasonably calm conditions, once the sails were properly trimmed, there was minimal pressure on her rudder. Sailor/author and lifelong student of boat design Roger Taylor noted that "the *Spray's* steering gear, based on a rope wound around a wooden drum turned by the wheel, was not self-securing, as would be, say, a worm gear attached to the rudderpost. With a worm gear, pressure on the rudder would not normally turn the wheel (though, to be sure, if, say, hove to in a gale, you'd lash the wheel hard down). But on the *Spray*, pressure on the rudder *would* turn the wheel, so Slocum had to hold it all the time he was

Prior to departing Montevideo, Slocum had used one of his many connections to gain an introduction to 60-year-old George Michael Mulhall in Buenos Aires. Like Dr. Perera in Brazil, Mulhall, an Irish émigré, owned a newspaper. Together with his brother, Mulhall had founded the *Buenos Ayres Standard*, South America's first English-language newspaper, in 1862. Thus, upon arriving in Buenos Aires, Slocum was met by someone who could not only report on the *Spray's* voyage but could also show him around the city. In *Sailing Alone*, Slocum wrote: "Mr. Mulhall kindly drove me to see many improvements about the city and we went in search of some of the old landmarks."

Slocum found the lemonade seller he remembered from previous visits and learned that the man had by now made a fortune selling his flavored drink concocted in a washtub at two cents a glass. But Slocum noted that "we looked in vain for the man who once sold whisky and coffins ... memory only clung to his name." Slocum didn't tell his readers why he had looked for a seller of whisky and coffins. It would have been too personal to relate that this was the man from whom, stricken with grief that endured still, he'd bought Virginia's coffin.

Another thing he neglected to mention was his discovery that the English Cemetery, where Virginia had been buried, no longer existed. By November 1892, the cemetery had been taken by the growing city, which used the ground to expand the Plaza 1 De Mayo, an important civic gathering place. Virginia Slocum's grave, and others, now lay beneath the square, while their monuments had been moved to a section of La Chacarita cemetery, the largest burial ground in Argentina. Slocum's feelings about this have not been revealed in correspondence, and remain unknown.

He now undertook yet another change to the *Spray's* rig. Preparing the boat for what was to come, he shortened the mast by 7 feet and the bowsprit by 5 feet—and he would soon wish he'd sawn an additional foot off the sprit. His primary goal now was to leave Buenos Aires behind. If he'd thought that visiting Virginia's grave might bring some comfort, he had found only more pain.

ON JANUARY 26, 1896, Joshua Slocum departed Buenos Aires for the last time. Just getting out to sea from the Río de la Plata was a challenge. He

---

steering. So, any time he wanted to leave the wheel, he had to lash it, but even with worm gear, you'd lash the wheel if leaving it in any sort of rough conditions."

needed a tow to clear the harbor and found, in the absence of wind, that the great river looked "like a silver disk." But the calm conditions were short-lived. Squalls arose, turning the water from silver to mud-brown. Seeking shelter, he anchored "in the best lee I could find near the land," but "was tossed miserably all night, heart-sore in choppy seas."

Lying in his bunk in his rolling boat, he was overcome by emotions that had been building through his stay in Buenos Aires. In *Sailing Alone*, he wrote that "weak as it may seem, I gave way to my feelings," but he didn't tell readers what those feelings were. In a March 4, 1954, letter to Walter Teller, Ben Aymar wrote, "Many years after mother died, father was looking at a photo of mother in my presence and tears streamed over his face." It seems odd that Slocum's editor didn't demand some explanation of this vague reference to "feelings." Perhaps an explanation was requested and refused. Instead, readers were left to imagine what he could be talking about.

It was clear, though, that Slocum wanted to distance himself from this place of heart-breaking memories and from the land itself. He wrote, "I resolved that I would anchor no more north of the Strait of Magellan." After hoisting anchor in the morning, the *Spray* took another 24 hours, until January 28, to make her way past Point Indio (Punta Indio), the river's southern headland, and emerge at last into Samborombón Bay (Bahía de Samborombón) and finally the South Atlantic.

Slocum now faced a passage of approximately 1,500 miles to reach Cape Virgins (Cabo Vírgenes), the landmass just north of the Strait of Magellan at 52° south, still more than 200 sea miles north of Cape Horn. When he wrote about altering his voyage route at Gibraltar, Slocum never said why he didn't stick to his idea for sailing eastabout, rounding the Cape of Good Hope in lieu of transiting the Suez Canal and Red Sea. The eastabout route was advantageous for getting around the great southern capes—including Cape Horn and the Cape of Good Hope—in the prevailing westerlies of those latitudes, but the westabout route had advantages, too, notably the downwind sailing to be enjoyed in the easterly trade winds of the tropics. But he had no intention of rounding Cape Horn and confronting in the little *Spray* the enormous seas that rush unimpeded around the bottom of the world in the Furious Fifties.

The timing was good for a Strait of Magellan passage, however. In a November 11, 1895 letter to Eugene Hardy, Slocum noted that the weather in Patagonia "will be growing better ahead for the next two months" as the southern hemisphere summer unfolded. Once he emerged from the strait, he could expect fair sailing in the Pacific trade winds, and his route would allow him to make stops at new places he wished to visit and others that held important memories. His timing for a reasonably smooth transit of the Strait of Magellan at the most propitious time of the year almost worked. But not quite.

CHAPTER 15

The Strait of Magellan

"All things considered, I believe there is not a more beautiful or better strait than this one."

—Antonio Pigafetta, chronicler for Ferdinand Magellan on the first voyage around the world, 1519–22

"We anchored in the fine bay of Port Famine. It was now the beginning of winter and I never saw a more cheerless prospect."

—Charles Darwin, *The Voyage of the Beagle*, 1839

JOSHUA SLOCUM'S PASSAGE SOUTH to the Strait of Magellan required him to bypass two vast gulfs, each of which lay ready to swallow unwary navigators who failed to stay well clear of their shoals and tidal races. Slocum wrote that he stood 50 miles offshore to pass the Gulf of St. Matias and the

142-mile-wide Gulf of St. George (Golfo San Jorge). His navigation down the coast was accurate, but he encountered a sudden and significant threat off Patagonia in the form of "a tremendous wave, the culmination, it seemed of many waves [that] rolled down upon her in a storm, roaring as it came."

Slocum managed to lower the sails and get himself "up on the peak hailliards,[1] out of danger when I saw the mighty crest towering masthead-high above me." The wave apparently broke over the *Spray*. "The mountain of water submerged my vessel." Slocum wrote that he "could see no part of the *Spray*'s hull for about a minute," more than enough time to make resolutions about future good behavior if he survived. Among other things, he thought he might dedicate himself to building a larger boat.[2]

But the great wave gave the oyster sloop one more chance to demonstrate her seaworthiness and prove Slocum's theory that her buoyant bow and stern with their lack of overhangs were ideal for offshore sailing. The *Spray*'s heavy construction proved itself again, too. Slocum wrote: "She shook in every timber and reeled under the weight of the sea, but rose grandly out of it, and rode grandly over the rollers that followed."

Thereafter, Slocum had uneventful sailing to Cape Virgins,[3] which he reached on February 11. His pulse may have quickened as the Strait of Magellan opened up ahead of him. Sailing ships took the outside route around Cape Horn, and there is no evidence of Slocum having been in the notorious strait before. His Admiralty chart would have been based on surveys made between 1826 and 1834 by Royal Navy captains Phillip Parker King and Robert Fitz Roy (of *Beagle* renown) and updated by Captain Richard Charles Mayne. The strait is a vastness of mountains, channels, rocks, glaciers, and islands, and no sailor could ignore the foreboding place names that mark its sea- and landscapes: Famine Reach, Crooked Reach, Breaker Coast, Useless Bay, and, looming at the western end, the Island of Desolation.

Rounding Cape Virgins, Slocum described the scene as "gloomy; the wind, northeast, and blowing a gale, sent feather-white spume along the coast; such a sea ran as would swamp an ill-appointed ship. As the sloop

---

1 The Thomas Fogarty illustration of this event in *Sailing Alone*, approved by Slocum, shows Slocum clinging to the portside shrouds well above the bulwarks. This makes more sense than hanging on to the peak halyard, because the natural result would have been to raise both himself and the mainsail, which he certainly would not have wished to do.

2 Although this was an extreme example of the *Spray*'s seaworthiness, she would prove herself, in Slocum's capable hands, able to deal with worse in the months to come. While cruising sailors today wisely tether themselves to their boats in bad conditions, Slocum never seems to have considered doing so.

3 Magellan found the cape on October 21, 1520, the day of the Festival of the Eleven Thousand Virgins.

neared the entrance to the strait, I observed that two great tide races made ahead, one very close to the point of the land and one farther offshore. Between the two, in a sort of channel, through combers, went the *Spray* with close-reefed sails."

Just as he had encountered a wrecked steamship upon his departure from Boston and entry into Massachusetts Bay, Slocum passed "the wreck of a great steamship smashed on the beach" as he entered the Strait of Magellan. If it was possible for his surroundings to be any more foreboding than they naturally were, this forlorn wreck, a rusty monument to the insignificance of man's technology in the face of nature, completed the picture.

Slocum, of course, had no engine to fall back upon in case of need. Instead, he would have to rely on his seaman's experience, the *Spray*'s abilities, and heavy anchors, which, when put to the ultimate test, would prove shockingly ineffective. He was at the wheel of a heavy-displacement sloop with no labor-saving devices save for an anchor windlass. The big gaff rig required significant energy and muscle to manage, and this would become an important factor in the weeks ahead. Work, stress, wind, and cold demanded that he consume adequate calories to keep up his strength. He wrote in *Sailing Alone*, "I insisted on warm meals."

To reduce the navigational demands, Slocum probably noted compass directions on the dotted-line course through the strait that was indicated on his chart. Doing so would have provided some relief from chart plotting during the approximately 350-mile passage, leaving him more opportunity to attend to his boat's needs, track his progress, and maintain a weather eye for dangers, both natural and human.

Having passed the wrecked steamer, Slocum found himself battling a head current in water shallow enough that he could see long, streaming sinews of kelp attached to dark rocks beneath the boat. *Sailing Alone* included a map of the strait with notations of wind encountered at various places, and this shows that Slocum faced winds from the northeast at the entrance, forcing him to tack back and forth, clawing to windward, *Spray*'s worst point of sail. The squalls had such weight that he had to triple-reef his mainsail and proceed with the remaining handkerchief of a sail plus a forestaysail. Sometimes he had to lower the sails entirely and then raise them again. He battled this way for thirty hours, making little progress.

At last, four days after entering the strait, Slocum anchored at Punta Arenas, labeled Sandy Point by eighteenth-century English explorers. Punta Arenas was then home to some 2,000 people and a Chilean navy coaling station, its growth having been spurred by the introduction of sheep farming on the vast, treeless grasslands north of the strait. It was at Punta Arenas that Slocum found someone who, like his supporters in Boston, Gloucester, and Gibraltar, was eager to help him in his venture. This time it was a sea captain named Pedro Samblich, whom Slocum identified as "a good Austrian of large experience." (He did not bother to note that Pedro would appear to be a singularly un-Austrian name.) Samblich's donations included a bag of carpet tacks that may later have saved Slocum's life and certainly accounted for one of the voyage's most talked-about incidents.

Samblich also donated a compass that Slocum said was better than his own, and a supply of smoked venison and biscuits. Noting that the *Spray*'s mainsail looked worn, Samblich further offered to donate the sail from his own sloop, but Slocum refused—a decision he would have cause to regret. Nor did he accept the offer to take as much gold dust as he wanted from Samblich's supply.[1]

Although the strait was patrolled by Chilean naval vessels, Slocum was warned that Fuegians, the indigenous people, were extremely treacherous. He had heard this already from his friend Captain Howard during their sail up the Río de la Plata, though Howard's claim that the Fuegians were cannibals merely echoed a false rumor. Still, the native people represented a threat, and Slocum was advised to take someone with him through the strait.[2] He did seek a crewmate for the passage, but found nobody willing to come aboard without making demands. What's more, he was not enthusiastic about having anyone sail with him, as he was always aware of doubters regarding his claim that he sailed alone. Later, in Australia, he would wonder if he needed to fumigate the *Spray* to prove he had nobody else on board.

So he set off by himself on February 19, with an arms locker that included two rifles and a carbine, his trusty Smith & Wesson revolver, Samblich's carpet tacks, and a fair wind. He anchored for the night in eight fathoms at

---

1 The discovery of gold in 1879 in Tierra del Fuego triggered a gold rush beginning in 1884, but yields were declining by the 1890s. Slocum gave no personal details about Samblich to indicate when and why he settled at Punta Arenas.

2 Confronted by missionaries, colonists, and European diseases, the native people of Tierra del Fuego faced a losing battle. Beginning in 1876, the Fuegians were decimated by measles, smallpox, and other sicknesses against which they had no resistance, in common with Native Americans throughout the two continents. The Selk'nam tribe of Fuegians were victims of genocide between 1884 and 1900 by sheep herders and cattle ranchers who wanted their grasslands. Large cattle companies paid a bounty for each dead Selk'nam—more for women than for men—as confirmed by severed hands, ears, or skull.

Nicolas Bay, and the next day—February 20, 1896—celebrated his fifty-second birthday while sailing off the southernmost tip of the American continent, Cape Froward. The *Spray* made an easy 30-mile passage to Fortescue Bay, and Slocum anchored on the south side of the strait near Charles Island, where he waited out a two-day gale.

In this area Slocum began encountering Fuegians. He'd been strongly advised not to let them approach too closely, to shoot as necessary but without trying to kill, and always to be on his guard. He did what he could to make it appear that he was not alone. He set up a dummy dressed as a sailor, and descended the companionway dressed in one set of clothes and emerged from the forecastle wearing something else.[3] "In this instance," he wrote, "I reasoned that I had all about me the greatest danger of the whole voyage—the treachery of cunning savages, for which I must be particularly on the alert." Yet his passage continued without serious incident.

By March 3, 20 days after entering the strait, Slocum hoisted anchor at Port Tamar and sailed the remaining distance to Cape Pillar (Cabo Pilar) and the Pacific. He carried a fair northeasterly wind out of the Strait of Magellan, but there his good fortune ended. The wind increased, forcing him to tie in his third and last reef, and then, on the morning of March 4, it backed into the northwest and blew even harder. He had no choice but to lower his mainsail, which was largely in tatters, and run before the storm under a reefed forestaysail with two long ropes trailing astern "to steady her course and break coming seas."[4]

Joshua Slocum was now in exactly the situation he had sought to avoid by making a passage through the strait. He was in the open ocean in the Furious Fifties, latitudes with a grim and deserved reputation as a graveyard of seamen and ships. The *Spray* was now in a world of mountains of fast-moving slate-gray waves laced with white foam that "rose and fell and bellowed their never-ending story of the sea."

---

3 Slocum delighted in telling of this ruse all his life. In a letter written to Walter Teller in August 1953, Reginald Martin remembered that when he was a boy of 11, he met Slocum who told him "about going through one hatch and coming out another to make it appear as though there were several men aboard."

4 Throughout this ordeal in the gale off Cape Horn, Slocum carried this sail. He did so almost certainly to steady the boat and give some measure of control, despite the fact that "even that small sail shook her from keelson to truck when it shivered by the leech. Had I harbored the shadow of a doubt for her safety, it would have been that she might spring a leak in the garboard [the planks directly abutting the keel] at the heel of the mast; but she never called me once to the pump." Regarding the mast, his concern may have been that the *Spray*'s shrouds would loosen enough to permit the mast to move a bit and, possibly, to jump in the mast step on the vessel's keel.

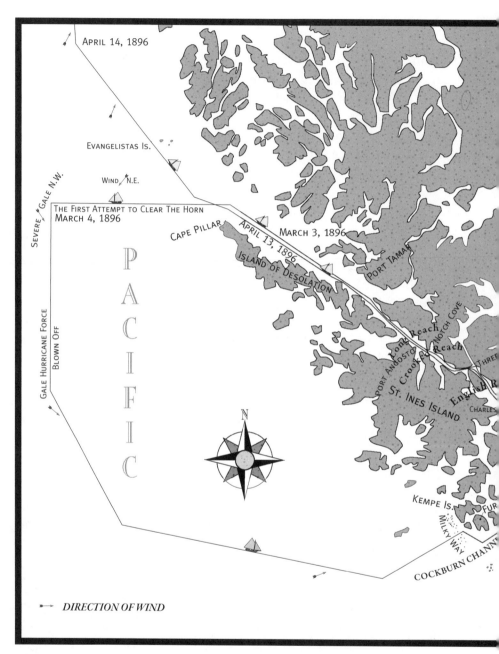

APRIL 14, 1896

EVANGELISTAS IS.

WIND N.E.

THE FIRST ATTEMPT TO CLEAR THE HORN
MARCH 4, 1896

CAPE PILLAR

APRIL 13, 1896

ISLAND OF DESOLATION

MARCH 3, 1896

SEVERE GALE N.W.

GALE HURRICANE FORCE

BLOWN OFF

PACIFIC

PORT TAMA

Long Reach

NOTCH COVE

PORT ANGOSTO

Crooked Reach

St. Ines Island

English R

THREE

CHARLES

N

KEMPE IS.

FUR

MILKY WAY

COCKBURN CHANNE

DIRECTION OF WIND

The Spray's *route through the Strait of Magellan testifies to Slocum's ordeal. A storm in the Pacific forced him south and east toward Cape Horn, and he was barely able to reenter the strait for a second try.*

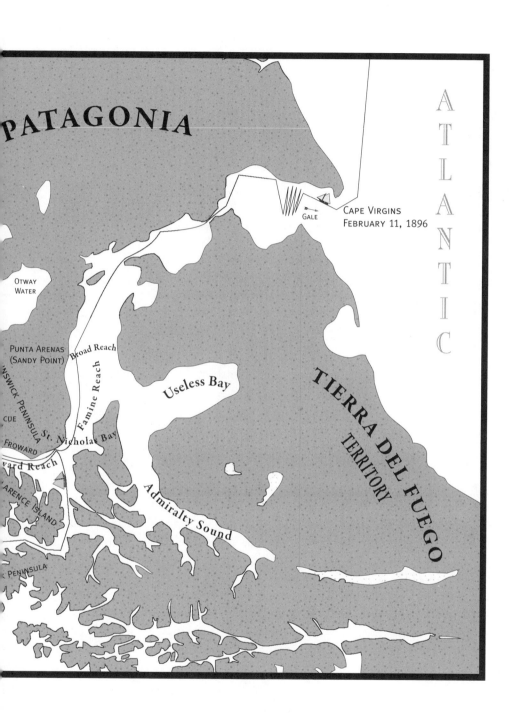

PATAGONIA

OTWAY
WATER

PUNTA ARENAS
(SANDY POINT)

Broad Reach

Famine Reach

NSWICK PENINSULA

CUE

St. Nicholas Bay

FROWARD

vard Reach

ARENCE ISLAND

PENINSULA

Useless Bay

Admiralty Sound

Cape Virgins
February 11, 1896

Gale

ATLANTIC

TIERRA DEL FUEGO
TERRITORY

Once he was confident that the *Spray* was holding her own, ever aware of the need to maintain morale and energy, Slocum made his way to the fore-cabin with its woodstove and somehow managed to brew a pot of coffee. He also planned to make himself a piping hot Irish stew. This bit of cookery, however, he postponed as, with some surprise, he discovered that Captain Joshua Slocum was actually seasick.

In *Sailing Alone*, Slocum wrote, "The first day of the storm gave the *Spray* her actual test in the worst sea that Cape Horn or its wild regions could afford, and in no part of the world could a rougher sea be found than at this particular point, namely off Cape Pillar, the grim sentinel of the Horn."

Helpless to do anything else, he guided his boat southeast toward Cape Horn, precisely the opposite direction from where he wished to go. At least, as he got farther offshore, he found the seas, while "majestic," posed somewhat less danger. He wrote that "the *Spray* rode, now like a bird on the crest of a wave, and now like a waif deep down in the hollow between the seas.... Whole days passed ... but with always a thrill—yes, of delight."

At some point, ever optimistic despite the conditions, Slocum managed to replace his ruined mainsail with the only thing he had aboard, what he called a "squaresail." Whether this was an actual square sail or an adapted piece of canvas, he didn't say. But the sail had reefpoints in it, and when the time came to set it, it would prove to be better than nothing at all.

By the fourth day of the gale, as the *Spray* neared what Slocum referred to as "the pitch of Cape Horn," he began to accept the real possibility that he might be swept right past the cape and back into the South Atlantic. He checked his charts and began calculating how long it would take to reach Port Stanley in the Falkland Islands, where he could rest, refit, and consider what his next step should be. As always, despite the terrible gale and the fact that he was losing so much hard-won ground, Slocum was unbowed and looking ahead.

It was at this point, just as the "fierce edge of the gale ... had blown off," that Slocum "saw through a rift in the clouds a high mountain, about seven leagues [21 nautical miles] on the port beam." With jubilation, he promptly hoisted his "awkward [square] sail reefed" and "headed for the land, which appeared as an island in the sea. So it turned out to be, though not the one I had supposed."

As he sailed, Slocum grew "exultant" over the prospect of getting out of the Cape Horn seas and back into the Strait of Magellan, even if it meant retracing much of his previous passage there for a second time. Unfortunately for him, the gale soon resumed and he was overtaken by squalls of such force that he lowered his square sail and continued under the reefed fore-staysail alone. In fact, the wind was so powerful that "Under the pressure of the smallest sail I could set she made for the land like a racehorse.... I stood at the helm now and made the most of it."

Fast as he was moving, it was not fast enough to get close inshore and verify his position before darkness fell. Suddenly, frighteningly, he was "feeling the way in pitchy darkness. I saw breakers ahead before long. At this I wore ship and stood offshore, but was immediately startled by the tremendous roaring of breakers again ahead and on her lee bow. This puzzled me, for there should have been no broken water where I supposed myself to be."

For the first time in *Sailing Alone* (or any of his other writings), Joshua Slocum admitted that he was unsure of his position. There would be two more instances during his circumnavigation when he would question his location, though in one, after a night of intense anxiety, he would learn that he was exactly where intended, and in the other he would be very close. But Slocum's problem off Cape Horn was of an entirely different magnitude.

It is hard to imagine how any sailor, even one with Slocum's uncanny instincts and ability to judge speed and distance without regular reference to his log and chart, could have known precisely where he was. He'd spent four days running downwind from Cape Pillar toward Cape Horn in huge seas and uncertain visibility, and he was battling seasickness and exhaustion. Then he had that snapshot glimpse of land, reckoned he had properly identified a specific island, and headed in.

Slocum believed he was headed for a channel that would take him back to the strait, but soon enough, alone in the roaring darkness, he understood that he had made a potentially fatal mistake. Instead of the channel he had expected to find, he was in the midst of "broken water" everywhere he turned. Now commenced a terrifying night made even worse, if possible, by the arrival of "[h]ail and sleet in the fierce squalls [that] cut my flesh till the blood trickled over my face, but what of that?"

In the darkness, Slocum could see the whiteness of broken water and little else. Absent visibility, he had nothing more to rely upon than sound. He could use the noise of the breaking waves to judge how far he was from the next rock that would surely sink him if he struck, and he spent the night of March 7, 1896, sailing to and fro in huge seas breaking on enormous sunken rocks in an area south of Kempe Island (Isla Kempe). The island is one of many that lie to the south of much bigger landmasses bordering the southern edge of the Strait of Magellan.

Throughout that night, Slocum had to wonder what error had caused him to enter these waters. He must have recognized early on that the island he had spied so briefly and used as his landmark was not the one he thought. He never named the island he *thought* he was sailing for, but he did name the island he had in fact spotted—Fury Island (Isla Furia). When dawn broke, he learned the dreadful reality of his situation—"the sloop was in the midst of the Milky Way of the sea."

In his *Narrative of the Surveying Voyages of His Majesty's Ships Adventure and Beagle*, Volume III, published in 1839, Charles Darwin described the area. The *Beagle* "passed out between the East and West Furies [a pair of rocky outcroppings], and a little further northward there are so many breakers that the sea is called the Milky Way. One sight of such a coast is enough to make a landsman dream for a week about shipwreck, peril, and death."

In *Sailing Alone*, Slocum quoted from Darwin's *Journal*: "Any landsman seeing the Milky Way would have nightmare for a week." And Slocum added, "or 'seaman' as well." Having survived a stormy night in the Milky Way, Slocum now at least had visibility restored. "What could I do," he wrote, "but fill away among the breakers and find a channel between them, now that it was day? Since she had escaped the rocks through the night, surely she would find her way by daylight. This was the greatest sea adventure of my life. God knows how my vessel escaped."

On the Admiralty chart, the words "Milky Way" appear to the northwest of the entrances to the Barbara and Cockburn channels, both of which give access to the Strait of Magellan from the Pacific. Based on Slocum's description of his ordeal, it is likely that he mistook Fury Island for the more distant promontories of the Brecknock Peninsula that lie east of the Milky Way and border the Cockburn Channel.[1] Had he made it inshore before nightfall, he could have corrected his course and carried on to the rocks known as the West Furies and mentioned by Darwin. He would then have found himself in the broad, largely unobstructed lower reaches of Cockburn Channel.

As it was, Slocum sailed out of his nightmare and wrote that "good

---

1 In *Sailing Alone*, Slocum included a map on which he re-created his passage through the strait into the Pacific and then, in the gale, to the Cockburn Channel. The course line indicates Slocum believed the sharp turn he took inshore led him directly toward a spot between Kempe Island and Fury Island and landed him almost in the center of the Milky Way. He escaped in an easterly direction to the Cockburn Channel.

luck followed fast. I discovered, as she sailed through a labyrinth of islands, that she was in the Cockburn Channel, which leads into the Strait of Magellan at a point opposite Cape Froward, and that she was already passing Thieves' Bay, suggestively named."

On the night of March 8, Slocum anchored in a "snug cove" near what he called "the Turn." This cove lies at the eastern end of Clarence Island, not far from where Cockburn Channel joins the Strait of Magellan. Weary, battered, lucky to be alive, Slocum was more or less where he had been three weeks earlier on his birthday. This time, however, the Fuegians noted his return.

Slocum wrote that he made himself a hot venison stew that much improved his frame of mind. Too tired to remain awake, he sprinkled Pedro Samblich's carpet tacks on the *Spray's* decks, made sure that many of them were pointing up, and went below to sleep. At midnight the tacks performed as intended, for Slocum was awakened by the howls of Fuegian boarders. He hastened their departure with gunshots, then went right back to sleep, awaking, he said, "on the morning of the 9th, after a refreshing rest."

Slocum ate breakfast and, remarking what a pleasant morning it was, sat down to turn his square sail into a proper gaff sail by sewing pieces of canvas to it. As he worked, he observed that there were no trees growing "on the slope abreast the anchorage," and not long afterward, he learned why. His pleasant morning ended in a williwaw that blew the *Spray* and her anchors "like a feather" right out of her cove and into the strait. "No wonder trees did not grow on the side of that hill! Great Boreas! A tree would need to be all roots to hold on against such a furious wind."

Fortunately, there was plenty of water between Slocum's anchorage and the nearest land to leeward, and he had time to raise both his anchors and redeploy them. He spent a quiet night and returned to sailmaking the next day, only to be struck by another williwaw that "picked the sloop up and flung her seaward with a vengeance … and swept the sloop by several miles of steep bluffs and precipices overhanging a bold shore of wild and uninviting appearance."

Slocum's woes in the Strait of Magellan were far from over. On March 10, he was sailing in rough water when another williwaw struck and the staysail sheet parted. The *Spray* headed directly for a sheer rock face with "breakers so close under the bows that I felt surely lost," but when he turned the wheel, the boat responded "and in the next moment she was in the lee of the land."

He considered but rejected the notion of returning to Punta Arenas to repair his boat and get help. In Brazil, after the loss of the *Aquidneck*, he had been determined to return home with no assistance and thus had built the *Liberdade*, and his present trials in the Strait of Magellan did not soften Slocum's insistence on self-reliance. Gradually he created a new mainsail, while dissuading more Fuegian boarding parties with his rifle. He met a steamship that generously resupplied the *Spray*.

After passing Cape Quod in the Crooked Reach of the strait, Slocum anchored for a time, as he was making little headway against a 3-knot current. When he got underway again, he sailed some miles west and anchored in Langara Cove, where, in the morning, he discovered something of a windfall. "I discovered wreckage and goods washed up from the sea." Despite the threat posed by the Fuegians, Slocum launched his half-dory and spent a day salvaging casks of tallow, hoping to earn some money from the tallow's later sale. But he never left the *Spray* without being armed.

Although he didn't mention it in *Sailing Alone*, Slocum had another encounter with the Fuegians, who were this time outfitted against carpet tacks. When he got to Newcastle, Australia, Slocum told a reporter that a second boarding party accosted the *Spray* toward the western end of the strait. "They came shod with thick skins and greenhide moccasins. I had in the meantime changed my plan of defense, and I caught three of them in my spring net.[1] Before they knew where they were or how to get out of it, I had them wound up to the masthead. One shot put their cowardly companions to flight."

In a letter to the *New York World* about this part of the voyage, Slocum wrote, "The fierce winds, the strong currents, and above all, the savage Indians, made difficult sailing through the Straits of Magellan. Two classes redskins infest the coast—the canoes who beg, murder, and steal: and the canoes who steal and murder. The *Spray* had experience with both varieties."

The *Spray* suffered another rigging failure when the mainsheet parted, and repairs were made at Port Angosto in the western reaches of the strait. There, too, Slocum fitted a mizzenmast to the brace he had built. In a letter to his Century Publishing Company editor Clarence Buel, Slocum said he made the mast from a "hardy spruce sapling" that he found "among drift-wood on the beach" at St. Mary's Bay off the strait. "[T]he boom projected over the stern 'til the jigger was stepped. Sufficient of the out end [of the

---

1 This net may well have been the same one he had "invented" for fishing in Buzzards Bay.

boom] was then sawed off to allow it to swing clear [of the mizzen mast]."
Finally, he added the mizzen lugsail, giving the boat her most classic appearance, the look and rig that readers most closely associate with the *Spray*.

The *Spray* was now technically a yawl, but Slocum wrote that "I called the boat a sloop just the same, the jigger being merely a temporary affair." In fact, the jigger remained with the *Spray* until the end. Slocum wrote that the yawl rig "was an improvement only in that it reduced the size of a rather heavy mainsail [from something over 700 square feet to 604 square feet] and slightly improved her steering qualities on the wind. When the wind was aft the jigger was not in use." Of the mizzen, Thomas Fleming Day, editor of *The Rudder*, wrote, "Captain Slocum never had a very high opinion of that jigger, and in his heart, I think, was a bit ashamed of it." Still, a reduction in the mainsail's weight was an advantage not to be discounted.

While Slocum was at Port Angosto a Chilean gunboat arrived, and her skipper offered to tow the *Spray* back to Sandy Point if only Slocum would give up the voyage. Instead, Slocum accepted a gift of some needed rope and warm flannel clothing. He tried time and again after that to break free of the strait and into the Pacific. With typical understatement, he called these attempts "little haps and mishaps." It was presumably the Chileans who took a letter from Slocum for the *Boston Post*. On April 4, the newspaper ran a single-paragraph update on the voyage noting that Slocum was in the Strait of Magellan and "had a rough experience since leaving Pernambuco."

Finally, on April 13, 1896, despite brushing some rocks, the *Spray* escaped the strait on a southeast wind, and by the next morning left Cape Pillar well behind. "Hurrah for the *Spray*!" Slocum wrote. That evening, a large wave broke over the deck and gave Slocum another soaking, but it did nothing to squelch his apparently indomitable spirit. "It seemed to wash away old regrets. All my troubles were now astern; summer was ahead; all the world was again before me…. Then was the time to uncover my head, for I sailed alone with God." He had been at the helm for 30 hours without rest.

CHAPTER 16

To "Lovely Australia"

"During the week the world renowned Captain Slocum and his cutter Spray *have paid us a visit. The captain looks well and hearty and, using his own words 'The old man is as well as ever he was in his life,' and judging from appearances there cannot be much doubt about that point."*

—*Port Denison Times*, May 29, 1897

TEN DAYS AFTER SLOCUM PUT the Strait of Magellan behind him, a shark approached the *Spray*. In *Sailing Alone*, Slocum wrote that during his ordeal in Tierra del Fuego, he'd "had no mind in the lonesome strait to take the life of any living thing." Now, though, he harpooned the shark without remorse "and took out his ugly jaws." He was back at the top of the food chain, back to his old self. The *Spray* was bound for Australia, where he'd met Virginia, fallen in love, and married 25 years earlier.

Five days after killing the shark, Slocum sighted Juan Fernández, the

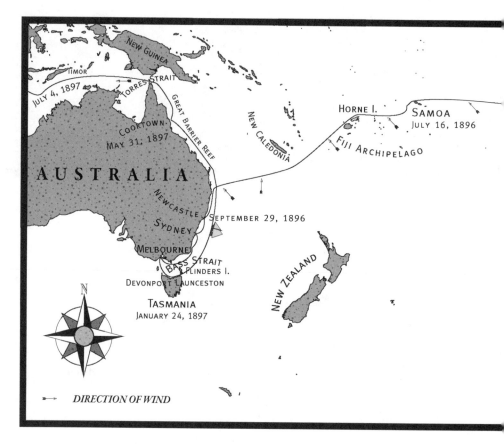

rugged island archipelago that included Robinson Crusoe Island, where Scottish privateer Alexander Selkirk had demanded to be left ashore rather than risk a voyage in a ship he rightly believed unseaworthy. Selkirk's tale of how he lived for four years and four months on the island is generally accepted as the inspiration for Daniel Defoe's novel, *The Life and Strange Surprizing Adventures of Robinson Crusoe*. Published in 1719, the book has captured the imaginations of readers ever since. Joshua Slocum, a student of solitude, wanted to see the island and "Robinson Crusoe's cave" for himself.

At Juan Fernández he showed islanders how to fry buns and dough-nuts and did a brisk business selling tallow. He also bartered tallow with a Chilean-born islander who sewed a new flying jib for the *Spray*. Ever sociable, he made friends ashore and recorded his observations of the islanders and the society they had evolved. He was favorably impressed.

"There was not a police officer or a lawyer among them," Slocum noted. He considered the lack of a school to be the island's greatest shortcoming.

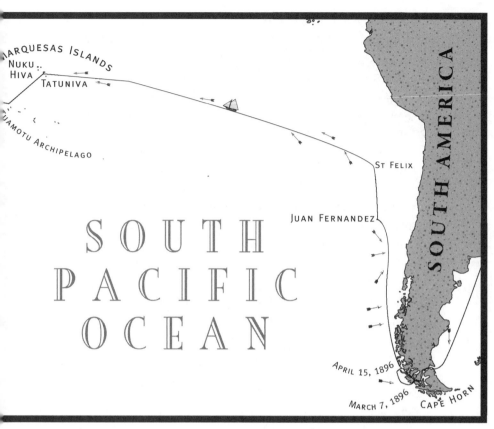

The Spray's track across the Pacific from the Strait of Magellan to Australia.

He spent his last day on Juan Fernández with island children, gathering wild fruit for the voyage ahead. Looking back on the experience after his return to Boston, he wrote that the day may have been "the pleasantest of the whole voyage." Though he wondered why Selkirk had ever left, Slocum himself departed on May 5, 1896, nine days after arriving.

Leaving the island behind, Slocum made a 43-day passage to the Marquesas island of Nuku Hiva (spelled Nukahiva in *Sailing Alone*), which he sighted when expected after discovering that his lunar observations "agreed within five miles of [his position] by dead reckoning." It was during this passage that Slocum, not believing his position according to the mathematical tables, discovered and corrected an error in the tables. At this point in *Sailing Alone*, Slocum devoted nearly three pages to his methods of navigation, noting with pride that "even expert lunarians are considered as doing clever work when they average within eight miles of the truth." He also explained how he found longitude "independent of chronometers" using lunars—a navigator's alchemy that yielded only to select practitioners.

Slocum did not stop at Nuku Hiva. He had established a pleasant routine, reading books, enjoying meals of salt cod, potatoes, and biscuits, and tracking his progress across the chart as the *Spray* steered herself to the next destination, Samoa. Driven by east or southeasterly trade winds, Slocum arrived there on July 16, 1896, 72 days after departing Juan Fernández. At Apia, he visited the home of the late Robert Louis Stevenson but, fearing it would be presumptuous, demurred when Stevenson's stepson invited him to write letters at the great storyteller's desk. He did, however, accept a sailing directory of the Indian Ocean from the author's widow, Fanny. Slocum rowed Fanny out to the *Spray* in his half-dory, although their combined weight lowered that rather miserable little boat's gunwale almost to the water.

Slocum spent just over a month at Samoa, making friends and delving into a culture that didn't revolve entirely around money. He sold the last of his tallow to a German soap maker, putting some cash in his kitty. Weighing anchor on August 20, however, he was unexpectedly overcome by "a sense of loneliness … and as a remedy for it I crowded on sail for lovely Australia."

An increase in trade wind strength forced him down to a triple-reefed mainsail as Samoa dropped astern. The *Spray* covered 184 miles on the first day out, though Slocum attributed 40 miles of that to a favorable current. He considered 145 miles to be a good day's run—an average of about 5.2 knots. Sometimes progress was slower, but sometimes the *Spray* did much better, not infrequently averaging 6½ knots noon to noon. She may not have been a thoroughbred, but she was no farm horse either.[1]

Slocum's original plan for Australia was to touch first at Brisbane. He told a reporter for the *Maryborough Chronicle*, "I wished very much to see Queensland for one thing because I read somewhere that it has no public debt. I wanted to see a country that was in that position." He would indeed visit Queensland—where he would learn that he was mistaken about its

---

[1] Based on his long experience in cruising sailboats, Roger Taylor said of the *Spray*, "I don't think a Westsail [a 32-foot full-keeled fiberglass cruising boat manufactured in the 1970s and credited with numerous ocean voyages] or a Tahiti ketch [a seaworthy double-ended ketch designed by John Hanna in 1935 and popular among long-distance cruising sailors] would be generally as fast as the *Spray*. A modern, lighter-displacement boat—like the 39-foot Bill Garden–designed double-ender *Moonshine* that Francis Stokes sailed in one of the round-the-world races—would be quite a lot faster than the *Spray*. A modern production cruiser like a Beneteau would likewise be faster until the crew got so beat up by her motion that they couldn't sail her anymore."

lack of debt—but his landing there had to be postponed because, off Cape Moreton, he failed in his effort to secure a tow from the pilot steamer. Light wind and a south-setting current having stymied his approach, he headed south toward Sydney instead. Forty days out from Samoa in deteriorating conditions, the *Spray* encountered heavy weather off Newcastle, and Slocum was happy to accept a tow by the government tugboat *Ganymede*. At 6 a.m. on September 29, the *Spray*, the now famous sloop from Boston bound around the world, was secured to a quarantine buoy.

Word spread quickly through Newcastle, and Slocum's warm reception included visits by the U.S. consul, the city mayor, and the harbormaster. He breakfasted with the harbor pilot, and when *The Newscastle Morning Herald and Miner Advocate* sent a reporter down to visit, the captain was welcoming. He told of building the *Spray* and pointed out that one of his water casks was still full of fresh water taken aboard in Yarmouth. Almost inevitably, Slocum gave his age incorrectly, stating that he was 51 rather than 52.

He was big news in Australia, but, as he rested in Newcastle and put the *Spray* in order after her long journey, Slocum learned that not all the news was good. Henry Slater, Slocum's mate aboard the *Northern Light* 13 years earlier, had moved to Sydney, and as word about the *Spray's* voyage captured the public's imagination, Slater began doing everything he could to besmirch his former captain. The *Sydney Daily Telegraph* was all too receptive to Slater's story, which it printed at length without first seeking to verify Slater's charges, review court documents from the trial or American newspaper coverage, or get Slocum's response.

Recognizing the need to rebut Slater, Slocum soon departed for Sydney. While being towed out of Newcastle Harbour, he was struck on the head by a heavy line, probably the heaving line attached to the tugboat's hawser. Although he didn't mention the incident in *Sailing Alone*, he was seriously worried that he might become incapacitated by the blow, and years later he would briefly wonder if it might have caused lingering problems. Nothing in his subsequent behavior or physical or mental abilities suggests this to have been the case, however.

Although Slocum wrote that he arrived in Sydney on October 10, he actually arrived on the afternoon of October 8, choosing to anchor in Manly, a secluded but comfortable spot in "North Harbour," the far northern portion of Sydney's sprawling waterfront. The next morning he was awakened by a reporter from *The Sydney Morning Herald*, who asked for an interview.

Slocum agreed. He was clearly still worried about the blow from the

Perhaps the most iconic of Spray photographs, this image was made at some time after Slocum's arrival in Sydney. Slocum seldom used his mizzen lugsail, but here he has everything up and pulling. The main is beautifully full as Slocum liked, for he knew that a full sail, not overtrimmed, was the best way to get the most out of his boat. The Spray sailed with modest heel and left an impressively smooth wake. (Courtesy the New Bedford Whaling Museum)

heaving line, for he mentioned it to the reporter while adding that he was feeling better. The reporter wrote, "Captain Slocum is an unpretentious man in both his style of address and his appearance and certainly not a man who would be suspected of a desire to traverse the ocean alone." When the reporter asked Slocum why he was sailing solo, he gave his stock answer: "Because my wife would not come with me." This seemingly lighthearted response may well have masked a resentment toward Hettie, but he had to know he was being unrealistic. Hettie wasn't Virginia. Nobody was. For her part, back in East Boston and looking after Garfield and Jessie, Hettie had her own reasons for resentment.

Slocum also told the reporter that his first visitors had been the New South Wales police, although he didn't say why. In *Sailing Alone*, Slocum noted that he "came to in a snug cove near Manly for the night, the Sydney harbor police-boat giving me a pluck into anchorage while they gathered data from an old scrap-book of mine, which seemed to interest them.... They made a shrewd guess that I could give them some useful information, and they were the first to meet me. Some one said they came to arrest me and—well, let it go at that."

Despite the vitriol and negative publicity spread by Henry Slater, Joshua Slocum had many fans in Sydney, and a welcoming committee had formed to greet the *Spray*'s arrival with appropriate ceremony. The committee chartered a steamboat named the *Minerva* so that all those who wished to welcome Slocum at Manly would have the opportunity. Among the 130 people aboard the *Minerva* were Virginia's sister Jessie and her sister-in-law, the wife of her brother George Walker, who had sailed with Virginia and Joshua to San Francisco and Alaska. When the *Minerva* reached the *Spray*, the two women were rowed over so they could have a few private minutes with Slocum. The three of them then returned to the *Minerva*, where Slocum received enthusiastic cheers.

The *Sydney Morning Herald* reported on Monday, October 12, that the welcoming committee "thought they were entitled to greet Capt. Slocum in this manner as a yachtsman and as an intrepid navigator who had achieved the feat of traveling round the world alone ... a task that not one of a million could accomplish.... A telescope and a badge were then presented to the captain amidst a considerable amount of enthusiasm." The only regret expressed was that Slocum had used his time at Newcastle to put the *Spray* "into exhibition order. It would probably have interested the company more to see the yawl in her weather torn condition, with the full traces remaining of her perilous travels."

The *Minerva* took the *Spray* in tow so she could be seen at several points around Sydney Harbour and by as many of Sydney's boat-crazy sailors as possible. Slocum, meanwhile, took careful note of the Aussie boats, observing that the "typical Sydney boat is a handy sloop of great beam and enormous sail carrying power.... Everybody owned a boat." It was a sunny, beautiful afternoon, and the *Spray* drew a lot of attention. A photograph taken that day during a stop at Shell Cove shows the *Spray* with several well-dressed visitors aboard and fashionable homes and manicured gardens in the background. Four rowing craft with curious onlookers are close by, and a big American flag waves in a gentle breeze from the *Spray's* mizzenmast.

But Slater's campaign did have an effect. When the *Minerva* arrived on the waterfront at Balmain, a suburb about 5 miles west of downtown Sydney, the committeeman on the bridge shouted, "'[H]ow then, Balmain people, three cheers for Captain Slocum.' This forcible appeal was answered by some hostile display, although some ... waved their hats. Another appeal only produced additional boohooing and although the receptionists on the *Minerva* lustily cheered at the same time, they were not of sufficient strength to outweigh the hostile demonstration."

Considering Henry Slater's disavowal in New York of what he called his attorney's unauthorized plans to further pursue Slocum after the judgment against him, his renewed prosecution of alleged past mistreatment may have taken Joshua aback. But Slater's allegations, belligerence, and threatening attitude induced Slocum to ask that a case against Slater be heard promptly in the Water Police Court. There a combative Slater lied in testimony, claiming he had not publicly threatened Slocum when, in fact, a Sydney detective and Slocum's own brother-in-law George Walker, who happened to be the court clerk, had been among those who heard him.

After listening to all sides, the magistrate ordered Slater to "keep the peace" for six months, by which time Slocum presumably would be gone, and to pay 80 pounds as a security deposit to ensure that he did so. While Slater continued making defamatory statements, the *Sydney Morning Telegraph* now reported Slocum's side of the story: "American papers go to support the captain's contention that Slater, and not he, was in fault in the trouble that took place on board the *Northern Light*.... [Slocum] readily admits that the American courts fined him $500 for his action in regard to Slater, the whole of which his underwriters paid; but he urges that the judge summed up in his favor when placing the case before the jury, and expressed the belief that he (Captain Slocum) did not act with malice or with motives of revenge, but was actuated merely by a desire to maintain discipline and to bring his ship safely into port. Copious extracts from newspapers published in America at that time to a large extent support Captain Slocum's statements."

Slocum put the matter behind him and began enjoying himself. In *Sailing Alone* he wrote, "Time flew fast those days in Australia." Sociable and outgoing as always, the captain welcomed many visitors aboard the *Spray* at one or another of its anchorages. Among them was Sydney department store owner and yachtsman Mark Foy,[1] who saw the condition of the *Spray's* sails and promptly paid for new ones. Slocum neatly folded the old canvas and stowed it in the hold, where it was joined by a handsome, varnished steering wheel given him as a keepsake.[2]

Two months after his arrival in North Harbour, Joshua Slocum sailed from Sydney on December 6, 1896. "My intention," he wrote, "was now to sail around Cape Leeuwin direct for Mauritius on my way home, and so I coasted along toward Bass Strait in that direction." He had rough sailing down to Cape Bundooro (Green Cape), and, after taking shelter along the way, sailed into Melbourne on December 23 and was towed up the River Yarra to the inner harbor by the steam tug *Racer*. Melbourne was the only port other than Pernambuco where the custom house charged Slocum tonnage dues despite his yacht license, but he recovered the six shillings and sixpence by charging visitors to come aboard. He also killed a 12½-foot shark, stuffed it with hay, and charged visitors to see it.

Southwest winds kept the *Spray* in port until January 24, 1897. Then Slocum got a tow back to sea, where, because of reports of ice and bad weather, he changed his plans. Instead of embarking on the long slog to Cape Leeuwin—Australia's southwest corner—he decided to cross the notorious Bass Strait to Tasmania instead. He faced rough seas in Hobsons Bay after leaving Melbourne but made the crossing to Tasmania in a few hours with "the wind being fair and blowing hard." Slocum's destination was Launceston, Tasmania's only inland city. Founded in 1806 and named for Launceston in Cornwall, it lies at the head of the Tamar River. Slocum's only comment about the 43-mile passage upriver was that "the tide driven in by

---

1 The store built by Mark Foy and his brother is now home to the New South Wales Supreme Court.
2 Slocum gave this wheel to his Martha's Vineyard friend, Captain Ernest Dean, who later presented it to the Boston Yacht Club, where it still resides. Although the brass plaque on the wheel suggests it was used on the *Spray*, there is neither pictorial evidence nor a statement from Slocum to back up such a claim. It was, essentially, a souvenir given to Slocum that he carried home with him.

DRAWN BY GEORGE VARIAN, FROM A PHOTOGRAPH.

The Spray *carried a long oar that offered Slocum enough leverage to maneuver his boat for short distances in harbor. This illustration from* Sailing Alone *shows Slocum working the* Spray *in Melbourne.*

the gale that brought her up the river was unusually high."

He secured his boat alongside a small jetty, where she lay high and dry after the wind-driven tide ebbed. When it came time to depart a week later, Slocum would need to dig a trench under the *Spray's* keel to refloat her. In the meantime, leaving his boat in the care of local children, he set off to explore. He "made journeys among the hills and rested my bones, for the coming voyage, on the moss-covered rocks at the gorge hard by, and among the ferns I found wherever I went."

"The Spray was berthed on the beach at a small jetty at Launceston," Slocum wrote in Sailing Alone. *It was there on the Tamar River that Slocum left his boat covered up and watched over by local children while he relaxed and explored ashore. This photo, probably taken in late January 1897, shows the Spray's bottom and rudder better than any other. The planking is smooth and fair with no fouling. A noticeable chunk appears to have been gouged out of the stem. The small shark that Slocum caught and then stuffed with hay hangs off the bow. A slender canoe is lashed to the rail. The photo was made by William Edward Masters, a solicitor (lawyer) and photography enthusiast. (Courtesy the Tasmanian Archive and Heritage Office)*

Thus began Joshua Slocum's pleasant interlude in Tasmania. From Launceston, he sailed back down the Tamar to Beauty Point, Georgetown, and then back to sea for a brief passage west to the Mersey River and Devonport on February 22. He wrote that the *Spray* was the first American-flagged vessel to visit the growing port. Word of his arrival had preceded him, and the local newspaper reported that "the beaches at Devonport were fairly lined by persons waiting to catch a glimpse of the tiny boat and its intrepid commander."

Slocum was glad to arrive at Devonport. He'd had "a slight accident on the run down. The *Spray* was going too close to some rocks and in making a rapid movement forward, he hurt one of his ribs rather badly," the newspaper reported. At Devonport, the *Spray* was hauled on a marine railway for refitting.

After arriving at Devonport, Tasmania, on February 22, 1897, the Spray was hauled. Some damage to her bottom was repaired and a new coat of Tarr and Wonson bottom paint was applied. The difference in waterlines from one side of the boat to the other suggests the photo was made before coating of the starboard bottom was completed. (Photo by W. Aikenhead; courtesy the New Bedford Whaling Museum)

Her bottom was closely inspected, and the Tarr and Wonson copper paint was found to have been highly effective, having allowed no growth and no worms. A fresh coat was applied to protect the *Spray* in the months ahead. Despite all that Slocum had endured on his voyage thus far, he had never thought of giving up on his grand plan to sail around the world until now. He was so "haunted" by the beauty of the country that he wrote, "If there was a moment in my voyage when I could have given it up, it was there and then."

But he was not going to quit until he completed what he'd set out to do. He must have asked himself, too, the same question he would confront after finishing the voyage: "If I stay here, what next?" It was in Devonport that he began, with considerable nervousness, to give lectures about his trip. On February 25, the local paper reported, "There was a fair attendance at the Formby Hall last evening when a lantern exhibition[1] was given by Captain Slocum of the sloop *Spray*. The venturesome skipper took his audience from Boston to Devonport, but did not deal very minutely with his voyage."

Slocum's Devonport presentation, augmented with "musical sketches" (piano and song) by local residents Mr. and Mrs. Frank Beverley, marked the start of his career as a presenter. He would eventually develop himself into a polished speaker but would always experience stage fright. When he wrote *Sailing Alone*, he noted that "I am not yet entirely cured." Apart from a single comment on the quality of a "magic lantern," which used an oil lamp rather than electricity as an illumination source, Slocum shared nothing about his photographic experience, never remarking on when or where his own pictures were developed or about photos he purchased to augment his talks.

On April 16, 1867, Slocum departed Devonport and sailed back to Sydney, arriving there on April 22 and anchoring in Watsons Bay, just south of Sydney Harbour. He was still not feeling entirely himself, writing that he was "nursing a neuralgia," normally associated with nerve pain in the face or neck. It was severe enough that he took a room ashore in a waterfront hotel, possibly either the Royal Hotel or the Palace Hotel. Both enjoyed prime locations overlooking the bay, with an ocean beach behind them.

Slocum was resting in his hotel when a bellboy arrived to tell him that

---

1 Lantern slides were the first way for photographers to share their work with a group. Manufacturers made kits available so that the photographer could convert a contact print of a photo into a glass slide. The slide could then be projected by a "magic lantern," the slide projector of that era. This feature of Slocum's talks would have put him on the cutting edge of the day's technology and would have been an important drawing card.

a steamship had collided with the *Spray*. Fortunately this was an overstate-ment, the only damage having been the loss of the anchor and chain, which were promptly replaced by the steamship skipper with an added 12 pounds in currency for what today might be termed "mental anguish." Noting that his lucky number was 13,[1] Slocum asked that the amount be adjusted up, and it was. In 1983, the Sydney Maritime Museum issued a challenge to local divers "to find the great Joshua Slocum's missing anchor" in Watsons Bay, but the anchor was not found.

Slocum had returned to Sydney because he had decided to forgo Aus-tralia's south coast altogether, instead planning to sail north to the Great Barrier Reef and the Torres Strait. Departing Sydney for the last time on May 9, he made his way back north past Newcastle, Port Stevens, Port Mac-quarie, and, on May 19, the Tweed River, at last rounding Great Sandy Cape and setting a northwesterly course that would lead him inside the Great Barrier Reef. "The *Spray* was now in protected sea and smooth water, the first she had dipped her keel into since leaving Gibraltar, and a change it was from the heaving of the misnamed 'Pacific' Ocean."

Although he was inside the reef, there could be no relaxation of look-out. "The sea itself might be called smooth indeed," Slocum wrote in *Sailing Alone*, "but coral rocks are always rough, sharp, and dangerous. I trusted now to the mercies of the Maker of all reefs, keeping a good lookout at the same time for perils on every hand." Despite the dangers, he delighted in "[w]aters of many colors, studded all about with enchanted islands."

He now considered himself homeward bound. He was in no hurry, but, as always, paid careful attention to his towed patent log, noting that the *Spray* was covering 110 miles daily. He anchored in the lovely bay at Port Denison on May 26, and soon enough, met seemingly everyone in town. The local magistrate convinced him to give one of his lantern-slide lectures on the second evening after his arrival, and it was well received.

Slocum headed next for Cooktown, sailing day and night with the help of his fine Admiralty charts. He had a fair wind and good weather and wrote that "the way through the Barrier Reef Channel, in all sincerity, was clearer than a highway in a busy city, and by all odds, less dangerous."

It was at this point in *Sailing Alone* that Slocum hinted at what hard work it had been for him to repeatedly raise and lower the *Spray*'s mainsail

---

1 Slocum was referring to the total of 13 men aboard the *Destroyer* when he and his crew had somehow avoiding sinking during their dreadful voyage.

during his ordeal in the Strait of Magellan. Now he avoided this task by the simple expedient of sailing through the night. He wrote: "The hard work, too, of getting the sloop under way every morning was finished."

Slocum reached Cooktown on May 31, 1897, a Monday. In *Sailing Alone*, he wrote that when he had been in Cooktown at least 31 years earlier during his near-fatal voyage on the *Tanjore*, he had been too ill to explore. Now he took the opportunity to visit the monument to Captain Cook. He also answered questions at an impromptu get-together at the Presbyterian Church.

He sailed from Cooktown on June 6, continuing his tactic of sailing through the night. On the night of June 8, after leaving the M Reef lightship astern, the *Spray*, "going at full speed … hit the M Reef itself on the north end, where I expected to see a beacon."[2] Had the beacon been operating, Slocum certainly would have seen it. In its absence, "Slocum's luck" saved him once more:

> She swung off quickly on her heel, however, and with one more bound a swell cut across the shoal point so quickly that I hardly knew how it was done…. I saw the ugly boulders under the sloop's keel as she flashed over them, and I made a mental note of it that the letter M, for which the reef was named, was the thirteenth one in our alphabet, and that thirteen, as noted years before was still my lucky number.

Slocum's next destination was Cape Grenville, well to the north. "The natives of Cape Greenville [sic] are notoriously bad, and I was advised to give them the go-by. Accordingly, from M Reef I steered outside the adjacent islands, to be on the safe side."[3] He stopped at Thursday Island where, on June 22, Queen Victoria's Diamond Jubilee was celebrated. Slocum ended his pleasant stay among the Torres Strait islands on June 24, and "the *Spray*,

---

2 What Slocum called "M Reef" was known officially in the *Australia Coast Pilot* as "emm (m) reef" and was described thusly: "2¼ miles long and one mile broad, lies two-thirds of a mile north of the north-west end of the E11 reef, with a channel between. On the north-west end is a sandbank which dries 6 feet and is 6½ miles, 174° true, from the extreme east end of Cape Grenville. The reef dries at low water. A patch of coral lies 2¼ miles, 65° true from emm reef beacon." As for the beacon that was missing at the time of Slocum's passage: "A square black beacon stands a quarter of a mile within the north-west end of emm reef, at 2 cables from the western edge." Emm Reef was later renamed Martin Reef, and E11 was renamed Linnet Reef.

3 These would have been seven small islands known collectively as the Home Islands. By the time the *Australian Coast Pilot Vol. IV* was published in 1917, the Cape Grenvillers were said to be friendly.

well fitted in every way, sailed on the long voyage ahead down the Indian Ocean."

Slocum was passing through the same waters he had known on the steamship *Soushay* so many years earlier. Recalling the time of his fever, he remembered Captain Airy and stopping at Booby Island. But the Joshua Slocum now sailing through the Arafura Sea was a far different man from the youngster he'd once been in these waters. He had a deep appreciation, as always, for the beauty of his sea world, noting that the *Spray* "sailed in water milky white and green and purple." On June 25, at last, the *Spray* cleared the Torres Strait and had only deep water before her.

To speed the voyage home, Slocum broke out the new flying jib he'd had made at Juan Fernández, setting it as a spinnaker poled out with a length of bamboo given him by Fanny Stevenson. As always, he maintained his meticulous log-keeping. The *Spray* covered 130 miles on June 26 after correcting for leeway—which he called "slip"—and current. He took noon sights and "sailed west on the parallel of 10 degrees 25 minutes south, as true as a hair."

On July 2 he sighted Timor, and on the 11th, his spinnaker still pulling, he raised Christmas Island on the *Spray*'s starboard bow. Perhaps remarking to himself how a boy from Brier Island, Nova Scotia, had come to be sailing across the Indian Ocean with sailing directions once owned by Robert Louis Stevenson, Slocum also recalled his first sight of Christmas Island years earlier. Then, sailing east aboard the *Tanjore*, he had been impressed by Captain Martin's navigation. Now a great navigator himself, Slocum set his course for Keeling Cocos Island, a dot in the Indian Ocean 550 miles to the southwest. Keeling Cocos is the main island in the 24-islet South Keeling archipelago of what is today simply the Cocos Islands.

In *Sailing Alone*, Joshua gave readers another example of his sailor's weather eye. Several hundred miles out from Christmas Island, "I saw antitrade clouds flying up from the southwest very high over the regular winds, which weakened now for a few days, while a swell heavier than usual set in also from the southwest. A winter gale was going on in the direction of the Cape of Good Hope. Accordingly, I steered high to windward, allowing twenty miles a day while this went on, for a change of current; and it was not too much."

His course allowances and ongoing navigation paid off when he spotted Keeling Cocos right on the *Spray*'s bow, having been forewarned by the appearance of white terns from the island that, he wrote, the islanders called "the pilot of Keeling Cocos." "[T]he sloop found herself at the end of the run absolutely in the fairway of the channel. You couldn't have beaten it in the navy!" Slocum anchored on the afternoon of July 17, 1897, after a passage of 2,700 miles and 23 days, an average of around 117 miles per day, the *Spray* doing about 5 knots. He had spent only three hours at the helm.

During this long Indian Ocean passage, the world lost track of Joshua Slocum. It is not entirely clear if he was still sending, or intending to send, his letters to the several newspapers that had initially indicated interest, but he may well have stopped. In an August 29 story that was partly truth but mostly fiction, the *Boston Journal* claimed that nothing had been heard from the "Pooh-bah of the seas" since November 1896. The headline was: "Capt. Joshua Slocum, the Missing Mariner, May Be in the Antarctic." The long article claimed that Slocum had been in San Francisco in April 1897, when the *Spray* was in Tasmania and Australia.

In New York, editor Joseph Gilder of *The Critic* had also lost track of Slocum. He read a *New York Times* article on September 22 claiming that Slocum had arrived in Mauritius and given up his voyage. The same article erroneously reported that Slocum had stopped in Yokohama, Japan, a year earlier and had been attacked by pirates off the coast of Japan.

With no better way to check, Gilder contacted the lone voyager's attorneys, but they hadn't heard from him for months, either. In fact, Slocum had written a letter to Gilder, but Gilder had no way of knowing. Nor did Slocum have a way to immediately post the letter. On August 20, 1897, a little over a month after his arrival at Cocos and 28 months into his voyage, Slocum wrote to Gilder noting that the *Spray* was "tied to a palm tree at Keeling-Cocos Islands.... Perhaps you did not expect to get a letter from this little kingdom in the sea." After describing at some length his navigation successes, and thinking of what he might do post-voyage, Slocum shared his idea for a "college ship ... to teach young people in the science of Nautical Astronomy."

Gilder didn't receive Slocum's the letter until November 3.[1] By then, however, the story about the *Spray*'s loss had been proved incorrect when, on September 21, 1897, the *New York Evening Post* reported that Slocum and his "Little Sloop" had arrived at Port Louis, Mauritius, some 2,600 miles from Cape Town. A half-world away from the *Spray*, Joseph Gilder read with in-

---

1 According to Walter Teller who, in 1953, had acquired the Slocum letter written at Keeling Cocos, it was postmarked Batavia (now Jakarta), 29 September 1897. Quite possibly, Slocum wrote the letter when a steamship headed east stopped at Keeling Cocos and could mail it for him at the first opportunity.

CHAPTER 17

Around and Home

"To succeed, however, in anything at all, one should go understandingly about his work and be prepared for every emergency."

—Joshua Slocum, *Sailing Alone Around the World*

ACCORDING TO JOSHUA SLOCUM, his around-the-world voyage and his life might well have ended at the "paradise on earth" that was Keeling Cocos. It was there that he accepted the offer of a ride across the island's lagoon in a rickety skiff owned by a man he called "a thoughtless African negro." The boat carried no oars or paddle, and when a sudden squall blew the sail to tatters, Slocum and his companion found themselves being carried out to sea. "There was an anchor to be sure, but not enough rope to tie a cat." Fortunately there was a push-pole aboard, and by paddling desperately with it, Slocum, thanks to "the merest accidental flaw in the wind," managed to get back to shore.

His interest in exploring the lagoon arose from a desire to load a quantity of exotic tridacna shells—giant clams with shells as large as four feet across and weighing up to 500 pounds—that he was confident of selling as curios upon getting home. He eventually loaded 30 of them into the *Spray*,

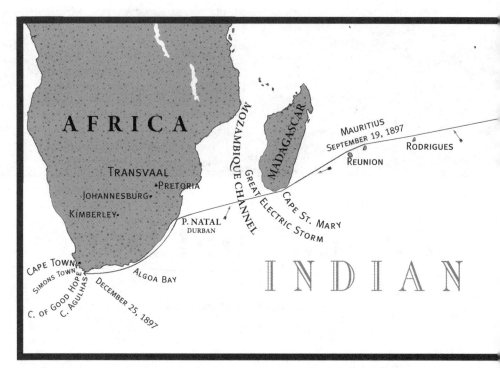

removing three tons of cement ballast to compensate for their weight.

By August 22, just over a month after his arrival at the group of two atolls and 27 coral islets, Slocum had his boat ready for sea. Conditions were rough and windy as he guided the *Spray* past the island's reef and set his course for Rodrigues Island (which he spelled Rodriguez), a speck in the Indian Ocean east of Mauritius, 1,900 miles away.

In *Sailing Alone*, Slocum gave his course to Rodrigues in points of the compass, as was common then: "The true course for the island was west by south, one quarter south … but I steered considerably to windward of that to allow for the heave of the sea and other leeward effects."[1] Slocum wrote that he sailed for days on his course with sails reefed in an uncomfortable beam sea.

He had long since developed an instinct for how fast and how far the *Spray* traveled each day, and on the passage to Rodrigues he began to feel a discrepancy between his own senses and what the dial of his taffrail log was

---

1 There are 32 points in a compass—eight points between each cardinal direction (north, east, south, or west)—and 11¼ degrees in each point. Thus, "west by south, one quarter south" is equivalent to 270 degrees minus 11¼ degrees, minus another quarter point or just under 3 degrees—or 256 degrees, more or less, on a modern compass card.

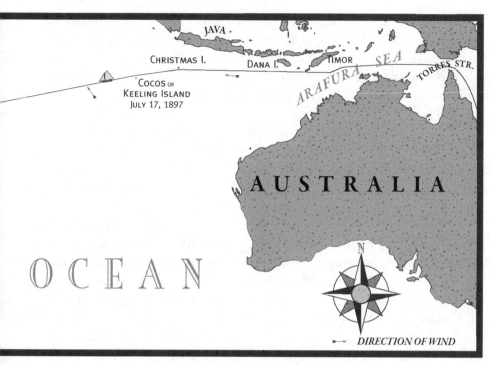

The Spray's *course across the Indian Ocean from Australia to South Africa.*

reading. After hauling in the rotator, he found that "two of the four blades of the rotator were crushed or bent, the work probably of a shark." His internal knotmeter told him he was 150 miles ahead of what the log was indicating, and he raised Rodrigues as anticipated 15 days after departing Keeling Cocos.

At Rodrigues, Slocum replenished his larder with beef, sweet potatoes, and pomegranates and filled his water casks with "pure and wholesome water" piped from a reservoir in the island's hills right to the jetty. The *Spray* remained at the island for eight days, then sailed for Mauritius (like Rodrigues, a British colony until 1968) carrying mail from Rodrigues and letters of introduction. At Mauritius, on two stifling nights, he brought in some cash by recounting his voyage to a crowd assembled in the opera house. Later he spoke at the Royal College.

He also took a party of island girls for a sail, going 15 miles out in rough seas and expecting his guests to become seasick and fearful. The opposite was the case. The girls had a wonderful time, even requesting, after returning, that the *Spray* be anchored near shore so they could go for a swim. Ever anxious to have witnesses to the *Spray's* self-steering ability, Slocum demonstrated it.

In a post-voyage letter written to Clarence Buel at *The Century* magazine, Slocum noted "that the seven ladies sailing on the *Spray* off Mauritius saw her come in on the home stretch with a fair wind and almost as straight as an arrow while the helm was lashed." The group stayed aboard for the night, dining on a big basket of provisions they had brought. Slocum was impressed.

The *Spray* had arrived at Mauritius on September 19, and Slocum stayed more than a month, waiting until the weather off the Cape of Good Hope could be expected to be most favorable. He departed on October 26, 1897, and found light winds until running into a four-day gale in the Mozambique Channel that began on November 6.

Slocum arrived in Durban on November 17 in yet another gale, and was led into port by a pilot tug. The local paper remarked on his skillful management of the *Spray*, but there were skeptics, as always, insisting that it would take three men to operate the boat and asking where the remaining crewmembers were hidden. In Durban's Hotel Royal, Slocum was introduced to the famous Welsh-born journalist and explorer of Africa Henry Morton Stanley. Stanley asked Slocum whether the *Spray* had watertight bulkheads and what would happen if a swordfish attacked and pierced the hull.

On December 14, Slocum departed Durban for Cape Town. It was a rough trip. Slocum wrote that at no time before or after had he been ducked more than once while on the bowsprit reefing the jib, but on Christmas Day 1897, the *Spray* ducked him three times. If he thought about the terrible storm that had caused so much damage to the *Northern Light* off South Africa, he didn't mention it in *Sailing Alone*. But once he had weathered the Cape of Good Hope in January and entered Cape Town's Alfred Dry-docks, he wrote, "The voyage then seemed as good as finished; from this time on I knew that all, or nearly all would be plain sailing."

At Cape Town he presented his illustrated lecture to an array of groups, and on March 2, he spoke at the Normal College in a presentation described in local press as follows: "He first, on a large map of the world, pointed out the route he had followed, and then proceeded to exhibit a large number of excellent Lantern Slides. The large audience was thoroughly appreciative, and heartily enjoyed and as heartily cheered the successive views and the Captain's descriptions—at once humorous, caustic and racy."

Thanks to a railroad pass given him by the government, he was able to travel about South Africa. Having encountered in Durban three Boers who insisted that the world was as flat as a Mercator projection map, Slocum now had the same experience in Pretoria, where he met Paul Kruger, the Boer president of the Transvaal Province. Kruger insisted that the world was flat and that it was "impossible" to sail "around" it.

In *Sailing Alone*, Slocum claimed that "the incident pleased me more than anything else that could have happened." He had read some of Kruger's pronouncements—such as "Dynamite is the corner-stone of the South African Republic"—and could now add his own experience to his picture of an ignorant but entertaining statesman. The encounter made the newspaper, though. On March 5, 1898, the Cape Town *Owl* published a cartoon entitled "The World According to Kruger." It showed Kruger sitting on a map, studying a book, probably his bible, and puffing a pipe. In the smoke emitted from the pipe was printed the word "ignorance." Slocum included the cartoon in *Sailing Alone*.

In South Africa, Slocum added Zulu assegai (light spears) to the spears and boomerangs acquired in Australia. Sailing from Cape Town on March 26, 1898, he found a southeast breeze on his second day at sea that sent the *Spray* homeward bound at 150 miles per day. He ran for days under single-reefed main, jib, and flying jib, finding the island of St. Helena, in the mid-South Atlantic, 20 miles ahead at twilight on April 11. He celebrated with "a long pull" from a bottle of port, and the *St. Helena Guardian* announced his arrival in an article in its April 14, 1898 edition.

There were still those in the United States who believed that Joshua Slocum must have been lost on his foolhardy voyage, but the U.S. consul at St. Helena, Robert P. Pooley, sent a dispatch to Washington announcing the *Spray*'s arrival. The news found its way into papers across the country. On May 21, 1898, the *Milwaukee Journal* ran a brief story with the subhead "Boston Man's Long Cruise Alone in a Small Yacht." The article read, in part, that "the news of his arrival at St. Helena will be welcomed by those who mourned him as dead. Consul Pooley's message seems to indicate that both the captain and his frail little boat have weathered many storms and tempests in the long voyage."

Slocum gave lectures and was feted at St. Helena, and he visited Longwood, where Napoleon had died in exile. Upon departing on April 20, he carried mail for Ascension Island—800 miles northwest—and gifts including a bag of coffee, a goat, and a lamb. The lamb promptly jumped overboard and drowned. The goat, once it got its sea legs, proved a terrible shipmate but provided two of the most humorous paragraphs in *Sailing Alone*.

Slocum discovered too late that no ropes aboard could secure the animal,

for it simply ate them. "Next the goat devoured my straw hat, and so, when I arrived in port I had nothing to wear ashore on my head." The goat also ate Slocum's chart of the West Indies, which he would soon need. The only animal that ever proved a good shipmate on the *Spray* was a spider that had come aboard in Boston. A tree crab from Keeling Cocos had shredded Slocum's foul-weather jacket before "finally threatening my life in the dark." A centipede had bitten his scalp, and two rats had tormented him, one of which he captured, while the other escaped.

He off-loaded the goat along with the mail at Ascension, and after

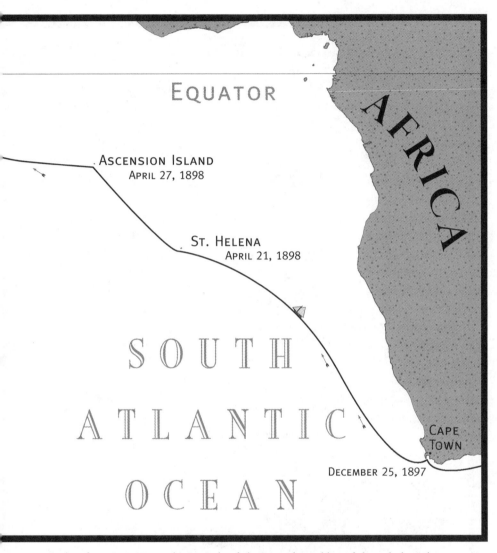

EQUATOR

ASCENSION ISLAND
APRIL 27, 1898

AFRICA

ST. HELENA
APRIL 21, 1898

SOUTH

ATLANTIC

OCEAN

CAPE
TOWN
DECEMBER 25, 1897

Sailing from Cape Town, the Spray *heads homeward, northbound through the Atlantic.*

acquiring a certificate attesting that nobody was sailing with him, put to sea once again on April 30. On May 8, 1898, on course for South America, Slocum crossed his southbound track of October 2, 1895. "I felt contentment in knowing that the *Spray* had encircled the globe, and even as an adventure alone I was in no way discouraged as to its utility, and said to myself, 'Let what will happen, the voyage is now on record.' A period was made."

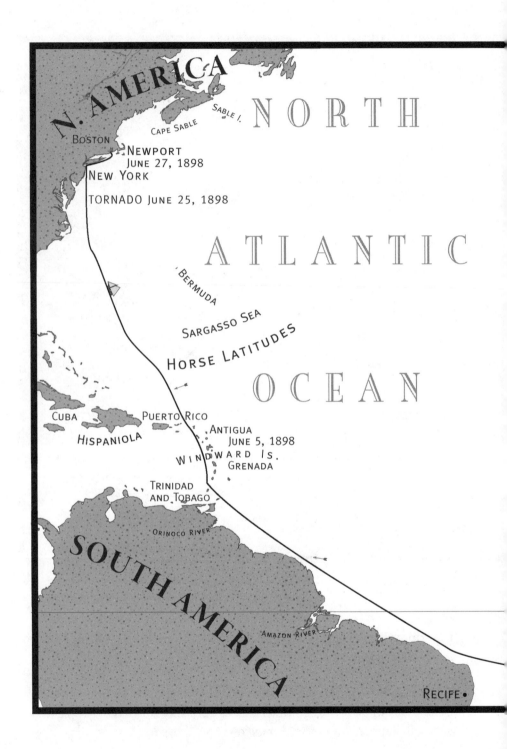

N. AMERICA

NORTH

SABLE I.

CAPE SABLE

BOSTON

NEWPORT
JUNE 27, 1898

NEW YORK

TORNADO JUNE 25, 1898

ATLANTIC

BERMUDA

SARGASSO SEA

HORSE LATITUDES

OCEAN

CUBA

PUERTO RICO

HISPANIOLA

ANTIGUA
JUNE 5, 1898

WINDWARD IS.
GRENADA

TRINIDAD
AND TOBAGO

ORINOCO RIVER

SOUTH AMERICA

AMAZON RIVER

RECIFE •

AZORES

MADEIRA

CANARY IS.

AN ANTONIO

CAPE VERDE IS.

EUROPE

STRAIT OF GIBRALTAR

AFRICA

EQUATOR

N

ASCENSION I.
APRIL 27, 1898

DIRECTION OF WIND

The last leg of the Spray's circumnavigation, homeward bound.

Joshua Slocum's lifelong study of the sea told him he was off Brazil's
Cape São Roque when he recognized "[s]trange and long-forgotten current
ripples [that] pattered against the sloop's sides in grateful music.... I sat quietly
listening to it while the *Spray* kept on her course." With current adding 40
miles a day to his progress, he was ticking off 180-mile runs. He calculated
that he was near the latitude of the Amazon River when he encountered the
battleship *Oregon* and learned that the United States was at war with Spain.
When the *Oregon* signaled to ask whether Slocum had seen any men-of-war, he
signaled back "No," then followed with flags suggesting, "Let us keep together
for mutual protection."

He passed Devil's Island (Île du Diable), French Guiana, on May 17,
and a day later had cause to lament the loss of his West Indies chart to the
goat. While sailing at night, he was shocked to find the *Spray* heading for
breakers that he seemed unable to escape no matter what direction he
steered. Only after hours of desperation did he recognize that what he was
seeing was not breakers at all, but mere reflections on the sea of the flashes
from Trinidad's lighthouse, 30 miles away. Despite his immense relief, Slocum wrote, "I could have nailed the St. Helena goat's pelt to the deck." An
unhappy stop at Grenada failed to produce a chart, and he didn't anchor
again until he reached St. John, Antigua, where he was welcomed and gave a
talk to a full house. Before he departed, his yacht license was validated one
last time so there could be no doubts that he sailed alone.

The *Spray* endured several more trials before reaching home, the first
of these being the eight days it took to cross the "smooth and monotonous"
sea of the horse latitudes. It was so calm that at night Slocum could read on
deck by the light of a candle. The calm was followed by a gale, during which
both the mainsheet strap and the peak halyard block on the gaff gave way.
Soon after, the jibstay parted.

Slocum repaired the damages and sailed on to the Gulf Stream, where
he was pelted by hailstones. Off Fire Island, New York, he encountered yet
another gale, this one so severe that he lowered his sails and set out his sea
anchor. He watched in some amazement as lightning bolts developed all
around him. At last, with the storm over, he rounded Montauk and headed
for Newport. There he faced the final threat of the voyage in the guise of
newly placed mines.

"The *Spray* hugged the rocks along where neither friend nor foe could
come if drawing much water.... It was close work, but it was safe enough so

Thomas Fogarty's illustration "Storm off New York" evokes the Spray *lying to her sea anchor with sails lowered and lightning flashing, the last ordeal of the voyage.*

long as she hugged the rocks close, and not the mines.... At last she reached port in safety: and there at 1 a.m. on June 27, 1898, cast anchor, after the cruise of more than forty-six thousand miles round the world, during an absence of three years and two months, with two days over for coming up." Slocum said he had gained a pound and felt 10 years younger than when he'd "felled the first tree for the construction of the *Spray*."

IMMEDIATELY UPON HEARING OF Slocum's arrival in Newport, Mabel Wagnalls traveled up from New York to greet him, arriving on June 28. She was among the first well-wishers, if not the first, to sign the *Spray*'s guestbook in Newport. By now, Slocum considered Mabel and her parents to be "old friends," and he had never forgotten her encouragement of his voyage plans at a time when many people were making fun of him.

Since meeting Slocum in New York some 12 years earlier, Mabel had used her social connections and financial means to pursue her many cultural interests. She nurtured friendships with people as diverse as William Sydney Porter (better known to his readers as O'Henry), Harry Houdini, the poet Edwin Markham, and Captain Joshua Slocum. "Because Joshua was close to her father's age," said Wagnalls scholar Carol Gaal, "I think she saw him as a fatherly figure and she respected his hard work and determination to make his dream come true."

When she had visited the *Spray* prior to Slocum's departure, Mabel had given him the books her father had ordered together with a little book she had written herself, *Miserere*, 'a musical story'. It was during this visit, according to Walter Teller, that Mabel Wagnalls "said to the grizzling seafarer, 'The *Spray* will come back.'" Mabel's encouraging statement would, along with her book, play a significant and rather uncomfortable role in the publication of *Sailing Alone Around the World*.

With genuine emotion, Slocum retrieved from the *Spray*'s bookshelves his copy of *Miserere*, which he now autographed and returned to her. His heartfelt inscription encapsulated key events of the voyage. It read:

A thousand thanks: Good wishes are prayers, heard by the angels:
 And so on June 28th 1898 the little book, after making the circuit of the earth in the single handed 'Spray' returns in good order and condition. And it is handed to the author, only on the condition that a copy is put in the Spray Library in its stead.

What ups and down Miserere, you have had, in your rounds! You have been twice through the Straits of Magellan; once off Cape Horn; you have seen Juan Fernandez, St. Helena and many more islands in the sea.

The Cape of Good Hope, called also the 'Cape of Storms' you have weathered unharmed.

Again you have lain quietly in your snug box while the skipper whistled for wind or spent a night on deck in the storm.

For weeks and weeks, again little Book no human voice has stirred the air to vibrate a chord among your leaves, and the only music you heard was the tune of the waves!

You saw the lonely atoll in the midst of the sea where the waves lashing and with eternal roar spent their fury on its trembling rim; which never grew less. Spite of the restless sea it grew more!

You have been read and reread by the captain and the crew of your ship, all rolled into one.

Henceforth little Book you will be in smooth seas while benefited old friend may still sail on.

Farewell, your story was well told! J.S.

New Port 28th June 1898

Also arriving to greet their father were his sons Victor and Garfield. Victor wrote that they "came from Boston at the first tidings of the sloop's arrival in port. My father's first hail was 'Vic, you could have done it,' and looking at me significantly, 'but you would not have been the first.'" Garfield offered no recollection of this visit, but he did indicate that his older brother was "taking care of me" in Canton, Massachusetts, during at least a portion of the time Slocum had been gone.

PERHAPS THE MOST important greeting Slocum received upon his arrival in Newport was not a visitor but a telegram sent on June 30 by Richard Watson Gilder, the 53-year-old younger brother of *The Critic*'s editor, Joseph Gilder. Joseph Gilder had followed with interest Slocum's voyage in the *Spray* and had given careful thought to Slocum's question in the letter written at Keeling Cocos: "Do you think our people will care for a story of the voyage around?"

Although *The Critic* was not an appropriate venue for publishing articles by Joshua Slocum about his voyage, the magazine edited by Gilder's brother Richard most certainly was. Richard Watson Gilder—Civil War veteran, poet, author, the ultimate sort of sophisticated, business-oriented literary man—was editor of *The Century Illustrated Monthly Magazine,* which had long since established itself as one of New York's (and the country's) leading literary publications. It had published works by Jack London and Theodore Roosevelt and had excerpted material from Mark Twain's *Adventures of Huckleberry Finn* and Henry James's *The Bostonians.*

As the magazine's title suggested, articles and stories were supported by illustrations, and these were done by some of the most skilled artists of that era. Indeed, fine illustration was such a stock-in-trade at *The Century* that the magazine would eventually come to be seen as old-fashioned, and its sales would decline as photography became ever more dominant.

How much Joseph Gilder and his brother Richard discussed the article potential of Slocum's voyage is unknown, but on September 22, 1897, the day after Slocum's arrival in Mauritius had been reported, an assistant editor at *The Century* named Clarence Clough Buel wrote Richard Gilder a memo suggesting that Slocum "might be able to make a lively story of his tens of thousands of miles in a forty-foot sloop." Buel had worked for the *New York Tribune* before joining *The Century,* and sailing was among his interests. He had a summer home on Long Island Sound, and his passion for boats would inform his editorial correspondence with Slocum.

Richard Gilder's telegram asked if Slocum would be interested in contributing his story to *The Century* magazine, and Slocum's response was written the same day: "I have a fund of matter to be sure; but have not myself had experience in writing magazine articles—I have very decided literary tastes and could enter into such parts as I am able to with a great deal of energy.... The most interesting and instructive part is never touched by the daily reporters. I am misquoted by them till I am discouraged.... A *thoughtful* magazine article would square me. If it should have some illustration I might help supply them.... I intend, of course, to publish the whole story in book form—if I can't do better."

As any good editor would, Richard Gilder asked Slocum how much he had already published about the voyage. The answer was less than comprehensive. Slocum did not mention his pre-voyage efforts to establish newspaper syndication as a means of earning money, nor did he note the few letters he had sent to the *Boston Globe* and other papers. He told Gilder only that "I have not written for publication more than one or two short letters to the *World* (N.Y.), these I discontinued for my own reasons long ago."[1]

Slocum's disaffection with newspapers in general and the *New York World* in particular seems to have been driven by tardy or skipped payments, demands for more personal details, and rather less interest in the trip itself. Slocum flatly rejected demands to reveal more of himself and his emotions.

Equally important, he felt that he had kept his part of a bargain with Joseph Pulitzer, publisher of the *New York World*. Garfield Slocum well remembered his father's response to Pulitzer, who "had a contract drawn up—he agreed to pay father for writing articles on his voyage and mail to the *World*. When father called for his money, Mr. Pulitzer tried to cheat my father out of a lot of money but father was very much disgusted and angry. He put the case in a lawyer's hands, father won, he got all of the money due him and was so pleased that he had the check photographed and hung up in the *Spray's* cabin."

Whatever Slocum "letters" were published during the voyage proved to be of little concern to Gilder at *The Century*. He and Slocum agreed to terms for the serial publication of the *Spray* story and its subsequent release in book form.

Not long after completing his circum-navigation, Slocum sat for a formal portrait at the Frommell studio in New Bedford. (Courtesy the New Bedford Whaling Museum)

---

1 No *World* clipping has been found.

Though he had arrived safely in Newport, Slocum would not consider the voyage complete until he had sailed the *Spray* up to Fairhaven. In his letter to the Century Company written on June 30, he wrote, "I am waiting at Newport for the fog to lift, when I sail for New Bedford. It may be clear tomorrow or it may be thick for several days here."

It would appear that the fog lifted by July 2 or 3, and when it did, Slocum sailed the *Spray* "home" and moored her in the Acushnet River to the same cedar post he'd used upon launching the boat almost exactly six years earlier. He was visited immediately by a reporter from the *New Bedford Morning Mercury*, which published an article about Slocum on July 4. The captain told the reporter that he "came to Fairhaven to get a little rest and put the *Spray* back as nearly as possible in the same shape she was when she went away and to spend a few days with my Fairhaven friends."

Joshua Slocum told the reporter that "I have made more money than I did when I was sole owner and commander of a little bark…. I am not ashamed to say that when I started my enterprise I had just $1.50 to my name. But instead of giving bottomry bonds[1] on my owners, I have lectured the *Spray* around the world. Anybody in this place who has befriended me need not lie awake for fear of not receiving compensation for I am prepared to pay all my bills with the legal rate of interest."

Slocum showed off his "hold full of curiosities, shells, sea fans, canoes, bamboo sticks" and scrapbooks full of clippings about his voyage and his lectures. Although he never once remarked about his photography, the camera he used, or the processing of his film, Slocum showed the *Morning Mercury* reporter boxes containing 300 lantern slides that he could draw upon for his lectures. As always, he was proud to point out that "[m]y craft does not leak a drop and I have not pumped her out since I was at Australia."

In fact, while the *Spray* was showing signs of wear, she could be methodically brought back to perfect condition. Her rigging could be renewed, her blocks overhauled, her topsides painted, her sails restitched as necessary. A bright new Stars and Stripes could readily be had to snap brightly in the wind from her mizzenmast. But what about Joshua Slocum? It was a question that would, as his post-voyage life moved ahead, begin to nag the aging captain.

---

1 Ever the captain, Slocum here used a term that referred to a ship (its bottom) being the collateral for any loan necessary for repairs.

"This Child of the Sea"

"I can do the work better away where it is quiet."

—Joshua Slocum, August 12, 1899 letter to Robert Underwood Johnson,
associate editor, *The Century Illustrated Monthly Magazine*

BY THE TIME HE RETURNED to Newport in June 1898, Joshua Slocum had
spent the better part of three years alone at sea in a stubborn, existential effort to complete what he had set out to do. Except for interludes at stopping
points along the way, he had lived for 38 months in solitude, his only companions the gracious ghost pilot of the *Pinta*, characters in the books he'd
read, his often painful memories, a spider, two rats, a lamb that jumped
overboard, a goat that ate his chart and hat, wild creatures of the sea, and
pelagic birds soaring overhead.

Now he would need to somehow integrate himself into a shoreside
world in which he had never comfortably fit to begin with. The long voyage
alone had worked on him. According to Garfield Slocum, who would spend
a significant amount of time with his father and Hettie during a roughly

four-year period after the voyage ended, Slocum was a changed man when he returned. "He was so different," Garfield wrote in a 1954 letter to Walter Teller. "He did not talk to me much. He appeared to be deep in thought."

There was a lot to think about, starting with the future. Slocum had never been a man who wasted time, and he knew instinctively that he needed to keep himself busy with new pursuits. But what would they be? Despite *The Century's* interest in publishing his story, Slocum, ever a man of action, explored other possibilities. He wondered whether he might be useful to the U.S. Navy in the Spanish-American War. In a letter appearing in the July 1 *New Bedford Morning Mercury*—even before his interview was published—Slocum wrote that "I burn to be of some use now of all times.... I spent the best of my life in the Philippine Islands, China and Japan.... Does Mr. McKinley want pilots for the Philippines and Guam?" But the navy saw no need for Joshua Slocum's services.

And what did the future hold for Slocum and his second wife? According to Victor, Hettie did not join him and Garfield on their trip to Newport to welcome their father home. Victor wrote that "Henrietta, was, of course, waiting in Boston for the skipper to report personally. So he left Garfield and me to discharge the *Spray's* cargo and to answer the multitude of questions asked by the constant stream of visitors that came to look and to watch us work."

However, Victor did not make clear whether this occurred at Newport or (more likely) Fairhaven or New Bedford, nor did he say how long Slocum stayed in East Boston when he went there to "report." Neither son offered details of Slocum's reunion with Hettie or even when it occurred. Garfield admitted that he didn't much care for his stepmother, nor did his observations of his father and stepmother in the coming months suggest a sympathetic marriage. Victor, who seemed always to have been mature beyond his years, kept silent on the matter. There was a reunion of some sort, and the result was that Joshua and Hettie decided to make the best of their situation and, in public at least, project an aura of congeniality.

Slocum had not forgotten his idea for a "college ship," which he had mentioned in the letter written to Joseph Gilder while "tied to a palm tree" at Keeling Cocos. The Coast Guard training ship *Salmon P. Chase* was well-known to Slocum—she was a fixture of the New Bedford waterfront—but his idea involved a broad, sea-based experience for students intent on civilian careers.

During the early days of August, he sailed to New York—with Hettie aboard—where he planned to pitch his ideas. Almost three months later, at the end of October, he presented his plans to a gathering in a room at Carnegie Hall. He spoke of a clipper ship specially adapted to carry 300 students and their professors on a two-year voyage around the world. The course offerings would be comprehensive and would include liberal arts, engineering, and seamanship. Slocum himself planned to instruct in nautical astronomy and navigation.

It was a grand, even visionary idea, but Garfield recalled that "he could not get enough people. He was very disappointed." The idea was well ahead of its time; beginning decades after Slocum's disappearance, school ships and seaborne instruction would resonate with young people and educators alike. Walter Teller noted that Irving M. Johnson, who could remember as a boy seeing his journalist father, Clifton, with Slocum, put Slocum's ideas into practice, albeit on a smaller scale: "In 1955, Captain Irving M. Johnson, and his wife, of the brigantine *Yankee*, completed their sixth round the world voyage with a paying crew of college-age men and women."

As other avenues closed, Slocum's way forward became clear. He needed to focus on speaking engagements and writing his story, a task he would soon discover was more challenging than he imagined. He and Hettie returned to East Boston and moved in with Hettie's sister Odessa, who had moved from Saratoga Street to 57 West Eagle Street. By the end of January 1899, Slocum's first draft had taken the *Spray* "around Cape Horn."

He moved ahead with speaking plans, too. In February, it was announced that "Capt. Joshua Slocum will tell how he built a boat with his own hands and sailed round the world." The talk was held at the Baptist Church on Central Square in Cambridge, Massachusetts, and admission cost 25 cents (roughly $7.50 in today's money). Prices would escalate at later, larger venues, with the most expensive seats being closest to the stage.

But Slocum's primary focus during much of 1899 was his writing. *The Critic's* 1894 review of *The Voyage of the Liberdade* had put Joshua Slocum's name between the same covers with literary giants of the day, including Julia Ward Howe (*Battle Hymn of the Republic*), Walt Whitman (*Leaves of Grass*), and poet, editor, and publisher James Russell Lowell. This was rarefied company, and Slocum had come to cherish it. He now felt the need to further develop his writing and would rely on the staff at *The Century* to guide him.

Slocum's contacts at *The Century* were assistant editor Clarence Buel and associate editor Robert Johnson. Throughout the evolution of *Sailing Alone* from rough draft to magazine serialization to the book itself, Slocum made it clear that he was not a professional writer. At various times, he revealed his respect for, and trust in, his editors. Writing from the *Spray* at Martha's Vineyard on August 4, 1899, he told Buel, "I am glad that my poor ms. fell into good hands. In *The Century*, it will appear far different to the ten fathoms of autograph which I first submitted.... [H]ow patient *Century* editors have been."

Buel and Johnson's correspondence was written on letterhead that read "Editorial Department, The Century Magazine, Union Square, New York." Most of Slocum's letters were written on blank or lined stationery. Sometimes he used a printed letterhead that showed a drawing of the *Spray* in the top left corner with the words "Round the World." To the right was printed "Yacht Spray,'" the year "1898," and a place to write the date. As time passed, Slocum usually remembered to update the year, but not always.

Although Slocum began writing his story in East Boston, he seems to have felt confined and uncomfortable in his sister-in-law's house. In April— as soon as the New England spring permitted—he sailed to New York and docked at Erie Basin in South Brooklyn. There, in the *Spray's* familiar cabin where he had written *The Voyage of the Destroyer*, he could focus entirely on his task. He was also near his friend Mabel Wagnalls, who could read portions of the manuscript as it developed and provide feedback.

He declared from the outset his desire to write the tale "without saying Slocum Slocum all the time—that I do not care for." This insistence contributed significantly to an absence of the personal revelations that readers would later miss. Slocum's primary concern, expressed time and again, was to tell the story truthfully and accurately. He offered his tracking charts to the editors to be sure the *Spray's* course was faithfully reproduced. He wrote Johnson on July 28, 1899, that he had given Buel the *Spray's* course "traced on a track chart; one of the best ever published." Almost certainly he was referring to a chart created under the direction of the U.S. Navy's Matthew Fontaine Maury.

As Slocum focused on telling the story of his voyage and received feedback from his editors, he began to understand the real labors the project required. In his July 28 letter, he begged Johnson to "be patient with me still." He had thought that writing would be compatible with wandering about Vineyard and Nantucket sounds during the summer months, but now admitted that "I find I must come to anchor and make a business of it if I hope to revise intelligently if at all." Among the revisions requested by Buel were rigorous details about the changes made to the *Spray's* rig and where they were made.

There is no way of knowing how similar the finished *Sailing Alone Around the World* is to its original drafts, for none have survived. Diffidently because he possessed so little schooling, Slocum showed the completed manuscript to a few educated friends outside the walls of *The Century*. One was his cousin Grace Murray Brown's father, Bernard, and Grace recalled that "Father was most emphatic in begging him not allow anyone, editor or critic to touch a phrase. He told him they could not approximate his style, charm or wit." Slocum's work reminded Mabel Wagnalls of Daniel Defoe's *Robinson Crusoe*.

But neither Brown nor Wagnalls was a professional editor or publisher risking time and money on a magazine series and commercial book. It's probable that significant editing was needed; Slocum certainly thought so. "I appreciate every touch of the pen given to my poor story," he wrote his editors. His goal, he wrote, was "to see a clear story appear in both Magazine and book with no superfluous matter."

The primary feedback from his editors was the need to be clearer and more concise. Slocum's professed abhorrence of "superfluous matter" suggests that he had an instinct for good writing. Like most beginning (and many experienced) writers, he struggled with wordiness—and wordiness was more in fashion in the nineteenth century than in the age of 140-character Twitter posts.[1]

On July 23, writing from Cottage City (Oak Bluffs) on Martha's Vineyard, Slocum told Robert Johnson, "I myself, upon reading ms. in cooler blood, wondered how I could have made some of the points so obscure." In his August 4 letter to Buel, he wrote, "I am trying to cut down the last installment of the *Spray* voyage. There is obviously a chance to consolidate." And in an August 12 letter to Johnson from Woods Hole, he admitted that "[a]bout three-quarters of the matter is greatly improved by the going over."

In characteristic fashion, Slocum managed to inject some humor into the matter of excessive wordiness, admitting to Johnson on August 14, "I fear that I have not condensed as much as you wished; but have cut some paragraphs. I find it rather difficult to condense the variety of experiences while sailing free over the smooth sea from Good Hope…. However the

---

1 Captain John Drew, "The Kennebecker," a literary inspiration for Slocum, was a master of verbosity. William H. Bunting, who is editing Drew's journals for publication, wrote, "My function is to dispose of excessive verbiage…. When Drew wrote of something that clearly interested him, his writing was very good."

editor will know how to slaughter my pet so as to keep the matter down to at least five installments. But it is a rule at Lloyds [Lloyds of London, the marine insurer] that one cannot have too much of a good thing." Only an old sea captain would have thought to equate the wisdom of carrying ample insurance (which Slocum himself had failed to do for his own vessels) with a writer's tendency toward excess wordiness. Perhaps he provoked a smile at *The Century*. Right to the end of the serialization, he struggled to pare down his work, but it was Joshua Slocum, not his editors, who did the writing and the revisions.

The editorial process was complicated by Slocum's frequent comings and goings. Manuscripts and galleys were mailed to New York from East Boston and various ports around Buzzards Bay and Vineyard Sound. Materials sent from New York sometimes arrived after Slocum had sailed on. Still, the work got done. Questions arose and were dealt with, and the first installment appeared in the September 1899 issue of *The Century*. (The lead story in that issue was artist and critic William A. Coffin's discussion of two Winslow Homer paintings.) Subsequently, Slocum's story unfolded in issues that included the work of Mark Twain and other literary lights.

The first installment of Slocum's article series was entitled:

Sailing Alone Around the World
Being a Personal Narrative of the Experiences of the Sloop Spray
on Her Single-Handed Voyage of 46,000 Miles
By Captain Joshua Slocum
With pictures by Thomas Fogarty
Twice Across the Atlantic

The illustrations were a hodgepodge. A formal photograph of Slocum (taken at the 518 Fifth Avenue studio of Hollinger and Company) was followed by an 1885 drawing by W. Taber of Slocum's *Northern Light*. (This was the only illustration that Slocum expressed displeasure with, noting that the vessel's sheerline had been inaccurately rendered, thus reducing the ship's beauty.) Next came a cross-section of the *Spray*'s hull with no attribution, followed by a number of illustrations by Thomas Fogarty (1873–1938), among the best-known illustrators of the day. In addition to creating his own art, Fogarty taught at New York's famous Art Students League. There, in 1910, he would influence a gifted 16-year-old named Norman Rockwell.

Perhaps because of schedule conflicts or workload, Fogarty was not the only illustrator whose work appeared in *Sailing Alone*. George Edmund Varian (1865–1923) was the other principal illustrator. Born in Liverpool, England, Varian moved to New York, where he studied at the Brooklyn Art Guild and the Art Students League. His work was a regular feature in *McClure's Magazine*, and he was well-known for his illustrations for Robert Louis Stevenson's *Kidnapped* (published in London in 1886 by Cassell & Company) and for Scribner's 1918 edition of *Treasure Island*. Varian had even worked with Slocum's Boston publisher, Roberts Brothers. A number of his illustrations for *Sailing Alone*, including "The *Spray* at Anchor off Gibraltar," are of exceptional quality. [1]

Some of *Sailing Alone's* illustrations are noted as having been drawn "after a photograph." Slocum had been thinking about photography right from the start of the voyage. In a letter to Eugene Hardy mailed from Yarmouth, Nova Scotia, on June 20, 1895, Slocum had written that the *Boston Globe's* publisher, Charles Henry Taylor, "had a camera to lend me for the voyage but I neglected to get it thinking I had a Karona[2] secured. But I was disappointed at the last moment. The camera seems to be the only thing lacking but I shall go without it and get along if I have to." He resolved the matter, never sharing how he did so, and many of his lectures were advertised with the words "illustrations in the way of lantern slides made by himself during his long voyage of 46,000 miles."

Many, perhaps most, of the illustrations in *Sailing Alone* were apparently drawn from Slocum's photographs or his descriptions of events or people. It would have been fascinating to hear Slocum describe to Fogarty the elements of one of the book's greatest pictures, the Chapter One illustration "It'll Crawl." The picture shows Slocum standing in front of the *Spray* and facing skeptical Fairhaven onlookers, one of whom warns that the caulking would not stay in place but would "crawl." For his depiction of the under-construction hull, Fogarty seems to have relied to some extent on an illustration published in the *Globe* and the New Bedford *Republican Standard* in December 1891. Slocum wrote to Johnson, "Mr. Fogarty is a careful

---

1 In addition to Fogarty and Varian, a third artist worked on *Sailing Alone*. This was German-born John M. August Will (1834–1910). Will, who was accomplished in a number of mediums, lived and worked in Jersey City. He frequently worked for *The Century*. Will did the maps for Slocum's book.

2 The Karona "Hand Camera" was introduced in 1894 by its designer, Gustav Milburn, who had formerly been sales manager at Kodak. Built in Rochester, New York, the Karona was a sophisticated 5-inch by 7-inch (negative size) view camera that could be mounted on a tripod or hand-held. It was beautifully made of wood and brass with a leather bellows.

"'IT 'LL CRAWL!'"

In Thomas Fogarty's illustration from Chapter One of Sailing Alone, *Joshua Slocum finds himself confronted by a bemused dog and Fairhaven waterfront skeptics who warn him that the caulking will "crawl." But Slocum's caulking method—cotton wicking coated with a mixture of cement and raw linseed oil—proved highly durable and contributed to a watertight hull.*

worker. He has sketched the spot the *Spray* returned to exactly as it appears: the old stake she tied up to and all."

The *Spray* story unfolded not in the five installments Slocum had mentioned in his letter to Johnson, but in seven. Appearing in March 1900, the sixth installment ended the voyage, and the seventh, an appendix, comprised Slocum's comments on the *Spray* and naval architect C. D. Mower's drawings of the vessel that would result in so much controversy.

Even as *The Century* was publishing the serialized story of Slocum's voyage, it was looking ahead to publishing the book version in March. Slocum continued to work at paring words and checking details for accuracy. On February 18, he wrote Buel to be sure that the *Spray's* length be given as 36 feet 9 inches (not 37 feet 9 inches) and that the depth of the hold be changed from 4 feet 4 inches to 4 feet 2 inches. The book was published on March 24, close on the heels of the final serial installment.

The first edition of Sailing Alone Around the World *was bound in navy blue cloth. The seahorses were stamped in lime green, and the title in white. (Courtesy the New Bedford Whaling Museum)*

In hindsight, *The Century's* press deadline proved overly aggressive. When Slocum got his copy of *Sailing Alone*, he found many details to refine in the subsequent printings he hoped would follow.[1] He wrote Buel on March 23 of "many improvements which I shall be able to make in the text: a touch here and there. Doing so would be no more than the great author of Ivanho did." Apparently, Slocum had read something about the editing process of Scottish novelist Sir Walter Scott.

Another letter from Slocum to Buel on March 30 reveals that it was *The Century* editors who had written the captions and the contents list that highlighted the subject matter within each chapter. Then, as now, such tasks were routinely performed by the editors. "The captions, I think you call them," Slocum wrote, "tickle us all. One sees by the table of contents that the editor read the story with care. My own is the only part with which I am not thoroughly delighted." Slocum referred to his book now as "this child of the sea."

The words Joseph Gilder had written ten years earlier to describe *The Voyage of the Liberdade* applied equally to *Sailing Alone Around the World*: "Ocean breezes shake the leaves of the book as you turn the pages.... The merits of the book ... are clearly attributable to the author. The thing has not been 'licked into shape' for him.'"

WITH SALES OF *SAILING ALONE* going well, *The Century* soon found itself in the happy circumstance of looking ahead to selling out the first press run of 5,000 copies before the end of the year. The planned second run of 2,500 copies gave Slocum an opportunity to make revisions. In May 1900 he wrote Buel, "I submit pages 12-31-108 of *Sailing Alone* with remedies for my bungling which I think you will agree should be made.... I beg that the changes may be made on the plates, especially on page 12."

Page 12 of both the 1900 and 1901[2] printings includes the most lyrical paragraph in the book. The changes are subtle, but they speak to Slocum's discerning and ever-improving ear for the English language. The Sheridan House edition of *Sailing Alone*, first published in 1954, is based on the text of the 1901 printing, as is the fine Penguin edition first published in 1999 and sensitively edited by Thomas Philbrick, a professor emeritus of English at

---

1 Paraphrasing Paul Valéry, W. H. Auden wrote in 1965, "A poem is never finished, only abandoned." The same can be said of a book moving toward publication.

2 In February 1901, 2,500 copies of the new edition were printed. Between May 1905 and February 1941, there were 14 smaller printings from The Century Company.

As the holidays approached in 1900, The Century Company placed this ad suggesting gift books in the New York Daily Tribune.

the University of Pittsburgh. Here is a line-by-line comparison of the two printings:

1900 Printing	1901 Printing
Waves dancing joyously across Massachusetts Bay met the	Waves dancing joyously across Massachusetts Bay met her
Sloop coming out, to dash themselves instantly into myriads	coming out of the harbor to dash them into myriads
of sparkling gems that hung about her breast at every surge…. Every	of sparkling gems that hung about her at every surge…. Every
particle of water thrown into the air became a gem, and the *Spray*,	particle of water thrown into the air became a gem, and the
making good her name as she dashed ahead, snatched necklace	*Spray*, bounding ahead, snatched necklace after necklace
after necklace from the sea and, as often threw them away.	from the sea, and as often threw them away.

Philbrick noted that "The text of that 1901 printing was faithfully re-produced in the more than twenty reprintings issued by the Century Company and the publishers who succeeded to the rights to the book before the copyright expired in 1956. Since that time, however, most editions of *Sailing Alone*, among them the one included by Walter Teller in his important compilation *The Voyages of Joshua Slocum*, have overlooked Slocum's last revisions and returned to the text of the 1900 edition."

Nor did all the illustrations that accompanied the serialization make

SAMOAN SEA-NYMPHS AT PLAY.

"Samoan Sea Nymphs at Play" was a Thomas Fogarty illustration that appeared in The Century's *serialization of* Sailing Alone Around the World *in April 1899 but did not make it into the book the following year.*

it into either the 1900 or 1901 printings. At least seven pictures are missing from the 1900 edition, the most unfortunate omission being a Fogarty illustration entitled "Storm off New York." It shows the *Spray*, sails lowered, lying to her sea anchor in rough seas kicked up by a tornado off Long Island. Illustrations missing from both editions include "The Captain's Dream" from Installment I, showing Slocum dreaming about a whale hooked by an anchor, and Installment IV's "The Merry-Go-Round" and fantasy-evoking "Samoan Sea Nymphs at Play." The latter shows Slocum in a dugout canoe propelled by long-haired Samoan girls.

The paper used by *The Century* for its editions of *Sailing Along* resulted in fine reproductions of the illustrations, measurably better in clarity and tonality than in all postwar editions. Slocum fans find much to enjoy when exploring one of the original editions or the magazine installments available online.[1]

While the timbre of the writing in *Sailing Alone* is similar to that of *Liberdade*, the narrative is more succinct and far more polished. Slocum's paring and wordsmithing sharpened the points, polished the imagery, and revealed the clarity that comes of economy. The prose flows easily and, like all good writing, is deceptively simple. This tale of a solitary man in his early fifties, living in a simple manner by wit and skill in sometimes ferocious surroundings was, and remains, a timeless story that seems to speak to most everyone who reads it.

Today the book mainly interests sailors, would-be sailors, armchair adventurers, and maritime historians, but the appeal of *Sailing Alone* was once much broader and more popular. Slocum's story was both an adventure tale—man in nature—and a travel memoir. The genres had wide appeal in that era long before the widespread publication of photographs, films, or, of course, television or the internet. (*National Geographic* didn't start publishing its famous pictures until 1896.) The illustrations in *Sailing Alone* gave readers a rare glimpse of exotic places and people they could hardly imagine and never expected to see in person.

NOTWITHSTANDING some discussion about whether Slocum's treatment of his meeting with Paul Kruger in South Africa could be construed as libelous, the most sensitive element of *Sailing Alone* prior to publication was its preface,

---

1 Inputting "The Century Magazine" should bring up more than one site on which the magazine can be read and the illustrations studied and even enlarged.

Mabel Wagnalls in 1904. Mabel and her family were longtime friends of Joshua Slocum, and he dedicated Sailing Along Around the World *to her. (Courtesy The Wagnalls Memorial)*

which Slocum had solicited from his friend Mabel Wagnalls.

Slocum's enthusiasm for Mabel's book *Miserere* had been echoed by her great enthusiasm for *Sailing Alone* when he shared the manuscript with her in New York. It was Mabel's admiration, and perhaps Slocum's awareness of her standing in the world of letters, that prompted him to ask her to write the preface (more properly termed a "foreword" when contributed by a third party). Thus began a saga that Slocum addressed in a two-page letter to Clarence Buel on August 18, 1899, as publication of the first installment in *The Century* approached.

There were two issues. First, Mabel's preface—submitted by Slocum with a portion of his manuscript—had elicited no reaction from the editors. Did that mean it had been mislaid? "I can understand," Slocum wrote Buel, "how a smaller paper even so important might get lost among the driftwood." He was being as diplomatic as possible for, in his memory, he had given the material to Buel himself. Second, and more to the point, Slocum himself had developed concerns about the effusive, congratulatory, overly dramatic tone of Mabel's writing[1] and had doubts about its appropriateness.

Mabel, meanwhile, was clamoring to know what was going on. Writing from Fairhaven, Slocum began his August 18 letter to Buel:

> A lady in your city is giving me the very deuce over a preface which evidently has been mislaid and, I think, in the Century office at that! … I send now the original—the other was a typewritten copy. I thought at one time that it would be a great lift to my poor book, if it ever got afloat; the editors may think entirely different.… Mabel Wagnalls I think is a good writer, clever and strong. In the case of the preface, perhaps too strong. One should be careful to not raise a debate and to be over-praised is worse than all. I would rather be pared down in the Century Brain Department than go out to the merciless world with a large head. But the dear lady is broken hearted!
>
> I value my friend's strong expressions of praise. My editors will know best whether or not the public will take kindly.… When I asked Mrs. Wagnalls[2] to write the preface, I did not think that the magazine

---

1 "Amid solitude and silence, with the keel of his little boat, he has traced the great circle—the emblem of eternity."

2 Mabel had married a likable Pittsburgh steel executive and lawyer named Richard Jones.

would print so much of the story.... I feel very sure that Mr. Buell will get me out of the difficulty that will come if the preface is not used.

It is unlikely that *The Century*'s editors ever seriously considered using Mabel's preface, but there were portions that, with editorial oversight, could have provided useful background for Slocum's voyage and could even have deftly touched on some of the personal matters readers sought to know more about. Whatever the preface's flaws, Slocum was profoundly moved by its author's support. It was to Mabel—"To the One Who Said 'The *Spray* Will Come Back'"—that Slocum dedicated his book. Of course, this raised another question: Who, if not the author's wife, was "the One," and what did she mean to him? It was, for readers of *Sailing Alone Around the World*, just one more question about the book's personable yet elusive author.

CHAPTER 19

Recognition at Last

"Captain Slocum's book Sailing Alone Around the World *(published by the Century Company) has had a large sale, which is still increasing."*

—James Burton Pond, *The Eccentricities of Genius*, 1900

IT IS EASY TO IMAGINE THE ANTICIPATION Joshua Slocum felt as he looked forward to seeing his name in each successive issue of *The Century*. The third installment, "Juan Fernandez and Samoa," was released in November, the same issue that included Mark Twain's retrospective article, "My Debut as a Literary Person." Twain's piece revisited a story he had written as a young reporter about the sinking of the clipper ship *Hornet* in the South Pacific on May 3, 1866. The article, which described how some of the survivors made it to Hawaii, would have fascinated Slocum and reminded him of his rescue of the Gilbert Islanders. He wrote Buel that this Twain article was "the best thing he has ever done in his long life of good work." In less than a month the admiring Slocum would meet Samuel Clemens in New York.

Even as *The Century* was working to get out the first installment of the magazine serial in the September 1899 issue, Slocum was making expansive plans for speaking engagements. His speaking career had taken off thanks to the gregarious and loquacious lecture organizer Major James Burton Pond. During the Civil War, Pond had served with the Third Wisconsin Cavalry. After the war, he pursued a variety of business interests before purchasing the Lyceum Theatre Lecture Bureau in 1874, which brought him into contact with many of the world's most famous people.

In 1900, Pond shared his impressions of his remarkable clientele in a book he called *Eccentricities of Genius, memories of famous men and women of platform and stage*. Of Joshua Slocum, Pond wrote:

> *What is most remarkable of all is that Captain Slocum is able to write and describe the incidents of the entire voyage and his wonderful experiences in a manner so graphic and simple that it absolutely charms and fascinates his hearers as few could ever do.*
>
> *The experiences of Captain Slocum have proved him to be one of the greatest navigators of the age.*
>
> *It is wonderful to listen to the descriptions of some of his hairbreadth escapes and to hear him answer, as quick as a flash, questions of every conceivable sort put to him by expert seafaring auditors. I have listened for hours to these seeming tournaments in navigator's skill, and never yet did the Captain hesitate for an instant for a reply that went straight to the mark like a bullet.*

Pond suggested that Slocum would have amassed a considerable fortune through his speaking had he been born 20 years earlier, but changes in the way lectures were being arranged would significantly reduce his earnings. Samuel Clemens believed from his own experience that Pond's forecasts of monies to be earned had always exceeded reality. That said, Slocum brought in cash with his lectures. When Pond closed his speaker's bureau, Slocum's reaction in a July 30, 1903 letter was, "God—we miss the Major."

Between his talks, the cash earned on the voyage, and payments from *The Century*, Slocum now had more than enough money to cover his financial needs. On November 4, 1899, he wrote Clarence Buel saying, "The Century did well by me. No one knows how much I have been paid ... enough to buy ... a house ... and as good a house too [as] I could wish to live in."

A month later, on December 5, Slocum was invited to a dinner celebrating Mark Twain at the Aldine Association, a prestigious organization composed of New York's publishing and art communities. The *New York Times* reported on December 15 that "The dinner was remarkable for the decorations of the rooms [which included] a pilothouse from the corners of which were suspended colored lights and the cornice of which bore the name of Alonzo Child, the name of one of the steamboats which Mr. Clemens used to pilot on the Mississippi River. The walls were festooned with hanging moss, and here and there were suspended oranges, gourds, and other Southern growths, while catfish were sailing about in aquariums."

Some 200 people attended this gala event, including publishers Charles and Arthur Scribner, George Haven Putnam, George Pratt Brett of Macmillan's, Frank Nelson Doubleday of Doubleday & McClure's, Richard Watson Gilder of *The Critic*, *The Century's* Clarence C. Buel, and Major Pond. Also present that night, on a speaking tour from England, was a correspondent who'd covered the Boer War and was now a 26-year-old would-be politician, Winston Churchill. Captain Joshua Slocum, who said he had used Mark Twain's writing to learn how to navigate Brazil's rivers, was among those who spoke.

Later that month, on December 14, Slocum wrote Buel that he'd had some much-needed dental work done and that this had improved his speaking. "I succeeded very well with my new teeth last, night, considering!" he wrote. On December 22, he wrote Buel that "Middleton, Annapolis County, Nova Scotia, will be my P.O. address 'til further notice." This speaking trip also took Slocum back to Brier Island, where those who had known him as a boy in Westport came to hear his lecture and see his pictures. He visited Tiverton on adjacent Long Island, 12 miles from Westport, and gave his talk there in Temperance Hall. Descendants of those who attended Slocum's presentations still speak of them.

The lectures continued when Slocum returned from Yarmouth on January 24, 1900. "Father and Hettie had an apartment in N.Y.C.," Garfield remembered in a letter written to Walter Teller in 1953. "I understood my father to say Hettie and he had rooms [on the West Side] in a building occupied by the Houghton Mifflin Publishers in 1900. Father used to go to schools, colleges and halls.... Father lectured in a large hotel on Fisher's Island. He gave lectures with lantern slides, the slides he had made from photographs he took and he bought some on his voyage. I remember that I operated the lantern a few times. Father gave a very interesting talk. He was *very good*. His listeners liked his interesting and educational talks."

While giving his well-received lectures, Slocum finished reading the proofs of the next-to-last chapter of the serialization. He suggested to *The Century* editors that they include several congratulatory letters from shipmaster friends in the book's appendix, but left the promotion of the book "in the hands of the masters." The letters never made it into print.

Once *Sailing Alone Around the World* was published, Slocum acquired a quantity of the books and, by springtime, was selling them aboard the *Spray*. On June 1, 1900, he was in Larchmont, New York, and planning to go from there to New Rochelle where, according to Garfield, Slocum was invited to dinner aboard Sir Thomas Lipton's magnificent steam yacht, the *Erin*. Back in East Boston, it was left to Hettie to greet the "enumerator" for the 1900 United States census. There is certainly no guarantee that, had Slocum been at home on June 1, he would have provided more accurate information about himself than Hettie did. At the time, the Slocums were staying with Hettie's sister Beatrice Elliott Ferguson at 184 Princeton Street. Hettie told the census taker that her husband was a naturalized citizen who had been born in Canada in April 1842 (rather than February 1844). For her husband's occupation, she gave "tugboat captain."

By July, Slocum was in Block Island and Jamestown, Rhode Island. Hettie had now joined him, and she was enthusiastic enough to enjoy row-ing a fine-lined tender—apparently a small, Whitehall-style boat—that Slocum had acquired. He named it the *Stark* after the little ferry he remem-bered from his time in Portland, Oregon. "She comes in for a large share of admiration," Slocum wrote Buel.

When in New York City, Slocum moored in Erie Basin and some-times, according to Garfield, on the New Jersey side of the Hudson at Fort Lee. Once, when the *Spray* was tied up at South Street, a minister from the Seaman's Bethel came aboard to see the boat. He invited Slocum and Gar-field to attend a service at the Bethel. "That was the only time we ever went to church together," Garfield remembered.

When Hettie was not with him, Slocum almost certainly lived aboard the *Spray* and did much of the editing and revising of his book in her cabin. On occasion he took friends sailing. Garfield remembered a daysail with Adam Wagnalls and "a young, pleasant lady, perhaps that was Mabel Wag-nalls. She was very nice.... Father steered toward a wharf near the entrance to [Spuyten Duyvil] creek.... I was standing on the port bow with two coils of rope in my hands to throw to a man on the wharf. The swift current threw the *Spray* against a pile under the wharf and I fell overboard. Mr. Wagnalls pulled me out."

In July 1900, Slocum received a letter from England written by Robert Bright Marston, publisher in London of *The Fishing Gazette* and one of the

The Spray *was an attention-getter in any harbor. This July 1900 photo was made off Newport during a cruise of R.A.C. Smith's motor yacht* Privateer *(formerly the* Buccaneer *under William Randolph Hearst's ownership) from Larchmont, New York, to Eastport, Maine, and Saint Andrews, New Brunswick. With Slocum at the wheel in light air, the* Spray's *jib is set and her topping lift wants slackening. (Photograph by Edwin Holmes; courtesy Bradley Williams)*

era's most influential journalists and scholars of fly fishing. Marston was the son of Edward Marston, a principal in the important London publishing company of Samson, Low, Marston & Company, which had published some of the biggest best-sellers of the period, including Jules Verne's *Twenty Thousand Leagues Under the Sea* and Sir Henry Morton Stanley's *How I Found Livingstone.*

After seeing a review of *Sailing Alone* in *The Nation,* R. B. Marston read the book himself and wrote Slocum that he wished *Sailing Alone* had continued on for another 40,000 miles. "Your fact is stranger than [Verne's] fiction." Marston showed the book to his father, and the decision was taken to release a British edition in the summer of 1900. It was reviewed by the great journalist and poet Sir Edwin Arnold in the *Daily Telegraph* on September 8, when Arnold was 68 years old. Arnold managed to succinctly sum up Slocum's unusual accomplishment: "The tale is true from first to last, written in a style plain as a marlin-spike, and yet full of touches which show what hidden poetry and passionate love of Nature were in the soul of this 'blue-nose' skipper."

GARFIELD SLOCUM SPENT the winter of 1900–01 as ship keeper aboard the *Spray* at Erie Basin. It was there that his father told him that he'd been invited to display the *Spray* at the upcoming Pan-American Exposition in Buffalo, New York. Slocum had hoped for an invitation to the Paris Universal Exposition in April 1900, but was rejected despite Buel's intercession because, as Slocum wrote Buel, "her [the *Spray's*] career is too new." The director general of the Pan-American Exposition Company was much more enthusiastic.

William I. Buchanan, whom Slocum had met during his stop at Rio, was in charge of the Buffalo Expo. "Because of his extensive connections in South America and his past experience with the World's Fair in 1893," said historian Susan Eck, "the Buffalo Exposition planners invited Buchanan to be the chief."

Slocum told Garfield that the Expo "would pay him for the privilege of exhibiting the *Spray*." The Expo—billed as "the first exposition of the 20th century"—would start in May. Recognizing a money-making opportunity when he saw it, Slocum promptly accepted the offer.

On January 20, 1901, the *Buffalo Express* carried a photo of Joshua Slocum on its front page and reported that the captain would indeed be present "next summer. The boat will ride upon the waters of Lake Park where it may be viewed or boarded by Exposition visitors. It will prove a great attraction.... His book, which appeared serially in *The Century*, entitled *Sailing Alone Around the World*, is an engrossing narrative of his adventures, that richly repays perusals."

Joshua Slocum, a dyed-in-the-wool sailing man, now did something entirely out of character. Foreseeing the challenge of taking the *Spray* up the Hudson River to Albany and then through the Erie Canal to Lake Erie, he bought a 24-foot lifeboat from the steamship *S.S. Crook*, which was moored at Erie Basin, and then journeyed to Cos Cob, Connecticut, home of the pioneering marine engine company Palmer Brothers. From the Palmers, Slocum purchased a 1½-horsepower, single-cylinder, two-cycle gasoline engine and had it installed in the lifeboat.

"I was instructed on the operation of [the engine]," Garfield remembered, "which towed the *Spray* from Erie Basin to Buffalo. The crew of the *Spray* was Captain Slocum, his wife Hettie, and Garfield."

Before departing from New York City, Slocum was presented with an expensive music box made by the Regina Company. These popular devices, the record player of their time, were made at Regina's big factory in Rahway, New Jersey. The company doubtless saw Slocum's Expo appearance as a good way to promote the music boxes. In Buffalo he was able to exchange his set of metal discs for others to gain more variety in the tunes he played.

A 1½-horsepower engine sounds small for towing a heavy 37-foot boat up the Hudson, but the trip went smoothly. "Father told me to hug the shore," Garfield remembered, "and he steered near the shore because the current running upstream helped. Every night we tied up to something. On arriving in port of Albany, newspaper reporters came onboard…. Father was honored by the Albany Yacht Club. They made him Honorary Commodore."

At Troy, the *Spray's* masts were removed for the trip through the Erie Canal. Garfield recalled the canal trip as a pleasant interlude and the passage through the five locks at Lockport as especially memorable to his father and Hettie. The most challenging part of the trip was hauling the *Spray* in Buffalo and transporting her to the 365-acre Expo site at the newly made 46-acre Gala Water, also known as Park Lake (now Hoyt Lake). Slocum had to search hard to find a mobile crane capable of lifting his boat, and then had to contrive a sling robust enough to lift her safely. Garfield recalled that his father made the sling from towing hawsers.

The *Spray* was placed on a substantial four-horse wagon and, with Garfield aboard, began making her way through Buffalo, detouring as necessary to avoid low overpasses. Once at the lake, Slocum constructed a launching cradle, and there the *Spray* sat while he touched up paint scrapes until 3:30 p.m. on June 1.[1] He built and greased a set of ways leading into the lake and, when the time came, used a sledge hammer to knock out retaining wedges. With the Stars and Stripes flying from her mizzenmast, the flags of countries she had visited flying in her rigging, and Hettie standing in the bow, the *Spray* slid into the lake in front of a crowd of onlookers.

The *Spray* became a popular attraction, an authentic throwback at a venue that, like all such events, celebrated the future. The Expo's grounds and buildings were illuminated by 2,000 electric lights, giving people their most dramatic experience yet of the promise of electricity. Visitors could climb aboard a steam-powered miniature railroad, take rides on futuristic electric and gasoline launches in the waterways, marvel at the electric fountain, visit sunken gardens, stroll an authentic street that evoked old Nuremberg, Germany, and experience a Civil War cyclorama where they were surrounded by a 60-foot-high, 360-foot-wide three-dimensional painting of the November 1863 Battle of Missionary Ridge.

---

1 An April snowstorm had delayed the opening of the Expo until May 1, and it closed on November 1.

"With a splash and a hearty cheer, the good sloop Spray, *Capt. Slocum commanding, slid down the ways and buried her nose in the bosom of Gala Water yesterday afternoon." That is how the* Buffalo Express *described the June 1, 1900 launch of the* Spray *at the Pan-American Exposition. An illustrator captured the colorful event for the paper's readership. (Courtesy Susan Eck)*

There was also "Venice in America," with palaces and bridges and gondoliers who took visitors on rides through the mile-long "Grand Canal," one of the several canals on the Expo site. Garfield was given a chance to learn to scull a gondola and found it harder than it looked. He remembered having "a wonderful time at the Exposition on the Midway. I was welcome in all of the shows.... I worked for a few weeks as a barker for a soft drink concession. People were nice to me."

As for the *Spray*, the *Buffalo Express* reported on June 2, "All summer the *Spray* will lie at her anchorage in Gala Water for the entertainment of exposition sightseers ... and everyone who visits Capt. Slocum on his own fo'castle will be assured of a good, hearty, mariner's welcome. There was no fee to visit the boat, but Slocum sold copies of his *Sailing Alone* ($2), *Voyage of the Liberdade* ($1), and a 48-page "Sloop *Spray* Souvenir" booklet (25 cents) that included a swatch of sail fabric from the *Spray*'s old mainsail. Regarding that bit of sail, the booklet noted that it had been "torn, beyond repair, in the gale off Cape Horn, 4th to 8th of March, 1896, a fierce tempest."

The "Sloop *Spray* Souvenir" was self-published, just as Slocum's first two books had been. A collection of favorable reviews from a wide variety of

This photo of the Spray *at Buffalo shows that Slocum had rigged a big awning over the deck to offer protection from sun and rain. (Courtesy Susan Eck)*

The Spray's *anchorage gave those walking along the shore path by the lake at Buffalo a good view of the boat. There is a chance that this amateur photo shows Slocum (and an indistinct Hettie) on the path with the* Spray *as backdrop. (Courtesy Susan Eck)*

newspapers, it presented an admiring portrait of Slocum, depicting him as "unique," "daring," "intellectual," and "impelled by high ideals." The booklet was commercially motivated, of course—a low-cost alternative for visitors too cheap to plunk down $2 for a copy of *Sailing Alone*—but Walter Teller wrote that it sprang from another, more personal motive too: "[Slocum] could not forget his detractors and disbelievers, nor disguise the hostility he increasingly felt."

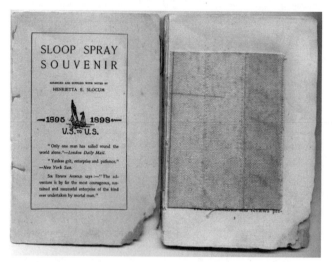

This rare copy of the "Sloop Spray Souvenir" shows the included swatch of the boat's original mainsail. (Courtesy the Millicent Library, Fairhaven, Massachusetts)

Hettie, not Joshua, was credited for the booklet's creation: "arranged and supplied with notes by Henrietta E. Slocum." Joshua's cousin Grace Murray Brown wrote Walter Teller on April 4, 1953, that Slocum felt "bitterness because of [his] wife's relations and thought perhaps the other cousins might feel as they did." It is unlikely that Hettie actually selected the reviews in the booklet, but putting her name on the title page in effect *made* her tell her sisters how wrong they had always been about her husband. "Just look at what the whole world has to say about Joshua Slocum and how blind you have been!" was the not-so-subtle message. One of the reviews included a reference to Mabel Wagnalls, although her name is not mentioned: "It is interesting to know that among Captain Slocum's nearest friends ... some one always said, 'The *Spray* will come back.'" The vote of confidence had come from another woman, not Hettie.

On June 10, Slocum took time from his exhibit routine to go to Buffalo's Central High School, where he gave one of his talks to a fascinated group of students. Although the *Spray* attracted her share of visitors, she seems to have garnered little publicity once the great fair opened. Certainly Slocum and his sailboat were an anomaly given the forward-looking themes of the displays—which included a marvelous trip to the moon that delighted everyone who experienced it—yet a steady stream of visitors were rowed out to the *Spray*, and Garfield Slocum wrote Walter Teller that so many people boarded the boat that a three-volume guestbook resulted.

In his letter to Teller, Garfield claimed that President William McKinley was among the visitors to the *Spray*, but there is no record of such a visit. McKinley visited the Expo on two successive days, September 5 and 6. He was greeted enthusiastically by the public on his first visit, lunched at the New York State building, was conveyed to the Government Building, and visited the Fisheries Building. He examined a display of the latest heavy artillery and the Philippine exhibit before having dinner at 5:45. Later that evening, he and his wife were taken by boat to the Life Saving Station, where they viewed a fireworks display. This would have brought the president in close proximity to the *Spray*, but Slocum never mentioned a presidential visit, and neither did anyone else. An overweight president trying to clamber aboard the *Spray* at night does not sound realistic.

At 4:07 p.m. the following day, in a receiving line inside the Temple of Music, a magnificent concert hall capable of seating 2,000 people, McKinley was shot twice in the stomach by an anarchist. He died eight days later from sepsis that had developed undetected.

By the time the Expo closed in November, an estimated eight million people had attended, but it was not a financial success. Luckily for Slocum, he did better than the organizers. He didn't say what he earned in his time anchored on Gala Water, but he did write that he received two-thirds of what the organizers had promised—meanwhile, of course, earning more money from book and souvenir sales.

With the Expo concluded, Joshua Slocum again confronted the question of what to do next. Never shy about thinking out loud, he told the *Buffalo Evening News* that "in the spring [he] will start upon a voyage through the Great Lakes." His plan for the winter of 1901–02, however, was to continue his lectures. Before he left Buffalo, the *Spray* was hauled from Park Lake and relaunched into the Erie Canal, where it spent the winter under the watchful eye of a boat keeper named Al Miller. Slocum sold his towboat to a Buffalo fisherman and departed with Hettie for East Boston. Garfield took a job making sand cores used for castings at the Pratt & Letchworth Steel Company in Buffalo, staying until sometime in 1902, when he left to make a voyage as a crewman in a steamship.

Slocum visited Washington, D.C., in February, stopping in to see former Massachusetts governor and then Navy Secretary John Davis Long. Although Long didn't get along well with his new boss, Theodore Roosevelt, he felt the president would want to meet Joshua Slocum. On February 8, the *New York Times* reported, "The Secretary insisted on taking Slocum over to the White House to see the President, saying that although it was Mr. Roosevelt's busy day, there was no one whom he would be so glad to see. The prediction was verified for the President, although overrun with work and visitors, was delighted and kept Slocum for some time talking about his adventures." There would be more meetings between Slocum and Roosevelt in the future.

PERIODICALLY OVER THE YEARS, despite his unhappy boyhood experiences at Mount Hanley, Joshua Slocum had mused about the possibility of buying a farm. Generally, the notion seemed to pop up after an especially bad experience at sea. Still, he had never acted upon the idea until now.

There can be no doubt that Hettie (and Slocum, too) had long since tired of staying with her sisters. Whatever disagreements and tensions the couple harbored toward each other, they appear to have been of like mind in believing that Martha's Vineyard would be a good place to settle down. Both had enjoyed their visits to the island aboard the *Liberdade* and, later, the *Spray*, and the island had attracted a number of Slocum's siblings, including his sisters Georgina and Ella and his brother Ornan and his wife, Annie, who, as of 1897, rented a tidy white cottage on California Avenue in Cottage City (Oak Bluffs). This area, known as Lagoon Heights, offers easy access to nearby Lagoon Pond.

Lagoon Pond was, and remains, a place of extreme beauty where, on calm, clear nights, one may see the stars reflected in the dark water. Slocum sometimes maneuvered the *Spray* through the little bridge that gives access to the pond. He took some delight in the fact that he could enter this slice of paradise that excluded yachts drawing more than 5½ feet. Anchored in the pond, he had a quiet place to edit his manuscript. There, too, at times, the *Spray* became a focal point for island children and parents who visited, asked questions, and swam off the boat.

Alice Longraker and her family were neighbors of the Slocums, and years later she shared her memories of them. "The Slocum family that we met that summer were all extroverts," she wrote Walter Teller, "and very soon indeed we were all eating our steamed clams or even lobster salad together."

Alice was 14 years old in 1899 when Joshua Slocum visited with the *Spray*, and she frequently saw the captain walking to and from the Slocum family's rented cottage. "It was a long time before I became aware that he had a wife," Alice remembered, "[for] he carried the relationship buoyantly. He always was the visitor and never seemed aware of [marital] ties."

A close observer, Alice remarked on Slocum's posture and dress. "I think he'd both literally and in his mind's eye had to telescope his neck in order to duck back and forth in and out of the galley or the cabin so often that it became simpler just to wear his head close to his shoulders.... I cannot remember seeing him ever in any but a blue serge suit. His hair and beard were gray and sandy—half and half I'd say at that time."

When Slocum returned to Buffalo in the spring of 1902 to take the *Spray* back to Massachusetts, the local paper's sub-headlines read: "Is Going to be a Farmer," and "Hand Which Held the Tiller is Soon to Hold the Plow—Satisfied With His Exposition Experience." Having sold his towboat, Slocum made the trip east through the Erie Canal the old-fashioned way, pulled along by a horse. According to the newspaper, this very same horse would, upon reaching Albany, be "enticed" aboard the *Spray* "and glide down the Hudson and through the Sound as far as Martha's Vineyard." There is no indication that this seemingly impractical plan was ever implemented.

On March 1, 1902, the *Vineyard Gazette* reported that Joshua Slocum had bought for $305 the West Tisbury house of the late John Manter and land belonging to Samuel E. West. Notwithstanding his affection for the Vineyard, buying a house there was something of an about-face for Slocum. Garfield remembered his father telling him, "If I settle down on land it will be on one of the Hawaiian Islands. I like the climate there much better than any country I have been in." But now, confronted with reality and with Hettie, Slocum adapted. The house was in close proximity to his seafaring friends the Clevelands, who, according to Grace Murray Brown, "induced him to settle near them on the island."

The house, a half-cape, was said to be among the oldest dwellings on Martha's Vineyard. Slocum reshingled it with shingles brought from the mainland aboard the *Spray*, and he was charmed by its sturdy construction and beams that reminded him of those in a ship. Grace Murray Brown remembered fondly the house's old paneling and doors and original hardware. She remembered that a painting of the *Northern Light* done by Liverpool artist William Howard Yorke "hung in gargantuan splendor in the tiny parlor."[1]

Clifton Johnson, who visited the Slocums that summer, described the house as "one of the most ancient on the island—an oak-ribbed ark of a dwelling with warped floors and tiny window panes and open fireplaces." According to the *Vineyard Gazette*, Slocum himself thought of his little house as "one of the coziest nests on the whole coast."

While making the move to the Vineyard, Slocum was shocked to learn that his dear friend Eben Pierce, the man who had given him the *Spray* and a place to live while rebuilding her, had died in an accident. Pierce, who was 86 years old, had been walking across the New Bedford–Fairhaven bridge on the evening of May 8 when he was struck and killed by an "electric car," as streetcars were then known. Slocum mourned his loss in a letter to his editor Clarence Buel. "He would have given any man a ship rather than take from any man the smallest thing," Slocum wrote.

On June 26, 1902, the *Martha's Vineyard Gazette* reported that "Capt. and Mrs. Slocum arrived Saturday and occupied their newly purchased house on the Sabbath." There are indications that Hettie may have arrived earlier, "preparing for him." But the new living arrangement could not change the essential dynamic between them. At some point after his not particularly successful steamship voyage, Garfield, too, moved to the Vineyard, where he found that whatever happiness the couple had displayed during the interlude in Buffalo was now past. Garfield recalled in a January 5, 1954 letter to Walter Teller that "Father and Hettie never talked about their troubles when I was near them, but whenever I came near, both of them were quiet. It was not pleasant so I slipped my moorings and went to another part of W. Tisbury." He remained on the island for a few years, working as a house painter and for the local phone company.

As 1902 drew to a close, on the evening of Thanksgiving Day, Joshua

---

1 The whereabouts of the painting, like the whereabouts of most of Slocum's manuscripts, scrapbooks, and other property, are unknown. On the Vineyard in June 1952, Walter Teller was told that Hettie "was a very neat housekeeper and was always throwing things out." Hettie had given away some porcelain vases to friends and had sold other items. Hettie herself told Teller that she had given books and papers to her sister. But the sister, Naomi (Mrs. James Tingley), who lived in suburban Boston, wrote Teller that Hettie "destroyed many of the Captain's letters, etc., before she left here the last time.... [H]er mind was failing during the last years." The painting's whereabouts probably came into question after one of Ben Aymar Slocum's several divorces.

Slocum gave one of his illustrated lectures at the Vineyard's Agricultural Hall. The *Vineyard Gazette* reported that Slocum "kindly offered to donate the proceeds of his lecture to the congregational church," of which Hettie had become a member.

When Slocum had departed Buffalo in the *Spray*, the local paper published an article about the voyage home that had ended on a hopeful note: "He intends to be a farmer, and only use the *Spray* for small trips on business." On Martha's Vineyard, soon after the start of the New Year, the *Vineyard Gazette* repeated this idea that Slocum was settling down. "With the earnings from his tour of the world, his lecture tours, and the royalties from his books, he had considered himself settled down to stay."

But the paper also reported that Slocum and his boat would be invited to the St. Louis Fair that would open in 1903. "It is to be hoped," opined the *Gazette*, "that after all the Captain will decide to remain through the summer at West Tisbury, where he has won many friends by his genial companionship."

Time would tell how long Joshua Slocum's avowed plan to settle down to farm life would last—and not much time, at that.

CHAPTER 20

The Shell Collector

*"We learned the stories and where the articles came from,
and how to blow the shells for customers as the captain did when
he needed a fog horn."*

—Mrs. Carroll W. Saley to Walter Teller, recalling her girlhood memories
of Joshua Slocum at Oak Bluffs in 1907

GARFIELD SLOCUM REMEMBERED: "Father told me he bought the old house because he liked the large timbers and the knees which looked like the hold of a ship and he intended to raise fruit trees." Did Joshua Slocum really believe he had a future as a farmer, or was he kidding himself and others? If the latter, he was successful, at least for a while. After journeying to the island for his article about Slocum in the summer of 1902, Clifton Johnson wrote that the captain had seemingly swallowed the anchor and "become an enthusiastic agriculturist.... Martha's Vineyard looks to him like Eden, and it is likely the sea will know him no more."

On January 15, 1903, the *Vineyard Gazette* reported that "Mr. Mark Foy, the rich Australian, a friend of Capt. Joshua Slocum, wants the Captain to sail again for the far-off continent." But Slocum had nothing so ambitious in mind. His actions during the spring of 1903 bolstered the impression that he was now shorebound. He invested in more property on Martha's Vineyard, purchasing three additional parcels and a tract of woodland. He wrote Clifton Johnson that he owned "160 acres of beautiful land. On some of these acres are stumps which I shall endeavor to hoist out putting in a hill of potatoes in its stead."

He even named his farm, calling it variously "Rudder Ranch" or "Fag End," the latter being sailor speak for the frayed end of an old rope. It might well have been a tongue-in-cheek reference to how Slocum himself felt. He had not lost his sense of humor.

Assisting Slocum in his attempt to become a "skilled agriculturist" was his younger brother Ornan, who had moved to Martha's Vineyard from Florida in 1900 at age 51. He had left the South because his flourishing alligator hide tannery in Orange City had been severely damaged during a freeze. When Joshua and Hettie moved to West Tisbury, Ornan was still establishing himself on the Vineyard. After helping to build the state-funded highway from North Tisbury to Gay Head, he would eventually establish a well-regarded shoemaking shop on Main Street in Vineyard Haven, returning to the Nova Scotia family trade.

But when Joshua arrived in the summer of 1902, Ornan had time to help him with the hop plants Slocum thought to pioneer on the Vineyard, just as he had once pioneered sales of Pacific cod in Oregon. Though never a beer drinker himself, Slocum thought he saw a strong market for hops and he may have been aware of successful harvests of the perennial in the Willamette Valley of Oregon. The brothers' alliance lasted until Slocum accused Ornan of allowing the plow horse to damage some of the hop plants. Ornan strenuously disagreed—it had been nothing more than an accident—and after the altercation he left Joshua to himself. For a time the brothers didn't speak. When they did reconnect—they ran into each other on a sandy island road—it was Ornan who made the overture.

During his visit to Martha's Vineyard, Clifton Johnson took photographs of Joshua and Hettie in front of their old house. In one image, Slocum is posed in the foreground with a hoe in his hands while Hettie is bent over in the background, possibly weeding or harvesting summer squash. The photograph suggests marital harmony and teamwork, and Rudder Ranch looks like an idyllic place, but Slocum was merely posing for the camera. He knew he was a round peg trying to fit a square hole. He must have suspected it right from the start, perhaps even as the horse plodded its way east from Buffalo with the *Spray* in tow and a farm on the near horizon.

Joshua and Hettie posed outside their Martha's Vineyard house in 1902. The image suggests a marital harmony that did not, in fact, exist. (Photograph by Clifton Johnson; courtesy the New Bedford Whaling Museum)

In the spring of 1903, Slocum was still telling himself he was a farmer. He wrote to a recent acquaintance, the distinguished naval officer Albert Gleaves,[1] "I am farming—planting trees at present—dug 50 holes yesterday and got dog tired. My wife is for chickens. If any of your friends in the fleet come to Menemsha this season, you may expect the *Spray* with complimentary broilers from Rudder Ranch." But as spring gave way to summer, the "agriculturalist" moved back aboard his boat, cruising alone in Vineyard and Nantucket sounds and in Buzzards Bay. For several weeks that summer, Slocum anchored in Marion, where he may have visited occasionally with *Century* magazine publisher Richard Watson Gilder, who had a summer home in the town.[2]

In the last months of 1903, Slocum seemed to be trying to acclimate

---

1 Gleaves had commanded the torpedo boat *Cushing* during the Spanish-American War and later the battleship *North Dakota*, but Slocum knew him as captain of one of the presidential yachts, the U.S.S. *Mayflower*. Gleaves may have fostered Slocum's acquaintance with Theodore Roosevelt, who had read and admired *Sailing Alone*. Despite his duties, Gleaves found time to write. At the time Slocum was corresponding with Gleaves, he was reading Gleaves's biography of Captain James Lawrence, who, after being mortally wounded in the War of 1812, famously uttered "don't give up the ship." In a June 1, 1904, letter to Gleaves, Slocum noted that "[a] relative of the brave Lawrence is a neighbor of ours."

2 Gilder's lovely wife, the former Helena de Kay, was an artist, a founder of the Society of American Artists, and a favorite of Winslow Homer. Helena's stone studio, which later became home to the Marion gas plant, featured a massive stone fireplace designed by architect Stanford White. During the Gilders' time in Marion, their home and Helena's studio were a gathering place for many celebrated artists of the day.

Slocum makes a pretense of hoeing while Hettie appears to be harvesting summer squash.
(Photograph by Clifton Johnson; courtesy the New Bedford Whaling Museum)

himself to the land and become part of the community. Years later, Haig Adadourian, pastor of West Tisbury's First Congregational Church, remembered that on a visit to the Slocum house, "the distinguished, genial seaman regaled me with the fascinating account of his lone but by no means lonesome circumnavigation of the globe and of his having been honored and entertained by well-known captains in the various ports where the sloop had anchored to restock his galley." Adadourian called Slocum a "congenial, companionable soul."

Despite his lengthy respite aboard the *Spray* in 1903, Slocum was still presenting himself as a farmer a year later. On June 1, 1904, he wrote Albert

During his visit to Martha's Vineyard, Clifton Johnson asked Joshua and Hettie to pose together aboard the Spray. The captain was 58 at the time; Hettie was 40. Her gold wedding band is visible. The Spray was well-maintained at this time, four years after her voyage and one year after her display at the Pan-American Exposition. (Photograph by Clifton Johnson; courtesy the New Bedford Whaling Museum)

Gleaves, "The *Spray* has not yet fitted. She is moored in the pond at Cottage City while I am having the most strenuous life on a farm—I'm as busy as the devil in a gale of wind." That fall, when he sailed into Boston Harbor, he was still talking about the farm. On October 4 he told a *Globe* reporter that "he had finished his farming for the year and remembering that he needed to renew his papers as sailing master, he decided to run up to Boston."

There was more on Slocum's mind than Rudder Ranch and renewing his master mariner's license. During one of his stays in New York, Slocum had met Dr. Edward R. Shaw, a career educator who was then dean of New York University's School of Pedagogy. The professor, who had previously arranged abridged editions of *Two Years Before the Mast* and *Robinson Crusoe* for classroom use, suggested a school edition of *Sailing Alone* to Slocum. Slocum (and apparently *The Century*) agreed, and Shaw completed his revision shortly before his death at age 48 in February 1903. The book was published the following year by the Scribner Press.[1] On June 27, 1904, the *New York Times* called it "an abridged and adapted school reader taken from the old sea Captain's book.... The children will sail with him hereafter."

In Slocum's preface for *Around the World in the Sloop Spray*, he wrote, "In launching the new literary packet I desire to commend it especially to the indulgence of children around and all over the world." The abridgement suffered mightily by comparison with the original, as abridgements usually do, yet Slocum seemingly considered the abridged and unexpurgated editions to be interchangeable. He acquired and sold copies of *Around the World in the Sloop Spray*, just as he sold *Sailing Alone Around the World*, and he didn't always bother to tell customers that the former wasn't the "real" book.

By 1905, Joshua Slocum's farm charade seems to have ended. On May 5, the *Spray*, on a voyage to Maine, tied up in Boston. A newspaperman who visited the boat wrote that she was "newly painted and looks to be as staunch as the day she was launched." It may have been on this voyage that Slocum stopped in Salem and was given a guided tour of the East India Marine Society's museum (today the Peabody Essex Museum) by its assistant director, Lawrence Jenkins. With its many objects brought back by Salem captains from China and the South Seas, the society's collection would have been of special interest to Slocum.

---

1 Walter Teller's research revealed that the Scribner Series of School Reading edition was bound in gray cloth. Another edition "printed on better stock by the Caxton Press, and attractively bound in maroon, was also used by school districts." It was entitled *Around the World in the Sloop Spray, A Geographical Reader.*

The Spray at Salem, Massachusetts, sometime between 1902 and 1905. The nicely shaped tender atop the cabin replaced Slocum's old half-dory after the voyage. The photo was taken from Derby Wharf looking toward Central Wharf. The houses in the background still stand. The location is close to the Custom House made famous by Nathaniel Hawthorn in The Scarlet Letter. (Courtesy the New Bedford Whaling Museum)

On June 21 he was in Boothbay, Maine, where he posted correspondence on the status of the *Liberdade*. His invitation to take the *Spray* to Buffalo for the Pan-American Exposition had included the *Liberdade*, too, and his original plan had been to rescue the boat from its mothballed purgatory at the Smithsonian Museum, install his gasoline engine in her, and use her as the *Spray*'s towboat. This idea, never implemented, became just another footnote in Slocum's prolonged, confused, and hapless effort to do something about his old "canoe."

Now he wrote Professor Otis Tufton Mason to arrange for the *Liberdade* to "be all sawed apart and bundled in some corner. I would gladly send the amount of the cost and as soon as possible get the bundles away. If not, let the executioner do his work."

In fact, the "executioner" had already largely done so. Five months earlier, in a January 28 memorandum to staff, museum curator George Maynard had written, "I am told the boat was never brought into the building. For several years, it lay outdoors on the east side of the building and, Sept. 25, 1899, was stored in the yard at the Ninth Street Annex. It is not sheltered from the weather and is considerably dilapidated and going to decay.... The accession papers include a list of tools, etc, as belonging to the boat.... I know nothing about these accessories.... I think the opinion expressed by Mr. Earle [who had argued that the *Liberdade* was not appropriate for the museum] is correct, and do not see that the boat can be of any use in this Division."

But Slocum appears to have been ignorant of his boat's slow-motion demise. On his way back from Maine—pausing to give lectures at the Hull Lifesaving Station on August 5 and in Boston on August 16—he mulled the *Liberdade*'s future, and on November 7 he wrote again to the Smithsonian, this time to director Richard Rathbun. Slocum reported that he had gotten as far as Newport on his way to Washington to fetch the *Liberdade* when events intervened, and he'd cancelled his trip to pursue some unspecified "remarkable venture."[1] He further explained that he had now "traded *Liberdade* off for a portion of Nomans Land [an island south of Martha's Vineyard] and a share in a harbor that Mr. Davis,[2] the present owner of the island is building for small craft. The plan is to put power in the old Brazil boat and

---

1 In a subsequent letter written to the Smithsonian's Professor Mason in October 1906, Slocum said he had been blown offshore and "couldn't fetch the capes of the Chesapeake."

2 Henry B. Davis's plan for Nomans Land never developed, and neither did his deal with Slocum.

run her as a packet between Nomans and New Bedford. She will want some repairs I know, but one week on her will make things look different."

Slocum's *Liberdade* correspondence would continue several more years without conclusion. His intentions were good, but he was merely thinking out loud. He simply could not focus long enough to follow through.

Around this time, Slocum unexpectedly received a job offer. Albert Gleaves had earlier introduced him to "the Carnegie Institution of Washington," now known as the Carnegie Institution of Science. On November 2, 1905, Slocum wrote Gleaves, "The President of the Institution pays me the great compliment to ask if I would consider the command of the *Galilee* in the service of the Institution. It may be only a compliment and if sincere not the best thing for me—I might not be just fitted for the place." Slocum knew himself well enough to recognize that commanding somebody else's ship might not suit him.

Another of Slocum's schemes was to escape New England's winters in the Caribbean, and this idea quickly evolved to a concrete plan. When reporters asked him about his upcoming voyage, Slocum responded as if Hettie would go with him, but in fact she remained firm in her resolve not to accompany her husband on any long cruise. By now the Slocums' neighbors on Martha's Vineyard could see that the couple's relationship was, at the least, unconventional.

Like small-town newspapers everywhere, the *Vineyard Gazette* reported the comings and goings of island residents and guests. When Slocum returned to the Vineyard on August 31, 1905, the *Gazette's* West Tisbury column noted that he'd been gone for months. Alice Longraker later remembered that Joshua cared little about staying in touch with his siblings. Speaking of her older brother's whereabouts once, Slocum's sister Margaret told Alice that he was "off in a sloop 'God knows where' as nobody ever hears from him!'"

In October, the *Gazette* reported a seven-day sailing trip by Slocum alone to Boston. Hettie, who had taken in paying boarders over the summer during Slocum's absence, made the paper on November 9. With the long, gray winter impending, Hettie, then 43 years old, decided she preferred to spend it with her sister. The Slocums closed their little house for the season, and Hettie went to East Boston while Slocum sailed alone for the Caribbean. Thus began another chapter in the dissolution of Joshua Slocum's marriage to his cousin.

According to Victor Slocum, his father told him that he sailed to

The Spray *became a familiar sight on Martha's Vineyard. The New England News Company of Boston published this postcard showing the famous boat sailing out between the jetties at Oak Bluffs, circa 1905. (From the collection of Melville C. Brown)*

warmer climes "to save buying an overcoat." Joshua Slocum, who seldom, if ever, complained about anything except ill-treatment by the press or ignorant yahoos, admitted to Garfield that he suffered from rheumatism and felt better in warmer climates. In a March 18, 1904 letter to William Tripp, his New Bedford banker, Slocum had written, "I became so interested in trying to keep warm these winter days that I forget all, except the wood-pile. I have an oak grove, fortunately, near my house."

The Slocums' little corner of Martha's Vineyard was no place for overwintering for anyone who dreaded the cold, and West Tisbury was also a subdued place socially in the winter months. Its paucity of year-round inhabitants gave Joshua and Hettie another reason to shut up the house during the bleak months. Nor did New York beckon him any longer. According to Victor, the New York clubs at which he'd been feted during the past few years "began to bore him, as did spike tails, white throat seizings and black ties."

In November 1905, Slocum departed the cold, gray autumn waters of New England for the warm, turquoise waters of the Caribbean. He sailed to Cuba, then to Kingston, Jamaica, and finally to Grand Cayman. On his

Staying warm became increasingly important to Slocum as he grew older. During his summer visit to the 58-year-old captain in 1902, Clifton Johnson made this photograph showing Slocum in front of the big fireplace in his old Vineyard house. On the mantle is a sea fan and a lucky horseshoe. The alarm clock does not match the one illustrated in Slocum's book. Barely visible is a copy of Sailing Alone Around the World *on the top shelf of the book case. (Courtesy the New Bedford Whaling Museum)*

circumnavigation, Slocum had collected a variety of exotic shells and corals that he believed would find a ready market upon his return. Perhaps he felt a connection to Virginia through this activity, for her older sons remembered their mother as an enthusiastic shell collector, scouring beaches in the Philippines and elsewhere. Slocum spent two months in the winter of 1905–06 collecting a hold full of conch shells. At the urging of some islanders, he also took aboard some rare orchids that they wished to present to President Theodore Roosevelt as a gift.

Slocum's route home that spring involved a detour. Instead of sailing up the coast to New England, he entered the Delaware Bay, the *Spray's* original home waters, and sailed with the tide up the Delaware River to Riverton, New Jersey, where he'd been invited to speak at the Riverton Yacht Club. He also took the opportunity to visit friends who summered on the Vineyard but lived most of the year in Philadelphia.

It was upon Slocum's return from Philadelphia to the *Spray* at the Riverton Yacht Club that he was arrested. A 12-year-old girl who had visited the *Spray* with a friend on the afternoon of Friday, May 25, told her father that she had, as the local newspaper put it on June 1, "suffered indignities at the hands of Capt. Slocum." This came as quite a shock to Joshua. The local paper, the *New Era*, reported, "At the hearing Capt. Slocum said he had no recollection of the misdemeanor with which he is charged, and if it occurred it must have been during one of the mental lapses to which he was subject."

His so-called "mental lapses" could only have been the occasional forgetfulness that accompanies advancing years or some lingering effect—real or imagined—from that blow to the head by the end of a heaving line in Newcastle, Australia. Although the initial charge was rape, it became immediately obvious, thanks to a doctor's examination, that the girl had suffered no physical harm. A letter from the girl's father clarified that "an assault ... appeared to misstate the facts."

The facts were that Slocum had neglected to button his pants—and not for the first time. At least two other visitors to the *Spray* noted that they had found Slocum careless in the same fashion. Given the possibility that Slocum was wearing no "undergarment," the girl's shock was understandable. Her father's letter stated that his daughter had been "greatly agitated by the indecent action and exposure of the person on this part of this creature now posing in the limelight of cheap notoriety."

It took almost a week for bail to be set, and when it was, Slocum couldn't afford the $1,000 cost and thus remained in jail. As days passed without an indictment, the charge was reduced to indecent assault. When, eventually, the case was heard before a judge, Slocum's attorney entered a plea of no contest and noted that there had been no intent to cause bodily harm. Neither the girl's family nor the judge believed any further action was appropriate. "Upon request of the family I can deal leniently with you," the judge told Slocum, but he admonished the captain never to return to Riverton. After spending 42 days in jail for his forgetfulness, Slocum was released on July 6 and, relieved to put the matter behind him, sailed back down the Delaware on the morning of July 7.

Years later, a letter to Walter Teller written by Percy Chase Miller, the son of Slocum's Philadelphia friend, provides a glimpse of Joshua Slocum just shy of the midway point of his sixty-second year: "Slocum was lean and hungry looking and gaunt. But he looked as though he could take care of himself. I was never disappointed in his appearance or behavior though I am quite sure he was a little cracked."

The notion of Slocum being a bit "cracked" or off-kilter was put forward by others he met in 1906–08. Mostly the comments were prompted by his eccentricities, such as cutting off big chunks off salt cod to eat in front of passengers on the rickety stage coach on the Vineyard or eating a bouquet of nasturtiums given him by a young visitor. But observations of Slocum's visitors in this period suggest that the captain had entered a period of decline. That decline was reflected all too obviously in the condition of Slocum's beloved boat.

Slocum took his time getting to Sagamore Hill, Theodore Roosevelt's house at Oyster Bay, Long Island, making one more passage of the East River en route. As soon as he arrived with his gift of orchids from the islands, he was greeted by 12-year-old Archie Roosevelt, who was sailing in one of the boats belonging to the presidential yacht *Sylph*. "The boy is a good sailor," the *Boston Daily Globe* reported in an article on March 4, 1907, "and when the family is at Oyster Bay in the summer months he spends a great deal of his time on the water."

Slocum promptly invited Archie aboard the *Spray* and showed him his shells and details of the boat. When Archie told his father about the visit, Roosevelt asked him to invite the captain to Sagamore Hill. Years later, in a letter to Walter Teller, Archie Roosevelt said that Slocum "proceeded to make friends of all of us, particularly my brother Kermit, and me. He was fond of Kermit because he and Kermit were great admirers of the poems of Rudyard Kipling. The captain could repeat much of Kipling."

As a result of this visit, Archie and a member of the *Sylph's* crew, a seaman named Obie, accompanied Slocum on the next leg of his trip home, a sail from Oyster Bay to Newport.[1] Roosevelt remembered fascinating details of the *Spray* and her captain in his letter to Walter Teller:

> *The boat was the most incredibly dirty craft I have ever seen. You can imagine how it offended Obie, who had been trained in the U.S. Navy. When we stopped at New Haven, Obie went ashore, and returned with a kerosene stove, which he bought with his own money, and jettisoned the filthy old relic that had served the captain, I don't know how many years....*
>
> *As a diet, he was fond of salt fish and every so often he would make us enormous pancakes, 'as thick as your foot,' he would tell us.*
>
> *The sleeping quarters were in the after cabin, and Obie and I slept on the top of a wooden chest, and the captain had his bunk.*

---

1 Slocum occasionally volunteered to take young people with him for a cruise on the *Spray*. In the summer of 1899, he'd taken the daughter of The Century Company's Robert Johnson for a sail out of Fairhaven "up Buzzards Bay or where else [she] may elect to direct her course."

In the hold, there was a quantity of miscellaneous equipment, and an enormous number of conch shell. Some of these had not been too carefully cleaned, and there was a fine ripe odor permeating the center of the ship.

While we were sailing, we would busy ourselves filing the points off the shells, and thereby making fog horns out of them. These, the captain would sell to visitors who came aboard when he was anchored in a port. He also sold his book, and charged, I believe, ten cents to every visitor. We learned, under his tutelage, to be pretty good salesmen of the shells and the book.

Of course we saw the famous alarm clock, which had to be boiled before it would run. Beyond my comprehension were his sheets of calculations for the lunar observation he had made single-handedly—a feat, I believe which is supposed to require three people to work out.

It is quite common for sail boats to sail on the wind with little or no attention paid to the helm, but the old Spray was, so far as my experience goes, unique in the fact that it would sail off the wind as well as on, without it being necessary to mind the helm after the course was set.

Regarding the *Spray's* rig at this time, Roosevelt recalled that "she carried a gaff-rigged main-sail, a stay-sail, and a jib set on a bowsprit. Now and then he would set a ballooner. Although rigged for a yawl, I never saw him carry a spanker." During the five-day cruise to Newport, the *Spray* encountered what the *Globe* reported as "all kinds of weather" before arriving on the morning of August 4. At Newport, Archie Roosevelt would be looked after by Albert Gleaves, then in command of the torpedo station. Slocum would, in the future, continue to enjoy a cordial relationship with the Roosevelts. The president sent him a note:

My dear Captain Slocum:
I thank you for your interesting volume, which you know I prize.
By the way, I entirely sympathize with your feeling of delight in the sheer loneliness and vastness of the ocean. It was just my feeling in the wilderness of the west.

Sincerely yours,
Theodore Roosevelt

The *New York Sun* of August 6 reported that "Capt. Slocum is on his way to Martha's Vineyard, but will make a short stay at Newport." Although he'd not seen Hettie in eight months, there is no indication that Slocum was eager to get home.

The truth was that the Slocums were now essentially separated. Slocum no longer needed a stepmother for his children. Jessie Helena had married in 1899 at age 24. Garfield had left the Vineyard in the spring of 1905 and found a job in Schenectady. Victor, still advancing his seafaring career, had added whaling to his résumé and was named among New Bedford's top harpooners in 1903. Benjamin Aymar was living in Lynn and pursuing what would be a successful engineering vocation; in 1906 he embarked on a short-lived teenage marriage. And Hettie, for her part, had long since abandoned any fond illusions of what life with a sea captain might be like. In June 1952, Walter Teller interviewed a number of Vineyard residents who had known the couple. A primary memory was that the Slocums were an "unusual family."[1]

During the summer of 1906, Joshua Slocum spent less than a month on Martha's Vineyard before departing for New Bedford and then Rhode Island, where he lingered for a time. As of September 28, he was at the Herreshoff yard in Bristol, perhaps doing some fitting out for the upcoming voyage south. He may have departed on October 1, which is when Captain Nathanael Herreshoff's daughter, Agnes Mueller Herreshoff, snapped several photos of Slocum and his boat.

During this Rhode Island interlude, Slocum once again contacted the Smithsonian about the *Liberdade*. On October 13, Slocum wrote Professor Mason from Providence:

> *If it is not asking too much I would very much like have Liberdad hauled away to some lot or down to the Potomac if any of your people know a place for her there or most any where. I would chance her, turned bottom up, under a tree, or alongside of a stone wall or fence. And will gladly pay for the trouble in the matter.*
>
> *I have written Archie Roosevelt about Liberdade. If Archie cares for her please deliver to him. Otherwise she might be hauled inland to some farm yard.... I feel guilt for not having carted this boat away and*

---

1 Divorce was still unusual at the time, at a rate of perhaps 8 percent. Because neither abuse nor infidelity were involved, the only reason Hettie might have cited according to then existing laws was abandonment. But the Slocums stuck it out.

after you have been so kind I have no right to ask it but if your people can lodge her somewhere for me till next Spring! Anyhow she must go from the present place.

At about this time Slocum received a letter from Dr. Charles Elihu Slocum, working as ever on his family genealogy. In a response written on November 15, Slocum apologized for being so hard to reach. "I regret that I have not been able to be, myself, a better subject among my kind—to have added an interesting line." But the material Charles Slocum gathered for Joshua's entry in his work was accurate, if lacking the flavor that a personal note from Slocum could have added.

Now, finally, Slocum headed the *Spray* for Washington, D.C., to deal with the *Liberdade* in person—but didn't bother to tell anyone about it. An internal memorandum at the Smithsonian addressed to director Rathbun on December 6, 1906, tells of the boat's removal. "Captain Slocum, when recently in Washington arranged with Cumberland's shipyard to receive and take care of the *Liberdade*. I have requested Professor Mason to prepare the necessary papers for your signature authorizing the removal of the boat. This transfer was authorized by you over a year ago, but we have never been able to get Captain Slocum to make any definite arrangements to remove it."

The memo included a "Memorandum of Packing" indicating that the *Liberdade*, or whatever was left of her, was ready for shipment to "Captain Joshua Slocum c/o Edward A. Cumberland at Cumberland's Wharf, 9th & Water Sts. SW, Washington, D.C." But it was not until some eight years later, on February 19, 1914, that the fate of the *Liberdade* was finally clarified after Victor Slocum sent a letter inquiring about her. At that time a Smithsonian curator paid a personal visit to the Cumberland boatyard to learn what had happened. By then, however, Cumberland had sold the yard, and the new owner had no knowledge of the boat. The curator's response to Victor picked up the story there:

The custodian of the adjoining wharf, occupied by the Capitol Yacht Club, knew Captain Slocum and saw him there looking after the Liberdade. Mr. W. K. Wimsatt, of the firm of Johnson and Wimsatt, wholesale lumber dealers, whose office is at the foot of Twelfth and Thirteenth Streets, S.W., was acquainted with Captain Slocum and saw him frequently some seven years ago when he was at the wharf with the Spray. I am told that Mr. Wimsatt states that your father at that time dismantled the Liberdade, cut it into pieces and put it aboard *The Spray*, after taking out the copper nails and other metal parts. It seems that your father gave the stem and stern of the Liberdade to Mr. Wimsatt, who still has the latter, but the stem he gave to the owner of a boat-building place nearby. Mr. Wimsatt, who may be addressed as above, and who perhaps knows more of the details connected with the last days of the Liberdade than anyone else, has expressed his willingness to furnish further information if you care to write to him on the subject.

It was a sad, shabby end to a cleverly designed and resourcefully built boat that had made an impressive sea voyage. Yet for all she represented, the *Liberdade* could not find a home in what is often called, affectionately, "the nation's attic." It is not hard to imagine Slocum's emotions as he dismantled the "old *Liberdade*" while, ever thrifty, saving her metalwork.

With the *Liberdade* matter finally resolved, Slocum sailed on for the Caribbean. He was still doing his best to keep busy, still trying to inject purpose into his life. Remembering the tridacna shells he had taken aboard at Keeling Cocos, he intended once again to collect shells in the Caribbean during the winter so he could sell them in New England in the summer.

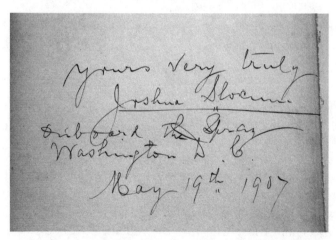

During his visit to Washington in the spring of 1907, Slocum sold autographed copies of books to visitors. This is the inscription in one of them. (Courtesy Chris Cunningham)

By now he suspected he was losing his faculties. In Kingston, Jamaica, in January 1907, he met a newspaperwoman from Philadelphia named Louise B. Ward. In a letter to Walter Teller in 1957, she recalled that Slocum said to her, "I can patch up the *Spray* but who will patch up Captain Slocum?" It was among the very few admissions he ever made that he wasn't the man he used to be and could perhaps use some help.

But even if he had had somewhere to turn for help—for company, for relief—it is unlikely he would have done so. It wasn't something that one did. It wasn't something a sea captain did. It wasn't something *he* did. Instead he carried on as usual, as best he could. In the spring of 1907 he was back in Washington, selling his book and making plans for the summer. On May 26 he answered a letter from Ben Aymar, who was now 34 years old, writing:

> *I am going ahead some again, with a vessel full of stuff worth something. My books are selling rather better than at first.*
>
> *I lecture Friday 31st at a fine hall here, and am promised a good house.*
>
> *The president sent down for me yesterday to meet him the Red Room, White House. Archie came and brought me in their market wagon.*
>
> *Archie will join me again at Oyster Bay and come further east this summer, perhaps to Falmouth or Woods Hole. You must find time to meet us in Aug.*
>
> *Your father*
> */s/ Joshua Slocum*

The planned cruise with Archie didn't work out, and Slocum sailed to the Vineyard alone.[1] There, at Cottage City, he opened up the *Spray* for business, selling his books, shells, and sponges and whatever other curios he had gathered. Sometimes he enlisted the aid of delighted island children in his sales efforts, and those who met the captain in this capacity would remember him fondly years later.

Slocum sailed south again in the fall of 1907, this time with a distinct

---

1 When Theodore Roosevelt later presented Archie with a sailing dory, Archie named it the *Spray*. Slocum sent Archie congratulations when he heard that Archie and the *Spray* had won a race.

The Spray in Washington, D.C., in 1907 after a winter in the Caribbean. The neglect visible here would worsen in coming months. This may be among the last pictures of the Spray with her gaff rig. The lazyjacks Slocum rigged were effective in keeping the big main sail contained as it was lowered. (Photograph by Winfield Scott Clime; courtesy the New Bedford Whaling Museum)

Looking worn but alert, Slocum stares into the camera during his stay in Washington in 1907. Behind him on the cabintop are big starfish brought back from the Caribbean. The Spray's boom displays deep fissures, but the sail, which has a seamanlike reef tied in, appears to be in good condition. (Photograph by Winfield Scott Clime; courtesy the New Bedford Whaling Museum)

purpose. He had been commissioned by the American Museum of Natural History to bring back a distinctive coral from the Bahamian island of Andros. Slocum's winter in the Bahamas was profitable. He loaded the two-ton piece of coral into the *Spray's* hold, and, in Nassau, gave a well-attended talk at the Colonial Hotel. His Vineyard friend Ernest Dean was on a yacht in Nassau at the time, and later told Walter Teller that Slocum made over $500 during his stopover there. Dean also reported what must have been the last example of Slocum using his big fist.

While he was splicing line aboard the *Spray* at the Nassau waterfront, Slocum heard several islanders disparaging his boat. One proclaimed that any man who said the *Spray* had sailed around the world was a liar. Dean told Teller what Slocum had told him: "I looked up in time to see which one said it, made a pier head leap, and with a couple of side-winders unshipped his jaw." Slocum's sensitivity to insult, whether to himself or the *Spray*, had not entirely mellowed with age.

The *Spray's* cargo was just one of 200 shipments of corals to the museum, part of an ambitious new exhibit planned by director Herman Carey

Bumpus. On May 29, 1907, the *New York Times* told readers what they could expect to see once the exhibit was installed. The plan was "to cut a section of the first floor of the museum building and reproduce below the level of the floor a representation of the bottom of the sea, showing the coral reefs in all stages of development. The section of the floor to be cut out will be 6 by 30 feet. When the reproduction of the reef and sea bottom has been completed, the flooring will be replaced by a rectangle of heavy plate glass."

Although details of the event are absent, Archie Roosevelt recalled that Slocum told him the *Spray's* gaff had been broken, presumably in the Caribbean during the winter of 1907. Slocum then rerigged the boat. Roosevelt recalled "a jib-headed or leg-o-mutton mainsail.... As I recollect it the jib-head was sort of a square jib-head with a little bit of sprit maybe a foot or two long and hoisted on what ordinarily would have been the throat halyard."

Such a sail would have been familiar in the Bahamian islands, and it dispensed with the heavy gaff. The sail itself—with a luff and foot about the same length—would have been lighter and smaller than the *Spray's* gaff mainsail. The new main had a small, curved gaff, the "sprit" that Roosevelt referred to, at its head, to which the halyard was attached. Slocum also replaced the mizzen lugsail with a triangular mizzen. This sail, with its much longer foot, required dispensing with the original elegantly curved, comparatively short boomkin. The new boomkin was a stout pole mounted much lower on the transom.

Whatever success Slocum had during his Bahamas cruise, he didn't share it with Hettie. In fact, he left her entirely in the dark about his whereabouts. Having nowhere else to turn, Hettie wrote Clarence Buel on May 11, 1908:

> *Dear Sir –*
> *Have just heard that the Spray is reported lost in the Maritime Register, have not heard any details.*
> *Personally have not heard from Captain Slocum since Nov. 1st, 1907.*
> *A Vineyard man reports he saw Captain Slocum in Jamaica a few weeks ago. I have doubts about the truth of the reports at this time. Will you kindly let me know if you have heard from him or of him of late. And greatly oblige.*
>
> *Very Sincerely,*
> *Mrs. J. Slocum*

The letter must have given the editor fresh insight into the Slocums' relationship.

Slocum arrived in New York with his cargo of conch shells and the museum's coral on June 2, 1908. While his movements in the period immediately afterward are uncertain, a likely scenario is that he sailed to Fairhaven and spent several weeks there alone aboard his boat. Eventually, in July, the *Spray* arrived at Martha's Vineyard. It was there, on July 23, writing from the *Spray* at Vineyard Haven, that he sent a letter to Herman Carey Bumpus at the American Museum of Natural History. Slocum thanked the director in advance for a photograph of the museum Bumpus said he was sending.[1]

At some point Slocum, or someone on the island, let Hettie know that her husband was back. It had been nearly eight months since she'd had word of him, but his visit to Rudder Ranch was a brief one. The notice that appeared in the *Vineyard Gazette*'s West Tisbury column on July 30, 1908, said all that one needed to know about the Slocum marriage: "Capt. Joshua Slocum of the sloop *Spray* is on the Island and has been a recent guest of Mrs. Slocum."

---

1 In addition to the coral that Slocum delivered, he gave the museum a gift of a wooden shield he'd acquired in Queensland. It was cataloged on June 18, 1908, as number 1908-33, 80.3783, and given accession number 5733.

The date and place of this photo of Slocum posed on a tree stump are unknown. What can be said with certainty is that the light-colored suit and hat were atypical. Slocum normally wore more practical dark suits, and he did not appear in this outfit in any other known photographs. (Courtesy the New Bedford Whaling Museum)

CHAPTER 21

The Disappearance
of Joshua Slocum

"In the sweet by and by,
We shall meet on that beautiful shore ...."

—*"In the Sweet By-and-By,"* 1868, lyrics by Sandford Fillmore Bennett,
sometimes sung by Joshua Slocum aboard the *Spray*

IN THE MARCH 1968 ISSUE of *The Skipper* magazine, lifelong sailor and
yachting writer Harold S. Smith (H. S. "Skipper" Smith) recalled meeting
and sailing with Joshua Slocum six decades before. Smith was 85 when he
wrote the article entitled "Quite Another Matter," but he had been about 23
years old when he and three friends went aboard the *Spray*. He did not recall
the exact year of the visit, referring to as being "[s]ome sixty-odd years ago,"
but the best guess based on the *Spray's* condition is 1908, probably between
mid-June and mid-July. Smith and his friends paid Slocum the usual 10
cents apiece to board the *Spray* where she lay in a Fairhaven creek.

Describing his first impression of the *Spray*, Harold Smith wrote,
"The little ship was filthy and almost everything aboard was dilapidated....

Also he had aboard a cargo of conch shells, most of them containing remains of their former inmates, all in a putrefying condition, and I can still remember that smell."

Smith's description of the 64-year-old Slocum likewise painted a distressing picture. "When we first went aboard, he had been sitting, or perhaps slumped is the better word, by the wheel in an attitude that betokened complete dejection. There was an air about him of abstraction and disinterest that was so deep it was as though he were living in a private dream world.... Captain Slocum himself answered our questions in a slow and hesitant way, indicating a kind of mental slothfulness or perhaps senility."

But Slocum's demeanor changed dramatically when his visitors, all experienced yachtsmen, asked if they could go for a sail by paying a dollar each. Slocum assented after the young men agreed they wouldn't mind anchoring at New Bedford on the way back so Slocum could row ashore to fetch some supplies. Perking up, Slocum "stayed by the wheel and gave his orders in a very crisp, sharp fashion without shouting—a far cry from his earlier hesitant mumbling."

Just getting the *Spray* out of her berth required clever boat handling, which Slocum directed. Smith recalled, "We ran out a small anchor on a long line so that we could haul her clear of the [mooring] stakes when ready. Then we made sail in true yawl fashion—jigger first, mainsail next, and cast off the jib gaskets. Oddly enough the sails, which I expected to find in bad shape, appeared in good condition and were very strongly and heavily made. We hauled *Spray* out to the small anchor, and at the proper moment, I hailed the captain: 'She's up and down, Sir.' Slocum came forward, hoisted the jib, belayed the halyard to a cleat at the foot of the mast, and held the clew in his hand until the ship's bow began to pay off. Then he let it go and walked aft to the wheel."

Slocum asked Smith to tend the jibsheet as he tacked the *Spray* out of the narrow creek to the Acushnet River. Smith felt the boat was moving at perhaps 4 knots in a light breeze and noticed that the mainsheet hadn't been trimmed. But when he moved to adjust the sheet, Slocum stopped him, saying, "No, don't. She sails better that way." The wind picked up steadily, and as they entered Buzzards Bay, the predictable afternoon southwester filled in. Smith noted that the *Spray* sailed at a very small angle of heel, wasn't bothered by the seas, and shipped only a negligible amount of spray over her bow.

As the *Spray* completed her long starboard tack across Buzzards Bay and neared Cape Cod, Smith wrote, "I was afraid that we might have a little trouble in stays, but she came around without any difficulty and without it being necessary to trim anything but the jib sheets. We then laid her off for New Bedford harbor, but the captain told us to keep well offshore.... On the run in, I watched *Spray* very carefully to ascertain how far she would hold her course by herself. She did not entirely, although the wheel was very light and required little attention.... Captain Slocum explained that, when running down wind, he usually doused the jigger to make her steer more easily."

After anchoring off the New Bedford wharves, the young sailors stayed aboard while Slocum went ashore for his supplies. Upon his return, they sailed across the river and, under Slocum's orders, "we dropped all sail at the entrance to the creek and let her ghost in between her mooring stakes. Slocum deftly dropped the bight of a line around one of the piles, and eased her to a stop, and we tied her up."

Harold Smith never forgot the details of the day he and his friends spent with Joshua Slocum. Blessed with the full experience of life by the time he wrote his article, Smith could convey his observations of the transformation in Slocum from the dejected figure who greeted him upon coming aboard to the commanding skipper alert to every detail.

"But the minute the lines were off and the *Spray* gathered way, he had turned into quite another man. He moved precisely, firmly, quickly, but not hastily, about the ship's business.... There was, I do believe, a sparkle in his eye, and there was little aboard that he didn't notice. He didn't say much, but you knew that he was a ship's captain, if from nothing else, from his confident bearing and from the quiet preciseness of his commands."

Ultimately, Smith concluded that Joshua Slocum "was one of that rare breed that is alive only at sea." Inevitably, perhaps, the sea would also be the place of Slocum's death.

GIVEN ALL THE MISSING and conflicting information about Joshua Slocum's early career and his readiness to provide vague or incorrect details about himself, it should not be entirely surprising that, in the end, he simply vanished. Four basic questions arose following Joshua Slocum's loss: When did he depart from Martha's Vineyard on his final voyage? When did the end come? Where did the end come? And how did he die?

Was Slocum's final going from Martha's Vineyard in 1908 or 1909? That at least, is a question that should have a simple answer, except that it does not. The relevant documents require interpretation, and Walter Teller's reading of the evidence led him to conclude that 1909 was the year. In her book *Alone at Sea, the adventures of Joshua Slocum,* Ann Spencer concluded that the year was 1908, and my own gathering and sifting of available evidence leads me to concur.

After his presumably brief stay in West Tisbury as a guest of Hettie in the summer of 1908, Slocum returned to the *Spray.* He spent some time at Vineyard Haven, but was at Menemsha on September 14, where he invited summer visitor Charles Harris and his children Nat and Catherine aboard. The Harris children kept a diary of their summer idyll on the Vineyard, and Catherine's entry for September 14, a day when the wind was "N.E. fresh" and the weather "clear," included remarks on her visit to the *Spray.* "We met Captain Slocum. We went aboard his boat. He gave me some shells and a piece of coral."[1] Ten days later, on September 24, the *Vineyard Gazette* reported that Slocum had gone to New York without mentioning the reason why. Possibly he had a speaking engagement.

By the time Slocum returned to the Vineyard, he would have been looking ahead to his voyage south in November. Hettie, too, was leaving for the winter. Despite the fractious state of their relationship, Slocum never gave up asking her to sail with him. Looking back on this time in a 1910 interview with the *Washington Star,* Hettie said, "He was anxious I should go with him saying he knew I would have a good time after we arrived in the West Indies: but I replied that I had not enough courage to take such a long voyage in the *Spray.*"

Hettie departed West Tisbury on November 12 for Wakefield, Massachusetts, and the home of her sister Mrs. James Elliott Tingley, and Slocum put to sea. Although she would later have lapses about the date of her husband's final departure, Hettie supplied the date to several newspapers in the following few years.

What may be the first notice of Slocum having gone missing appeared some 11 months after Joshua and Hettie left the Vineyard to go their separate ways. The *Fairhaven Star* printed a brief notice of Slocum's disappearance that was picked up by the *Vineyard Gazette* of September 30, 1909: "It is feared that Captain Slocum is lost.... The return of Captain Slocum's mail unopened from a foreign port to which he directed it to be sent when he sailed from this port last November on one of his long cruises on the *Spray,* and the fact that no word has been received from him since he sailed, has led

---

1 *Martha's Vineyard,* May–June 2005, "The Living was Easy," edited by Tom Dunlop

his wife and relatives to believe that he has been lost."

On July 25, 1910, the Boston *Daily Globe* ran a story datelined New Bedford, July 24, and including a quote from Hettie: "I believe beyond all doubt that Capt. Slocum is lost.... He sailed Nov. 12, 1908 going south for the sake of his health.... We expected to hear from him when he reached the Bahamas."

The *New York Times* picked up the story on July 26, 1910, with a headline and subhead that gave unequivocal evidence of Slocum's departure time: "Sloop Master Missing. Capt. Slocum Sailed for Antilles November, 1908— Wife Thinks He's Lost." The *Star*, the *Gazette*, the *Globe*, and the *Times* all gave the departure date as November 12, 1908.

In an August 28, 1910 letter to her Nova Scotia friend Mrs. Albert McNutt, Hettie reaffirmed the year of her husband's sailing, although she changed the date: "He sailed from Vineyard Haven the *Spray's* home port on Nov. 14th,[2] 1908 bound to the West Indies, and to my knowledge nothing has ever been heard from him since that date."

On November 13, 1910, the *Washington Herald* reported that Slocum had gone missing after leaving the Vineyard almost exactly two years earlier. "Hundreds of Washingtonians will remember his visit to this city in May and June 1907 on his return from the West Indies.... On November 14, 1908, Captain Slocum sailed alone from Vineyard Haven, Mass., the *Spray's* home port, bound for the West Indies to escape the severe New England winter.... His wife tried to persuade him not to attempt the voyage in 1908, but he replied that he could not live through another cold winter at home.... From that day to this, a period of nearly two years, no word has come from the bold navigator."

Six months after the *Washington Herald* story, on May 27, 1911, the New Bedford *Standard* published a note about Slocum prompted by one of many spurious rumors that he was still living. This little story claimed that a white man seen on the Orinoco River[3] might just be the lost captain who "left here in November 1908."

The preponderance of evidence thus supports a departure date of

---

2 Why Hettie used November 14 here is unknowable. It is possible that Slocum had not yet sailed when she herself left the island on November 12, and that she expected him to sail later that same day or within a couple of days.

3 The Orinoco River Delta can be reached by island-hopping south through the West Indies to Trinidad and Tobago, then making a short hop to Venezuela. It was a plausible destination that would have had allure for Slocum, and he seems to have mentioned it as a possibility—but that might have been another instance of thinking out loud.

November 1908 for Slocum's final voyage. The evidence for the 1909 alternative is shaky by comparison and doesn't hold up to scrutiny.

The first such document is a typed copy of a letter sent by Joshua Slocum to his son Victor. Slocum wrote, "We are pulling out of it [West Tisbury] for the winter at least and would sell if a purchaser should turn up." The letter is dated September 4, 1909, but that is either a typo made during transcription from the original or a lapse on Slocum's part. Victor Slocum may well have been unaware of the *Star* article or even the incorrect date on his father's letter. At any rate, Victor used 1909 in his book, which also gave his mother's death incorrectly as occurring in 1885 rather than 1884. Having accepted 1909, Victor also used that as the year when Slocum stopped for a brief refit at the Herreshoff yard on his way south. Like all sailors, Joshua Slocum appears to have held Nathanael Greene Herreshoff in high regard. The great yacht designer had visited the *Spray* during a chance encounter at Woods Hole. Slocum, who didn't immediately recognize Herreshoff, later sent him a signed photograph of the *Spray*, inscribing it: "To the man I mistook for a farmer." Subsequently, in 1906 (and perhaps at other times), Slocum had sailed the *Spray* to Bristol, Rhode Island, and did some refitting at the Herreshoff yard.

Capt. Slocum.

The Spray was no stranger to the Herreshoff Manufacturing Company wharf. On October 1, 1906, Captain Nat Herreshoff's daughter, Agnes Mueller Herreshoff, snapped this image of Slocum wearing the big straw hat he used to protect his bald head from the sun. (Courtesy the Herreshoff Marine Museum)

In Bristol, Slocum met with both Nathanael Herreshoff and Captain Nat's son, Francis, who was 18 years old in 1908. Both Herreshoffs were more impressed by Slocum than by his worn-looking boat, to which they donated paint and cordage. Francis wrote Walter Teller, "My father did not think much of the *Spray* but he had great admiration for Captain Slocum's ability to go around the world in such a poor vessel." Francis later used 1909 as the date of the visit, but there is no record in either Herreshoff's papers that gives the year of Slocum's final visit. So Francis Herreshoff, who was many things but not a diarist, was writing based on memory 36 years after the fact. The greater evidence suggests that he was off by a year.

The strongest support for a 1909 departure date comes from an "official document" based on testimony supplied by Hettie. On April 12, 1912, Hettie filed a petition in the Dukes County Probate Court to have her husband declared dead, but for some inexplicable reason, the petition stated that Slocum had "disappeared, absconded and absented himself on the 14th day of November A.D. 1909."

Why, after all Hettie's previous references to a November 1908 departure, the month and year consistently published in the newspapers of the time, did the year change to 1909? Perhaps she had a simple memory lapse that went unremarked. Perhaps she felt that the year of Slocum's presumed death at sea was more to the point than the year of his sailing from the Vineyard. Perhaps she grew embarrassed that almost a year had elapsed between her husband's departure and her report of his absence.

Once Hettie got 1909 in her mind, it stayed there. On November 27, 1923, when Hettie was finally appointed administrator of Joshua Slocum's estate, the date of Slocum's final departure from Martha's Vineyard was once again given as November 14, 1909. If, at the time of her 1923 filing to be named administrator, Hettie remembered 1908 as the correct year of her husband's departure from the Vineyard, she didn't bother to call attention to her earlier error. Perhaps she felt it would have added a needless complication. Thus, the date of Joshua Slocum's departure from Martha's Vineyard as officially recorded is one year later than the event itself.

ONCE IT WAS MORE OR LESS obvious that Joshua Slocum had been lost, a variety of people emerged to claim they had been the last to see the famous mariner alive. More than one commercial fisherman from the Vineyard, sailing his catboat in nasty November weather in Muskeget Channel, believed he had seen the doomed skipper heading out. Up and down the coast, others voiced a similar conviction. L. Francis Herreshoff wrote Walter Teller, "I shouldn't be surprised if I were the last one to speak to the captain for I saw him off on the morning that he departed."

Even years later, people readily told how they'd waved good-bye to Joshua Slocum or were convinced they'd been the last to see him. In the April 1940 edition of *The Rudder* magazine, Toni Culler shared with readers the reactions that the fine *Spray* replica completed in 1930 by her husband, boat designer and builder Pete Culler, often evoked:

> At Nantucket we were greeted by the last man to see Captain Slocum alive ...
>
> At Moorhead City we were boarded by an old sea captain who was a friend of Capt. Slocum and who had seen him off on his last voyage ...
>
> At Charleston we met the same man only he was a different man ...
>
> The other day at Lauderdale another stranger (the sixteenth I believe) dropped in to tell us he'd waved goodbye to Slocum on his last voyage.

In addition to the many people who believed they were the last to see Joshua Slocum, the mystery of how he was lost prompted some to believe that he was still alive. The *Washington Herald* story in 1909 about Slocum being seen on the Orinoco was but one example. But all such sightings were fictions. In an October 6, 1952 letter to Walter Teller, Grace Murray Brown mentioned "an explorer on the Amazon River [who] was positive in his identification of Captain Slocum. He said he was living with natives, etc. Several rumors reached Hettie and his family but I heard her say 'no one can make me believe that because, first of all, Josh would not go native—he just would not mix with them in any sense, especially living among them.'"

Slocum's brother Ornan heard the Orinoco story, which went on being repeated for years, and in 1913 he told Alice Longraker what he thought of the tale. Knowing of his brother's long interest in the Panama Canal, he told Alice "that if [Josh] is alive he will 'turn up' at the celebration of the Panama Canal." But no Slocum and no *Spray* appeared on August 15, 1914, when the canal finally opened.

The Rudder magazine editor Thomas Fleming Day was almost certainly correct in suggesting that he and the magazine were well-placed to report a definitive sighting of the *Spray*—*if* there been one. Day was familiar with Slocum's suggested plan to sail for the Orinoco, and in January 1911, he wrote: "But there is no news that he ever made the river or any port, and surely some of my correspondents would have seen *Spray* and sent word."

AN IMPORTANT MEMORY shared by those who saw Slocum and the *Spray* before and after he left the Vineyard in 1908 was that the *Spray* was looking poorly. Slocum's friend Ernest Dean told Walter Teller that the *Spray's* bowsprit had been forced upward several inches when it settled on a stake as the tide fell. "Captain Mayhew said that to his astonishment all Slocum did was take an axe and drive the bowsprit back in place."

Harold S. Smith, who knew boats, was relentlessly critical of the *Spray*. "No two planks appeared to be of the same shape, size or thickness, or even the same kind of wood.... [T]he shape she was in would give the horrors to anyone who went to sea." Smith was too respectful to query Slocum on these matters, and it is unfortunate that Slocum never remarked on what work was necessary to keep the *Spray* going during her voyage.

But there is no reason to believe that the *Spray* as rebuilt by Slocum didn't have the uniformly sized Georgia pine planks he proudly reported, or that Slocum was not a better shipwright than Smith gave him credit for. Smith considered Slocum a "hammer and nails carpenter. He was the kind of craftsman who, if a four inch nail driven with a hammer would not send a plank home, would use a six inch spike and a maul. If the timber split in the process, it was just too bad. The whole ship gave mute testimony to that variety of wood butchery."

Dilapidated as the *Spray* was when Smith inspected her (and he was not alone in his assessment of her deplorable condition), the boat's performance and appearance in previous days suggest that Slocum was a better boatbuilder than Smith knew. The many repairs Slocum had had to make during and after his great voyage may have been rough and ready, but the *Spray* had never been of yacht construction, and Slocum sought only a rugged workboat build and finish.

Observers noted that the *Spray's* rigging was frayed in places, and that her standing rigging needed to be tarred and adjusted. Some lines appeared too small in diameter for their purpose, while others were too large. Photos of the *Spray* in her decline show a mainsheet that looks too thin and sail lacing that looks too thick: a hodgepodge. Slocum seemingly never found the money to rig his boat as he might have wanted. The *Spray* suffered failures of both rigging hardware and cordage at several times during her voyage, and but for "Slocum's luck," those failures could have had fatal consequences.

On his way south in 1908, Slocum stopped in Miami to refit the *Spray* to some degree and to lecture, and it was there that 32-year-old yachtsman and writer Vincent Gilpin[1] met him. Gilpin was interested in everything related to the history and development of South Florida and boats, and his appreciation of small craft and the sea, coupled with his writer's insight, enabled him to provide a concise summation for Walter Teller of the *Spray* and her skipper as he found them. Both man and boat were looking worn, he told Teller. The *Spray*, he said,

> was very simply fitted out, rather bare, and very damp from many soakings with salt water, and Slocum kept a little wood-stove going to help dry her out…. He was rather shabbily dressed in civilian clothes, with a ragged black felt hat…. On the whole, I felt him a good example of the old-line Yankee skipper, competent, self-reliant, not talkative. But perfectly friendly and ready to answer questions. He was obviously a first-class boat handler—which is something quite different from being a ship captain; apparently he was both, beside being a shipwright a very capable man and a lonely, unhappy man.

Thomas Fleming Day had also expressed concern about the *Spray's* condition. He wrote that when he last saw her—Day did not give the date—she was "considerably dozy," by which he meant that her wood had become soft with rot. Day was among those who conjectured that the *Spray* may have suffered structural failure. In a June 10, 1923 article in *Motor Boat*, Charles Mower, the naval architect who did the drawings of the *Spray* that appeared in *Sailing Alone*, wrote that he had been impressed by the boat's sturdy construction but believed her deckhouses were flimsy. He suggested that boarding seas could have breached the houses and sunk the boat. But those were the same deckhouses that had survived the circumnavigation.

Despite all such testimony about the *Spray's* problems, it cannot be assumed that she sank because of neglect. For his part, Slocum was still espousing his boat's virtues in the summer of 1908, telling a reporter, "I caulked

---

1 Gilpin was a great friend of Miami pioneer Ralph Middleton Munroe, whose gracious home and boathouse at Coconut Grove represented early efforts to settle the area. Gilpin wrote *The Commodore's Story*, about Munroe's adventures settling Biscayne Bay. (Munroe's title derived from his long service as commodore of the Key Biscayne Yacht Club.) In addition to articles about Florida history, Gilpin also wrote *The Good Little Ship* about Munroe's practical sharpie design known as the Presto, a shallow-draft craft well-suited to the waters of Biscayne Bay.

Shot in 1908, this may be the last photograph of Slocum and the Spray. *Slocum had the boat hauled at the Miami Boat Works so he could perform some maintenance before continuing on what would be his final voyage. Slocum is dressed in coveralls, tie, and hat. The photo clearly shows the* Spray's *long boomkin that replaced the original, and the absence of a gaff for the recut mainsail. (Photograph by Vincent Gilpin; courtesy the New Bedford Whaling Museum)*

her myself, fourteen years ago, and she has scraped mud and sand off the land of a hundred coasts. I never knew her to leak, and the caulking is as tight and as secure as the day I put it in."

Slocum's pride in the *Spray*'s tightness was unfailing. In a February 25, 1954 letter to Walter Teller, Garfield wrote, "Father told me the *Spray* had not leaked since the day she was launched. I poured a bucket of water down the pump well occasionally to sweeten the bilge and pump ship."

There is, of course, a difference between a boat's cosmetic condition and her structural condition. Poor cosmetics can certainly suggest more serious underlying issues, but they do not prove it. The *Spray*'s loss may or may not have been due to a stove-in cabin or a sprung plank. What is verifiable, however, is that Joshua Slocum, who had always taken such pride in his boat, no longer had the energy or will to maintain her. They had aged and declined together. Possibly, when he looked at her, he could no longer see her as she was.

It is also possible that Joshua Slocum no longer particularly cared about his boat's condition or even if the *Spray* remained seaworthy. The worst that could happen was that she would sink and end 24 years of loneliness and the disappointment he felt after a career that never amounted to what it should have. Despite his efforts to remain involved in life, Slocum may well have been the "lonely, unhappy man" that Vincent Gilpin perceived. It is possible that, at some fundamental level, his eternal optimism had deserted him and what lay ahead of him was mainly emptiness.

Still, Joshua Slocum remained a great sailor, and he had always been concerned about the safety and well-being of those who sailed with him. It would be distressing to think Slocum would have asked Hettie to join him aboard a boat he knew to be unsafe, but given all the testimony of eyewitnesses who knew boats, and Slocum's possibly depressed emotional state, one can't entirely rule out such carelessness.

WHAT WAS THE EVENT THAT ENDED Joshua Slocum's life? It is unlikely that the circumstances will ever be known. Victor Slocum's conjectures were no better, no worse, and little different than anybody else's:

> Four things may have happened to the vessel and her skipper: Foundering in a gale, which is unlikely, as there was no seriously bad weather which that pair could not ride out to the sea anchor which was always ready: second, the possibility of fire, a hazard imminent on every vessel everywhere; third, collision at night; and last, shipwreck.
>
> Collision at night has always seemed to me the most likely of any of the things that may have happened.

Victor's brother Ben Aymar had a different take on the matter. He believed his father had ended his own life. In a March 4, 1954 letter to Walter Teller, Ben Aymar wrote, "I will always believe that father decided to join my mother—he could not live without her." In fact, it is not hard to imagine that the decline in the *Spray*'s condition in later years was a reflection that Slocum no longer cared if the boat suffered a serious failure at sea.

Nine years after Victor's book was published, an article appeared in the Quincy *Patriot Ledger* that matched exactly Victor's guess about the reason for his father's loss, if not the location. "Solution of Sea Mystery Indicated In New Facts" was the story's headline. It was published on April 8, 1959, and carried the byline of Edward Rowe Snow.

Long before he became a *Patriot Ledger* columnist in 1957, Edward Rowe Snow was a widely celebrated historian who specialized in stories about maritime New England, pirates, and lighthouses. He had an undergraduate degree from Harvard and a master of arts degree from Boston University, and was well-known as "the Flying Santa" who delivered Christmas presents to New England lighthouse keepers—and sometimes keepers outside New England—and their families. That he copyrighted his story about Slocum is a measure of the seriousness in which he held the piece. He clearly believed what his source told him about Joshua Slocum. Snow's lead paragraph was as follows:

> *One of the world's greatest sea mysteries, the loss of the* Spray, *rivaling in importance the enigma of what happened to the ship's company of the* Mary Celeste *in 1872 and the disappearance of the collier* Cyclops *in 1918, may have been solved yesterday at the offices of the Quincy* Patriot Ledger *by the disclosure that Capt. Joshua Slocum, who vanished at sea in 1909, may have been run down by a steamer off of the Lesser Antilles within a relatively few hours after he had left the home of a farmer in the vicinity.*

Snow named his source as Captain Charles H. Bond, "a master mariner whose background and references are such to make his statements unimpeachable."

Although Snow's article contains factual errors, and although he could have asked more questions of Captain Bond than he seems to have done, he did apparently take the time to check out Bond's veracity. Bond told Snow a story that he said was related to him by Felix Meinickheim, a onetime planter on Turtle Island.[1] When Bond met Meinickheim, both men were living in New Jersey. Nobody involved in the story who might have been impacted by what Meinickheim revealed was still alive.

According to Meinickheim, Slocum had stayed at Turtle Island for a few days prior to departing for Venezuela's Orinoco River, which he planned to follow to the Rio Negro and the Amazon. In retrospect, it sounds like a dubious adventure concocted by someone with nothing better to do. But merely spending winters collecting shells and corals in the Caribbean was no

---

1 Although there are a number of "Turtle Islands," this one, Île de la Tortue, or Tortuga, is located off the north coast of Haiti.

longer enough for Joshua Slocum. In fact, he had mentioned exploring the Orinoco during one of his "thinking-out-loud" interviews with a newspaper in 1907.

Two days after Slocum's departure from Turtle Island, Meinickheim boarded a 125-foot interisland steamship, noticing as he did so "a deep cut in her stem, just above the waterline." When Meinickheim asked the ship's captain about the damage, he was told "that the craft had run down a native boatman the night before." Snow reported that Meinickheim asked how the captain could be sure it was a native craft that had been struck. The captain's answer: "'Who else could it have been?'" Meinickheim thought he might have the answer to that question. As Captain Bond told Snow:

> Meinickheim now had a terrible feeling and asked when the incident had taken place. He was told it had been during the graveyard watch, the midnight to 4 a.m. watch always taken by the second mate.
> Meinickheim then interviewed the second mate, who admitted that it had been a terribly dark night, overcast, and at the moment of contact with the other craft, there was definitely no one at the wheel of the other vessel.

Having gotten that far in his statement to the planter, the second mate contradicted the steamer's captain regarding the vessel having been a native craft. "In the few seconds when I saw the other craft, I made out that she was not a native of this area," the mate said.

Captain Bond told Snow that "Captain Slocum and the *Spray* were the only outsiders anywhere in the vicinity as far as is known and the island steamer ran down its victim right in the area where he would have been. Of course it was decided that there was no use in publicity at the time for the officers would have lost their jobs for not going back and looking for survivors."

Key details are missing from Captain Bond's story, and there is no way of knowing whether Snow (who was more historian than reporter) asked about the dates of Slocum's Turtle Island arrival and departure, the name of the steamship, Meinickheim's relationship with or impressions of Slocum, in what direction the steamship and the *Spray* were headed at the time of the collision, and why the steamship skipper did not stop after colliding with another vessel. That said, the second mate's admission that the vessel struck was not local and that there was nobody at the helm are chilling clues that the story could be true.

"Father told me that he wanted to be buried at sea," Garfield Slocum wrote Walter Teller, "and he got his wish."

Perhaps "Slocum's luck" finally ran out in the nighttime waters off Haiti. He would have been sleeping in his familiar cabin while sharks prowled the darkness beneath him and the *Spray* faithfully steered herself toward the Orinoco River and their next adventure. Then, out of the night came a steamship. As the sea closed over him, perhaps Slocum saw his beautiful wife Virginia, the love of his life, beckoning to him from that beautiful shore where she'd been waiting all those years, waiting to welcome him to that sweet by-and-by.

Epilogue

THE OCEANS ROLLED ON. TIME MARCHED ON. "Peace to Captain Slocum," wrote *The Rudder's* editor Thomas Fleming Day in January 1911, "wherever he may sleep, for he deserves at least one whispered tribute of prayer from every sailorman for what he did to rob the sea of its bad name."

In a time when small-boat voyaging by people of modest means was little more than a crazy idea, Slocum helped show the way. He proved that the sea could be sailed—respected but not feared—by those in small craft. The *Spray* herself became an inspiration. As a yacht for offshore voyaging, the *Spray* has had many detractors, and for good reason. Besides the Cullers' *Spray*, however, many other replicas would be built that, despite modifications, were reasonably faithful to the original. They have generally displayed the seaworthiness and self-steering ability that Slocum attributed to the original.

Sailing Alone sold reasonably well, and Hettie eventually renewed the copyright in 1927, although ownership of the publishing rights was retained by The Century Company. Neither Hettie nor Slocum's children could afford to buy the rights when The Century Company offered them for $5,000 during the Depression. The records of the company and its successors show that the book sold through 17 printings totaling 27,760 copies. In the 1930s, New York reprint publisher Blue Ribbon books printed, according to Teller's research, 16,200 copies of a lower-priced, lower-quality edition. Editions of *Sailing Alone* were published in England, Poland, France, and Germany.

In 1954, Sheridan House issued its edition of *Sailing Alone*, this one containing an introduction by Walter Teller that offered information and insights aimed at imparting to readers some sense of Slocum the man and the importance of his writing. The Slocum estate was still receiving a small royalty—$650—in 1962 that covered a period starting in 1957. Those monies were paid by Appleton-Century in London and Sheridan House.

Despite Joshua Slocum's misgivings about how his book would be received by critics, it garnered good reviews. Renowned English journalist and poet Edwin Arnold followed up his glowing review with a letter to Slocum: "Never will your achievement be surpassed until all sail together across those wider and ever more wonderful seas that separate planet from planet and star from star."

Sailing Alone's literary worth was still recognized three decades after the book's first publication. In 1934, Princeton's renowned professor of English J. Duncan Spaeth[1] and his associate, Joseph Brown, included *Sailing Alone* in their book *American Life and Letters, a reading list.* Among their other recommended "Narratives of the Sea" were Richard Henry Dana's *Two Years Before the Mast* and three Melville novels, including one of the greatest works of American literature, *Moby-Dick.*

On May 10, 1921, Hettie married 65-year-old Ulysses E. Mayhew of West Tisbury. Mayhew was an entirely different sort of man from Joshua Slocum. He'd been a successful store owner—S. M. Mayhew, in Chilmark—and banker on the Vineyard, and a state representative. Hettie was widowed for a second time in 1939.

After the death of her second husband, Hettie remained on Martha's Vineyard, where she continued to attend the Congregational Church of West Tisbury, belonged to the West Tisbury Grange, and took part in civic affairs. She busied herself making elaborate hooked rugs. Suffering from what is now known as dementia, Hettie Slocum Mayhew died at age 90 on Martha's Vineyard in October 1952. She had by then become a figure of interest to her fellow islanders. Years earlier, on September 23, 1927, she had been the subject of a *Vineyard Gazette* article that referred to her as "a wonderful woman … who speaks quietly of death and disaster without a tremor in her voice as she sits in the peaceful surroundings of her home."

The *Gazette's* reporter recounted Hettie's early life as a dressmaker and gown fitter in Boston after she left Nova Scotia. The story told of her marriage to Captain Joshua Slocum and of the trials of the *Aquidneck* and *Liberdade* voyages, and the reporter remarked on the curios Hettie had saved from her life with the late sea captain and adventurer. Among them were "sea shells of bewildering beauty."

---

1 Spaeth (1869–1954) graduated Phi Beta Kappa from the University of Pennsylvania, where he played tackle on the football team and was a swimming champion and varsity oarsman. He received his Ph.D. from the University of Leipzig, coached Princeton's crew, organized courses for illiterate soldiers during World War I, and was said to be "the most versatile man on the [Princeton] faculty."

Slocum biographer Walter Magnes Teller interviewed Hettie at West Tisbury during research for The Search for Captain Slocum, *published in 1956. (Photo by Roy Stevens; courtesy the New Bedford Whaling Museum)*

Appendix A

Ships and Boats of Joshua Slocum

Vessel Name	Type	Length × Beam × Depth of Hold (ft.)	Tonnage	Builder/Date	Owner	Remarks
S. J. Sanderson	brig	—	312	Registered at Yarmouth, NS	G. and George G. Sanderson	Slocum was Able Seaman, 1864
Agra	ship	174 × 34½ × 22½	850-951	J. T. Foster & Co., Medford, MA/1862	Thomas B. Wales & Co., Boston	Slocum crew c. 1864-1865, Renamed *Heinrich*
Tanjore	bark	—	907	J. T. Foster & Co., Medford, MA/1862	Thomas B. Wales & Co., Boston	Slocum crew 1865-1866, Sold foreign c. 1867 and renamed *Anna.* Sold to Holland, 1874, renamed *Betzy and Arnold*
Montana	schooner	—	93	Oakland, CA/1866	Anderson (1879)	Slocum's first command, c. 1869
*Cesarewitch**	bark	—	394	Lubec, ME/1851	Russian-American Co.	Original name of vessel unknown
Constitution	bark	—	362	Philadel-phia/1850	N. Bichard (as of Nov. 1869)	Slocum's first square-rig command, 1870
Washington	bark	—	332	—	Merrill and Bichard	Slocum was master when wrecked in 1871, Alaska

Vessel Name	Type	Length × Beam × Depth of Hold (ft.)	Tonnage	Builder/Date	Owner	Remarks
Page	schooner	81 × 15 × 10	110	Barnstable, MA/ 1831 (rebuilt 1866)	N. Bichard (1871) Sea & Wright (1879)	Slocum was master Feb.-March 1872.
B. Aymar	bark	128 × 27 × 14	516-531	John Carver, Searsport, ME/1840	Benjamin Aymar & Co.	Slocum was master, 1872-1875
Pato	schooner	72 × 15 × 9	65 (English) /95 (American)	Hull by Philippine builder. Slocum built deck and house. Edward Jackson design, 1876	Slocum	Sold at Hawaii, 1878
Amethyst	bark	100 × 28 × 18	340 (approx.)	John Robertson, Boston, MA/1823	Slocum**	Among the oldest U.S.-flagged merchant vessels in 1878. Sold by Slocum in 1881 and converted to a whaler.
Northern Light	ship	233 × 44 × 28	1,795	George Thomas, Quincy, MA/1871	Slocum, et al	Bought a share in June, 1881. Sold share Jan., 1884
Aquidneck	bark	138 × 29 × 13	365	Hill and Grinnell, Mystic, CT/1865	Slocum	Lost in Brazil, Jan. 1888
Liberdade	sampan-dory, junk rig, 3 masts	35 × 7½ × 3 Draft 2' 4"	6	Joshua Slocum, Brazil/1887	Slocum	Voyaged from Brazil to U.S., 1888
Destroyer	steam ironclad	150' long. 1,000 hp		John Ericsson and C. H. Delamater, New York/1878	Brazilian govt.	New York to Brazil. Dec. 1893-April 1894

Vessel Name	Type	Length × Beam × Depth of Hold (ft.)	Tonnage	Builder/Date	Owner	Remarks
Spray	sloop/ yawl	36′ 9″ × 14′ 2″ × 4′ 2″	13 gross, 9 net	Unknown/ Slocum rebuilt, launched 1892 at Fairhaven	Slocum	Eben Pierce gift to Slocum, 1891

* *Cesarewitch is an anglicized version of Tsesarevich referring to the heir apparent to the Czar of Russia.*

** *The Amethyst was built for Lewis & Co. of Boston.*

Notes

This table is based on the most complete available data at the time of publication. The name of the drogher on which Slocum is presumed to have sailed on his first voyage from Saint John, New Brunswick to Dublin, Ireland, has yet to be discovered, and that vessel is not included in the table. Only vessels with which Slocum had a known or presumed connection as crewmember or captain are included in the table.

Vessel Types: A brig had two masts (foremast and mainmast) and was square-rigged on both. A fore-and-aft sail was also typically carried on the mainmast. A bark or barque had at least three masts. While the fore- and mainmasts were square rigged, the mizzenmast was fore-and-aft rigged. The term "bark" or "barque" is believed to originate from the word "barge." Bark is the common United States spelling. A bark-rigged vessel typically required a smaller crew, carried less canvas and fewer spars, and had more modest cordage needs than a ship-rigged vessel, yet performance was similar at tonnages said to be around 1,200 or less. Although the term "ship" was, and is, regularly applied to all sorts of vessels, a vessel in the age of sail was said to be "ship rigged" if all three masts carried square sails. The mizzen might also carry a fore-and-aft sail rather than a lower course (square sail.) Schooners are fore-and-aft-rigged vessels with two or more masts.

Tonnage: Tonnage was (and is) not a measure of a ship's weight but of its rated carrying capacity. The word "tonnage" is misleading, as it derived from a much earlier term, "tun." "Tunnage" reflected the number of wine barrels of a given size that a ship could carry. In *Tonnage measurement of ships, historical evolution, current issues, and a way forward* (World Maritime University, 2010), Aji Vasudevan summed up tonnage in its historical context "as the basis for collecting ships' dues [a portion of which in the U.S. was used to fund lighthouses]. Over a period of time, tonnage was to be a convenient basis for various other purposes such as shipping statistics, regulatory application, manning, and insurance."

Tonnage reflected the size of a vessel but could vary significantly as reported in different sources. There were English and American formulas for calculating tonnage, and each underwent changes over time. The American system was based on the English system from colonial times until 1865, when the Moorsom system was adopted. Like previous methods, it was based on a mathematical formula involving a ship's length and beam (breadth).

Appendix B

The *Spray*'s Lines Controversy

SOME YACHTSMEN AND NOT A FEW naval architects have been critical, sometimes highly critical, of the *Spray*'s design. After all, her shallow-draft, internally ballasted hull was broad and low-sided, a form well suited to her original purpose as a Delaware Bay oyster boat but, seemingly at least, not deep-sea cruising. Slocum's modifications, chiefly raising the height of the *Spray*'s topsides and eliminating her centerboard, were important but didn't change the basics. And yet, there would prove to be far more to "the basics" than met the eye.

Debate about the *Spray*'s plusses and minuses as an ocean cruiser, and suggestions for improvements—notably in her ultimate stability—has continued to the present day. It is doubtful that the discussion will end anytime soon, and the *Spray* is likely to be subjected to ongoing computer analysis that leads to refinements of a basic shape that few, if any, naval architects would recommend for offshore sailing.

All this said, in December 1908, naval architect Cipriano Andrade, Jr., himself skeptical, sat down to analyze the *Spray*'s lines as drawn some eight years earlier by naval architect Charles Mower. It was those lines that were included in the appendix to Slocum's article series and book. With no computer software to assist him, Andrade described his analysis this way: "I attacked her with proportional dividers, planimeter, rota-meter, Simpson's rule, Froude's coefficients, Dixon Kemp's formulae, series, curves, differentials, and all the appliances of modern yacht designing."

His article was published in *The Rudder*'s June 1909 issue with the title: "Critical Analysis of the Yawl Spray." His primary and surprising conclusion, after all his study, was that "she emerged from the ordeal a theoretically perfect boat. For when she is underway, every element of resistance, stability, weight, heeling effort, and propulsive force is in one transverse plane, and that plane is the boat's midship section. I know of no similar case in the whole field of naval architecture, ancient or modern."

Of the *Spray*'s absence of a centerboard, Andrade wrote that "Spray is a much better boat to windward than her form of midsection would at first glance indicate. To the casual observer, it would seem almost impossible to drive her to windward at all without a centerboard.... But on careful analysis it will appear that there are three reasons why *Spray* should be a fairly good boat to windward." The reasons were that the boat's hard bilge and flat sides acted like a large leeboard even at a small angle of heel; the long, fairly deep keel raking downward from stem to the stern was much more efficient than a straight keel; and the hull provided "a large lateral plane" in absolute terms and in relation to the sail area.

Too much focus on the potential windward ability of the *Spray* is unwarranted. Joshua Slocum knew he would be plotting courses similar to those he'd sailed in square riggers. He would be sailing off the wind in the trades for thousands of miles.

Some have pointed out that a wide, shallow, internally ballasted boat like the *Spray* would be just as stable upside down as right side up, and these critics have offered ways to improve her ultimate stability. Andrade's analysis reached a different conclusion:

> *The curve of stability shows that Spray is theoretically uncapsizable, because [at] 90 degrees of heel, she still has left a righting moment of over 20,000 foot-pounds or over 9 foot-tons. This is most remarkable for a boat of her shallow draught, doubly remarkable in view of the fact that she carries no outside ballast whatever, and even her inside ballast consists merely of cement blocks. Her maximum stability is at about 35 degrees of heel, where she has a righting moment of 75,000 foot-pounds or over 33 foot-tons.*
>
> *As she should never be sailed much lower than 10 degrees of heel, it will be seen that she has an ample margin of safety at all times.*

Andrade also examined the *Spray*'s speed potential in light of Slocum's claims—disbelieved by many—that his boat could, at times, achieve 8 knots. Andrade wrote of this claim, "I thought he must be mistaken.... I next swept in two diagonals ... which are omitted from the lines as published in Slocum's book, and then I realized that he was justified in his claim of 8 knots."

In his fine book, *In the Wake of the* Spray, scholar Ken Slack quoted from a letter he had received from R. D. "Pete" Culler, who had built a *Spray* replica. "Captain Culler said: 'Best speed I ever got out of her was eight knots even—did it on three occasions, twice in smooth water where one could overcarry on sail, and once coastwise between buoys, so think it's about top for that vessel." Slack also noted that a *Spray* copy called *Igdrasil* once did 204 miles in 24 hours in a strong sou'wester with mizzen furled. "That works out to an average speed of 8½ knots. But about 25 miles of the distance was said to be abetted by current. I think 6½ knots a fair average for *Spray*."

Despite Andrade's favorable analysis, criticism of the *Spray* went on, and Andrade's work itself was called into question. Why did this happen?

In *Sailing Alone*, Joshua Slocum wrote that "No pains have been spared to give them [the *Spray's* lines] accurately." In fact, however, the lines-making process was flawed thanks, in part, to the need to meet *The Century's* publishing deadline of March 1900 for the final installment that included the lines. In his impressively researched book *In the Wake of the Spray*, Kenneth Slack quoted from a Howard Chapelle letter that illuminates the lines subject. Chapelle's source was Charles Mower himself, for whom Chapelle had worked as an 18-year-old apprentice draftsman in 1919.

AT THE TIME OF THE *Spray* lines episode, Mower was employed by Thomas Fleming Day at *The Rudder*. Although Slocum never mentioned it, he had once approached Day about publishing *Sailing Alone*, and it was Day who suggested that the captain should stick with a larger, more general-interest publisher. Probably wanting to be helpful, Day asked Mower to accompany Slocum and take off the *Spray's* lines for use in The Century Company's magazine and book efforts. Unaccountably, however, the boat was not hauled at the time, so Mower could only measure the deck plan, rig, and above-the-water profile. Mower asked Slocum to let him know when the boat was hauled so he could return and properly measure the hull beneath the waterline.

In fact, the actual measurement of the *Spray's* hull by Mower never happened. Instead, Slocum presented Mower with a half-model built by Henry B. Robbins, who owned a boatyard on lower East Main Street in Bridgeport, Connecticut. Robbins, well-known locally as a builder of sandbaggers and other vessels, had hauled the *Spray* and, apparently assisted by members of the nearby Park City Yacht Club, took what measurements he felt were needed to create an accurate inch-to-the-foot model. Slocum was so impressed with the result that he called the model "a poem." But the poem was certainly not the same as lines capably taken from a hauled-out boat.

Chapelle recalled that "upon applying the model's lines to the measurements made afloat, Mower found many discrepancies.... Upon inquiry the yard owner told him they had not actually taken off the lines but had taken some measurements and made the model by eye.... Day instructed Mower to work up the plans as best he could and the result was published as the drawings of the *Spray* .... Mower felt badly about this as he knew many people had accepted the plans as the accurate record of the *Spray.*"

The information that the *Spray*'s lines were an "approximation" was enough reason for Chapelle to write that "they were not accurate enough to justify the Andrade analysis." Was this overly critical? Probably, since a hull like the *Spray*'s is unlikely to be sensitive to the modest inaccuracies possessed by the half-model. An experienced boatbuilder like Henry Robbins must be due some credit regarding the measurements he and his crew took.

In an effort to resolve the matter, Ken Slack painstakingly drew his own set of lines, spending two years of part-time effort on the project. "My method was to compare the scale measurement of each and every part of the lines with that of a feature whose actual size was known—for example, the overall length of the boat. With the latter serving as a standard, the former could readily be calculated.... I measured the lines both in Slocum's own book and in his son's biography [as calculated by Andrade].... Altogether, eighteen separate tables of offsets were prepared and, finally, an average table, in which each figure was the mean of eighteen different measurements."

After all his careful labors, Slack concluded that the Mower lines "were probably accurate to within a few inches ... a fairly conservative estimate." All that said, Chapelle was correct in pointing out that the *Spray*'s lines were never taken off the vessel itself and that a "true" record of the boat does not (and never will) exist.

Slocum, of course, didn't have the luxury of choice in his boat. He took what he was given and made the changes—eliminating the centerboard and raising the topsides—that he thought were appropriate. Nor did Slocum "care a rope yarn," as he put it, about "mathematical calculations," but made clear his belief that the *Spray* would stand up well to analysis. He was proved correct.

Of course, criticism of the *Spray* has been based not so much on whether her lines were precisely taken but on the alleged unsuitability of a

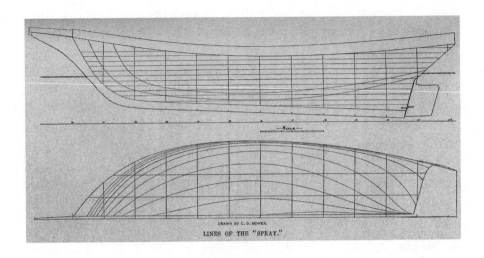

LINES OF THE "SPRAY."

These Spray lines—based on those created by Charles Mower—were originally drawn ½ inch to the foot by naval architect Cipriano Andrade, Jr. The lines, he concluded, revealed "[t]he inner mystery of Spray's design…the extraordinary focusing of her centers [of buoyancy, gravity, lateral resistance, and effort]. Here lay the secret to the boat's good balance, easy handling, and self-steering qualities."

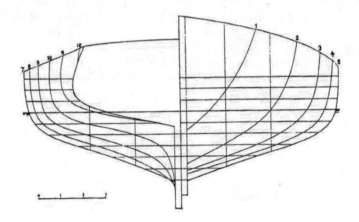

wide, shallow, internally ballasted hull for offshore voyaging. Certainly there have long since been cruising boats far more suitable for deep-sea voyaging than the *Spray*, but *Spray* copies built, more or less, to the published lines have been reported by their owners to possess the same seaworthiness, good balance, and self-steering qualities reported by Slocum. Ultimately, of course, there is the testimony of the *Spray* herself.

The Spray under sail, most likely in Sydney Harbour showing off new sails donated by wealthy department store owner Mark Foy, who greatly admired Joshua Slocum. Only the first reef pennant at the sail's clew (after edge) has thus far been rigged. As usual, Joshua is proudly flying the Stars and Stripes. His visitors, standing beside the cabin, are unknown, but Joshua is at the helm in a dark suit and hat. (Courtesy the New Bedford Whaling Museum)

Appendix C

Sail Plans of the *Spray*

Joshua Slocum made several changes to the *Spray*'s rig between his departure from Boston in April 1895 and his final Caribbean voyage in 1908.

Boston, April 1895
Mast with topmast
(for flag halyards).

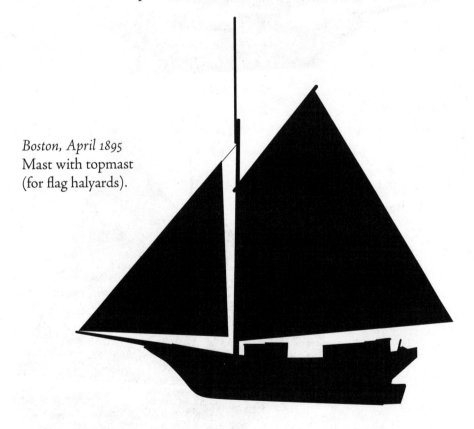

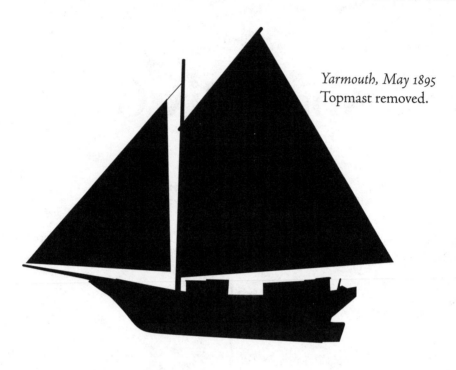

Yarmouth, May 1895
Topmast removed.

Recife, Pernambuco, October 1895
Boom shortened 4 feet.

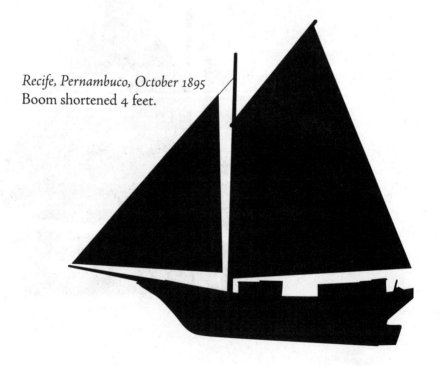

Buenos Aires, December 1895
Bowsprit shortened 5 feet;
Mast shortened 4 feet;
Arch brace added for mizzen
(not shown).

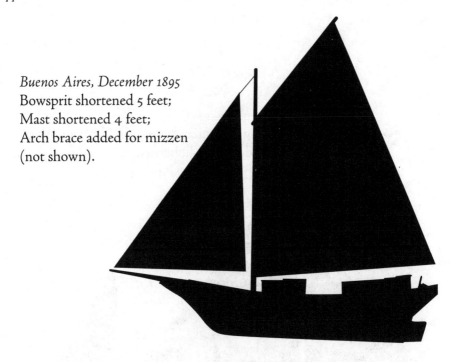

Port Angosto, circa February 1896
Mizzenmast and (presumably)
boomkin fitted;
Sail plan here shows voyaging
headsails—flying jib and
staysail.

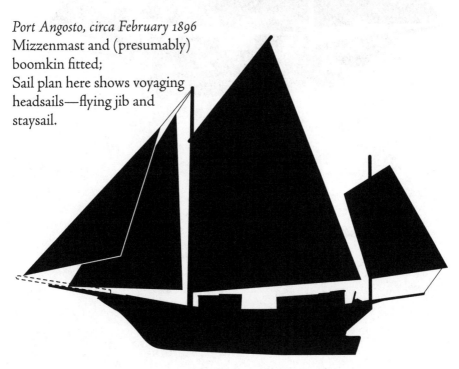

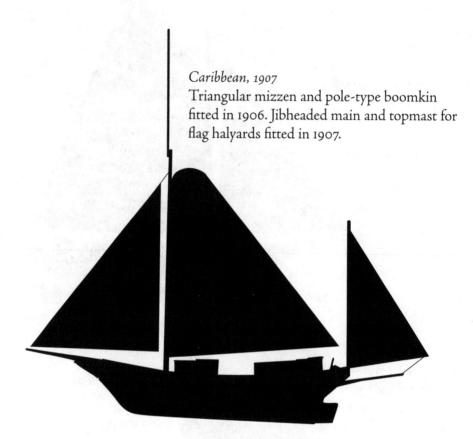

Caribbean, 1907
Triangular mizzen and pole-type boomkin
fitted in 1906. Jibheaded main and topmast for
flag halyards fitted in 1907.

Appendix D

Henry and Joshua:
Walden and *Sailing Alone Around the World*

THOUGHTFUL READERS HAVE LONG LINKED Joshua Slocum's *Sailing Alone Around the World* and Henry David Thoreau's *Walden*. If asked to sum up *Sailing Alone*, a devotee might well suggest that Slocum's book is a kind of waterborne *Walden*. In fact, after the release of Walter Magnes Teller's *The Search for Captain Slocum* in 1956, the *New York Times* published a July 29, 1956 review by critic Brooks Atkinson under the headline: "Biography of a Sea-Locked Thoreau."

Multifaceted British-born writer and critic Jonathan Raban concluded in 1995 that *Sailing Alone* was "so full of echoes of *Walden* that it reads like *Walden*-on-Sea." The echoes are there, but did Slocum hear them? Did he ever read *Walden*, or do the two books simply happen to share important themes while remaining profoundly different?

Journalists and others who visited Joshua and Virginia Slocum aboard the *Northern Light* were impressed and charmed by the ship's beauty, the obvious care given to every detail, and the well-equipped living quarters complete with a piano. Slocum's son Victor remembered, "One of the cabins of the *Northern Light* contained a library of at least five hundred volumes representing the standard works of the great writers."

But while Victor enumerated many writers his father had read and enjoyed—Dickens, Coleridge, Tennyson, Stevenson, and Mark Twain among them—he did not mention Thoreau. At the time, *Walden* was far from being widely read or recognized. In 1885, a year after Slocum sold his share in the *Northern Light*, slow-selling *Walden* showed up in a rare-book catalog published in New York by Leon & Brothers, the first such catalog devoted to American authors. The cataloged value for *Walden* was $4.50; its original selling price had been $1. (By 1999, the best first edition examples were commanding a price of $10,000, according to knowledgeable antiquarian booksellers.)

There is nothing to indicate that Joshua Slocum had read *Walden* before or during his voyage in the *Spray*. When a new American[1] edition of *Walden* was released in 1897, Slocum was half-a-world away in Tasmania, Australia, and later the Indian Ocean. Nor is there anything to suggest that he encountered *Walden* during the decade between his return from the circumnavigation in 1898 and his final departure in 1908.

SUPERFICIALLY AT LEAST, *Walden* and *Sailing Alone* may seem as different as their authors, one a graduate of Harvard College, the other a seaman with three or four years of back-country schooling. Thoreau was inwardly focused, an observer and philosopher. *Walden* urged readers to live simply, to be guided by their own intuition, to avoid the trap of materialism, to live in harmony with nature. This was such stuff as made Thoreau a champion of Transcendentalists. Although Slocum would come to exemplify some of these same ideals, he was by nature a doer, ever in the thick of things. When times were good, his success was reflected in well-appointed ships and fashionable clothing for himself and the wife he so loved.

Thoreau not only never married but, after a youthful proposal was rejected, appears to have avoided intimacy with women of marriageable age while maintaining friendships with other men. In consequence, his sexuality and possible homosexuality have become topics for examination by scholars. Joshua Slocum was recognized by the insightful Grace Murray Brown as "ardent." There was nothing of the ascetic or the chaste about him. He married the love of his life, Virginia, and fathered seven children, four of whom survived to adulthood.

Thoreau seldom ventured far from Concord. He moved briefly to Staten Island. He made a river journey from Concord, Massachusetts, to Concord, New Hampshire, with his brother. He visited Quebec, took four trips to Cape Cod, and made three camping excursions into Maine's woods. But other than his time in Cambridge while a Harvard student—a mere 15 miles away from Concord—Thoreau was never away from his hometown for more than six months at a time. He traveled farthest through his reading.

As a boy, Joshua Slocum couldn't wait to leave home. His first baby steps

---

1 An English edition was published in Edinburgh in 1884 using sheets sent from America. In 1886, in London, a purely English-made edition was released.

took him from Brier Island to Yarmouth, then to Massachusetts, and then across the Western Ocean. Subsequently he became, literally, a man of the world.

Thoreau explained to readers what lay behind *Walden*. He moved to his cabin to "live deliberately" and "front only the essential facts of life, and see if I could not learn what it had to teach, and not, when I came to die, discover that I had not lived." Joshua Slocum didn't have time for such a made-up experiment in living. He couldn't afford, as Robert Louis Stevenson wrote of Thoreau, to leave "all for the sake of certain virtuous self-indulgences." Nor did Slocum have to worry about discovering at life's end that he had not lived.

Slocum said little in *Sailing Alone* about why he embarked on his solitary adventure. He wrote, with something less than candor, that after rebuilding and launching the *Spray* for possible use as a fishing vessel, he learned that he "had not the cunning to properly bait a hook [and] resolved on a voyage around the world." There was much more to it than that, but Slocum wrote a book about a voyage, not a work of philosophy that required first establishing what he planned to do and why. Although this is clear from the beginning, Slocum eventually made his intent explicit in the next-to-last sentence of his narrative: "I have endeavored to tell just the story of the adventure itself."

DESPITE THE MANY PROFOUND differences in their authors, *Walden* and *Sailing Alone* are curiously alike in several ways. In March 1845, 28-year-old Henry David Thoreau borrowed an axe from one his fellow townsmen in Concord, Massachusetts, and hiked about a mile-and-a-half south into the woods.[2] He had already selected the site near Walden Pond where he planned to build a little cabin and there conduct an experiment in living, thinking, and writing. The cabin would be constructed on land owned by Thoreau's friend and mentor, Ralph Waldo Emerson. To make a start, Thoreau wrote that he "began to cut down some tall arrowy white pines, still in their youth, for timber."

In 1891, 29 years after Thoreau's death, Joshua Slocum found himself in Fairhaven, Massachusetts, standing in front of a decrepit boat owned, like the property where it rested, by his friend Ebenezer Pierce. Regarding the

---

2 Whether the axe belonged to Thoreau's friend Ellery Channing, to his mentor Ralph Waldo Emerson, or to his neighbor Amos Bronson Alcott is a matter scholars have explored. The minute details of and behind Thoreau's book have fascinated readers in much the same way as Slocum's readers have sought details related to *Sailing Alone* and its author.

start of the *Spray's* rebuilding process, Slocum wrote,"My axe felled a stout oak-tree nearby for a keel and Farmer Howard, for a small sum of money, hauled in this and enough timbers for the frame of the new vessel."

Thus, *Walden* and *Sailing Alone Around the World* share a common endeavor early in the narrative, the felling of trees that will be transformed into self-made shelter. Thoreau's 10-foot by 15-foot cabin was a place of repose where the "self-appointed inspector of snow storms and rain storms" could take refuge from neighbors who recognized him as that odd young man who might spend hours staring at a duck. He was the unpredictable fellow who, while others worked hard on their farms, might set off on river outings in his self-made, blue-painted rowboat with no purpose other than to enjoy being on the water. He was this tousled, thin, round peg of a fellow who didn't fit the square hole of Concord.

Observers in Fairhaven who watched Slocum working on the *Spray* recognized him as unusual. Slocum may not have seemed as far out to them as Thoreau did to his neighbors, but he was an unemployed captain rebuilding an apparently worthless boat with no purpose in mind and, all the while, living apart from his wife and family. Slocum was commonly asked if his endeavor would "pay." He had no answer to the question, and, perhaps, didn't really care. Ultimately, the whole effort worked out better than he could have imagined thanks to book sales and the curiosity of people who paid to hear an unconventional man speak about a voyage no right-thinking person would have ever imagined, much less undertook.

What besides the felling of trees and the building of shelter do *Walden* and *Sailing Alone* have in common? By the time Slocum launched the *Spray*, the boat's cabin—smaller than Thoreau's at about 10 feet by 12 feet—represented a refuge from a world in which he had lived large, even heroically, but in which he no longer fit. Thoreau didn't fit easily into society, either, and a result is that an exploration of solitude is a theme common to both books.

In Chapter V of *Walden*, Thoreau examines solitude as if viewing the subject through the prism of a many-faceted gem, always seeing something new to reflect upon. "I love to be alone," he wrote. "I never found the companion that was so companionable as solitude." Such comments have led some critics to negative assessments of Thoreau as, at the least, antisocial and supercilious.

Slocum's book has no single chapter devoted to solitude or any other single theme. The book's title, of course, makes clear the essence of what Joshua Slocum was doing—embarking on a great adventure, and doing it alone. Prior to the voyage, Slocum had never said or done anything to suggest that he enjoyed being alone or preferred his own company to that of others. He was a sociable man who made friends easily and everywhere. Nor does he ever suggest that he gave any thought beforehand about how he would react to being alone for extended periods. He confronted the matter for the first time after departing Yarmouth, Nova Scotia, when, for the first time, he was not looking ahead to a snug harbor at day's end.

As he left Sable Island behind in the mists, reality set in. Soon enough, Slocum found himself talking to the man in the moon, who, perhaps to bolster his own spirits, Slocum judged to be "smiling." Afterwards, in thick fog, the enormity of his venture engulfed him. Of facing the Western Ocean alone, he wrote that "I felt myself drifting into loneliness, an insect on a straw in the midst of the elements." But the emptiness soon passed, blown away during an ensuing gale. "The acute pain of solitude experienced at first never returned," he wrote.

As for Thoreau, he claimed in the chapter "Solitude" that "I have never felt lonesome, or in the least oppressed by a sense of solitude, but once, and that was a few weeks after I came to the woods, when, for an hour, I doubted if the near neighborhood of man was not essential to a serene and healthy life." That hour of doubt soon ticked past, and Thoreau then claimed that he found all the comfort and company he needed "in Nature."

Thoreau spent two years and two months at Walden Pond, a period he condensed into one year in the tightly structured world of *Walden*. Slocum spent three years and two months on his voyage, and he framed his narrative to cover the whole period. It must be noted that Joshua Slocum's solitude was of an entirely different magnitude than Thoreau's. Thoreau's cabin could be visited by townsmen and passersby. Walden Pond was close to Concord and the comfortable Thoreau family house, where he could take his meals, not to mention his dirty clothes.

Thoreau's solitude, such as it was, was easily broken. The sociable Slocum's solitude was absolute. What is more, Thoreau's not-so-solitary surroundings were benign by comparison to Slocum's. Slocum's ocean world and the Strait of Magellan were, given one wrong move, one dragged anchor, one parted sheet, one unseen rock, one rogue wave, one sprung plank, one misjudgment, potentially deadly.

BOTH *WALDEN* AND *SAILING ALONE* espouse the virtues of living simply and economically, thus putting a premium on self-reliance. Chapter I of

Walden is entitled "Economy." In it, Thoreau ruminated in some detail about the virtues of sticking to the basics when it comes to food, clothing—he considered fashion to be nothing more than folly—and shelter. He kept a careful record of how much he paid to buy the mostly repurposed materials used for his cabin. He spent $8.03½ cents on "mostly shanty boards." He paid $4 for "refuse shingles for roof and sides." The cost of two "second-hand windows with glass" was $2.43. He paid $4 for one-thousand "old brick."

As for Slocum, in his prime, he was always well-dressed and looked the part of a successful sea captain. By the time he arrived in Fairhaven, however, those flusher times were long gone. If Eben Pierce hadn't given Slocum the *Spray* and a place to stay while rebuilding her, the whole adventure would never have happened. But Slocum worked hard to earn the capital needed to rebuild his boat. Like Thoreau, he gives an accounting of the cash outlay, though not so detailed. The materials cost him $553.62 and 13 months of his own labor.

Among the most uncanny and peculiar points of commonality between *Walden* and *Sailing Alone* is, of all things, a discussion relating to navigation. In a long paragraph in which he espouses forming good business habits based on self-reliance, Thoreau uses as a metaphor a Salem ship owner trading with the Celestial Empire, as China was then known. He urged that every detail of the business be overseen personally, that charts "be studied, the position of reefs and new lights and buoys to be ascertained, and ever, and ever, the logarithmic tables to be corrected, for by the error of some calculator [meaning the person who created the tables of figures and the typesetter who prepared them for printing] the vessel often splits upon a rock that should have reached a friendly pier."

In Chapter XI of *Sailing Alone*, Slocum uncharacteristically allows himself to boast just a bit about how "[u]nique was my experience in nautical astronomy from the deck of the *Spray*." Slocum used his sextant to take lunar sights as a means of obtaining longitude using mathematics, said to be the most difficult of all aspects of celestial navigation. After taking sights that put him "many hundreds miles west of my reckoning by account [by which he meant deduced reckoning, and for which he towed a patent log during the voyage]," Slocum took another sight with the same result.

"I asked myself why, with my boasted self-dependence, I had not done at least better than this." He found the answer in the column of tables: "[A]n important logarithm was in error.... The tables being corrected, I sailed on with self-reliance unshaken." Slocum proved, literally, Thoreau's metaphoric point about not trusting "some calculator."

PERHAPS THE MOST FREQUENTLY noted theme shared by *Walden* and *Sailing Alone* is a reflection upon nature and man's relation to it. Both Thoreau and Slocum found comfort and inspiration in nature. "There can be no very black melancholy to him who lives in the midst of Nature and has his senses still," Thoreau wrote in "Solitude." "We can never have enough of nature." Thoreau was stout in his view that nature is never a threatening force but instead a sustaining one.

Slocum knew differently, but he never lost his appreciation for the sea no matter what it dealt out. Whatever its threat, Slocum believed the sea was to be "sailed over," and he celebrated "the pleasure of sailing free over the great oceans." Following his near-fatal ordeal of being forced back toward Cape Horn after leaving the Strait of Magellan the first time, Slocum—resilient as ever—wrote of triumphantly reentering the Pacific on his second try:

> *The waves doffed their white caps beautifully to her in the strait that*
> *day before the southeast wind, the first true winter breeze of the season*
> *from that quarter, and here she was out on the first of it.... One wave,*
> *in the evening, larger than others that had threatened all day—one*
> *such as sailors call 'fine weather seas'—broke over the sloop fore and aft.*
> *It washed over me at the helm, the last that swept over the Spray off*
> *Cape Horn.*

Slocum put the strait behind him with this sentence about that big, soaking wave: "It seemed to wash away old regrets. All my troubles were now astern; summer was ahead; all the world was again before me." This cheerful anticipation of summer weather is evocative of *Walden*'s final chapter, "Spring," with its emphasis on renewal and its next-to-last sentence full of delicious imagery and optimism: "And so the seasons went rolling on into summer, as one rambles in high and higher grass."

Thoreau celebrates nature not only for itself but for the advantages it offers compared with the society he found wanting: "In the midst of a gentle rain, these thoughts prevailed, I was suddenly sensible of such sweet and beneficent society in nature, in the very pattering of the drops, and in every sound and sight around my house, an infinite and unaccountable friendliness all at once like an atmosphere sustaining me, as made the fancied advantages of human neighborhood insignificant, and I have never thought of them since."

Slocum enjoyed "porpoises gamboling about" or approaching, for example, the island of Pico, in the Azores, "completely hidden by the white, glistening haze that shone in the sun like polished silver." But Slocum didn't see nature as a replacement for human society. He was pleased to make landfalls and, in contrast to Thoreau, sought the warm companionship of newfound friends. When he arrived at Rodrigues (which he spelled Rodriguez, perhaps referring to the island as identified in his sailing directions), east of Mauritius, Slocum wrote, "My first day at this Land of Promise was to me like a fairy-tale…. [H]ere was I in a bright hall, surrounded by sparkling wit, and dining with the governor of the island!" Such a sentiment would be rather hard to imagine coming from Thoreau.

Of course, not all of Thoreau's thoughts on nature as recorded in his journal—the raw material for *Walden*—made it into the book. On April 23, 1857, about three years after *Walden* was published, Thoreau wrote in his journal: "How rarely man's love for nature becomes a ruling principle with him, like a youth's affection for a maiden, but more enduring. All nature is my bride."

Joshua Slocum was that rare man who embodied what Thoreau was talking about. Both before and after Virginia's death, Slocum had another bride. Early in *Sailing Alone*, he wrote: "I was born in the breezes; and I have studied the sea as perhaps few have studied it, neglecting all else." The sea was Slocum's first and, after Virginia's death, perhaps his only love. All the oceans were his bride.

BOTH SAILING ALONE AND WALDEN are still in print as commercial editions after 117 and 163 years, respectively, as of the time of this writing. Sometime before 1900, the New York State Library began compiling an annual "Best 50 Books" list. Starting with as many as 500 titles, librarians winnowed down the total to just 50. In 1900, when *Sailing Alone* was published, the first book on the list was *To Have and to Hold*, a historical novel written by Mary Johnston, then a bestselling author. Ninth on the list was *Literary Friends and Acquaintances*, written by one of the country's leading men of letters and a star-struck admirer of Thoreau, William Dean Howells. Twelfth was the popular Booth Tarkington's *Monsieur Beaucaire*.

Sailing Alone was among four books tied in the librarians' voting for fiftieth position, along with Samuel L. Clemens's *The Man That Corrupted*

Hadleyburg; *The Redemption of David Curson*, a bestselling novel written by a clergyman named Charles F. Goss; and a collection of Theodore Roosevelt speeches entitled *The Strenuous Life*. Joshua Slocum thus found himself in impressive company. It is fair to conclude, however, that *Sailing Alone* remains among the few top books published in 1900[1] that is still read outside universities, if at all. Certainly, given that he was not a professional writer or celebrity, Slocum's literary accomplishment and his book's staying power are impressive.

The New York State Library wasn't opened to the public until 1855, and there was no "Top 50" list of the books published in 1854, when Ticknor and Fields released *Walden; or, a Life in the Woods*. That said, *Walden's* first year's sales of fewer than 800 copies were insignificant when compared with one of that year's bestsellers by an American writer.[2] *The Lamplighter*, a first novel by 27-year-old, Salem, Massachusetts–born Maria Susanna Collins, sold 65,000 copies in the five months following its publication in Boston by John P. Jewett. Even this substantial figure was enough only for second place in sales to Jewett's previous massive hit, Harriet Beecher Stowe's *Uncle Tom's Cabin*, published two years earlier. Also released in 1854 was the second edition of Nathaniel Hawthorne's *Mosses from an Old Manse*, a collection of allegorical stories. But in the generations since, while better-selling titles of the 1854 cohort faded into obscurity, *Walden* went on to influence countless millions of readers and spark ongoing debate and commentary by students and critics.

BESIDES THEIR RESPECTIVE SUBJECTS, which remain compelling, the styles of *Sailing Alone* and *Walden* have much to do with their longevity. A century after the books were written, their prose does not appear old-fashioned and, thus, off-putting. Slocum's language is surprisingly "modern." His relentless paring down of excess wordiness reduced *Sailing Alone* to an engaging simplicity. The story is easily approached, the reader soon engrossed. Economy of language is always in fashion.

Readers need only peruse one of English author John MacGregor's

---

1 The first printing in January 1900 was 5,000 copies. In November a second printing followed, numbering 2,500 copies.

2 It took roughly five years—until 1859—for Ticknor & Fields to sell its 2,000-copy first edition of *Walden; or, a Life in the Woods*, printed in August 1854. A second edition, called only *Walden* because Thoreau didn't want the book to be mistaken for a guide to rustic living, was printed in 1862 with a run of only 280 copies.

(1825–1892) books about his experiences in his *Rob Roy* canoe and yawl to get a flavor of the Victorian-era prose so absent in Slocum. "The beautiful phosphorescence of the sea on this occasion was an attractive sight, and I could follow the line of my hemp cable by the gleam of silver light which enfolded it with a gradually softened radiance from the surface of the sea, down to an unseen depth where, in sooth, it was dark enough."

In his reminiscence of Joshua Slocum published in *The Rudder* in January 1911, editor Thomas Fleming Day wrote: "Slocum's story is a remarkable one; I do not mean as the story of a voyage but as a piece of writing. It is written in a pure narrative style, absolutely devoid of any disfigurements betraying effort, and flows from page to page like a wind-favored tide. It is worthy to be placed beside any narrative writing in our language, even beside the work of the great master of that style, De Foe."

As for Thoreau, scholar Walter Harding called him "one of the major American prose stylists." In his introduction to *The Variorum Walden*, first published in 1962, Harding noted that although many sentences in Walden are long, some a half-page or longer, they are "so carefully constructed … that the average reader has no difficulty with their syntax and is hardly aware of their complexity." That said, there are plenty of short sentences in *Walden*, for Thoreau had a good writer's appreciation for rhythm in language and for the delightful patterns and images that artfully assembled words can create.

Slocum's vocabulary is far less likely to send readers to the dictionary than Thoreau's, which includes words such as "fluviatile" and "integument." Yet Thoreau's word choices, even when challenging, contribute to the vividness of his images. *Walden* is chock full of metaphors, allusions, paradoxes, symbolism, riddles, and other devices that enrich the text and provide endless fodder for students and critics.

Slocum managed to employ more allusions and metaphors than one realizes upon a first reading, illustrating how much he had learned about writing from reading others' books. These devices work fine in *Sailing Alone*, although one of them, at least, is slightly askew. In Chapter XII, Slocum refers to his patched-up mainsail, "which, like Joseph's coat, was made of many pieces." The reference is to Genesis 37:3, but anyone who has read the story of Joseph knows that his coat was of many *colors*.

WHATEVER THEIR DIFFERENCES and similarities, what *Sailing Alone* and *Walden* have most in common is that they influence and inspire their readers. How many of those adopting today's Tiny House lifestyle would find inspiration in Thoreau and Slocum? How many successful nature writers owe a debt to *Walden*? How many fine prose stylists, whether their primary themes involve nature or not, have had their ear for language adjusted, as if by some linguistic tuning fork, by Thoreau's prose? How many *Walden* readers have at least tried to adopt aspects of the Transcendentalism reflected in Thoreau, including an ecofriendly lifestyle informed by respect for the natural world?

Perhaps Slocum's most lasting influence has been to inspire land-lubbers to dream and cruising sailors in untold numbers to venture forth while always appreciating the sea and preparing for any eventuality. To find a profound example of Slocum's influence, one need only think of the great French sailor, environmentalist, and writer Bernard Moitessier. While leading the 1968 *Sunday Times* Golden Globe round-the-world race, Moitessier quite suddenly dropped out and sailed to Tahiti to live the simple life. The name of Moitessier's boat was *Joshua*.

Others have read Slocum and made their own circumnavigations. Many *Spray* replicas or near-replicas have been built and proved largely satisfactory. Nor can any reader escape Slocum's message of how much can be achieved with little cash outlay if one lives simply in a self-sufficient manner. Slocum learned this the hard way, going from modestly prosperous to broke, but he did learn.

WHO WROTE THE TRUER book, Thoreau or Slocum? Self-centered Thoreau lived a life of the mind that seemingly left little room for sympathy toward others, for those who had farms or stores to tend, families to support, and the material, emotional, and physical needs of what Thoreau thought of as your average "John and Jonathan." These were the people who, he believed, lived lives of "quiet desperation." *Walden* was Thoreau's way of preaching—"as lustily as Chanticleer"[1]—a lesson intended to awaken readers to their deficiencies and provide ideas about the ways in which they could improve themselves.

Slocum, by contrast, never preaches. He is more direct in his approach and never holds himself morally superior to others. There is only one sentence of advice in *Sailing Alone*, and it doesn't come until the fourth paragraph from the end of the appendix: "To young men contemplating a voyage I would say go." (It must be noted here that Slocum wasn't advising

---

1 The rooster of a medieval fable, who also appeared in Chaucer's *The Canterbury Tales*.

others to circumnavigate or even to go cruising as the term is meant today. Rather, he was talking about a before-the-mast merchant voyage.)

Walden is more complex and intellectually challenging than *Sailing Alone*, but *Walden's* essays reflect Thoreau's ideas more than the reality of his life, and the ideas often clashed. This dance of competing and opposing ideas give the book much of its fascination, but they require readers to puzzle through, taking tidbits here while leaving others there. In *Writing America: Literary Landmarks from Walden Pond to Wounded Knee*, English professor Shelly Fisher Fishkin wrote: "*Walden* is an exhilarating and infuriating book—a sermon on simplicity that was far from simple, a celebration of honesty that hid or masked as much as it revealed; a book that sometimes pretended to be what it was not and at other times turned out to be exactly what it claimed to be; a book that was supremely humble and supremely arrogant at the same time."

Such comments could never apply to *Sailing Alone*. Slocum wasn't straightforward about why he made his voyage, but his book is never mean-spirited, never condescending, and doesn't pretended to be anything more or less than it is. During his voyage, Slocum really did live the solitary, self-sufficient, simple life that Thoreau espoused but didn't quite manage. On his voyage, Slocum gathered firewood, cooked his meals, mended his boat, made his decisions, navigated his way. He accepted the generosity of strangers and ignored critics of the *Spray* and of his plan to do what others deemed foolish or impossible.

In the end, Joshua Slocum, in love with the sea and with sailing, embodied one of the most famous passages in *Walden*: "If a man does not keep pace with his companions, perhaps it is because he hears a different drummer. Let him step to the music which he hears, however measured or far away."

Appendix E

The Children of Joshua and Virginia Slocum

Raised aboard their father's ships until the passing of their mother, the four Slocum children had unconventional childhoods even by nineteenth-century standards. They were home-schooled by multitalented Virginia until her death, then educated in public schools thereafter. The three youngest—Ben Aymar, Jessie Helena, and Garfield—faced challenging childhoods. With their mother gone and their father away at sea, they were looked after either by Hettie or by an aunt on the Slocum side. They would cherish what memories they had of their father, but they knew relatively little about him. Even when home, Slocum had little time for them. Jessie, the daughter, said she never received a letter from her father.

Despite and perhaps in part because of the circumstances in which they grew up, the Slocum children displayed inner strength, self-reliance, and the willingness to make independent decisions as they entered adulthood. Certainly those traits reflected their parents. The children developed interests in the arts and possessed a can-do attitude, self-sufficiency, courage, and, to varying degrees, ambition. Whatever Joshua Slocum's shortcomings as a father, his children were proud of him. None would have been disappointed to know that their obituaries invariably noted that they were the offspring of the famous captain.

Victor

VICTOR SLOCUM was born aboard the *Constitution* at San Francisco on January 10, 1872, and was the only Slocum offspring to follow a career at sea. Educated primarily by Virginia, Victor learned seamanship and the basics of navigation from his father. Joshua Slocum eventually made his oldest son mate aboard the *Aquidneck* sometime before or just after his sixteenth birthday.

Victor Slocum. (Courtesy Melville C. Brown)

Victor learned responsibility at a young age.

Victor's career included a stint as a whaler out of New Bedford, and he was considered the city's top harpooner in 1903. The sheath knife he carried had, by 1904, 22 notches cut into its handle for the whales he'd harpooned. In 1904, in a clear effort to mimic his father, Victor was reportedly building a C. G. Davis–designed ketch that was 30 feet long overall with a 24-foot waterline, 10 feet of beam, and 6 feet of draft. Victor named this boat the *Fox*, and Davis wrote an article in the March 19, 1904 issue of *Sail and Sweep* magazine saying that Victor planned to "penetrate the far north" in the boat. The idea was to go to St. John's, Newfoundland, and then to Upernavik, on the west coast of Greenland. From there, "Mr. Slocum intends to visit the retreats of the great polar whale, the most inaccessible animal in the world."

If Victor ever embarked on the *Fox* voyage—or even if he completed the boat—he never remarked upon it. During World War I he served as navigating officer aboard the U.S. Navy's transport ship *Monongahela* and sailed from Sandy Hook as one of the pilots who guided ships into the Port of New York. In 1931, at age 59, Victor Slocum received his unlimited master's license in both steam and motor ships, and was employed by what his brother Ben Aymar called the Roosevelt Lines (probably the Roosevelt Steamship Company).

On August 17, 1937, in a feature story about Victor, the *Brooklyn Daily Eagle* reported that he had inherited many of his father's traits and his mother's talents. At the time of the article, a display of his paintings of Chinese junks was being shown at the Franklin Avenue branch of the New York Public Library. The *Eagle* also noted of Victor's career that "at every port a camera and drawing board would go with the Captain to see the sights of the town instead of a whisky bottle." At the start of World War II,[1] 70-year-old Victor was retained by the navy as an inspector of wooden-hulled vessels. Postwar, he served as a night captain in New York for the United Fruit Company and taught courses in navigation.

While there is no document indicating that Victor had a middle name, at some point he began referring to himself as Victor Joshua Slocum. In retirement, perhaps thinking of his mother, he learned to play the piano. He continued his painting, built model boats, and wrote several books, the best-known being *Castaway Boats* and *Capt. Joshua Slocum, The Adventures of America's Best Known Sailor*. Victor married Estelle Woodruff, who died in 1946. Victor was living on Lexington Avenue in New York at the time of his death at age 77, on December 10, 1949. "Son of Famous Captain Slocum Dies at 77," read one of the headlines.

---

1 During the war, one of the 2,710 Liberty ships built—hull #3082—was christened the *Joshua Slocum*.

Benjamin Aymar

BENJAMIN AYMAR SLOCUM was born December 21, 1873, in Sydney, Australia. Named for the ship of which his father was then master, Ben spent his childhood years afloat. Of all the Slocum children, Ben Aymar shared the most detailed memories of his mother with Walter Magnes Teller. "My mother," he wrote Teller on March 4, 1954, "was very talented in many branches of art at which she was always engaged—also a good pianist." Ben never forgot the riding equipment and whip that Virginia retained among her possessions even years after her days as a horsewoman had ended.

Ben was not interested in a life at sea and asked to be left with his aunt in Natick when Slocum and Hettie, together with Victor and Garfield, departed for the *Aquidneck* in February 1886. During the *Aquidneck* and *Liberdade* period, Ben had no contact with his father, other than through his aunt. Ben told Walter Teller, "As I review the past, my early life was rather a tough one and my mind seemed to be occupied on improving my position in worldly affairs—self-preservation."

Ben Aymar Slocum with his family in 1902. Left to right: daughter Mildred, wife Florence, and son Ralph. This photo may have been taken in the Lynn Woods Reservation, which was established in 1881 and remains the second largest municipal park in the country. (Courtesy Melville C. Brown)

Ben Aymar posed on the running board of a 1920s-vintage phaeton. (Courtesy Melville C. Brown)

He said that he "attended a preparatory school [which he did not name] where my fundamentals of art were taught me." Ben used his artistic talent to create portraits of his parents based on photographs. Into his early adulthood, he considered himself a painter; that is the profession he claimed at age 18 on his certificate of marriage to Florence A. Sherman, on August 12, 1892. But Ben Aymar knew that he needed a means of earning a living. On March 4, 1954, he wrote Walter Teller that Grace Murray Brown's father Bernard "was very much interested in my future—had advised me to become a c.e. [civil engineer] but I was mechanical minded and became m.e. [mechanical engineer]—this shows the mind of B. Murray [Bernard Murray] who saw in me—at 16—the stuff to develop."

He described himself as a "self-taught mechanical engineer." He worked initially in Lynn, Massachusetts, as a "machine designer and development engineer." The Slocum-Sherman marriage produced two children, Ralph and Mildred, but the union ended, and in 1910 Ben married a second time, to Ida M. Sanson of Saugus, Massachusetts.

Ben had developed an early interest in photography, perhaps inspired by his father, and he owned a 5-inch by 7-inch view camera. By 1913, Ben and Ida moved to Rochester, New York, where the couple was living at the time of the 1920 census and where Ben worked at Kodak—initially at least—as a draftsman. He later invented an automatic film-spooling device for dental X-ray machines.

Subsequently Ben moved to Binghamton, New York, where he married for a third time on May 18, 1927. His new wife was Florence ("Fawn") Cole Ordway. While living in Binghamton, Ben built a model of the *Spray* that he donated to the De Young Museum in San Francisco. On January 22, 1931, he wrote a letter to Lawrence W. Jenkins, long-time assistant director of the Peabody Museum in Salem, Massachusetts, offering to build a similar *Spray* model for that institution.

Jenkins wrote back on January 26, 1931, saying: "We would certainly be delighted to have [the model]. I remember meeting your father here a good many years ago and spending an enjoyable two hours going over the museum with him. We have a model of a whaling boat presented by Mr. V. J. Slocum who, I presume, is your brother."

On May 14, 1931, the *Daily Boston Globe* featured a photograph of the model with the headline, "Model of Sloop That Circled Globe Given to Salem Museum." The model, built at a scale of ¾ inch to 1 foot, is still owned by what is now the Peabody Essex Museum. In a letter to Jenkins, Ben noted that the model was based on the *Spray*'s lines as printed in *Sailing Alone Around the World*, and he regretted that he didn't have a more complete photographic record of his father's boat. He built a third *Spray* model for the New Bedford Whaling Museum.

Ben Aymar left Binghamton and his third wife by July 1934, spending time subsequently in Randolph and Beverly, Massachusetts. The war years found him back in Rochester, working as a tool designer for Delco Appliance Division of General Motors.

Shortly after the end of World War II, Ben Aymar traveled to Sydney, Australia. Family memory and correspondence do not reveal why he made the trip, but in Sydney, on November 21, 1945, 72-year-old Ben Aymar married for the fourth and final time. His 59-year-old wife's name as listed on the marriage certificate was "Virginia Hagen also known as Dose." Virginia was said to be the daughter of George Walker, Virginia Slocum's younger brother. While some confusion exists about this union of first cousins, it seems not to have lasted. Ben Aymar returned to the United States in 1946.

It is thought that Ben retired by 1949 and either moved to or spent significant time in Damariscotta, Maine. He was still there as of March 1958, but later moved to Greece, New York, where he lived for a time with his son, Ralph G. Slocum. Ben Aymar Slocum died in a Rochester, New York nursing home on April 8, 1965. Besides his son Ralph and his daughter Mildred, by then Mrs. George Ansell of Pompano Beach, Florida, Ben Aymar Slocum left nine grandchildren and 23 great-grandchildren. He was buried in Pine Grove Cemetery in Lynn. When it learned of Ben's passing, the *Vineyard Gazette* headlined its obituary, "Joshua Slocum's Son Dies at Age of 91."

Jessie

JESSIE HELENA SLOCUM, named after her mother's sister—a contralto in the Sydney Opera—was born in the Philippines on June 10, 1875. Letters to Walter Teller written in 1952 and 1954 reveal that Jessie retained certain clear memories of her parents. She said her mother "was very talented. Did very fine fancywork, played the piano, harp, guitar, sang, and was a very fine dancer." She remembered looking through her father's scrapbook with him, and how he would cut out newspaper stories with his penknife and paste them in. After Virginia's death, when Jessie was nine, she was raised at various times by one of Slocum's sisters in Natick and by Hettie. Subsequent to Hettie's remarriage, Jessie referred to her in correspondence with Walter Teller as "Mrs. Mayhew."

In a May 3, 1953 interview with the *Santa Cruz Sentinel-News*, Jessie said that after the *Northern Light* voyage, "My life has followed a very conventional pattern ever since. I attended [Massachusetts] public schools, then worked for a short time in a jewelry store where I met and married [in Attleboro, Massachusetts on July 3, 1899] my late husband, Arthur Joyce. We were in the poultry business for many years, retiring here [in Santa Cruz] in 1940." The couple had one child, a son named Arthur.

Jessie told Walter Teller that she believed her father had corresponded with Jack London, who was an admirer of Slocum. London wrote that Slocum's voyage had prompted him to make one of his own in his wastefully expensive schooner, the *Snark*.[1] If there were letters between the two men,

---

1 Jack London's *The Cruise of the Snark* was published by the Macmillan Company in 1911.

Joshua Slocum's daughter, Jessie Slocum Joyce, is seen here in Santa Cruz, California.
(Courtesy Melville C. Brown)

none have yet turned up. Jessie collaborated with writers on a magazine article about her father and a book written by Beth Day called *Joshua Slocum, Sailor*, published in 1953 by Houghton Mifflin.

On August 6, 1953, Alice C. Longraker, who then lived in Carmel, wrote a letter to Walter Teller describing a visit she had made to Jessie Slocum Joyce. Together with her granddaughter, she drove over to see "what relation Jessie Slocum Joyce might be to those dear friends who had played such a major role in the happiness that now still shines from those summers on Martha's Vineyard. We found a short and stocky little body who claims 78 years, living in a tiny white cottage not unlike that first one on California Ave. in Massachusetts, way back over the hump that divides this century from the last. Her face is weathered and lined and her features are quite pronounced, but above all her smile is the most noticeable feature and the cordiality with which she invited us (perfect strangers) into her living room and showed us portraits of the Captain himself and Jessie's mother—his first wife and the Mother of his many children."

Jessie Slocum Joyce died in Santa Cruz, California, on June 27, 1960, at the age of 85. She had long referred to herself proudly as "the captain's daughter."

Garfield

JAMES GARFIELD SLOCUM was born at Hong Kong on March 3, 1881. Garfield may have sailed more with his father than any of the other Slocum children. He was born aboard the *Amethyst*, sailed with his parents on the *Northern Light*, sailed with Victor, his father and Hettie on the *Aquidneck*, made the

Garfield Slocum aboard the Spray, *circa 1901. He was 20 years old at the time. (Courtesy Melville C. Brown)*

voyage from Brazil home in the *Liberdade*, and made the *Spray* trip to Buffa-lo. He also cruised to Maine with his father in the *Spray*. Memories that Garfield shared in letters to Walter Teller provide among the most detailed information that survives about the *Spray*'s cabin post-voyage. "On the star-board side, a mattress on the transom boards—no springs.... Starboard side on the wall; brackets holding a carbine, Zulu assegi spears with a holder for throwing the spears, boomerangs from Australia, a .45 revolver, a bookcase on the wall the foot of his bunk ... two chronometers, two sextants, a ba-rometer, thermometer, lots of charts."

Joshua Slocum made some decisions about Garfield's education that echoed *his* father's demand that he quit school to work in the boot shop. In a letter to Walter Teller, Garfield remembered:

> *Father told me he wanted me to go to sea for a career, he taught me a little navigation, he did not let me remain in school, kept me with him so I was unable to study navigation with mathematics, the principal of the Tarrytown, N.Y. high school asked him to leave me with him and put me thru school, father refused, he needed me he said. When I left Buffalo I landed in N.Y.C.—father had an old friend, Capt. Shackford, he was Supt. of the American Line, pier 14, he took me as a deck cadet, served on the Philadelphia and St. Paul mail steamers until I became 21, which was the age limit, that was 1903, from there to father's, if I had gone onboard the nautical training ship St. Mary I would have been properly educated, father could not afford to send me there.... I love the sea, wanted to follow it, I wanted an education and [to] become an officer.*

Garfield made one voyage as crew on a steamship, but it was the only one.

As the youngest of Slocum's children, Garfield may have felt the loss of his mother even more keenly than the others. He was also a frequent witness to the coolness between his father and stepmother at home. A cer-tain plaintiveness emerges in some of Garfield's letters, and he seems always to have been appreciative of the kindness showed him by others. In the spring of 1905, at age 24, Garfield moved to Schenectady and found a job. In August 1906, he married Grace May Davison, and the couple had four chil-dren: Arthur, Winston, Virginia, and Doris. The daughter, Virginia, was killed by a drunk driver at age 33. After that event, Garfield and his wife raised Virginia's three children.

Garfield had a long career working in an office capacity at General Electric in Schenectady. He called the city home for 45 years and died there on January 21, 1955, not long before his seventy-fourth birthday. His wife Grace died in Schenectady on April 3, 1982. In later years, Garfield sometimes referred to himself as the "ex-bosun of the *Spray*."[1]

---

1 In the family genealogy, and occasionally elsewhere including on his marriage certificate, Garfield's full name is given as James A. Garfield Slocum. The "A" is presumed to refer to President Garfield's middle name, Abram. In the Slocum genealogy, however, the "A" is mistakenly said to be for Abraham. The initial does not appear either on Garfield's birth or death certificates. He normally referred to himself as J. Garfield Slocum.

Appendix F

Joshua Slocum's Recipe for Fish Chowder

This is Slocum's recipe as he related it to Clifton Johnson. Johnson included it in his article about Slocum published in *Good Housekeeping* in February 1903:

> *My method is so simple people would hardly believe it would give such appetizing results. Put some pork and sliced onion in the pot and let that cook awhile. Then put in a layer of potatoes and next a layer of fish, and so on up to the top with a seasoning of salt and pepper. Then add enough water to barely cover it and cook for twenty minutes. When it is about done, put in milk and bits of cracker or bread and let it simmer a little. Your codfish must be cut in chunks and you must have the skin on and the bones in it.*

Acknowledgments

A book like this represents a journey of many, many steps. All along the way, individuals and institutions responded to my requests for information relating to Joshua Slocum. Two Massachusetts researchers in particular, both resourceful and dedicated and both now deceased, assisted with very important materials. They were Robert "Bob" Birely and Slocum family genealogist and Joshua Slocum student Melville C. Brown. A special thanks also to Mel's wife Carol Brown. A word is due to the late Slocum researcher Leon Fredrich of Portland, Oregon, who shared some of his important findings with Walter Magnes Teller and Mel Brown. Thanks also to researcher Bruce Williams of Bridgeport, Connecticut; to Pan-American scholar Susan Eck, and to Carol Gaal of The Wagnalls Memorial. They all maintained contact with me over time, sharing and clarifying regarding areas of their particular expertise.

In Alaska, thanks to Freya Anderson at the Alaska State Library, Joan Anderson of the Alaska Dept. of Natural Resources, Toby Sullivan of the Kodiak Maritime Museum, and historian Shana Loshbough of Anchor Point.

In Nova Scotia, a very special thanks to Dorothy Outhouse of the Islands Historical Society in Freeport, Joanne Head of the Western Counties Regional Library, Joanna Otto of the Mount Hanley Schoolhouse Museum, Nadine Gates of the Yarmouth County Museum and Archives, the Public Archives of Nova Scotia, and to the Halifax Public Libraries. Also in Canada, Stephen Bornais of Fisheries and Oceans Canada, Maritimes Region, and David Bradley, Maritime History Archive, Memorial University of Newfoundland.

In the United Kingdom, thanks to Douglas Paterson at the Fishing Boat Heritage Museum, Aberdeen, Scotland, John Winrow, Maritime Archives, Merseyside Maritime Museum, and Glenn Mitchell, Senior Book Specialist at Peter Harrington, Ltd., London.

In Australia, thanks to the State Library of Queensland, The Australian National Maritime Museum, Bill Bourke of the Sydney Heritage Fleet, The Tasmanian Information and Research Service, and to Rhonda Banks and Anne Hoogvliet at the Great Barrier Reef Marine Park Authority.

The following libraries all responded with needed information: Chris Glass and his fellow reference librarians at the Boston Public Library, Cynthia Harbeson at the Jones Library, Amherst, Massachusetts; Kathryn Arinaga at the Hawaii State Library; the Multonah County Library; Carolyn Longwood and Deb Charpentier at the Millicent Library, Fairhaven, Massachusetts; the reference staff at the Abbott Public Library, Marblehead, Massachusetts; the Morse Institute Library in Natick Massachusetts, the Mystic Seaport Museum Library; the New Bedford Free Library; the New York Public Library: Olivia Larsen at the Aquinnah Public Library; Hilary Wall, Archivist and Librarian at the *Vineyard Gazette/MV Magazine*.

Museum curators, librarians and historical societies also turned out vital information in response to my queries. Among them were The California Historical Society; Dan Finamore, Russell W. Knight Curator of Maritime Art and History at the Peabody Essex Museum (PEM) in Salem, Massachusetts, and the Phillips Library staff at the PEM; Chesapeake Bay Maritime Museum librarian, Lynne Phillips; Halsey Herreshoff and Norene Rickson at the Herreshoff Marine Museum; the Chesapeake Bay Maritime Museum, the Lubec Historical Society, the Maine Maritime Museum, the Medford Historical Society, Ben Fuller of the Penobscot Maritime Museum, and Mark Procknik, librarian at the New Bedford Whaling Museum.

Others who responded with timely information included Carol Wilson at the National Archives, San Bruno, California; Geoff Robertson in Australia; Thad Danielson, student of traditional boat-building methods and materials; Chris Richard, Director of Tourism, Fairhaven, Massachusetts; family genealogist Mike Suthern, Lisa Crunk of the Naval History and Heritage Command, and Chris Cunningham, editor of *WoodenBoat's Small Boats Monthly*, wire-rope-industry historian Don Sayenga, and Judy Lund of the New Bedford Whaling Museum. Thanks to Robbert Das, whose wonderful drawing of the *Spray* appears on page 166. Thanks also to my wife Constance who assisted with researching the logbook of the *Tanjore* on which Joshua Slocum sailed during his 21st year.

Finally, thanks to James Russell, President and CEO of the New Bedford Whaling Museum for his belief in, and generous support of, this project; to Walter S. Teller who shared with me information about his father; to co-publisher Jon Eaton at Tilbury House for his thoughtful editing; to sailor and writer *par excellence* Roger Taylor; to maritime historian W. H. (Bill) Bunting, who clarified important matters relating to Slocum, Captain John Drew, and the *Amethyst*; and to Llewellyn Howland III, whose breadth of knowledge and concise suggestions did much to sharpen and enrich the text.

Sources

The most important single repository of Slocum's correspondence is the Walter Magnes Teller Collection at the New Bedford Whaling Museum. The New York Public Library also has some letters. The Peabody Essex Museum (Salem, MA) has several letters of Benjamin Aymar Slocum relating to the donation of his model of the *Spray*.

The following newspapers, magazines, and books were searched. Most references to specific issues are included in the text. As appropriate, additional information is included below.

NEWSPAPERS

The *Bismarck Daily Tribune*

The Boston *Daily Globe* and the Boston *Sunday Globe* various issues 1889-1922

The *Boston Herald*

The *Boston Investigator*

The *Boston Journal*

The *Boston Sunday Journal*

The *Daily Alta California*

The *Daily Astorian*

The *Daily Picayune* (New Orleans)

The *Daily Shipping News*, Sydney

The *Daily Telegraph*, Launceston, Tasmania, Feb. 10, 1897

The *Fairhaven Star*

The Galveston *Daily News*, Jan. 18, 1884

The *Hawaiian Gazette*, Feb. 2, 1897

The *Honolulu Friend*, May 16, 1878

The *Iola Register*, Aug. 11, 1882

The *Maitland Weekly Mercury* (New South Wales), May 15, 1897

The *Hobart Mercury*, Feb. 25, 1897

The *Milwaukee Daily Journal*, Feb. 2, 1889, May 21, 1898, Oct. 15, 1897

The *Milwaukee Sentinel*, Sept. 4, 1899

Nautical Gazette, New York, Dec. 1874

The *New Bedford Standard*, May 27, 1911

The *New Haven Evening Register*, Jan. 17, 1884

The *New York Times*

The *New York Herald*

The *New York Sun*, Aug. 8, 1882

The *Oregonian*, 1877

The *Pacific Commercial Advertiser*, May 4, 1878, May 18, 1878

The Quincy *Patriot Ledger*, April 8, 1959

The *Salt Lake Semi-weekly Tribune*, Sept. 27, 1898

The *San Francisco Daily Evening Bulletin*, Feb. 19, 1883, Jan. 13, 1863, Feb. 3, 1863, March 16, 1868

The *San Francisco Chronicle*

The Baltimore *Sun*, Feb. 7, 1884, "Shipping Notes," July 7, 1885

The Sydney *Evening News*, Oct. 10, 1896

The Sydney *Morning Herald*, Oct. 9, 1896, Oct. 12, 1896

The *Vineyard Gazette*, Edgartown, MA, July 29, 1909, Sept. 9, 1909, Oct. 14, 1962, et al

The *Washington Herald*, Feb. 26, 1892

The *Weekly Monitor*, Bridgeton, Nova Scotia, Dec. 1889

MAGAZINES AND BOOKS

Australia Pilot Vol. IV, The, First Edition, the Lords Commissioners of the Admiralty, London, 1917

Barrett, Walter, *The Old Merchants of New York City*, Carlton, New York, 1885

Clark, Arthur H., *The Clipper Ship Era, 1843 – 1869*, G. P. Putnam's Sons, New York and London, 1911

Culler, Toni, "We Live Afloat and Like It," *The Rudder*, April, 1940

Day, Beth and Jessie Slocum Joyce, "Joshua Slocum Was the First," *True*, July, 1952

Dolin, Eric Jay, *Brilliant Beacons: A History of the American Lighthouse*, Liverwright, New York, 2016.

Gleason, Hall, *Old Ships and Shipbuilding Days of Medford 1830-1873*, Medford, MA, 1936

Hearn, Chester G., *Tracks in the Sea: Matthew Fontaine Maury and the Mapping of the Ocean*, International Marine/Ragged Mountain Press, 2003

Hill, Hamilton Andrew, "Boston and Liverpool Packet Lines, Sail and Steam," *The New England Magazine*, January 1894

Jackson, Edward, letter to the editor, *The Engineer*, May 23, 1873, London

Johnson, Clifton, "Captain Joshua Slocum, the man who sailed alone around the world in a thirty-seven-foot boat," *Outing*, Boston, October, 1902

Johnson, Clifton, "The Cook Who Sailed Alone," *Good Housekeeping*, Springfield, MA, February, 1903

Kochiss, John, *Oystering from New York to Boston*, Wesleyan, CT, 1974

Laing, Alexander, *Clipper Ship Men*, New York, Duell, Sloane and Pearce, 1944

MacDonnell, Kevin, "Collecting Henry David Thoreau," *Firsts* magazine, September 1999

Martin, Captain James P., Logbook of the ship *Tanjore*

Matthews, Frederick C., *American Merchant Ships 1850-1900 Series Two*, Marine Research Society, Salem, MA

Raban, Jonathan, "Walden-on-Sea," *The New York Review of Books*, April, 1995

Sources

Schulz, Kathryn, "Pond Scum: Henry David Thoreau's Moral Myopia," *The New Yorker*, October 19, 2015

Shea, Phil, *Brier Island: Land's End in the Bay of Fundy*, Lancelot Press, Hantsport, Nova Scotia, 1990

Slack, Kenneth, *In the Wake of the Spray*, Sheridan House, White Plains, NY, 1966

Slocum, Charles Elihu, M.D., Ph.D., *A Short History of the Slocums, Slocombs, and Slocumbs of America*, Syracuse, NY, published by the author, 1882

Slocum, Joshua, *Sailing Alone Around the World*, Penguin Books, New York, 1999

Slocum, Victor, *Captain Joshua Slocum: America's Greatest Sailor*, Sheridan House, White Plains, NY, 1950

Smith, R.A.C., untitled cruise scrapbook of the vessel *Privateer*, 1900

Spencer, Ann, *Alone At Sea, the Adventures of Joshua Slocum*, Firefly Books, Buffalo, NY, 1999

Stephens, William Piccard, *Traditions and Memories of American Yachting*, Wooden-Boat, Brooklin, ME, 1989

Teller, Walter Magnes, *The Search for Captain Slocum*, New York, Scribner's, 1956

Teller, Walter Magnes, *Joshua Slocum*, Rutgers University Press, New Brunswick, NJ, 1971

Teller, Walter Magnes, *The Voyages of Joshua Slocum*, Sheridan House, Dobbs Ferry, NY, 1985

Wagnalls, Mabel, *The Light in the Valley: Being the Story of Anna Willis*, Funk & Wagnalls, New York, 1925

Whipple, A.B.C., *The Challenge*, William Morrow & Co., New York, 1987

Index

Writer/historian Stan Grayson is widely
recognized for his nonfiction storytelling.
After earning an M.A. in English from
Pennsylvania State University and serving
in the U.S. Army in Vietnam, Grayson
pursued a career that has included stints
as a reporter, editor, photographer, auto
industry consultant, publisher, and writer.
He is the author of numerous books and
articles on American automotive and yachting history and is a regular contributor to
WoodenBoat magazine. He has studied and
reflected upon Slocum's life and career for
some 40 years.